Dysfunctional One

John Davies

www.dysfunctionalone.net

Copyright © 2015 John Davies
All rights reserved
First Edition

PAGE PUBLISHING, INC.
New York, NY

First originally published by Page Publishing, Inc. 2015

ISBN 978-1-63417-904-1 (pbk)
ISBN 978-1-63417-905-8 (digital)

Printed in the United States of America

Preface

One of my favorite biblical characters and role model is Joseph, the blessed son of Jacob who was sold by his brothers to Egyptian merchants. In comparison, however, I must admit that there is a great difference between us. Joseph recognized his callings and was obedient to God from his early youth, throughout all his adversaries up to his adult life, while it took me much longer to sort things out. Unlike him, I would have responded favorably to Potiphar's wife without a second thought since she asked for it. That was how far my waywardness would have gone without conscience. From early childhood throughout my teenage life, I was a fearless risk taker who blindly hopes for positive results without consciously submitting to God's will. In all my shortcomings and the very troubling choices I made in my life, God still continued to demonstrate incredible love for me in special ways, even in the midst of all the troubles that I caused others and the ones that society forced upon me. Amazingly in my maturity, when I look back, I only see someone else in all of it and not me; for if it were me, surely I would not have been alive to tell this story. It is befitting to say therefore that part of this story you are about to read is about a boy who died in the man who wrote it.

Chapter 1

I was born in a small village called Kissy Mess-Mess located in the suburb of Freetown, Sierra Leone, in July 1954. One of the major landmarks Kissy Mess-Mess was known for was the country's only metal health institution called in colloquial terms as Kissy Crace-Yard meaning "a yard for crazy people." During my early troubled years, some people would jokingly reference to my place of birth to describe or measure my behaviors. In my early teens, my parents, who were separated when I was eight, argued once about my birth date when I asked both of them for a copy of my birth certificate. My mum thought it was July 21, but my dad believed it was July 23. After they argued about it, they then resolved that it might well be another date in July 1954 other than what they remembered. I then choose July 22, to stay in the middle.

In the feud that separated my parents in 1962, my mother willfully set fire on most of my dad's belongings. In one of his wooden trunks contained my birth certificate that was burned to ashes then. My parents were married at the cathedral church in Freetown, and they had both agreed to move from a leased house in Kissy Mess-Mess, east of Freetown, where I was born to my mother's house at 24 Berwick Street in western Freetown. It was a two-story wooden house she inherited from her father, who died when I was four years old in 1958. My grandfather was said to be one of the richest men in the ethnic Kru tribe who migrated and settled in Sierra Leone from Liberia. As a seafarer and money lender, he built wealth for himself and owned several homes that he willed to the many children he had by a number of wives. That was how my mother inherited the two-story home at 24 Berwick Street where my parents moved to when I was four years old after the death of my grandfather.

My mother happened to be my dad's second wife. He divorced his first wife, Jakay, following his demolition from the British Royal Navy in December 1946. He had fought for the British in the Second World War and rose to the rank of chief petty officer. Some people who knew him then still called him by his naval title and number, CPO 623. His first marriage was blessed with three children, all of whom were separated from him and taken away from Sierra Leone to live in Liberia with their mother after their divorce in Freetown. In one of his many testimonials issued by the British naval base officer and secretary of the famous warship HMS *Barbrooks* II, Dad's performance was rated as "Superior," and he was described as an excellent disciplinarian who was honored and decorated five times during his seven years' service in the British Royal Navy. Among the accolades bestowed upon him were the British Defense Medal, the Victory Medal, the 1939 and 1945 Stars, and the prestigious Atlantic Star, which only a handful of black men from Africa merited. The testimonials also commended him for his honesty and acknowledged his physique and command ability, having successfully carried out assignments with 1,700 men under his command, described as a notable feat. His marriage with my mother was blessed with four children and lasted a little over ten years before they were separated in 1962. It was well known by all in the family that Dad loved and favored me the most among all of his children from his previous marriage and also my other two brothers and sister. My mother's favorite was their firstborn, my elder brother, Princer. I was the second child in the family. After me came Samuel and then our sister Victoria. They had another girl child after Samuel, but she passed away at age two, I guess. We were two years apart in age except for our sister Victoria, who was four years from Samuel. Our family was relatively healthier and happier, living a middle-class family life in the community.

My dad worked as a policeman in the Sierra Leone Police Force after he was demobilized from the British Royal Navy, and he rose up to the rank as inspector of police. He later became a labor unionist and an entrepreneur. He had a piece of land that he sold and used the money to buy a Hillman for our family use and a Bedford lorry, which he used to buy and distribute firewood in the community, and that was bringing home a good income.

My mother too had rental income from the second floor of her house, and our family lived on the first floor. She was not educated and never worked aside from being a housewife, which was customary at the time. She was by far younger to Dad and a very dedicated mother, caring and being there for her family. At our family home in the late 1950s my dad set up after-school study programs for children in the community. It was a very strict military-type tradition where students who did well were portrayed and treated as superior officers to those who don't. My brother Princer and I were very sharp, clever, and confident because Dad was always challenging and inspiring—ready to throw some type of quizzes at us to challenge our IQs at all times. For example, if he wanted any of us to do something, he would spell every word in his sentence, and you are to figure it out to know and to do what he meant, and some other times we would have to do the spellings to communicate what we wanted to say. With him, we were always in readiness to take a quick arithmetical quiz or some type of spelling or brainstorm other subjects. He would not easily settle for second place when we come home with school reports. Because of his rigorous preparations, I was registered to attend school one year younger than the accepted age, and my parents and teachers were very proud of my performance. I remember telling my parents that I would like to become a lawyer and a musician when I grow up.

My dad's best friend at the time was a big-time lawyer named Aaron Cole. On weekends our family would visit the lawyer's family home, and together with the Cole children, we would learn to play piano or act like judges and lawyers in courtroom. It was fun. On Sundays, after church service, we spend most of the evenings at Lumley Beach.

When I was about seven years old, the Louis Memorial Church on Adelaide Street, in Freetown, where my mother sang in the choir, put up an announcement for humanitarian assistant to a young man named Sylvanusy Pynee Jacksony who needed a home to live. My parents then volunteered to assist this young man. He was brought into the comfort of our home and was treated relatively well. My dad provided him with basic assistance to improve his living condition. He was also given stipends for helping out with the after-school study program that my dad created for children in the community.

When I was eight years old, my mother was expecting a baby, so she was taken to the Cottage Hospital on Foray Bay Road in Freetown, where she gave birth to a baby girl. My dad hurried back home from work to pick us up to go visit Mum at the hospital that afternoon. We drove in the Hillman to PZ Shopping Center where he bought the needed items for the newborn baby, and then we drove to the hospital to see both Mum and our newborn sister. When we arrived at the hospital, the young man Jacksony was there in the maternity ward with his head buried in the local *Daily Mail* newspaper, facing the window that overlooked the street. Excited, we placed the items down, and all three children went over Mum's bed to hug and kiss her and the baby.

Suddenly, the joyous mood we came with turned ugly as Mum sat up to speak directly to dad and uttered words in our Kru dialect.

"This child is not yours," she said repeatedly with her face frowned.

I guess my father could not believe his ears as he asked in a shaky but troubled voice whose child it was.

"It is Jacksony's child," replied my mother as she lay on the bed with the baby in her hands. Those words and that moment drastically destroyed our family forever and would eventually change my life for the worst. At the time I could hardly grasp the meaning and weight of those words that were exchanged between them and the bitter exchanges that ensure thereafter, but as I grow older and the weight of those words began to weigh upon my heart and the endless consequences they imposed on my life, I became convinced that both my mother and Jacksony were heartless, wicked, and vicious with impunity. Given my analogy of Joseph with Potiphar's wife, I would not have been that brave or wicked to be present when and where she tells her husband, Potiphar, that the child she begot was mine. Both were united in arrogance in the midst of their wrongdoing, lustfully foolish, blind in their little world of betrayal and unfaithfulness.

Dad's joy instantly transformed into rane and anger, and there was some heated exchange of words between both parents to the extent that the doctors and nurses had to come in to quiet down the place and beg Dad to leave. Before we departed from the hospital, Mum gave him an ultimatum for him to vacate her house by the time she returns home from the hospital. Despite all these, Dad went calling on members of the clergy to resolve the matter. I guess because of his status in the community, he tried to quiet down the scandal, for he offered to adopt the child and to move on with our family.

But Mum, stone-hearted and infatuated with Jacksony, rejected every talk and counseling from the clergymen and the elders of the community.

A week later Dad came home from work to find his belongings put on fire and burned down to ashes in front of the house on the street, and he was not allowed to enter the house. This was when my birth certificate burned to ashes, along with the precious contents in the trunks, especially celebrated memorabilia that the former chief petty officer brought back from England. When Dad returned from work that fateful evening and found the damages done to some of his most precious treasurers, neighbors who rescued him explained that he collapsed, paralyzed, and was taken to a nearby hospital.

After his recovery and discharge from the hospital, the man felt so humiliated that he disappeared for three years, away from the western area of Freetown where most of the Liberians residing in Freetown lived at the time. I would not see Dad in the next three years. Those were the most agonizing and very difficult years for me in particular because I was very attached to him. Maybe I could have overcome our separation over time then if he was dead rather than knowing he was alive but not knowing where to find him. Surely, he must have missed his family too because he was a very loving and caring dad. He was also influential and had many friends in the community. Years later he was quoted as saying that his disappearance helped in subduing temptation and also helped him heal the wounds. As an ex-service man who commanded 1,700 at war, it was obvious that he was capable of taking revenge against two smaller targets, Mum and Jacksony, but he did not. Instead, he just simply disappeared.

Mum's infatuation with Jacksony grew without reasoning at the expense of losing her family and losing her lovely responsibility as a mother. Jacksony, in turn, hated me in particular for various reasons: I missed my dad so much so that I would talk and inquire about him frequently all of the time, asking when he would come back; second, I carried my father's name as his junior, and each time my name was called, Jacksony would be tormented, eyeing me evilly; and third, I refused to recognize him—a man whom I have known as a servant to my dad—as stepfather or some sort of a father figure. So he ill-treated me, beat me up several times a day, found fault at me, and made me restless and hopeless in my family home, so I ended up leaving to live in the street at age eight.

For the most part of the three years of my father's disappearance, I was living on my own on the streets, sleeping in old wreck cars in garages or on the pouch of neighbors. I became a school dropout and began to learn how to withstand and overcome starvation and to practice some of the survival skills my dad would talk about during his warfare naval days. Then I began to learn how street boys lived: to steal bread from the bread shop and began doing dirty jobs for people around for food or for money.

My brother Princer, who was my mother's favorite, was in and out, sometimes coping with the situation with a little sweet talk here and there from Mum who, though uneducated, was smarter than the average educated women I knew then.

Samuel was living with one of our aunts, who took him away to Ghana for nine years when he was about a year old, so he was not around until in 1966 when he returned to Sierra Leone.

Victoria, our younger sister, was about two years old and had no idea what was going on. Mum in those three years of my dad's disappearance begot two bastard children for Jacksony and was sponsoring him at a seminary school at the Milton Margai Teachers College, where he was studying to become a teacher and a minister of the gospel of Jesus Christ, preparing to pastor the Lewis Memorial Church on Adelaide Street, in Freetown.

I guess here was where my whole concept of Christianity and the Bible became shady and confusing at an early age, and it all seem like I or Dad had done something wrong for which we were being punished. I had attended church with my parents, and at school, Bible knowledge was one of the compulsory subjects in our curriculum, and we learned how to read scriptures during devotion and read stories in the Bible. My knowledge of the Bible was elementary, and my understanding of things that were happening in everyday life in relation to what the Bible teaches was also elementary. I knew then that the Bible says Lucifer entered the Garden of Eden and deceived the first family, but Lucifer was not going to preach the word of God to anyone. Instead, he was going to stand against God's word. At least that is the way I understood it. Like Lucifer, Jacksony had just entered the comfort of a family that provided him shelter, and he destroyed them against the will of God, and now he was going to become a reverend to preach God's word and to pastor a church.

But the Davies family would not be Jacksony's only victim; there would be many more women and families to follow before he graduated and was ordained to pastor the Lewis Memorial Church. Jacksony, the would-be pastor and playboy actor, was a womanizer who puts asunder many marriages and destroyed families. Some of the marriages he destroyed were the ones that he officiated over. He bore children in adulterous relationships with many women in the congregation.

In the early days with Mum, on weekdays, he lived on MMTC campus studying theology and on weekends. Friday nights to Monday morning, he would be home with Mum. Both of them, along with their friends, would drink beer, get drunk, and sing Christian hymns, which they were good at. They both would go to church on Sundays, and after church service they would go get drunk and come home singing and ended up vomiting some of the times and mess up the house.

For the most part of those three years of Dad's disappearance, I hardy went to school or to church. My dream to become a lawyer and musician began shrinking as I became preoccupied with where, when, and how I would get my next meal or where to sleep when night falls. I sometimes sneaked into the house to steal whatever I can lay my hands on when he was not there. Mum, the loving and caring woman I knew then, was gone, and Dad, the most affectionate person I needed in my life then, had disappeared, leaving me in a vacuum quenching, seeking, searching, and looking in the wrong places for all the good things I lost: love, affection, care, security, etcetera. The place I once knew as home was no longer. Then life was a mess; the home study and my regular schooling were also now messier, and the challenges in caring for myself at age eight was the messiest. Sometimes I wished I was never born in Kissy Mess-Mess.

Chapter 2

It was about a month after my parents separated in 1962 that I began the strange journey of looking after myself. I rapidly degenerated from that promising kid full of confidence and intelligence into a frightening and more problematic kid. Within a month of Dad's disappearance, I was framed unworthy and faulty in the eyes of Jacksony, my supposedly bastard stepfather, and once he expressed his displeasures, Mum would support him and get flogged. They both united with each other over punishing me for anything they considered my wrongdoing, even though it was apparent that these two were delusional sinners who needed counseling and repentance themselves. In fact, these two had a way of explaining things to justify their conspiracy against Dad to make it look like their actions were righteous and acceptable in the sight of God.

Mum started punishing me by withholding food from me for a day or two, so the streets became my resort. I had to find ways and means, and so I spent most of my time as a boy in those three years in the streets of Freetown, serving other people for food or for money and sometimes stealing mostly foodstuff to eat. Sometimes I would join other street boys to go garbage-picking for food at the PZ dumpsite or at dumpsites at Hill Station, where the wealthiest people lived.

Periodically, the police would find me sleeping in wrecked cars in the streets or at the national park overnight, and I would be brought back home where they would be told about my waywardness and branded as a bad boy. When they turned me over to Mum and Jacksony, I will get flogged and punished for living in the streets. Mum and Jacksony would make things look before the police like I was just a bad boy who liked running away from the comfort of home life to live on the street. I would be scared and tongue-tied when asked by the police why I like living in the streets. My confidence and boldness had dissipated, replaced with fright, shame, a deep feeling of guilt, and inferiority.

During the period when my parents were together, none of their children dared go on the street unprotected without authority or supervision. But things were different now. Oftentimes it would be Jacksony who would ask me to leave house if I do not want to see him. Other times it would be my brother Princer and I who would be thrown out of the house. Although our exit to live in the streets was being triggered by ill treatments at home under Jackson's reign, very few people in the neighborhood knew that. Many of the neighbors witnessed our belongings in carton boxes thrown over the window, but not all of them understood the root causes. Many who had no answers concluded that we were just bad boys, and that was why we were frequently being thrown out of the house. Some parents in the neighborhood branded us bad boys and treated us with cold shoulders, sometimes ignoring and rejecting us or repelling their children from playing with us so as not to stained them or influence them.

By the time I was age nine in 1963, I was well known as a street boy in most part of the western area in Freetown, and I learned lots of street-living survival skills and techniques, none of which was a good thing. I lived constantly with physical wounds over my body, and I suffered internal pains as well. Street life was like living like animals in the jungle. There was a great deal of lawlessness. The bigger boys do not need any cause for beating up younger boys or bullying them. After all, it was their way of asserting power and somehow derived some excitement and pleasure. Sometimes they would like to watch a fight, so, like promoters, they would just coax two of other young boys and set up a fight while they amuse themselves as they watch. So I had my share of that piece of the pie.

At some point being beaten up meant nothing to me anymore; in fact, they labeled me with the name Borborpain, a slang in Creole for anyone who, like sponge sucking and holding water, can withhold pain constantly. In my world, beating was as good as money to pay in exchange for goods, so I had to submit myself for beating in exchange for food or anything I needed. If I was desperately hungry, I would go to any of the restaurants and order food and soda, and when I was done eating without any money to pay for the food, I will take whatever punishment instead; usually a few kicks in the ass and knocks on the head and the bill is paid. Other punishment might be to do some hard-labor jobs, cleaning up for a couple of hours.

I recall a particular incident when a cook shop owner held on to me in front of her cook shop on Kroo Town Road. Coincidentally, Jacksony was passing by, and someone beckoned to him that I was being held. He came over, looked at me, and shook his head. Then he told the woman something that immediately prompted the woman and others to flog me. Later that evening, I was seating among some people on the street corner at the intersection of Berwick and Pricilla Streets when suddenly, older boys grabbed me, and before I knew what was happening, my mother appeared, and I was taken home by force.

At home Jacksony was waiting prepared with two canes socked wet and with some pepper water. They both claimed that I was a disgrace to the family. My mother socked my eyes with the pepper water so that I won't see as I was stripped naked. Jacksony viciously struck my bare skin with those canes to his satisfaction until I lost my voice and could not cry any more. After they were done, I knew not how to position myself to sleep or to seat or to stand on my feet for a number of days. My body ached everywhere, and I promised myself that I must kill them both at the least chance. By this time in my life when I think of doing something, I just do it without a second thought or without weighing the consequences. But after a few days before I took the street again, one night I had a terrible dream that deterred me from doing what I planned. What I planned to do was to stab them multiple times while they were in bed drunk and sleeping, but miraculously I dreamed the exact plan in my sleep, and I was terrified when I jumped out of the dream sweating and shaking, and for a moment I thought it was real, that I had stabbed them both about a hundred times each, and a couple of birds, vultures, were waiting for me to leave so they can take care of the mutilated bodies. The figure of two men appeared in pure-white clothing, and the vultures fled away at their arrival, and one of them stretched out his hand, and I let go the knife, and the other handed me a white handkerchief. Together, before my eyes, piece by piece, the two mutilated bodies were coupled up, and both of Mum's and Jacksony's bodies became whole as if nothing had happened. This dream followed and terrified me for a long time thereafter.

My wounds healed over time, but the scars remained, and my hatred for them both deepened all the more. On days that I go to school, the whole school would be staring at me, and I would be so embarrassed thinking of what they already knew about me. By now the teachers were all disappointed with me. Some of them remembered me as a very clever boy few years back, and now I am so irregular and disconnected that even my own friends looked at me as a freshman.

I remembered something went wrong in my class one day, and the teacher whipped the entire pupils in the classroom except for me. When it was my turn to be flogged, the teacher just looked at me with all the wounds and marks on my body with no shoe on my feet, and he said, "You know, John, I am afraid I won't touch you because you look already half-dead. I don't think that you even bath this morning before coming to school after so many absences. You are filthy and sick. You need to have your parents take you to the hospital to take care of all these wounds on your body."

He was right. I came from the street that morning before going to school. I did not even wash my face, and my uniform was dirty and rumpled. The only reason I went to school that day was because the National School Authorities had given foodstuff—cornmeal, milk, bulgur, and butter oil—to each school for distribution to the children, and if I did not go to school that day, I would not get my portion of the ration. The whole class ridiculed me during recess and after school that day, so that was my last day in school for that year.

I sold a large portion of my supply and reserved the others, which I ate straight without preparing them. I put the bulgur in my pocket and ate little by little over time. I also ate the powder milk dry, and I sold the cornmeal and butter oil.

One Ramadan evening in 1965, I was seating among a group of elders on the street corner listening as they argued on various topics about rich people and pioneers of businesses in the country. A few people who initiated meaningful projects in our community came up, and I was surprised and very proud when my father's name was mentioned as the first person to start bringing firewood to the doors of people who needed it. Others who had lorries did the same thing but differently. They would go get the firewood from the rural area and bring it to town, but they would sell to the people from one terminal where the firewood would be packed. JC, as my dad is affectionately called, decided to have an apprentice in the truck shouting, "Woodea. Woodea"—meaning "wood is here"—as the truck drives slowly from one street to the other. This way people living on a particular street, interested as they often were, would call out loud, and the apprentice would ring a bell for the drive to stop, and the sales would be made right near the buyer's home, a much easier system that lifted the burden of carrying bunches of firewood on heads and walking long distances.

When Dad started that system, his truckload of firewood would be sold within a few hours. Over 90 percent of the local population, including most bakeries, used firewood; therefore it was a fast-moving commodity in that country's economy. One of them said JC had not been seen for years in the area, and everyone agreed except for one man who claimed to have seen him and spoke with him just a couple of weeks ago. This caught my interest. I dared not interrupt the elders, so I just listened and waited for them to retire.

When it was approaching prayer time, the men dispersed, and I followed the elderly who claimed to have seen my dad to speak to him in private. When I introduced myself as JC's son, he was glad to speak with me and confirmed seeing him frequently at Kissy Mess-

Mess, and he believed that my dad lived and worked there, but he did not have an address. That night was a sleepless night for me as I started planning to go in search of my dad. The good news now was that my dad was still alive, and he returned to Kissy Mess-Mess. For the first time in my life, I found myself taking the initiative to pray, sincerely asking God to help me find my dad.

Chapter 3

I woke up very early the next morning at five not only because I planned to start the long journey to Kissy Mess-Mess but also to comply with the policy of one of my friends in the area in whose house I slept. His parents would punish him if they found out I slept in their home or if they spotted me in their home any time between 5:30 a.m. to 7:00 a.m. when his dad leaves the house for work. He had slicked me into his room once in a while to sleep. I would have to walk barefooted to cover the six miles to Kissy Mess-Mess. For an eleven-year-old-kid at that time, traveling alone to cover such a distance was unusual. In fact, until then, my street life was limited to the western area of Freetown. I barely traveled past the Cathedral Park, where I seldom go to have fun.

I started off my journey at around 6:00 a.m., and in a matter of few minutes I reached the intercession of Kroo Town Road and Andrew Street where I usually help petty traders early in the morning or late evenings with casual jobs to carry their loads on my head from there to wherever. A woman hired me to carry a bag of peanuts from there to Lumley Street for ten cents. On the way I stripped open the sack and grabbed some of the nuts, making sure all my pockets were full. The woman who was walking ahead of me did not notice, so she paid me, and I walked away to find the first shop and ate breakfast. I bought bread for two cents, one cent butter, and a cent sugar; then I borrowed an empty bottle and fixed me what street boys called "sugar ray": a bottle of water loaded with sugar, shaken until the sugar dissolve. This quick drink goes well with hot bread, hot enough to melt the butter in it. This was every street boy's dream in the morning before the hustling and bustling began. After I had breakfast, I rested for about an hour. The bag of peanut was very heavy, and the woman was reluctant to let me carry it, but I insisted. I suffered neck pain, so I rested three times on the way before I finally arrived to make the delivery, and after the load was taken off my head, it feels as though it was still there. At around midday I continued with the journey.

Four hours later I was at Wellington where I saw some children playing soccer, so I joined them, and by the time we were done, it was getting dark. I asked the children if there was a nearby street pump so that I could drink, but two of them invited me to their house to drink. Once we entered the yard, I realized they were Muslim children. A large group of Muslim men were preparing for prayers before breaking fast, and the smell of food and busy women were in the yard bringing large bowls of food to the mat. One of the boys went in and brought me a cup of water. I was going to ask him if I could stay to pray with the elders and to broke fast with them, when he suddenly suggested that I joined them to eat after the prayer. It was as though he read my mind. I stayed, and minutes later the crowd of men and women went to the mat to pray, and feeling guilty that I was sitting alone, I joined the children's group at the back, and we all prayed. It was so funny to me that for the first time in my life I became a Muslim for the food. One of the women asked my name after the prayers, and I had to give her a Muslim name: Musa. There was enough food, and as we ate, the women kept bringing more and more food. In my mind I was feeling guilty and funny that I suddenly became Muslin for a moment. I do not think that the Muslim people would have send me away because I belong to the Christian faith, but I was indecisive, scared, and lost esteem for myself. I was always thinking that people would find fault at me if I spoke the truth, so I told them what I thought they would respond favorably to just to fit in. Anyway, I told myself that a little flavor of Muslim blended with Christianity should not be harmful. After all, trying to find your way to Kissy Mess-Mess when you are already in a mess, anything can happen.

For a brief moment I asked myself what religion I belong to. In three years I have not entered a church. My dad had all his children baptized in an Anglican Church, and I had been attending church regularly with my parents before Lucifer himself visited our family and brought things to where they were. I wondered what Christianity would look like after Jacksony graduated, ordained as a reverend, and pastured a church. I imagined how many people would be led on the road to hell if the Lord withheld his grace and mercy. The meaning and purpose of religion at that moment was ambiguous and too complex for me to understand. What matters to me was to eat well, be energized, pick up the pace, and continue my journey. After all, in Sierra Leone, Christian and Muslims amicably lived side by side without any major incident. Muslim children attended Christian schools and prayed to God Almighty. School-going children in Sierra Leone at that time, be they Muslim or Christian, took BK as a subject in class, and they all participated in devotions with the holy Bible being the textbook. Intermarriages between Christians and Muslims were popular as they are today. Part of each of these marital rites is conducted in a Church and the other part in a Mosque. Christians would celebrate Muslim holidays, and Muslims would celebrate Christian holidays, vice versa.

Now it was night, and I was full and lazy to walk, so I decided to look around for a place to sleep after I left my new friends. I remembered seeing an old unfenced garage with defective vehicles near where we played soccer. I decided to go back there to sleep. I settled in one of the several wrecked cars and fell fast asleep. But that was one bad night for me. I was awakening in my sleep in the early-morning hours by a distant noise that came closer and closest toward me. Some people were chasing a burglar, and the burglar had made his way into the garage and jumped from the back into a small valley. I was fully awakening but lying flat in the backseat of the wrecked car. I started hearing voices around the garage. It was only a matter of time when they will fish me out and give me the trashing of my life. I have heard of the people of the east of Freetown. They would kill a thief it they caught one. There was a popular saying in the west that folks in the east would push lime with pepper in the rectum of thieves after they are severely beaten up. Fear gripped me and I began to shed tears in the dark, praying not to be seen. Suddenly the torchlight started flashing around the area where I was in the garage. My heart sank, and my stomach somersaulted as the light flashed on me. The one who had the light flashed on me called the attention of the others that the burglar was in there, I started crying out loud and pleading that I was only sleeping in the wreck car.

But before they could hear me in the commotion, I have already received a cut at the back of my left hand along with some punches. Then the men realized that I was only a boy. They believed the burglar was a heavily built adult. But one of them said we could have been together. Now they asked if I saw or heard something. I did not see him, but I heard a loud sound like someone landing from a jump. I pointed to the direction where I thought the sound I heard came from. Few of the men went around the fence and, there they found the burglar lying flat in the bushes. I had never seen such beating before in all my life. This burglar himself was crying out for the police to come rescue him. He sustained several wounds on his head, bleeding as they dragged him under the streetlight.

More people came struggling to take a strike at him. The burglar was taken to the Kissy Police Station, and the crowd followed. One of the men held my hand and took me along. He said it was dangerous that a little boy like me should be sleeping in that place. There were too many people entering the police station, but the police disperse the crowd. After the burglar was placed in the cell, the man pulled me forward, and the told the police about me. He told the police I am a witness, and I also needed help because they found me sleeping in one of the wrecked cars at the abandoned garage.

It was around 3:30 a.m., and the crowd dispersed. After all the police formalities, the burglar was thrown in a cell with all the wounds he sustained. I thought that they would have taken him to the hospital, but they did not. Now the station officer called me to his desk, along with some of the men who caught the burglar. He asked my name, and for a moment I thought I had seen him at the Muslim's place where I ate. If this is the case, then my name is Musa, I thought, but that would only make matters worse if the police eventually found out who I was. So I told them my real name. The officer asked what I was doing sleeping in a wrecked car at the abandon garage. I told him I was in search of my dad whom I heard was leaving in Kissy Mess-Mess, and I was on my way there from the western area when night caught up with me. He wrote down the information; then he lifted up his head and asked my father's name. Upon hearing my father's name, the officer's eyes brightened, and he stretched his hands across the desk toward me, excited. He repeated my dad's name and asked if the JC Davies I was talking about was once a police inspector. I said yes, and the officer stood to his feet and placed his hands over his mouth in astonishment that a son of the former inspector, who was his boss, would be in this predicament, sleeping in wrecked vehicle. Then he told the men who brought me in that he got his police training under my dad; then he said my dad was living in Kissy Mess-Mess and working as a tug master at the Kissy Dock Yard.

"I know where he lives and where he works also," he said. "I cannot take you to his house now because it is far away in the village, but I can take you to his workplace after my shift ends in the morning when I am off duties. You will stay here with us, till in the morning."

Finally I found a possible link to finding my dad. The police used their first aid kit to take care of my wound, and they gave me a drink and a stretcher to pass the rest of the night. This night was a fearful one, but God was really with me. There was no way I could take half of the beating that that burglar took and survived.

Chapter 4

The station officer finished his shift turnover formalities by 9:00 a.m., and then we drove together with few other offices in a Land Rover Jeep to Kissy Duck Yard where my dad worked as a tug master. The work site was a large compound by the seaside with couple of tugs, small speed boats on the pier, large oil tanks, warehouses, and large trailers and trucks on land. We were taken to a small conference room to wait for my dad. Some of his coworkers thought he may have had some problem for the police were there, but the senior police officer broke the ice.

"Mr. Davies is my former boss in the police force, and I am here to see him to seek his advice. There is no problem," he said, laughing.

My dad entered the room moments later and apparently did not see me sitting in the corner. He recognized the officers and started calling them by name, and all of them upon his entering simultaneously stood to their feet and saluted him military style. My dad smiled at them, and as he was about to ask what brought them there, he looked my way and recognized me. Surprised and excited, he called me by my middle name, which is his middle name too.

"Chea!" he shouted out, throwing both hands over his head in amazement. "This is my son!"

Simultaneously, we both reached out for each other, embraced, and wept. There was a moment of silence; then he explained to the officers, who sobbed as they listened, the reason why he exiled himself from his family for three years. He fought back tears as he was explaining, and I was inconsolable, seeing my dad and remembering the good man he was and the good times that were taken from us, which were replaced with three years of misery. I was so overwhelmed with emotions that I did not know what to do with the moment. There were many things to cry for: the new wounds and pain I sustained from the night incident, the old sores on many parts of my body, the blisters under my feet, the psychological pain and sufferings and exhaustion of street life, etcetera. I had been weary, tormented, and isolated. I needed the warm embrace and comfort of someone who truly loved me and cared about me, and my dad also needed that. This was the moment and the only person in the world God had given me to fulfill this need.

I felt like I have found a precious jewel. For once in three years I felt secured like a child should. The head police officer sobbed as he gently tapped me on the back and said good-bye. My dad thanked them, and they left. Some of his coworkers where delighted to see us together, and my dad was given the rest of the day off. Before we left the company compound, I was taken to the cafeteria, where a hot bowl of cassava leaf soup with rice was served. My dad asked if I needed a second round. Without hesitation, I went for it. Then I was taken to a barbershop, where I got a nice haircut, and then he took me to Bata, the shoe company, where he bought me about six pairs of footwear: shoes, snickers, and slippers. Then he bought me clothes. When we went home; he bathed me and treated the wounds on my body. I put on some nice clothes, and we went out for dinner at one of the place's popular restaurants. It felt good and reassuring once again to know that no one would have to beat me up for the food I was eating.

We stayed up that night till 3:00 a.m., talking before sleep took its turn. I wanted to make him feel justified for his action, and he also wanted me to understand it could have been worst; he could have been in jail as a convict awaiting his execution for murdering his wife and her boyfriend, and that stigma would have lived with all of his children for the rest of their lives. He repeated what he said to the officers that if he had not exiled himself, he could have done some damages that would have destroyed his reputation. In my mind, at the time I thought that was what he was supposed to do, because I hated Jacksony, and I was disgusted at the treatment I received from him.

For a year I stayed with dad at Kissy Mess-Mess, but he was not the same man I used to know. He gave me everything I needed, but I was left alone most of the time. He had a girlfriend who also had children, and he spent most of his time at her place, and I had to live alone at his house. I needed more of his attention and affection to help me heal, but I had to share him with this other family, and it was not satisfying for me.

He registered me at Kissy Primary School (KPS), where I made good friends at school and around where we lived. I always needed someone to keep my company and never wanted to be left alone, but I did not know how to communicate this with dad. When I was at home alone, especially at night, I sometimes get nightmares, and it felt like the situation I was in when I was living as a street boy. The phobias never really went away. I started buying and smoking cigarettes and sometimes stayed in the streets after school and would return home about the time I knew Dad would be off duties. Although I do not go eating food without paying likes before because this time I always have money from Dad, and plenty of food and provisions were always at home. My father loved good food so he always made sure there was enough food home, and he also maintained an account with a nearby provision store where he introduced me and made a standing order for me to be given anything I wanted on the account.

There were few homeless boys I played soccer with on a nearby playground that I empathized with their plights. I would take food from home for them some of the times, and that made me feel good that I reached out to a community of vulnerable people whom I related to despite the way they were branded in the community. I became popular in the community, and Dad had no idea because he was seldom around to see what I did daily after school or on weekends when he would be gone for a couple of days either on assignment at sea or spending time with his new family.

He was confused one Saturday during a big community event when elders in the community commended me for building bridges between some troubled families and folks referred to as wayward boys

DYSFUNCTIONAL ONE

in the community. It all started between two neighbors who entered a feud over their children's association with so-called wayward street boys. It was because of a watch that was said to have been stolen from one member of one of the families and sold to a member of the other family. The matter culminated into physical fights between the two families and their children. The chief and elders in the area tried to resolve the many matters that degenerated from this one watch issue.

It turned out that one of the homeless boys whom I used to feed was the one who sold the watch, and it was given to him by a son in the family who owned the watch. It was his dad's watch, and it was sold to his neighbor. I came from school one afternoon to find the big crowd on the street, and when I inquired from one of the homeless boys, he told me exactly where it all started and named the son who stole his father's watch and the one he gave it to, who in turn sold it to the other family member. It turned out that it was not the watch alone that this boy stole from his home but also his mother's necklace, which was not yet sold.

My sense for fair play kicked in, and I decided to talk to the boy who sold the watch, and he was honest with me by explaining exactly how it happened, and then he showed me a necklace that no one knew about yet except the son of the family who stole his father's watch. The necklace belonged to his mother. I got involved and spoke to the homeless boy who released the necklace to me, and I was able to convince him that we should return the necklace and expose the boy who stole his father's watch, because eventually at the end of the day when the police got involved he, the street boy, would be the one who would be framed, and he knew that because of his street boy reputation, no one would believe him then.

He agreed and I took the necklace to the chief and some elders and explained things to them. Moments later the brawl between the two families and their relatives subsided, and they all converged in a compound before the chief and elders, and the two families understood where the problem started from. The son who stole his father's watch came from school that evening and was punished. His family and relatives apologized to their neighbors, and the watch and necklace were returned to them. The tribal chief and elders thanked me and the homeless boy for having the courage to come forward to resolving the problem. The elders advised and encouraged some of the homeless boys present to restrain themselves from temptation. People in the neighborhood were warned not to label the homeless or street boys, as they are called, bad because of who they were.

A couple of days later, a woman tapped at my door and asked for my help. Some street boys in the neighborhood had threatened to beat up her daughter if they saw her on the street. I accompanied the woman and her daughter to the street corner where I talked to the boys, and the matter was resolved. So when Dad witnessed the tribal chief and some elders recognizing me at the community events that weekend, he was stunned and proud of what he was hearing about me. But all that was short-lived.

In September 1966, Dad was transferred to work at Pepel, a little island near Freetown, and he would not let me stay all by myself at Kissy Mess-Mess, so after careful thought, he decided that we were going back to western Freetown.

We moved out from Kissy Mess-Mess to a one-bedroom apartment at Upper Waterloo Street in Freetown next to Samaria church. Dad rented a room in Pepel where he lived for the most part while he worked at sea near Pepel. He would spend weekends in Freetown and rest of the weekday at Pepel. Shortly thereafter, he fell in love with another woman who had divorced her husband, and the competition I feared from sharing my dad with another family continued, making me a loner.

In Kissy Mess-Mess, we never received local news about what was going on in our Kroo tribal community since there were hardly anyone from our tribe living in that part of the country. We were isolated from the Kroo community to the extent that my younger brother, Samuel, returned from Ghana at age nine in 1965 shortly after I went in search for Dad, and both of us had no idea until when we moved to the area. When we learned that Samuel was back from

Ghana, Dad and I were eager to see him, but he had to go back to sea to work, so we planned that when he returned that weekend, we would both find a way to get Samuel to visit us and spend the weekend together. But when Dad left and I was alone, I was tempted to go find my brother to introduce myself.

When I arrived on Berwick Street that afternoon, no one recognized me easily because I was different. I was dressed in a navy-blue khaki pants, white long-sleeves shirt, white socks, and a crape. I had a nice haircut, and there were no sore on my body, and I was looking very healthy, and I had some change in my pocket that Dad left me.

When I arrived at my mother's house, the whole place went ablaze, and neighbors who heard the noise came to see me. My mother was excited as much as I was, but that was just for a little while until I asked for my brother, Samuel. My mother said that Samuel left and was living on the street like I was. I learned that no one had even reported me as a lost child for the year that I was not seen. My mother just assumed that I must have found my dad or maybe gone to Liberia to live with relatives there. I knew right away that Samuel must have had some issues with Jacksony.

Poor boy, I thought, *just arrived in the country and being initiated.*

It was Samuel's third time to be thrown out of the house in a period of ten months. I left immediately to search for him even though I did not know what he looked like. Some of the street boys in the area knew him, and they showed me where to find him. As soon as I saw him that evening at the marketplace at Government Wharf, where I was told he frequently went to carry loads for marketers to make a living, I sensed who he was. We looked alike. I called him by his middle name. "Ynogbay!"

He looked at me wondering where he knew me from. Then I introduced myself, and he dropped the bag on his head that he was carrying for someone, and we hugged each other and cried as marketers looked on. Together we left, and when we got home at Upper Waterloo Street, there was plenty of food and a place he can call home.

Samuel told me countless stories of Jacksony and Mum, about drunkenness on weekends and fighting and altercations and how everything he did was evil in the eyes of Jacksony, who beat him up many times. Each narrative of Jacksony's cruelty made me feel like going back to my mother's house to attack him, but somehow I resisted the temptation but not for a long time. Samuel and I shared a lot in common. We were not just brothers with physical similarities, but in our characters and instinct, we were also a team in many ways and deeds: good, bad, and ugly.

Dad would leave us alone, and for the most part we had to do things by ourselves without supervision for a long time. Dad had so many girlfriends that he would spend time with even when he was not working on weekends, and Samuel and I would decide what we were going to do.

Sometimes we would gather a sack full of rocks and go to wreck war with Jacksony. We would impose curfews on him, and so if he was in our mother's house, he would never leave to go anywhere else, or if he was out, he would not come back to the house. We would be at two strategic places, and on sight of Jacksony anywhere, we would throw rocks on him so hard that he either ran for his life or took cover. Even when we were not around, neighbors would watch him looking over his shoulders or running his way in or out.

Chapter 5

From 1962 when my parents broke up to 1968, Dad struggled with one relationship after another. Samuel and I had difficulties coping with some of his girlfriends and their children. At times, we would move in with him into his girlfriend's home, and suddenly the challenges of trying to adjust or cope with living with their children would take its toll. Some of them were from different tribes and different cultural backgrounds.

But Mum and Jacksony were still together though he fed on her rental income to support his womanizing lifestyle, which he was very good at. He was notorious for having multiple affairs with several women from the same church, some of them were Mum's own friends, but somehow they were still together until his graduation from Foray Bay University in 1969. He and Mum have had four children by then: the first was the girl child, whose birth was in the center of my parents' separation. Her name was Munah, and she lived six years and died mysteriously in 1968 at age six. Their next child was a boy named after Jacksony. He was Jacksony's junior just like I am my father's junior. He was born retarded in 1964 and never was able to creep, sit, stand up, or walk until he died mysteriously later that same year, 1968, at age four. Those two mysterious deaths in 1968 and the fact that Jacksony Jr. laid stiffed in bed for four agonizing years from the day he was born to the day he died should have sent a clear message to both Mum and Jacksony: a message that he simply cannot put asunder what God had put together and under the same breath display hatred toward the children whose lives he sought to destroy and expected to have a son named after him from the same womb. Those were four agonizing years for these two, but apparently they did not get the message, or they were in denial.

Their third child, Princes, was the one that Providence spared but for a purpose. She was destined to turn the table around on her parents for life. Her life would be like a long-term payback vendetta in multiple ways, and she played her role very well to the point where both Mum and Jacksony and a lot more people in the vicinity feared her till this day. She would become a witch at an early age and later became notorious for three of her signature accomplishments: (1) She carries around on her person a cobra and a ritualistic handkerchief in her purse; (2) she killed her sister, Jacksony and Mum's child, Sylvia, in 1992; and (2) she slapped her dad, Rev. S. P. Jacksony, and pulled him down to the ground from the pulpit before his congregation while he was delivering his Easter Sunday sermon in church in the early '80s.

By the time Sylvia was born in 1968, Jacksony had graduated with honors from MMTC and started attending Foray Bay College and at the same time taught Bible knowledge part-time at Albert Academy, one of the prestigious high schools in Freetown. That same year my elder brother, Princer, who was living between Mum and our grandmother at 37 McDonald Street in Freetown passed his common entrance examination and started attending Albert Academy.

Princer was very ambitious and wanted to advance in his education, but there was something conflicting between him and Dad. Because of our unstable way of life, living between two opposing parents, the culture of trying to do things or say things while in the presence of one parent just so one can be favored was prevalent. Princer had shown support for Mum to gain favor in the eyes of Jacksony, so he and Dad would not see eye to eye.

But trying to gain favor in the eyes of Jacksony was like building one's foundation on quicksand. The Bible instructor would put his student stepson out of his class at school if there was something wrong between then or any of us either at home or on the streets.

One weekend in 1969, Jacksony beat up our younger sister, Victoria, who was then nine years old. He was drunk then and took off her tooth. Victoria, bloodied up, came running to Dad's house apartment at 13 Charles Street, Freetown, where Dad had settled down with his new girlfriend and three of her children. It was a one-bedroom apartment that we all had to share at the time. Dad brought in his new girlfriend, who already had about three of her own children. On that weekend, Dad was home when Victoria came crying with swollen face, bloodied up with her tooth knocked off her mouth.

That was the day that Samuel and I were going to get into our first major trouble. We went in search of Jacksony while Dad took our sister to the police and then to the hospital. But Jacksony smelled what was coming, so he escaped and went into hiding by the time Samuel and I came looking for him, armed with knives and cutlasses. He was arrested the next day, but Mum posed a bond and bailed him out, and when the case came up, she testified in favor of her boyfriend and told lies that she ordered the flogging as a disciplinary action and that Victoria's tooth was already shaking and came out the day before the flogging. She said it was just a plot growing out of jealousy. The judge acquitted Jacksony in his final ruling. There was no question that some sort of bribery had taken place.

During these times, Jacksony would undermine our older brother, Princer, at school and threw him out of his class and influenced other teachers to do the same or to be hard on him. This frustrated Princer, who moved out from Mum's home to live with our grandmother. Our grandmother then arranged for him to go to Liberia to live there with her brother, Counselor Daniel Draper. So Princer dropped out of school and traveled to Liberia in the fall of 1969.

In that same year, Sylvanusy Paynee Jacksony graduated from Foray Bay College, and the church, which partly sponsored him, sadly decided to have him ordained to pastor the church amid the damages he had already committed: his womanizing reputation, having multiple secretive relationships with married and single women and fathering children who would never know who their real biological father is.

In preparing Jacksony for his big day, he was placed in the church's property up the road on Adelaide Street, where his neighbors there expressed their disgust at the many women who came in and out to see the would-be pastor in seclusion. The doors and window to that house were locked most of the time when he was in there busy with any of the women who were also attracted to him.

But there was a big objection hanging over the playboy pastor's big day. As a rule, he cannot be ordained to pastor the church as a single man, so he was given a couple of months to marry before being ordained; otherwise, the church would have someone else to the throne. Too bad forMmum that she could not get divorced fast enough to marry her playboy Jacksony, who needed the position so badly since that would give him the total control and monopoly he needed to continue his womanizing with impunity. Besides, the divorce laws favored Dad since he did not cause the separation, and he could delay the proceeding for as long as wanted as a payback, just so that Mum would be hurt. Ordinarily, divorce cases took a long time anyway, sometimes a year or more to conclude.

So Jacksony, seeing that chances for his big day may never come if he waited on Mum, made his decision and selected his bride-to-be from his collection of women; it was one of Mum's best friends whom he had been sleeping with secretly. Their marriage did not only devastated Mum and the other disappointed women in the church, but it also polarized the congregation to a point of no reconciliation.

However, Mum found consolation in other playboys who were both members of the same church. One of them, Sylvesternus Mosesi, a married man, who was also a policeman, betrayed his wife and bore a son with mum in 1970, not long after Jacksony was ordained reverend and installed as pastor of the church. Soon, news spread about the policeman's relationship and the bastard child he had with Mum, and the policeman's wife took offense, and trouble began to brew in the community among them.

A year later, Mum entered another relationship with a seafarer named Lawrenzo Davis, and a year later in 1972, she bore him a child. That man's wife who sang in the choir took offense, and the scandal, and all the gossips it garnered took its toll. It would appear that Mum's relationships with the policeman and the seafarer were in retaliation to hurt Rev. Pastor Jacksony for what she might have considered as his betrayal. But I was confused when later they renewed their relationship, and Mum bore the pastor's fifth child in 1974.

Rev. Pastor Jacksony was slicker than slick and a shameless spinster who saw himself as a warrior, spreading his wings around as he took pleasure in adulterous relationships, sleeping around with so many women, and breaking homes, which he was notorious for. The church became polarized in a variety of ways until it became smaller and smaller for the pastor to effectively lead or deliver a reasonable sermon. In fact, most sermons were framed, tailored to justify and suit his purpose, just to make his agendas righteous in the eyes of the women, many of who were illiterate. And to those who were educated, his favorite quote would be "Do as I say, but don't do as I do."

It is not known how many people received salvation under Jacksony's pastoral wings over the next few years, but it is well known that over time, he became a laughingstock as more and more women became united against him, and he strived harder to disappear especially so after his daughter, Princes, walked up to the pulpit on that fateful Easter Sunday and slapped the pastor as he was delivering his Easter sermon, pulling him by his robe down to the floor, and pandemonium broke up as the pastor struggled to free himself from an angry but fearless daughter who dared anyone to intervene as she dealt with the pastor.

"It was a blessing that the police station was just a block away, and there was also a 'policeman' in the congregation," recalled one church member.

Police had to intervene to keep the peace in the church; after which an assistant to the badly beaten-up pastor delivered the convocation to a handful of traumatized members of the congregation, while the other members stood on the street, wondering what has just happened.

Chapter 6

By the time I became seventeen years old in 1971, my life had been so restless that the consequences of unprepared challenges had emboldened me to take and engage risky ventures, mostly without second thoughts or with little or no concern for my reputation. When Dad and I moved to Freetown from Kissy Mess-Mess, in 1966, we lived at Upper Waterloo Street for about six months, then something happened, and Samuel and I moved back to Mum's house for a few days, after which she kicked us out, and we ended up at our grandmother's one-room apartment at McDonald Street.

Dad came from work one night and had a couple of beers, which was the case whenever he got paid. He was lying in his room sleeping when Princer came in to visit. From one thing to another, he convinced us to steal some money from Dad's salary that was in an envelope in his coat pocket. The amount was about twenty-eight pounds, and that was a considerable amount of money at that time. The amount could have paid Dad's rent for at least six months with yet some change left, so it was a big deal. For some stupid reasons, I had always wished and dreamed that my parents would get back together again and things would be as exactly as they were before, but Dad had sold his Bedford and Hillman to foot the bills for his recovery from paralysis and post-traumatic stress disorder he suffered from the violent separation.

However, Samuel and I joined Princer, and we took the amount to our Mum, who instantly became very nice toward us. She convinced us to go back and get our belongings from Dad's place before he was awoken and to come live with her once again, and we did. When Dad woke up the next morning and was sober, he checked for the envelope containing his salary, and he could not find it, and he could not find Samuel and me who used to live with him.

He had no idea that Princer had visited us the evening before, and he would not imagine that the two of us would have the guts to go back to our mum to live.

However, Dad went in search for us and got hold of me playing soccer on the street. As soon as he got hold of me, I confessed and lied that it was Princer alone who took the money to his mother, and Samuel, who was not there when I confessed, gave the same narrative as mine when he was grabbed. Dad involved the police, but Mum denied receiving any amount from us, and Prince also denied, saying he never even visited us at Waterloo Street. Nothing came out of the case after long hours of interrogations. Dad was so annoyed that he asked Samuel and me not to come back. Now we could not go back to Mum's house to live, and so we ended up living at our grandmother's house for a while and subsequently in the streets.

Grandmother was a very nice and caring person, who loved all of us, but living with her was living in the remotest parts of the world in the 1700s. She did not have electricity in her apartment, and nights were longer than usual and boring. Her doors are closed at 7:00 p.m. latest, and that was bedtime for her. She was always fighting for us to the extent that her own daughter (Mum) once beat her up at her house in Berwick Street.

On the day Mum beat her mother, Jacksony had beaten me up, and a neighbor who witnessed how badly I was being beaten informed my grandmother while she was on her way to the market, so she came to her daughter's house to chastise Jacksony, and Mum took offense and slapped her own mother. Then she jumped on her, threw her on the ground, and sat on her belly while striking her on the head and face.

The Morris family was a tenant at her house at the time, and they intervened to separate them. Since that time both Mum and Jackson maligned Grandmother, and that went on for years even though they all attended the same church on Adelaide Street.

Somehow down the road, Samuel and I settled our differences with Dad, but he was no longer living at Upper Waterloo Street.

He was living with his new girlfriend then on Dundas Street. She had four children living with her. Then Samuel and I lived there for a while, but things were not the same anymore. Dad's relationship with that woman was short-lived, and he left the house. Samuel and I could not continue to live there anymore after Dad left, so we stayed on the streets for a while, but we were always visiting our grandmother to eat in the evenings and then disappeared before 7:00 p.m., or else we would be locked in until 7:00 a.m. the next day.

Samuel and I lived on the streets for a couple of months before we learned that our dad was living with another girlfriend on Steward Street. She had only one son. Dad spoke to the woman, and she allowed us to live at her place for a while, but that was short-lived as they broke up soon after, and Dad finally rented the one-room apartment at 13 Charles Street and settled down with the woman he spent the rest of his life with until his death in September 1993.

By the time Dad settled down with his new girlfriend at Charles Street, Samuel was done with street life. He started learning auto mechanic and was adopted by a middle-class Creole family called Benjamin on Little East Street. The Benjamin family ran a bakery business, and Samuel volunteered with their jobs overnight while learning to become an auto mechanic during the day. None of these activities offered any stipends, but he was consistent and for a long period of time I was sure to get bread and cake from him every time I visited him.

Dad's new girlfriend was a single parent raising three children fathered by three different men, and two of her children were older than us. Dad and this woman had four children: three boys and a girl in the 1970s. Life was never going to reverse for me to get back the childhood I missed, and our parents were never going to be the same anymore as there were too many children and too many conflicting interests and challenges involved.

With the instabilities that Samuel and I had to deal with, our school attendance record wasn't that great; though we were ambitious to learn, we were discouraged, and the longer we stayed out of school, the more difficult it was to catch up.

Dad's new girlfriend surely did not like us. Resources were scarce, and she would prefer to favor her children over us, and we were always in some problem with her; then we moved out to live with our mother, and when she kicked us out, which was inevitable, we would briefly live with Grandmother and then back on the streets. This was the routine before Samuel became stable, leaving me to decide my fate at some point.

By 1970, I stumbled into class 7 by surprise at St. Thomas Primary School and found myself slated to take the common entrance examination to enter high school. This was three years past due, and so I was excited with the opportunity even though I had no idea where I was going to get the support from to get all that was required to enter high school if I made it.

As fate would have it, I was living with my mother then. Traditionally, students slated to take this selective examination would go into intensive study weeks before the exams, but I did not have the leverage and the facility. I had to fetch water from the street pump about fifty yards away to fill three large drums. Each of those drums takes about twenty buckets to full, and this is done every other day. Then I would wash clothes with my bare hands and hang them to dry and then iron them. Then I had to clean up the yard in the morning, and by the time I was done, exhaustion would have taken its toll.

Two days before the exams, I refused to do any work, and so Mum staved me for those two days, which was not a strange thing to me then because I have been used to that. But what she did to me on the morning of the exams was something that I would never forget. I went to bed early the night before and woke up early that morning like all candidates were advised to do. Common entrance examinations are taken at designated facilities around the country, and St. Thomas Primary School candidates were assigned to join other candidates to take the exams at Methodist Girls' High School facility near Congo Cross.

The exam started at 8:00 a.m., and since I was going to walk approximately two miles to get there, I decided to leave the house at 6:30 a.m. When I was ready to leave, I tapped at Mum's room door and woke her up and then asked her for my entrance pass, which I gave her earlier for safekeeping. That contained a set of numbers that the National School Exam Board provided their candidates, with emphasis that every candidates must provide that at the entrance before they would be allowed to enter the examination.

Mum was woken, opened her room door, looked me in the eye, and said, "This is where I knew I was going to get you since starving you does not mean anything to you anymore. For your refusal to fetch water for the house in the last two days, I am also going to seize your exam pass as a payback." And she slammed her door in my face. Those words cut through me like a knife.

I began sweating and crying, and I ran to neighbors and begged them to come to my rescue. Some of them came to talk to her, but she refused. As the clock on the wall struck seconds and then minutes passed by, it was like ripping off my heart. When there was no progress being made at around 7:15 a.m., I ran out of the house to call an elderly woman who was the treasurer of their church living in the neighborhood. The woman left everything she was doing and came with me to speak to my mother, but her heart was hardened, and she refused until when it was around 8:30 a.m.

I was sitting on the step to the front gate with my head buried between my legs crying and wondering what sense to make of this, when suddenly she threw the ticket at me from the window upstairs. I was already humiliated, disoriented, and disconnected. I picked up the ticket and my folder containing materials such as pens, pencils, ruler etc.

I started running, but my feet were too weak and heavy to carry me as fast as I would like to. By the time I arrived, it was a few minutes to 10:00 a.m. The whole place was as quiet when I suddenly appeared at the entrance of the examination hall. One of the officials sitting behind a desk at the entrance could not believe what she was looking at, me standing before her with tears running down my cheeks. She beckoned to me to wait, and she went into the hall and called other officials, who came running, surprised with their hands covering their mouth, gesturing that they can't believe that I was coming only now.

One of them asked what had happened, and the only thing I could respond with was a loud cry, for it was difficult to explain what had happened. No mother on earth would do this to their son, and I felt that no one would believe me then if I told them the truth, so I lied on myself that I misplaced the ticket and was looking for it. That made me look even reckless in their eyes, but I had not thought of any better lie than that. An elderly woman came from opposite direction, and she took me to a nearby office where I was processed and warned that the exam was in progress and that candidates were on the second paper. I was then led to the seat designated in the large hall where the exam was taking place. I lost my composure, and looking at the papers before me, I could hardly spell my own name correctly. I had to write and erase it until there was a little hole in one of the papers. I looked around me and saw candidates with heads bowed and writing, and for a moment I lost consciousness.

As I struggled out of that nightmare, I convinced myself that it was no point coming, I should just get up and leave, but my feet were heavier, and the weight of shame tied me to the seat. It was troubling to know beforehand that I have failed the exams before even trying. As I sat there all the papers that were put before me were all blank for I read nothing, understood nothing, and wrote nothing except my name and my ticket number on all the papers. For each time my eyes met with any of the administrators or any of the candidates in the hall, my heart pounded, and my mood showed that I was nervous, disconnected, and disoriented. The little self-esteem I had left just flew through the window, replaced with shame, degradation, and fear.

As I sat there shocked, nervous, and lost, I decided there and then in that hall that I would go to Liberia to join my elder brother there, though our relationship was like cats and dogs and we were always fussing and fighting.

Chapter 7

Before the common entrance exam results came out, I dropped out of school and was living full-time on my own, no other place to live but on the streets, determined to raise funds to cover my first trip to Liberia to live there. Samuel and I talked about my experience with Mum and about the exam, and he blamed me partly for even giving her the exam ticket for safekeeping:

"You should have predicted that with her, setbacks are common," he emphasized.

There was a contrast between Samuel and me. I was paradoxical in character. I was quick to forgive and to pretend nothing bad had happened, and sometimes I resolved to blame myself for the way I was treated by others, including our parents. And when I can afford to give gifts, I would do so hoping that that would change the attitude of people toward me. It was a real struggle for me trying to gain favor in the eyes of people. But Samuel was the opposite. He had always said that Mum's nature was like that of sugar ants, seeking and sticking where sugar is and disinterested when and where there was no sugar. He vowed that he was done with our parents and now focused on learning to become a motor vehicle mechanic, which he mastered later in his adult life.

As a mechanical apprentice during those days, Samuel had been lucky if he got stipend from the bosses, who got all the money and gave apprentices anything they feel like if and when they wanted to. If Samuel needed some money, he would skip the garage and do some hard-labor jobs like towing merchandises for marketers or helping to upload or offload commercial trucks at one of the nearby marketplaces.

On Saturday nights when there were no bakery activities, Samuel would sneak me into their storeroom where he slept, and I would spend the night there with him since there would be no activities that night, and all the cakes and breads that he hid in various hiding places would be placed in a sack for me to carry with me on Sunday morning.

Survival for the rest of the week was solely on my own initiatives. I would spend some time at the library during the day reading and sometimes borrowed novels to read in secluded places. Two of my favorite writers then were Perry Masson and James Hadley Chase. I would isolate myself most of the time and hid from anyone I knew, especially my schoolmates. My determination to raise funds to take me to Liberia to join Princer and to be able to survive there was burning inside me. Life in Freetown was humiliating for me after the exam. I was a smart kid, and I knew that despite my irregular school attendance, I could have pulled that off and promoted myself to high school, but sadly that was not the way I was perceived by the people in the community. Most grown-ups I dealt with then knew I was better than that. The foundation that Dad instilled in me together with the practicalities in surviving street life in early childhood had contributed to my maturity level above children of my age. I worked hard to pay my own school fees and to buy books at times.

My first and second terms' school fees for class 7 were generated from working as a casual worker at the local Coco-Cola Company near Jomo Kenyatta Road. But I was banned from working there by the management after a disgusting incident that I was involved in there. The company hired casual workers weekly to pack bottles in crates, stock pile crates of soft drinks, clean up factory equipment and the premise, etcetera. During the times I work there, I once created a small sleeping place at one of their storage where crates of finished products were stored and slept there for about two weeks. During those two weeks, I drank soft drinks overnight when I was alone in the store until I took sick. One of the company's inspectors found me sleeping during his inspection after working hours when no workers were allowed. That incident led to my interrogation and subsequent ban.

The following week when I got better, I went back to speak with Mr. Williams, the general manager, and apologized, but he would not accept any apologies, and he asked me outright never to return for casual work.

So when I was brainstorming how to raise funds for my Liberian trip, I thought about the company but not in any sense of working there but how I could defraud the management. I knew how their casual workers system worked, from the hiring process to attendance to the weekly remuneration process of their casual workers. I figured that I could infiltrate the system and get paid not as a casual worker but as a middleman between the management. It was an exciting challenge for me to see if I could put a plan together to delude those educated and experienced administrators to have them pay me in place of as many casual workers as possible. The maximum laborer pay per week then was around four Leones, which was equivalent to five US dollars, and that was a good amount of money for a single average citizen.

The weekly recruiting was usually carried out outside the main gate by a team of middle factory managers selecting casual workers for the coming week on Saturday afternoons, choosing among hundreds of job seekers. The casual workers would then work from Sunday to Friday, and on Saturday morning they would go individually into the finance office upstairs, announced their names to the paymaster, who sees hundreds of casual workers only on Saturdays. He would look for their names on a spread sheet and then they would sign on the sheet and collect their pay in sealed envelopes handed to them. From there, those who wanted to continue being hired would go into one of the middle managers' offices and bribed them one Leone so that their names would be highlighted on the new recruiting list for the following week.

During recruiting process at the main gate where hundreds of job seekers would be scrambling, the middle managers would first call into the gate those who already bribed them, and when that list is exhausted, then they would begin to handpick others and take down their names and addresses. On the first Saturday after my failed Common Entrance Examination attempt, I decided to execute the plan that I constructed. I went to the Coco Cola Company in the afternoon and watched the recruiting, and I wrote down the names and addresses of at least ten new casual workers, who were all easy to note since they were among the handpicked. Then I went up to Temgbeh Town at Brookfield, which was near a valley where some indigenous people from Limba tribe lived. Most of them were illiterates who came from up country and could hardly speak the local Creole language. They formed a community of palm wine and local gin brewers. They got more indigenous fellows coming to find better life or somewhat civilized life in the city.

I went there and recruited ten men, the youngest in their late twenties and the oldest in his midthirties. I told them that I wanted to return a favor to some people who helped me in the past, but since they were no longer there, I do not mind helping them out. I told the made-up story that I had been made a supervisor at the CCC and that I needed to recruit ten people to replace ten others who abandoned their work. The jobs, I said, were paid weekly and that they would have to work in the names of the guys who abandoned their jobs for a week and then returned to their actual names. They were excited, so we went to a secluded place where I tutored them their roles. We had three rehearsals that week to prepare them. They would wait for me to pick them up on Saturday morning to take them to the site where they would perform the role they were prepared for.

On Friday evening I went to a local bar on Campbell Street where Mr. Williams, the CCC general manager, hang out with his girlfriend who lived not far away from the bar. They usually met there on Friday evenings. He would park his car on Dugan Street to dislodge his wife, who frequently chased him around. On a few occasions, he had sent me around with messages for her, and she had prepared food for him, which I picked up and delivered to him at his office. I wanted to meet with him in that relaxed environment where he was drinking, socializing, and flirting with his girlfriend or with other girls. My plan was to tell him something to have him remove the ban placed on me so that I can have access into the compound and not have the security guy at the gate stop me from entering the CCC compound.

As fate would have it, his girlfriend who had no idea that I was banned spotted me first and tapped his shoulder as she pointed to me. I went straight to their table with a big smile on my face and whispered something in his ears.

"I know you are mad at me, but I just want you to know that your wife is around," I said.

And without waiting for me to end my statement, he immediately pulled his chair underneath him and stood up like a soldier standing at ease, and he asked where she was. I said she and others set a dragnet at the corner of Dugan Street where he parked his car.

"You won't believe who is passing information on you to your wife," I said.

By this time, the girlfriend was concerned and had excused herself after she heard him asked where his wife was. I said that I was afraid that I was not chanced to disclose things right there, but if he would allow me to see him tomorrow morning, he would be surprised about what was going on.

They both left their drinks, and he asked that I walk with him, but I said that I dare not do that right away, and then he walked away quickly without saying good-bye to any of the people in the bar.

As I was leaving in the opposite direction, his nervous and very shaky girlfriend came running behind me to catch up with me, so I slowed down my pace, and she got closer; she started pounding questions after questions at me.

"What is the matter? Where is she? Was she heading for the bar?" she asked as she looked around, nervous.

We walked together crossed the road toward her home, and I told her all the lies that scare the devil out of her—things like if I had not diverted Mrs. Williams's attention elsewhere, she would have caught them red-handed. To keep her in suspense, I said that there was someone very close to them who was passing information to Mrs. Williams, but I will tell him all about it tomorrow morning if he would allow me to see him. She was concern and eager to know more, but I had to work to keep her in suspense. I, however, told her that I was banned by Mr. Williams, but if he would allow me to see him tomorrow morning, it would be to his best interest, and he would know how to watch his steps. She said it would be no problem for him to see me in the morning because she would call him at the office first thing in the morning to let him know that he had to see me by all means.

Early on Saturday morning, I led the eight men team to the CCC. All seven men had mastered their roles to satisfaction, and they waited for me at one of the nearby booths while I went ahead to the main gate to meet the security. In my hand was a paper bag I prepared overnight to convince the security that I brought Mr. Williams's food. But that was not necessary as Mr. Williams already instructed the security to allow me to see him any time I came in. Apparently he gave the instruction even before receiving any phone call from his girlfriend. He must have been eager to speak to me, which was what I prompted.

As soon as the security waved me to pass through, saying that the boss wanted to see me, I knew that the game was on. I returned to the booth pretending to buy something from there and told my guys to proceed in ten minutes after I went in.

When I went inside the compound, I did not go to see Mr. Williams but waited in the workers' restroom for a while; then I came back out just in time to see my guys entering the gate. All they needed to say to security was that they were there to see the paymaster. The paymaster usually received any casual worker who showed up to receive their pay any day of the week, from 8:00 a.m.

My guys came in, and I led them up the stairs to the paymaster's office. At the office entrance I stood and allowed them to go in. The paymaster was on the phone when they got in. I heard him putting whosoever he was talking to on hold to attend to my guys. I heard him saying they came earlier than usual; then I heard the flipping of pages as he asked their names one after the other. Each provided the name and address I provided them, placed their thumb print on the signature list since they could not read or write, and then they came out of his office one after another.

As they got out, I collect the envelopes from them and dropped them into the bag and gave them a ticket with their real name on it with some set of numbers I assigned them. Then I asked them to go back to the booth and wait for the next step in the process. As the seven of them walked away down the stairs, I went to the opposite direction to Mr. Williams's office, where his secretary told me to wait a little as the general manager was on the phone. I then left to use the restroom and never returned.

In the restroom, I folded each of the envelope and placed them in an inside pocket; then I went through the main gate to the booth to congratulate my guys and told them that all of them have been registered and would start work under their real names a week from then.

Excited, they left while I pretended to go back to my office at the CCC. A couple of minutes later a loaded truck was leaving the building to make delivery, and I asked the driver for a ride to the main road, and he let me in. Moments later I was heading for Berwick Street to pick up some of my belongings, which one of my neighbors was safely keeping for me in order to start my journey to Liberia.

Just at that moment when I was leaving, an elderly woman who owned and ran a bar at the intercession of Berwick Street and Pricilla Street called me and asked if I would go buy three crates of beer for her, and she gave me twelve Leones. I took the money and bided her farewell in my heart. Then I took a taxi to Dan Street in the eastern part of Sierra Leone where there was always a vehicle going up country.

DYSFUNCTIONAL ONE

In the backseat of the taxi, I checked my net worth. It was fifty-two Leones and the rate of exchange at the time was eighty cents to one American dollar, which was the currency in use in Liberia then. I rode in a cargo truck to Bo District, and from there I took a cab to Kenema District where I spent the night. By the time I arrived at the border the next day before changing my money to dollars, I had spent about four Leones on transportation, food, and motel.

Chapter 8

I arrived in Monrovia, the capital city of Liberia, late in the night and the cab driver lodged me till the next morning then he dropped me off at Waterside Market where people from the kroo tribe finally directed me where to find one of my relatives. Coincidentally, that relative happened to be one of my mother's elder sisters at whose place my elder brother, Princer lived. He once lived with Counselor Daniel Draper, our grandmother's brother that he was sent to but something happened and he was kicked out so he came over to live with our aunt at Gibraltar Town. His version why he was kicked out was because the lawyer's wife, who happened to be a senator, was very skeptical of him, and thought of him as an outside child of the lawyer. He said he was stranded, depressed, and forced to become homeless so he decided to commit suicide in one garage where he slept but someone accidentally intervened and rescued him and he later found out about our aunt and so he was brought there to live. Our aunt was living in a three-bedroom house with her family (husband and two little children), including two other distant relatives with their own children and grandchildren living in the same house. The small house was congested so Princer and I slept on the floor in the seating room and had our wardrobes underneath chairs in the seating room. Things were looking good and promising during my first two weeks of stay after which Princer and I started fighting each other over little things. He had always been picking fights ever since we were little kids. There has always been some jealousy for the extra favor I enjoyed from dad and that often sparked off some difficulties for me when he was not around. Princer felt it was payback time for some of those difficult times in his past and when he was taking it on me; he would make references of one incident after another. "This is a different terrain" he would say, "there is no dad around here and we are both responsible adults". I was sixteen at the time while he was eighteen. The children in our aunt's house were school going children while we were both school dropouts from Freetown. I met him working as a storekeeper at Volvo Garage on the main road to Via Town. The only thing that our aunt provided us was a sleeping place and once in a while if there was sufficient food we would eat dinner there. The money I took with me lasted about a month and for a good while I stayed broke. Princer wasn't making much money to be independent at the time. I later found a way to make some money joining some boys to search everywhere for various types of metals, brass and aluminum to sell to merchants in the metal export business near Free Port of Monrovia. But that was hard work, too burdensome and the amount generated from it was insufficient to help get me back in school, which was my most pressing heart desire. In March 1971, I decided to go to Sinoe County to meet with Counselor Draper for assistance but unfortunately he was in Monrovia with his family and I had no knowledge then. Then I was stranded in Sinoe County and lived on sugarcane and other fruits from the Draper's yard while lodging there with the house keeper. When President William V. S. Tubman died in July 1971, I rode free with a group of sympathizers to Monrovia where I was taken to live with the Drapers at their Sinkor resident. But my stay with them was brief. There were so much domestic work to do and many errant to run but there was no assistance for my schooling that I sought. I gathered some money from tips received from their many visitors to enroll myself at Lincoln Secretariat Institute on Gurley Street where I started taking classes in bookkeeping and accounting, typing and business English. There was a young woman named Sarah who lived with the Drapers at the time. She was taking classes at the same institute and when I disclosed my intention to her she helped save my money and used it to have me registered for those classes, but I hide this from Counselor Draper and his wife until one day his wife noticed that each time she came home I was out when she asked for me. Then Sarah told her that I was attending Lincoln Secretariat

Institute with her and she felt betrayed. According to her, I should have asked her instead of making it looked like they don't care about me so she gave me an ultimatum: I must be home when she returns home from work each day and the day that she came home and I was not there, then I should not return to her house. My classes at the institute were from 3:00 p.m. to 7:00 p.m. and she comes home sometime at 4:30 p.m. Besides she had instructed the cook to keep an eye on me and report to her anytime I left the house on my own. This restriction was not for me, even though it was a hard decision for me to make. Living conditions at the Drapers was compared to none that I had experienced then: there was always enough food and drinks and I was sharing a room in the basement with two other boys who lived with them. There were nice furniture and fixtures, TV or VCR to watch but I had to give it all up to continue with my schooling. So I moved back to my aunt's house in Gibraltar Town while attending school but that was short lived. The monthly fees at the institute for all my courses were paid for three months in advance before I left the Drapers so I was not anticipating a dropout soon, but my attendance at the institute was short lived.

Gibraltar Town and Clara Town were situated in slumming area along United Nations Drive in Monrovia and the two towns are next to each other. They shared many natural landscapes: swamps, sand and many homes that did not have toilet so some of the inhabitants went to the swamps to shit. As though the two towns possesses some mysticism or competing in witchcraft or voodoo powers, there were some kind of mysterious happenings always on a daily basis that created a sense of fear in me. Most weekends when I was not in school, I will join other children in the area to play soccer on a field near a swamp in Clara Town. I was warned to live the area as early as 6:00 p.m. or face anything that happened to me. Stories of lost of children were told and photos of some of them had been displayed to me. I was warned not to eat food from even those that I think that I knew. One Saturday evening around 5:30, I was in the mist of some boys coming from Clara Town after a soccer match that took place there. A few boys and I were throwing the ball at each other as we walked in the crowd and at one point I missed catching the ball and it went into a nearby bush on the sidewalk, I jumped into the small bush to pick up the ball. But what I picked up was not the ball but the head of human. A woman's head had been severed and left lying in the bush and I thought it was the ball so I picked it up but it was heavier than the ball and as I looked to see what it was that I pickup, I realized it was a human head with blood dripping from it. I dropped it and ran out of the bush like a mad man, screaming my guts out as I ran into my aunt's home and straight into one of the rooms confused. Few of the boys saw the object in my hand before I dropped it and started screaming, they also ran and so did most in the crowd. Some came after me to find out what it was. They pulled me underneath the bed and all I could say was that I wanted to go back to Freetown. I repeated that many times as many people kept pouring in the little house to see what was going on. Then someone came with the information that it was a woman's head that I found in the bush along the road and the police had been called in to investigate. Not long thereafter the police came to interrogate me and all I wanted was to go back to Freetown. The full story was in the national news on TV and radio the very night and throughout the next morning. The narrative that was aired was that a man chopped off his wife's head with a new cutlass he purchased from a nearby store two nights ago in Clara Town and he went to one of the swamps where he committed suicide by drinking acid. I was troubled the whole night as images of the head appeared to me in fearful ways to a point where I cause noises that woke many in the household up several times overnight. All the stories about mysterious happenings that I have heard and all the children I knew that disappeared within a short period of time I lived in Gibraltar Town, coupled with stories of ritualistic killings which was rampant in the news, took their toll on me that night and my decision to return to Freetown was eminent. The next morning, before sunrise, with just $2.00 in my pocket, no passport, no police clearance, no visa and no medical papers, I was at the terminal at Waterside where I quietly boarded a private transportation leaving for the border, and, just like I entered Liberia without any documentation, so I made it back into Sierra Leone without any documentation.

Flaws in the border system were basically due to greed, lust and negligence of the officers on both sides order than the system itself. The officers loved flirting around with women passengers and competing amongst themselves as to who had the most women. Secondly border officers believed their post is to make money for themselves so that is what they concentrated on rather than the process. I have heard stories after stories from people travelling to and fro Liberia about the security system on both sides of the border, but it was all a wide perception then until the moment I starting planning my first trip to Liberia. I knew then that I could beat the system there the moment I arrived there. I had learned that people living in villages near both sides of the border usually interact on a variety of levels and crossed border lines without any documentation. So when I was coming to Liberia, I took the role of palm wine vendor once I arrived at the Sierra Leonean side. I met a couple of palm wine vendors and told one of them that I was sent by some of the elders from the Liberian side to have one of them supply ten gallons of palm wine. Excited, he took me to a nearby hut where he had two large containers filled and I had to carry one of them as we went pass through the securities on both sides. I had my small bag hanging on my shoulder with the large gallon on my head when we crossed. Some of the securities were calling the palm wine vendor by his name and asking to taste or to buy but he told them that we were delivering the gallons. They took me for his son or as a helper and no one ask me any questions. Once we crossed over to the Liberian side I sat him down at the entrance of the small village with the two gallons while I cross the road to where the administrative offices were located, pretending I was going to get the elders who sent me. Moments later

DYSFUNCTIONAL ONE

I entered the commercial vehicle heading to Monrovia and when that vehicle was leaving I saw the man patiently smoking his pipe, waiting, and I ducked my head like I was picking up something as we approached where he was waiting. This was how I entered a country that my parents are citizen of and that I was supposed to be a citizen of. On my returned to Sierra Leone, the transportation I took from Waterside stopped at the border where I said was my destination so when we arrived at the first checkpoint before arriving at the border, as passengers were displaying their travel document to officers there, the drive just told the officers that I was a relative of one of the custom officers at the border where I was sent to deliver death news of another relative. The driver had earlier named several of the officers at the border that he knew and I choose one of the names as my relative so when one of the securities at the check point asked me I just called that name, which apparently was the name of a very popular custom officer who seem to have many friends in the area. At the border I dropped off at the last village just where I left my palm wine friend and I paid the driver a dollar. He drove away to the main terminal. As I walked further down slop at the village entrance I saw a woman sitting near bags of produce. She asked if I can wait a little for her sister who was using the restroom to come so that I can help lift the bag on their heads to carry to the Sierra Leonean side. They had been waiting for a mini truck for a while but the truck was being repaired and it was taking longer than expected. I asked where they were going with the produces and I became excited to learn that they were heading where I wanted to go. "I can carry one of the bags for you guys if you are willing to pay", I said. The elder sister was nice to offer me twenty cents and we agreed on the deal. I helped put one of the bags of produce on her head and I carried the other one while the younger sister carried my small bag. When we approached the bridge, the Liberian soldiers and security personnel were joking with the women and touching their butts. The younger sister was playfully furious and threw curses at them and they were laughing and joking while they tried to hold her back and the older sister and me went ahead but she caught up with us in the middle of the bridge and we all reached the other end together. Then we go pass all of the Sierra Leone officers until we arrived at a nearby market place where I later left them but not until after eating some of their foodstuff, in addition to what I was paid for the job. I was now on the Sierra Leonean side where I wanted to be. I then got a job as apprentice for a Toyota truck driver plying the area. They were loading his truck with produce and I volunteered to help and at the end he asked if I wanted to work and I agreed so I slept in the back of his truck on top of produce with another apprentice that night at the market place at the border and early the next morning we left for Kenema District where I disappeared the next morning after we offloaded the truck, ate breakfast and I got paid one Leone. I jumped into another lorry heading for Freetown and worked in return for the fees I was to pay. I found myself that evening on Dan Street in Freetown like a dream. I had been away for about eight months and the only people that missed me were my grandmother who had been searching all over Freetown for me out of her unflinching love, my brother, Samuel, who knew where I was but would not tell anyone, and of course, Mr. Williams and his management team at the CCC who wished to lay hands on me together with the ten decoys. My grandmother had been going all over Freetown to search for me out of her unflinching love for me while Mr. Williams only wished he could see me once more to lay hands on me.

Chapter 9

Magnoose, as Samuel was nicknamed, went ballistic when he saw me. We spent our first night sleepless in a little room that the Benjamin family gave him in their compound next to the bakery. I explained to his amazement my experiences and adventures in Liberia, and he briefed me about what had happened while I was away.

There was an intensive search for me by the CCC. The men that I used went back the following Monday to look for me for the job promised. That was when the cat let out of the bag, and the CCC management realized I outwitted them and beat their system. They had to evaluate their system and made some adjustments. The company began to issue to their casual workers a special-made ID ticket with two signatures on it with the company's official stamp. The two signatories on the ID ticket are that of the factory manager and the holder. In addition, the ID ticket carries a serial number that the paymaster checks and matches on his newly reconstructed spreadsheet to warrant the release of casual workers' pay.

As for the woman who owned the bar at the intercession of Berwick Street and Pricilla Street, Mum refunded her money after some harassment that Mum could not put up with. For Mum to have refunded the woman's money was strange and out of character. She would have asked the woman to leave her premises and that she was not responsible for my actions. Something must have happened, but I dare not show up at her house any time soon to find out, so I stayed with Magnoose for a couple of weeks.

Because we were not to let the Benjamin Family know that I was there in their compound spending time with my brother, I had to hide all of the time, sometimes leaving the compound early before sunset and returning late at night.

Although living on the street most times meant no schooling, I was very fond of education. I was always moving around with novels or some literature books to read. I was always reminded of the decision I made as a kid to become a lawyer and a musician. My favorite novel writers were Perry Mason and James Hadley Chase. I was always reading about some cases of criminal, detective, or legal nature. The way I get these novels was pretty amazing, for I never did go to any bookstore to buy one. I signed up for books from the library that were never returned, not because I intended so but because I was unstable and lost many of those books, so I was banned from taking any books. But I will spend some time reading or writing there.

Somehow I joined a group of older folks who were in the novel-exchange business. The way it works was that when one is done reading a particular novel or novels, he or she would exchange it to someone else in the group for another. Once I joined their conclave, one thing was certain: I always had a reserved novel to keep my company during the day and some nights I will go to the movie theater just to kill time before joining Magnoose late in the night when all the Benjamins were asleep.

I tried avoiding many people who knew me but not for long. One Saturday afternoon, I went to watch soccer and bumped into several people who knew me, and before long word circulated that I was in town, and it was rumored that the search for me was on.

Magnoose and I talked about it late one night, and after he dose off to sleep, I remembered uttering a word of prayer. I never wanted Magnoose to hear me praying so he won't laugh at me and use that as a joking point on me in the future. After all, we never prayed together anytime before. Street boys do not pray or go to church. They just live. The first thing I told Magnoose when we were up in the morning was that I was going to telephone Mr. Williams or go to the Central Intelligence Department (CID) to ask why they were looking for me.

Magnoose stood up with a puzzled face. "Are you crazy? I don't get it, what is the idea, and what are you going to tell them?" he asked as he looked inquiringly at me. Magnoose knew that I was the brain behind most of the things we did together, and he knew that I was full of ideas, daring ones too.

Went I left him that morning. I went to the Post & Telecommunications Department where Dad's former driver worked and asked him a favor to use their telephone. He placed me in a booth, and I dialed the CCC number, and posing as a CID agent, I asked to speak with the general manager. I had my T-shirt over the mouthpiece to conceal my voice as I spoke to Mr. Williams.

I asked him the latest he heard about John Davies, and he said it has been awhile since he heard anything about him except for rumors that he was seen recently. I asked about the other seven people who had cooperated with the investigation where they can be found, and he said they should be at Temgbeh town. Three of the ten decoys had disappeared on the very Monday that the deal was exposed at the CCC. They probably fled back to the villages where they came from for fear that their dream for civilization in city life would be ruined, shattered if the police was involved. I said that we are hearing that John is around, but we do not know where he lives, and we checked on the seven men he used in the havoc, but they too have returned upcountry where they came from.

He took a deep breath and said, "Well, you have their statements on file, right?"

I conceded and said that it was not enough and that they needed to physically identify John as the person who actually planned the theft and led them to take someone else's pay and the person to whom they handed the money after they received it.

"In the absence of these, the evidence against John is weak," I said.

He agreed and started using curse words. "That bastard," he said, "needed some good beating if grabbed, and that is my interest at this point, good whipping on his buttocks is what he needed."

I had to suppress laughter and then cut in to say, "He is only a sixteen-year-old boy to pull that on your management, which might be an embarrassment for you in court especially before our juvenile judges. My bosses at the CID have been talking about how embarrassing it might be for your paymaster and other members of your management."

Before I was done, he interrupted me and said, "That is the very reason I needed this brat grabbed and his buttocks severely whipped. We do not have any interest standing in court with him to argue that he came here and infiltrated our system. We have since then fixed all the loopholes and regulated some of the functions to prevent future occurrences." He went further to talk about casual workers' IDs, signatures, etcetera. Then he said something along the line that he was surprised that I was giving him a call after he and my bosses concluded months ago that the CCC was not interested in pursuing the case but that we would have John disciplined when we grab him.

"I am sorry," I said, "the case file must have been mistakenly placed on my desk among other cases assigned, and that was why I went on to find the seven men and to call you for any information you might want to share to assist me with the investigation, but I will send the case file back to be closed."

Then I added, "Actually, you guys can discipline John if you get hold of him so long you don't kill him."

We agreed on that, and before we hung up, he promised to call my boss in the afternoon to ensure that the case is closed. I assured him that that was not necessary and that I was going to do so right now after we were done talking. I clenched my fist in a gesture of victory as we said good-bye, and just when I was about to hang up, he said, "Oh, one more thing Agent Steve [which was the name I gave], if by chance you hear anything about John, where he lives and things like that, please feel free to give me a call back."

"Yes, sir," I said and hung up. I could not believe my conversation with Mr. Williams. If only he knew who he was really talking to, I thought, but it was a great relief upon my heart to know that, after all, no CID agents were in the lookout for me as rumored.

Chapter 10

My street life was suspended in the fall of 1971 when I went back to stay with Dad at 13 Charles Street. He and his new girlfriend then had two younger children, and she had three older children of her own who lived with them in the one-bedroom apartment. Dad had just been employed as a tug master for Shabro Minerals in Moyamba District in the southern province of Sierra Leone. The company engaged in bauxite mining, and as a tug master, Dad's job was to escort large ships carrying these minerals in and out of the company's harbor and to transport large group of workers at sea.

I accompanied him to the remote village called Gbangbatoke, the home of Sierra Leone's first and second prime ministers, Sir Milton Margai and his brother Sir Albert Margai.

For a city boy like me at the time, the town was boring. The population was probably around one to two thousand people predominantly from the Mendi ethnic group. There was a small airstrip where a miniplane landed once a month; one primary school that children in the town attended, a marketplace, and an administrative office under the control of the chiefdom.

There was no high school in Gbangbantoke village then. Children who graduated from the only primary school in the village were sent to bigger towns like Moyamba to attend high school if their parents could afford the costs involved. During school breaks the village was flooded with students returning from bigger towns for holidays, and there would be lots of sports and entertainment activities.

The nearest clinic was about twenty-five miles away from the village in a bigger town called Mokanji. Electricity was rationed in the town from 7:00 p.m. through 6:00 a.m., and there were only a few homes in the chiefdom that received power in addition to the six streetlights at strategic intercessions. Water was fetched from wells and from rivers.

Besides farming and a small trading community, most of the men who lived in the village and its surroundings worked for either of the two mining companies: Seronco or Shabro Minerals. Both companies were several miles apart from Gbangbantoke, but the companies provided transportations for the workers early in the morning to pick them up from surrounding villages and to bring them back home in the evenings.

Before Dad leased a house in Gbangbantoke, we lived in one of the smallest villages called Foryah near the company's worksite. There were about twelve houses in Foyah at the time, and the population there was around fifty people. It took us two days to know everyone who lived there facially.

After three months when Dad's probation period ended, he decided to bring in his girlfriend with their two children along with her ten-year-old niece called Nyohswen. Her older children were left behind with her sister and mother in Freetown for schooling. It was at this point we moved out from Foryah to Gbangbantoke.

Life for me in these villages was really tougher than I had imagined. There were snake-infested bushes everywhere on compounds and footpaths, and the bushes grew fast. It was my job to cut the bushes, mow the grass around the house and footpaths, which led toward the main street from our home every weekend. This job was done manually using cutlass, hoe, shovel, and rake. In addition to this endless task, I fetched water on my head with a-four-gallon container from wells about twenty-five yards away from our home. I have to go several rounds fetching water daily because that was the only way we can have water for cooking, bathing, drinking, etc.

In addition, we used firewood to cook, so I had to go in the forest to find dry wood, cut and tie it up to make a bunch, and carry it on my head. Then on Saturdays I will wash the family's dirty cloths and beddings at a nearby river and wait for them to dry before I go home, and then on Sundays I iron them.

On some weekdays when Dad would be working late, I would walk four miles from Gbangbatoke to Fohyah to drop off Dad's meal at his worksite and sometimes walked back four miles back to the village. The palm of my hands became harder like a steel worker, and gradually I became weary of the routine jobs as weeks turned to months and months turn to a year. But Dad's girlfriend was never satisfied with my performance. Surprisingly she complained about everything, and that often resulted to my being spanked by Dad. Dad was a strong, hefty man like a wrestler, and he had such a mighty hand that I saw stars for each slap that landed in my ear and sent me falling down on the ground. For the most part of the year and half I stayed with them was like living in a prison.

There was no school for me and no books to keep me company. Even if there were books to read, time would not have permitted me since there were always some undone task waiting its completion.

Things had changed for the worse. Dad was showing love and care for his children while everything about me seem unpleasant to him. I was constantly being insulted, mistreated, and told that my life was a shame and I would never become anything good in life, so I wanted to return to Freetown, but it was not easy to leave the village as there were only two commercial vehicles leaving the village for Freetown twice per week, and Dad knew both the drivers and owners. They were all given strict orders not to allow me on board outside of the knowledge and consent of my parents. Besides, money was hard to come by in the village, where most people rather give some produce in return for work done for them.

Dad's girlfriend had some of the Jacksony's character, and she constantly reminded me of him. But she was an eccentric and unpredictable in character, and I hardly know what she would complain about until Dad is around. She would never say "I will tell your dad about this or that," and some of the time she would exaggerate things to my amazement. I thought maybe she had not forgiven me for a group fight we had in Freetown against her older children shortly before Princer left for Liberia. All three of us—Princer, Samuel, and I—entered into a fight with her children, and she took side and aggravated us, so we fought back harder with sticks and rocks, which we were good at, and they fled indoors and locked themselves up.

Dad was admitted at the hospital at the time, suffering from hypertension, and when he heard the news, he ordered that we should leave the house immediately. But all that was gone, and I had apologized to her as Dad instructed me to do before he and I made the trip to Moyamba District, and she claimed she had forgiven me, but the current trend of events did not show any forgiveness.

Dad and I had related well with each other during the short period of time we spent together until his new family arrived. I also thought that the traditional rite of heritage to bearing the name of Dad as his junior was equally troubling as being born in Kissy Mess-Mess. In our tradition, women would fight with their rivals over the rite of heritage by naming their boy child after his father. When it comes to Dad, I bear his name and carried his heritage, and I do not think Jacksony likes that nor do I think Dad's girlfriend likes that either. The only way any woman's child can be traditionally named after Dad, nullifying the existing heir to his heritage, was in the event that I was no more alive.

In March 1973, my relationship with Dad and his girlfriend had become completely sore. It was going downhill, but it was during Christmas season in 1972 that things went bad after I rebelled and refused to work for anyone if my schooling needs were not addressed. The family left me in the village and went to Freetown to celebrate the holidays. They locked up the house and left me lonely without any food since I refused to work. I used to survive by playing checkers, which I was good at, with elders in the community. But in their absence, I opened up the ceiling from the outside boys' room where I lived and then travelled through the ceiling and descended in Dad's store room where all their food was stored. I opened up a new bag of rice and transported half of it through the roof, along with some other foodstuff into my cabin. I sold some of the rice through bata system and got fish and other ingredients to cook and ate well those days they were in Freetown. When they came back and discovered that I indeed entered the main house without key and stole some of the food stuff, Dad easily tracked and nabbed me in the small village where hiding was forbidden.

I was jailed at the chief's court, and after being detained for a week with hardly any food to eat, the chief released me and turned me over to Dad, who took me home to forge a new beginning, but that new beginning was not to come since his girlfriend had insidious plans.

Dad left for work the next day, and his pregnant girlfriend was preparing to take their two children to the clinic and also to attend to her prenatal checkup. Before leaving that morning after Dad left, she asked me to go fetch water for her to bath, but there was enough water in the drum outside that she could have used. I could not understand why she wanted me to go fetch water. However, I took the bucket and came through the back door, but something else held me up, so I spent some time behind the house fixing fishing net that one of the neighbors had asked me to fix. Apparently she thought that I had already gone, so she came walking very quickly into the kitchen, which was at the back of the house, and then she came to an abrupt stop as she saw me standing there patching the fishing net. She yelled at me, and then she returned into the house. Then I ran quickly to fetch the water after I protested that there was enough water in the drum, to which she said that she wanted it fresh, which was strange.

So I ran as fast as I could down the road where the well was and fetched the water, but as I returned with the bucket of water on my head and about to turn from the side of the house to the backyard I saw her in the kitchen, her hand coming from my food that was in the pot. The metal top of the pot made a loud sound as she was covering the pot. This made me uneasy, and I started wondering what she was doing with my share of the morning food. There was nothing else in the kitchen besides the three stones, the wood between the stones, and my share of the rice that was in the pot on top of the stones. The kitchen was an open one that was outdoors, detached from the house. It was built with few sticks in four corners without walls, and palm leafs were used for its roof and to fence it about two feet high without a door but a little opening space to enter and exit. Anyone standing from any angle at the back of the house could see inside the open kitchen. Simultaneously as her hand came from the pot and the sound of the pot cover came ringing in my ear, she hurried into the house through the back door. I wondered what she could be possibly doing with my food, and I became alerted.

Then I asked myself why did she insist that I should go fetch water when there was enough water in the large drum at the back of the house to bathe everyone in the house. That second question baffled me and left me with no answer, and therefore the act of tampering with the food meant something out of the ordinary to me.

The only thing that was kept in that kitchen was firewood and the three rocks placed in triangular position as fireplace for pots to sit on. That morning I warmed up the leftover food for breakfast, and she had taken her portion along with that of her niece's, Nyohswen. The more I tried to find answers why I had to go fetch water and what was she doing tampering with my food, the unease I became.

Moments later, the minibus came, and she left with the two children. I was left alone with her niece, Nyohswen. Deeply troubled and perplexed about the situation, I became hesitant about eating the food. But the question that was more troubling was, How would I know that she really did something to the food if no one ate it, and I threw it away?' Then it occurred to me that if it was good for me, then it should be good for Nyohswen, her niece. So I asked her if she would like to eat some of my food, and she readily answered yes. So I told her to take it, and she went over to the kitchen, took the whole pot into the house, and ate up three quarters of the food; then she was full. I then kept an eye on her, and after a while I left to uproot cassava from the nearby farm to eat. When I returned an hour later, I met Nyohswen struggling in the seating room, squatting on the floor and crying stomach pain while vomiting green thick fluids. Even though it may looked hypocritical that I asked what was the matter with her, I was genuine, unbelievably shocked but real.

When she could not speak but only grunted, suddenly fear gripped me that I knew something was wrong with the food but yet offered it to her. After all, I was convinced that her aunt did put something in the food for me, why then did I offer it to her? I thought. The next thing that happened frightened me so badly that I ran away, leaving her to die there, in the seating room. She grunted heavily as she squeezed her belly and at the same time threw up thicker greener fluid, and she began to shit.

Scared and shocked, I ran in and out of the house several times hardly believing what was happening before my eyes. I went out to see if I could find help, but then I halted and asked myself who in the world would believe me if I told the story what had happened. Her aunt might turn the table on me, and the whole village would call me a witch and probably punish me for killing a little girl. So I left her there and went up the road where I usually play checkers with some older folks and stayed there until when it was around 1:00 p.m. I saw the minibus bringing my dad's girlfriend back from the clinic; then I followed the vehicle running as fast as I could to get to the house.

Her aunt barely descended from the vehicle when I arrived and started helping her with one of the children. She stopped and looked at me in astonishment and asked if I have eaten yet, and I said I was just about to. Then we entered the house together, and she almost dropped the other child who was sleeping in her hand when she saw her helpless niece lying in a pool of green fluid with a little blood dripping off her mouth, and the house smelled with human feces. She lay the child in her hand down quickly and rushed to her niece and then looked at me, then back to her niece, and called out her name loud several times, but she did not respond. Then she picked her up and shook her so hard that she began to move body parts a little, showing signs of life left in her.

I stood there blank face looking straight at her, but she avoided looking into my eyes. But when our eyes finally met, they spoke more than words could express, and we both understood. Then she went into her room and grabbed a bedspread, towel, and a bucket of water and stripped her niece cloth off her body and poured some water on her. I was just standing there, fixed, looking and thinking that this could have been me.

After she cleaned her up, she dragged her into her bedroom, and I went outdoors around the house to her room window where I peeped, watched, and listened to her speaking to her half-dead niece. "So you ate Chea's share of the food this morning, right?" she asked. But I could not hear Nyohswen responded.

"You are going to die," she continued. "You are very greedy. I fed you well this morning before leaving. Why must you eat of his share of the rice?" she went on and on.

I stood there frozen as I listened, and then I heard the door opened, and she went through the back door with the remaining part of the rice in the pot and emptied it on a piece of rag, and then she threw it in the latrine and made her way into the bushes. Then I followed her, but she did not know.

Deep into the bushes she picked three different types of leaves and then came back running. She passed by me as I hid behind a tree, and she came to the house and picked up a bottle of palm oil and a little pot. Then she went into the kitchen and made fire and put some of the leaves into the small pot and boiled them. Then she took fever leaves and some other stuff that she grinded and laid on the hop stone until they were slightly withered, and then she rubbed them between her palm and squeezed until liquid was extracted. Then she poured the liquid into a cup and poured palm oil in it and stirred it up. Then she took it into her room and forced her niece to drink it. Nyohswen was totally helpless to the point where her aunt lifted her head and forced her to take it. I could hardly believe what was going on. She made warm water and cleaned her niece up in the bedroom and then she went into the sitting room and cleaned up the mess there.

I was standing by the door when she was done, and she said to me, "You and I are in for long ride, and we shall see who will win in the end."

I took a deep breath, looked straight into her eyes, and then I quietly walked away.

Chapter 11

Dad came back from work that evening at 7:00 p.m. with his usual container of palm wine. His girlfriend had prepared food for the day and dished out my usual portion, which was untouched on the dining table till the next day. Miraculously, Nyohswen survived the poison, and she was recovering gradually but still appeared weaker, and she was asleep when Dad returned home from work. He settled down, took his bath, and went to the dining table to eat his food. Usually it was when he would be eating dinner that she would be sitting by his side explaining what went on during the day at home and sometimes lodging complaints against me. She talked about her trip to the hospital and about their children's health and her prenatal status, but she never said a word about the poison. She kept a close watch at me, and I also would looked straight into her eyes.

I was hesitant each time I wanted to say something about it to Dad especially when he asked about Nyohswen, and his girlfriend said she had malaria and was asleep."

Would he believe me or his girlfriend? I asked myself knowing that she could deny flatly and turn the table at me.

So she never brought it up and never allowed Dad and me alone by ourselves that evening, and the next day when I was supposed to take his meal to him at work she prevented it from happening. During the night, I was thinking about a way to go back to Freetown. I just could not figure out how I can cover the four hundred miles without any money and food, and besides, I already looked like a laughingstock with no shoe to wear and no decent clothing. I was worried about food because she would be the one cooking and dishing out the food. I decided and made sure that I was present whenever she was cooking, especially when she was dishing up the food.

DYSFUNCTIONAL ONE

The next plan that I executed each time before I ate food that she cooked was to share the food first with the two little children she had with Dad. One was about five years old, and the other was three. Before I ate anything in the house, I will call the little children, who were very fond of me, and fed them first in her presence while looking at her, and she would be also sometimes looking at me, and we would be both smiling because we understood each other well.

I have my own bowl where she usually dishes food for me. Whenever she dishes food for me before I ate, I would make sure that she was present and that she sees me feeding her two little babies with the food, and when I do not see any reaction from her other than the usual smiles that we exchanged, I will go ahead and eat. If the children were sleeping when she dished the food, I will wait until they are up, or I will not eat the food if they don't want to eat. She could not keep the children away from me because naturally children are attracted to me. When the children get the slightest chance, they would come to me because I love playing with them, and we always had fun.

Nyohswen never ate any food from me again, and for a while the entire episode became a secret among the three of us: Nyohswen, her aunt, and me.

One day I fell ill and became weak and thought maybe it was malaria or fever, but when I started feeling my stomach pinching inside and started throwing up some light-green fluid, I ran straight into the bushes to pick some to the leaves I saw her used for her niece and came back and stole some palm oil. I was fixing the same thing when she came to the entrance of the back door to watch what I was doing. Then she came and grabbed the oil bottle from me, but she was too late, for I had already taken the quantity I needed. I locked myself in my room and took the medicine over again and slept throughout that evening till the next morning; then I felt better, but I was still feeling weak.

Dad came to see me in the morning and brought me two chloroquine tablets for malaria and a cup of hot tea that his girlfriend made for me. He urged me to drink the hot tea, but after he left the room, I just wasted it. Even though I had been very careful not to fall in her trap yet, somehow, I was lying there, weak and experiencing similar faith as Nyohswen. Though I was weak and hungry that day, it was the day that I made the decision never again to eat any food from my father's household.

It was exactly one week after my full recovery when Dad came home from work early at lunchtime to break the news that the company was transferring him permanently to the eastern province over the weekend so we should all pack up our belongings and prepare to leave the next day for Freetown, where we would wait until he settles down in the new district; then we would join him. He said that the company had arranged for one of its vehicles to transport us to Freetown in the morning. Suddenly, both Dad and his girlfriend were being nice to me, encouraging me to help take care of the little children on the long journey to Freetown. He then gave me some money for myself to buy some clothes and shoe, and he asked me to come back with the company vehicle so we can leave together for his new assignment over the weekend.

I thought this was the miracle break I needed. In the last couple of days I have been cooking for myself overnight when everyone was asleep. I would join hunters or fishermen to hunt and to fish, and whatever was my share of the gain, I will spend the night cooking and eating and then hiding any reserve food up a tree at the back of the house. I always fetch fresh water for me and never used any leftover that I wasn't sure of. We spent the rest of the day packing our personal belongings, just the things his family needed for a week or two as Dad gave the impression that the reunion with his family would be short.

The trip to Freetown took two days because of the roads, and everything went well. We arrived in Freetown around 8:00 p.m. the next day, and Dad's girlfriend went into her parents' house with her two little children, while Nyohswen carried one of her bags on the head following her. But when she entered her parents' house, she found out that after all, Dad was not being transferred as he said he was. It was a telex he received that his girlfriend's mother had passed, and sensing the kind of uproar that it might cause him if he broke the news to her in Gbangbatoke, he came up with the transfer story, and none of us had any idea until when we arrived there.

When my dad's girlfriend entered the house, her sister received her with the news of their mother's death and that she sent a telex to Dad at Shabro Minerals to inform her and to ask her to come for the funeral. She started crying and rolling on the floor, and I just politely put her personal belongings down and expressed my sympathy to her as our eyes spoke once again, and I left.

With my bag hanging on my shoulder I walked slowly to my mother's house. The company's driver showed me where to meet him in the morning for our trip back to Gbangbatoke, and I happily took down the address and told him if he did not see me, it meant that I might be on the plane flying there.

Chapter 12

Mum was a little excited to see me after a long time. I told her all about my experience with Dad's girlfriend, but she said that she was not surprised because she knew the woman's background, whatever that meant. Mum had been greatly disappointed and depressed over her lover boy Jacksony's choice for marriage to be ordained reverend to pastor the Louis Memorial Church on Adelaide Street. He could not marry her not because Mum and Dad were still married by law, but Jacksony, like a parasite, was only interested in drawing blood: exploiting and/or seducing the women.

When he selected from his playboy binder a woman who happened to be one of Mum's best friends and married her, rumor had it that he only married to fulfill the requirement to be ordained as a reverend and to pastor the church, but not because he was prepared to settle down or because he was in love or prepared to respect and abide with the solemn vow that comes with marriage. This rumor was overwhelmingly true as Jacksony's wings of seduction spread like the tentacle of an octopus after he was ordained and appointed to pastor the church. He used many women in the church as sex slaves, hypnotizing them and having sex at different places almost daily. After their separation, Mum entered two separate relationships with married men who were also members of the same church, and she had children by both men.

As Mum and I sat in her sitting room, talking on the night of my return from Gbangbatoke, I thought that after all Jacksony, whom I considered a demon, was no longer in her life, at least, so I thought until around 11:00 p.m. when I saw the tall black male figure leaving her bedroom and saying good-bye. The voice was unmistakable, and it produced goose bumps all over my body that all the while Jacksony was in her bedroom, probably listening to our conversation. In fact, Mum was pregnant again for him. If I were not tired, sleepy, and disoriented, I would have left her house immediately, but I needed to sleep, so I slept there that night and disappeared early the next morning. I had asked earlier if I could stay in her home, and she agreed, but with Jacksony still sneaking in and out, I rather not subject myself to any more parental complications, which I had enough of already.

Early in the morning I went to my grandmother, to stay at 37 McDonald Street. I was at Grandmother's place when Mum gave birth to Rev. S. P. Jacksony's fifth child named Glorie in early 1974. Later that same year Mr. Lawrenzo Davis, one of the men whom she had a child for in 1972, came back into her life again. At this time, life for me was regrettably stagnated with no progress in advancing my education other than just reading novels. Later that year, Mum wanted some work done in her yard and asked me to assist.

When I arrived, I met Mr. Davis and some of his friends drinking. I later learned from Mr. Davis's wife that he was an honorable man before he involved himself in adulterous affairs with my mother, who by then had lost her self-esteem. Mr. Davies may have had some bumps along the way in his marriage, which is not my place to speak about since there are no bumpless marriages I know of, but unlike Reverend Jacksony who never once bought me a piece of candy in all the years he was in the relationship with Mum or even once wish me happy birthday, Mr. Davis was a man with generous heart, and he showed concern for me as a fatherly figure.

When Mr. Davis saw me that day, he asked me questions about my life and what I would like to become and things like what I was doing to achieve goals in life. He was a seafarer who worked for international shipping companies in Europe through the local shipping agency. On that day, he sent me to buy some more drinks to entertain his friends.

When I returned with the drinks, I met them in an argument. The argument was all about me, and I had no idea until they waved me to a seat. Mr. Davis had asked my mother about her expectations about me and how she sees my future. Mum had given him an answer that I was already spoilt, foolish, and had no future. Few of his friends who either had a little alcohol in their head or were just trying to align with Mum supported her that I was a wayward boy beyond repair. Mr. Davis sat me down and asked me to be candid with him because he said he wanted to prove the others wrong. Then he asked what I would like to become in life. I thought for a while, while everyone waited for my response. It was the second time someone asked me that question. The first time was Dad, when I was maybe five or six years old, and my response then was that I wanted to become a lawyer and musician, but I dared not give the same answer now.

So I said, "Right now I am struggling to see myself clearly, but I want to make use of any meaningful opportunity that comes my way now to determine my future."

Mr. Davies then asked, "If I arrange for you to become a seafarer like myself, would you consider this as meaningful opportunity on the road to shaping your future?"

My eyes went wide open, and I stood up and energetically answered, "Yes, sir."

Then he asked, "Would you not let me down, Chea?"

"Of cause not," I replied.

He then told me to keep the change from the drinks he sent me to buy and made an appointment with me to meet him at the local shipping agency the next day. Mum and the others reserved their opinion and resorted to a mere "we shall see."

The next day Mr. Davis and I met at the local office where he introduced me to Mr. Hamilton, the boss at the agency who happened to be his friend. About a week later, my paperwork was completed, and within two weeks I signed my first contract for three months as a steward trainee with Elder Dempster Shipping Lines, one of United Kingdom's largest shipping companies. The first vessel where I started the training was named MV *Mano*. Mr.

Davis shouldered all the costs to make that happened in my life. But before I left for the first training circle at sea, he signed a year contract and left the country. The advance payment I received was my first big money that I ever handled, and it was enough to make me excited.

As a custom when one receives their first money earned from working life, the amount must be shared to family members, so I went first to my grandmother, who was very proud of me and gave her some money. Then I shared the remaining money with all of my little brothers and sisters and then with some of my friends.

It was on board of MV *Mano* that I learned to play chess. As a trainee steward, my job was to serve the officers their food and to clean up their rooms, fix beds, and set dining tables. I had seen chess being played in movies, but I never had any idea what it meant or how to play it. Some of the officers, including the captain, were chess freaks, and in addition to the many different chess sets on board, there was a small chess library.

On my third day on board, I fell in trouble with two of the officers. They had an unfinished game that I packed up during my cleaning their mess room. The game was not recorded, or it was recorded, but they lost the record, and they both claimed having the upper hand in that particular game. There was a wager at stake, and once again I found myself in trouble, especially when I was told to put the game back together as I met it, and I simply did not know what that meant.

That night before going to bed I took a beginner's book in my cabin and started reading about the game. Then it occurred to me that I needed a chess set too, so the next day during my lunchtime, I grabbed one of their chess set and took it into my cabin, and within a week's time, it was as though chess had replaced everything in this world that I had lost. I became glued to the game that I ran into so many problems with my work time, but it was one incident a month later that corrected all of the problems recorded against me.

A chess tournament was going on at the bar, and I was assigned there to serve participants who were all white men. Racism was not an issue; participants were all white because no black man on board could play the game at the time. In fact, the black men on board said the game was too difficult for them, and they accused me of trying to be white because of my kin involvement with game. At the tournament finals, which took place on a Sunday evening, I volunteered to work overtime just to witness the games, but I was constantly being interrupted by spectators whenever they ordered drinks. Deep into the final game, I took spectators' orders, but instead of going to the counter to get their orders, I was consumed by the games and just stood there watching, and to my disappointment, the elderly man playing the black pieces resigned, and everyone applauded the winner, who was a much younger man.

I stood there with a perplexed face, and someone tapped me on the shoulder and asked for their drink, and I jerked. The others who first placed their orders expressed disappointment and chastised me, but the chief mate present placed his hands around my shoulder and said with a mocking smile, "Can you tell me what you know about this game that you have forgotten to do your job, young man?"

I hesitated and looked around me, and then I said that black should not have resigned. Instead, he should have forced a possible zugzwang position in the twenty-ninth move and drew the game. That sparked a loud laughter among them, especially the two whose game I discarded weeks ago and could not put back together; they were the loudest who laughed in the bar. One of them came over to the board and discarded the position along with the board, and he asked that I set the board from the beginning and replay the moves to where I claimed a zugzwang existed.

I was nervous, and with trembling hands, I went to work setting up the board, the pieces, and move by move I recreated the game using the descriptive notation, which was used to record the game, and on the twenty-ninth move, I pointed out the possible zugzwang. The place went quiet as I reenacted the game move by move, and when I was done, everyone was not only convinced but amazed as I revealed the sugzwang.

As they marveled at the moves, I went to the counter to put in the orders and I could hear the two officers saying that just weeks ago I must have pretended that I knew nothing about chess, and so when I returned with the drinks, one of them, perplexed, asked how was it that I had shown not knowing anything about chess just weeks ago and then showing extraordinary skills in the game.

I simply replied, "That was then, and this is now."

For me at the time, I did not know how big a deal that performance was and the respect and favor I earned from it. But to them as Europeans it was an outstanding feat for an African youth to show them a move that they challenged was not there in that game. It became a talk that they shared throughout that week. The following week I was taken from being the steward on the ground floor to the third floor where most of the officers who played the game were, and then I began to be in the company of the officers playing chess and kicking asses for the most part. I stocked my cabin with many advance chess books, read them, and replayed world championship games—looking in the minds of great players like Bobby Fischer, Boris Spassky, Paul Murphy, and others.

The three months training contract ended, and I was returned to Freetown with good report sent to the local shipping agency. The captain even made a special recommendation for me, but Mr. Davis was then in Kuwait working on an oil tanker there, so he was not present when his friend at the agency congratulated me for a job well done. Yet I had to give the head of the agency one-third of my earning from the contract so he can put me back on another ship. This was the culture: bribery for consideration to be given another contract.

A month later, I signed another three months contract with Elder Dempster Shipping Lines and boarded another ship called MV *Freetown*. This trip was not as encouraging as the previous one, but it was worth the money, and most of my free time was invested either in chess studies or in the corresponding courses in bookkeeping and accounting, business, math, and English I had enrolled into from England.

Before I signed that second contract, I had fallen in love with a girl named Leticia Anderson. Our romance, which was short-lived, landed me to experience firsthand how a broken heart felt. Because of my struggles in life, I had not really fallen in love, or shall I say no girl in their right mind was interested in loving somebody like me, so my first love, Leticia, meant a lot to me, and I was deeply in love with her to the extent that it was difficult for me to go work at sea, leaving her for months in that unfaithful environment full of Jacksonys. She was such a pretty girl, and I considered myself lucky to have her, but when I returned three months later from sea, she was pregnant for someone else, and that devastated me, and I made a vow later not to go back to sea when I was in love. I understood firsthand how Dad felt when Mum betrayed him. It was difficult for me to let go of Leticia even though she was pregnant for someone else that her parents wanted her to marry. I felt discouraged, frustrated, and depressed; it was as though the whole world shut down on me.

A month later I decided it would be good to go back to Liberia to pursue my studies there. I could not be a seafarer anymore, for when I love someone, I wanted to stay close to that special someone to be a family and not to be far away at sea travelling from one country to another and having affairs with prostitutes from country after country as most seafarers do. Conversely, I had seen so many seafarers' wives engaged in unfaithful acts behind their husbands' back. I needed a land job where I see and be with the one I loved. Those seafarers whose wives are pregnant before they leave to work at sea are less worried about their wives having affairs behind them. These are issues that seafarers themselves discussed when at sea, and I was not prepared to go on with my life in that direction of a broken heart because I knew who I was; I was someone looking for someone to love me unconditionally, someone I can give my heart to in return wholeheartedly. I needed a family of my own, children to play with, a family to live or die for out of pure love, and the only thing that healed my broken heart was my interest in the game that captivated me, chess. Chess represented the contrast against every disappointment in life, every words of degradation that people threw at me.

I left Freetown for the second time in 1975 and went to Liberia to continue my schooling there. There was a great improvement in Princer's life. He was now a custom officer working as secretary to the collector of customs at the Robert International Airport, and he was living by himself at one of the nearby towns called Smell-No-Taste. At the airport, custom officers made a lot of money from tips, bribery, in addition to their salaries, so Princer was living well, and he was very excited to see me once again. We discussed my intention to continue my schooling at Lincoln Secretariat Institute, and he assisted me to attend the school once more in Monrovia. So I had to come back to live with my aunt at Gibraltar Town, in Monrovia, while attending school, learning bookkeeping and accounting, economics, business, math, and typing.

On weekends I would go to Smell-No-Taste to spend time with Princer and returned to Monrovia to attend school during weekdays. Princer and I fell out after two months thereafter, and he ceased supporting me, so I searched and found Dad's older children from his first marriage to see if they could help me, but they were already brainwashed by their mother not to recognize us or to even consider us as blood-related. At my aunt's house, things became very difficult as more distant relatives came to stay and the place became crowded and noisier, seriously affecting my studies. The lack of space and food, together with the increase in noises became unbearable problems for me. So, like the adventurer I have always been, I backed up my bag and took to the streets after relations between Princer, and me fell out as usual.

I found a distant relative named Richard Pattern working as a supervisor at Liberian Produce Marketing Corporation inside Freeport of Monrovia. Their corporation provided lunch for their laborers on weekdays, so he offered that if I was around when lunch was served, he would make sure I eat with the laborers; therefore, I went to this place at noon on weekdays to eat by day and slept at an abandoned garage near the police station at Point Four. I struck a deal with the management of Lincoln Secretariat Institute to serve as janitor to offset the monthly fees for my courses, so I had to stay when the last classes ended at 10:00 p.m. to clean up the various classrooms, toilets, and the offices. Once in a while when no one noticed, I sneaked and slept in the building, but for the most part, I had to sleep at the garage. It was in that garage that a figure I believed to be Jesus Christ was revealed to me. It was a terrifying experience. I sneaked into the garage one weekend and lay in the backseat of one of the old cars where I usually slept. I was not sleeping, but all of a sudden as I was looking up the sky through the window, the clouds began opening, and I could not believe my eyes.

Curios to see what was about to happen as the cloud wide opened apart, I then saw the most fearful thing in my life. A multitude of people in various colorful robes appeared, walking in the opened sky like they were coming down, and gradually as the cloud cleared and the multitude of people swept into view, it became vivid that they were all following the man in white robe leading. The whole experience took a little over a minute, and as the man in the white robe placed a part of his robe that seem to be dropping off his shoulder, he pointed directly at me as many of those following him looked on, and I felt a chill all over my body, paralyzed for a moment and unable to move or speak.

Everything disappeared before my eyes as I looked on; the cloud came back and covered everything, including the finger that was pointed at me, and it took a little while before I was able to move my body and to speak. I jumped out of the vehicle and ran into the police station. The officer behind the counter asked what I wanted, and I was just mute. I could not tell him that I was in the garage, for I would have been exposing myself, and I could not say what had happened, for there was nothing he could do about it. I left the station and walked down the road to Madam Duclay's Temple of Heaven Church where a prayer service was in progress, and some of her members were testifying. I entered and joined the line for testimony, but when it was my turn to testify, I took the stand, but again became muted. I could not utter a single word. I just stood there, scared and nervous that I might be perceived as being insane.

Madam Duclay led me to the far corner and asked that I kneel there and pray. That experience left an indelible imagination with me that cannot be erased. From time to time I would be frozen and pensive as I tried to figure out the meaning of that experience, but one thing was clear: It led me back to church after a very long time, and I obtained a Bible to read and to pray.

Chapter 13

By early 1977, I completed the last of the courses I was taking at Lincoln Secretariat Institute and was certificated just in time when the then world largest rubber plantation, Firestone Plantations Company (FPCO), posted two accounting positions for their Accounting Department; one was to fill the position of a senior bookkeeper in their accounts payable section, and the other was to fill the position of a junior bookkeeper in the accounts receivable section. I was a bit timid in applying for the position since I had no working experience and the sociopolitical makeup of the society at the time favored mostly the elites over people of so-called country origin when it comes to jobs especially in the biggest company in the country.

Moreover, most daughters and sons of the elites were educated abroad in the United States, and they are connected, looking out for one another's interest. So for a homeless person like myself who had no one to back me up and the fact that my accent was foreign made all the more intimidating to compete with these types of job seekers. However, I applied for the junior bookkeeping position and mailed my application since I could not afford to go up to Harbel, Margibi County, where the company's headquarters were situated. Since I was homeless and still had to continue working as a janitor to offset the arrears I owed the school, I used its address: 10 Gurley Street, Monrovia.

A few days later I received a reply from the company's personnel manager reiterating the requirement for the jobs as posted in the newspapers and inviting me to join other candidates in a few days to take and pass the company's accounting aptitude test to be considered for the position. The letter stated that all accounting candidates must take company's aptitude test in addition to the degrees. This meant that I had to travel to Harbel, near Smell-No-Taste, to take the test in a few days. I was so excited that I took the letter to my accounting instructor, who then rallies others to raise $2.50 for me to go there to take the test.

I went to Smell-No-Taste on a Saturday to make sure I was close by Harbel, which was just two miles away. When I arrived there, one of Princer's neighbors disclosed that he had been dismissed from his custom job, and I was saddened to hear that even though he had given me strict instructions never to come near him. But surprisingly the neighbor told me about another elder brother of ours who was working at the Electrical Department at FPCO. I decided to go search for him, and when I found him that very day, he admitted that we are brothers. He was one of Dad's many children before he even married his first wife.

George Nagbeh Davies, as he is named, was born in the early 1940s and reared by his grandmother. George then lodged me that Saturday evening up to Monday morning when I took the FPCO accounting test. For two weeks, candidates were scheduled to come in to take the test. On Monday morning we were about twelve candidates who took it. Four candidates had their accounting degrees from the United States, and the few others were graduates from Booker Washington Institute and the rest from the University of Liberia. We were told that the company would contact us the following week. As we walked outside, I noticed that some of the candidates came with their own private vehicles, while I trekked my way back to my newfound brother's house. He was at work when I arrived, but his wife and grandmother wanted me to stay with them in Harbel to wait for the result instead of going back to Monrovia to wait, so I returned the next day to notify the Personnel Department of the change of address.

That week, George and I got to know each other better, and he told me how disrespectful Princer had been toward him and that they both did not speak to each other. I was never bored when I was alone because I had my portable chess set with me together with a few world-class games to analyze. On Sunday they took me to the Assembly of God's Church to worship, and they were excited to introduce me to their friends.

On Monday afternoon while George was at work, he got a call from the personnel office asking if I was available to come in on Wednesday at 10:00 a.m. There were other candidates for different positions in the conference room that morning while we all waited. Then at around 10:30 a.m., the door swung open, and a Swedish national named Peter Burgie, who was the assistant to the chief accountant, entered the room, and after he greeted us, he asked, "Who is John Davies?"

My heart pounded as I put up my hand, and he looked in my direction and took a few step toward me while looking in the paper in his hand, and then he offered his hands and said to me, "Congratulations, you have not only passed the company's aptitude test, but you had also set a new record with the marks you made. Therefore, you are selected for the senior bookkeeper position instead of the junior position you apply for."

Then he asked for the next person, Calor Coker, a university graduate, who made it next after me and was slated for the position of junior bookkeeper. Speechless, I sank back into the chair with my head in my hands unable to process what I had just heard from the second man in command in the Account Department of the world's largest rubber plantation. I had to fight back tears that nobody in the room would have imagined why, at the time, I should be happy. But I was just overwhelmed with emotions that only I understood, and I just wanted to leave the room to cry it out and relieve myself.

A secretary who came in with Mr. Burgie handed me a folder containing some documentation and a checklist of the employment process. I have a week to complete the process, which begins with medical examination by the company's doctor and then an optical checkup to be followed by labor department clearance before the personnel department would finally conclude the employment process. It was just difficult to conceal my emotions.

Mr. Burgie noticed that as I was leaving the room. He came after me and massaged my shoulder and whispered, "Congratulations."

It was apparent that I was crying in the inside, and he watched me walked away in tears. I cried, sang, and praised God as I trekked my way back. I stopped at the Electric Department, and when George saw me, he knew that I looked different, and together with some of his coworkers, we all rejoiced.

At his house, his grandmother and wife danced with me, and we sang hymns of praises. The old woman took me to their prayer meeting at church later that evening, and we testified and gave thanks to God Almighty for what he has done. The church then set a committee to help me out with the things I might need to make me look presentable at work until I was able to buy the things I wanted and to provide me with a temporary shelter until the company assigned me a house to live in when my probation ended.

One of the women in the committee had a used-clothes business, so she took me to her storage the following day and provided me with shirts, ties, suits, socks, and shoes. Another woman's son had a barbershop, and she took me there for a free haircut. The committee gathered linings, beddings, etc., for me to start with. The whole church became involved with my preparation with members praying constantly for me even before I took the test.

I went through the medical process the next day—physical and optical checkups—and was cleared, and then I proceeded to the company's Labor Department the following day to obtain labor clearance. The staff responsible smoothly processed the paperwork, and after I signed, he took the file to department director, Mr. Joe Dawh, for approval.

Mr. Dawh then held on to the file and kept me waiting till closing that day. I waited for hours, and each time I asked about the process, one of the staff would say my file is before the boss for approval and he has not yet released it to show if I was cleared or not.

At the end of the day most of the staff signed out and left the office, while I was still waiting for Mr. Dawh, who was still in his office. He finally came out, and I approached him and asked about my clearance. He shouted at me and ordered me to leave the premises right away. I became afraid, baffled, and confused, so I hesitated and asked if it would be ready by the morning.

Mr. Dawh grinned and scornfully looked me in the eye and said, "I will never approve any clearance for you because I know very well that you are not a Liberian. You have a Sierra Leonean accent, and unless I have proof of your citizenship as a Liberian from the highest Kru authority in the country, you are wasting your time here."

I was shocked and disappointed at his statement because I know that while it is true that I had a Sierra Leonean accent, that should not disqualify me as a bona fide Liberian.

"You guys leave your poor country to come here to take jobs from bona fide Liberians," he barked at me.

There was no way I was going to let him take away my dual nationality from me, so I left his office disappointed but determined to fight back. I went home and told George and his grandmother what had happened, and they were all offended. The old woman took me over to their church where they had a weeklong prayer meeting, and a group of women, upon hearing what had happened, formed a delegation that very night, and they took me to Mr. Dawh's house where they vouched for my citizenship, but Mr. Dawh was very rude and disrespectful to the women just as he was with me at his office. He asked us to leave his premises before he loses his temper, so the women then challenged him that they would fight back, and we left.

The next morning, George called Mr. Dawh to inform him that I was his younger brother and that we were born of Liberian parents who migrated to Sierra Leone, and he told him that if he is allowed to work for the same company, why then was his brother discriminated against, but Mr. Dawh was resolute with his decision.

The church officially took up my case and found some prominent Liberians to intercede for me on Friday afternoon, but

Mr. Dawh was still defiant. Then word came out from one of his staff who was related to one of the people from the church that Mr. Dawh was not happy because his nephew who got his degree in the United States took the accounting aptitude test and maybe the next person on the line if I was disqualified.

That Friday night, like a difficult chess position, I cracked my brain on how to solve the problem, and by 4:00 a.m. on Saturday morning, an idea emerged. Dr. Forh, born in Sierra Leone, was an influential Kru man in Monrovia, who taught at the University of Liberia and was currently working as assistant minister at the Ministry of Labor. He grew up with my mother in Freetown and knew my entire family, so I thought he could be the one positioned to bring Mr. Joe Dawh to his senses now that I know that he was trying to disqualify me for his nephew. I had only slept for about two hours. I remember I was once introduced to him at the time he was lecturing at the University of Liberia. He had given me his address and asked that I visit him when I fine the time. I was convinced that if I can find Dr. Forh, this problem would be solved. He frequently travelled abroad, and I can't think of any way to find out if he was in the country or not. I thought that while the church would be working on my issue tomorrow, it would be stronger if I can also get Dr. Forh involved.

I woke up and tapped at George's room door and told him that I was leaving for Monrovia to see the Dr. Forh. George knew that I did not have the fare to take me to Monrovia, so he asked me to wait on Monday; he would have raised enough fund to make the trip. But I insisted that I was leaving, and he was puzzled how I was going to make it. I told him that I had always taken risk in my life especially when it was necessary, and I knew that God would make a way.

So at 5:30 a.m., I left to go to the main terminal at the marketplace. On my way toward, the terminal I met three men trying to jumpstart a pickup truck. Two of the men pushed the pickup down the slope, but it could not start, so they were trying to push it backward up the hill to try it again. I saw that it was difficult for them, so I went over to give them a hand. The vehicle almost started, but it did not. So the driver encouraged us to try one more time. We went backward and then forward down the slope, and this time the engine roared. One of the men was the apprentice, and the other was just a volunteer like me. The driver thanked us and wanted to give us each twenty-five cents, but I asked if he could give me a ride to Monrovia; he said they were heading for Paynesville near Monrovia. I said that was fine, and I jumped in.

From Harbel to Monrovia is forty-five miles, and from Paynesville to Monrovia is only two to three miles. I then took a bus from Paynesville to Third Street in Sinkor, Monrovia, where Dr. Forh lived. The time was around 11:15 a.m. when I arrived at his house.

Dr. Forh was in the shower when his wife opened the door and received me. After a while, Dr. Forh came fully dressed, and we greeted each other. He was concerned that I looked pale and dirty. His wife served me a sandwich and fixed me a hot malt drink. I told the story why I came to see him. He interrupted me a couple of times to clarify one point and another. Then he went to a stock of newspapers and fished out the *Liberian Age* newspaper and looked at the FPCO job posting for the bookkeeping positions and he placed the paper on the table and pointed to it.

"Are you talking about one of these jobs as yours, John?"

"Yes, sir," I answered. And then I pulled out the folder in my small bag and showed him the rest of the papers that the company provided me to complete the employment process.

Dr. Forh became immediately upset, and he picked up his telephone and dialed a number and spoke to someone. I could hear him calling the name of the company and using words like *nepotism, segregation, discrimination, unfair labor practices, violation of the Employment Act of 19———, the constitutional rights of a citizen*, etcetera.

After he hung up, he came over to me and said, "Hurry up, John, you are going with me to the Kru Tribal Council meeting at New Kru Town right away to present your case before the Kru community." He said that I was very lucky that that meeting was to be held that very afternoon and that he served as secretary of the council head by the Kru governor, Counselor James Nagbeh Doe. When he said this, I knew right there and then that my being there was not a coincidence. I was led by the Holy Spirit to the right person and the right place and at the right time.

We drove to the town hall at New Kru Town where the Kru Tribal Council meeting was being held. After the first agenda item was disposed of, which was the reading of the minutes of the previous meeting, Dr. Forh introduced me and effectively explained my situation to the council. There were probably three hundred tribal elders in the hall who keenly listened, and they were all uncontrollably furious. As emotions and tension in the hall grew louder, it took the chairman several minutes calling for order before the place was calmed. A section of the council called for a petition to remove Mr. Joe Dawh from the position, labeling him as one of those who suppresses the indigenous and practiced nepotism. Others were calling for a movement to instigate strike to protest these types of inequalities, segregation, and discrimination in the society, claiming that most of the children of the elites came back from America with accents, and they get all the good jobs, and their children who struggled in nearby African countries and most of those who grew up in Liberia are marginalized.

After all the opinions were expressed, one of the governor's advisors stood up and suggested that a letter would be written with the Kru Tribal Council letterhead, stamped and sealed, then addressed to the managing director of FPCO, and a copy should be sent to Mr. Joe Dawh, attesting unequivocally that "John Chea Davies is a Kru man to the backbones" and that "he is an original bona fide Liberian to the letter." He said it was about time that actions against these types of unfair practices, nepotism, and discrimination be addressed in drastic terms but that the current individual situation should be addressed independently and urgently in order not to jeopardize my interest. His wise words carried overwhelming support, and

Dr. Forh was advised to draft a letter immediately, which the clerk typed, and the governor signed, stamped, and sealed it. Two copies of the letter were given to me plus my own copy with forwarding orders attached to each envelope, and I was instructed to have both letters hand-delivered to their respective addressees: the managing director and labor manager of FPCO. And I was to send back to the council the signed forwarding order and provide progress report of my employment. The sum of $20 was raised to assist me. I thanked them and left the meeting but not before angry members of the council expressed their intensions to call Mr. Joe Dawh on Monday to express their concern or to dare him any further procrastinate of my clearance for employment.

Chapter 14

I arrived in Herbel on Saturday night and showed George, his wife, and the old woman what I accomplished. She also told me that they had the elders of their church fully involved, and a delegation would be going to see the managing director of the company on Monday morning. In addition, their prayer group announced a one-day fast and prayer for me on Monday. It was exciting to know that so much support was garnered behind me.

On Monday morning when I went to deliver the managing director's letter at the administrative building where the Accounting Department was also situated, I found out that it was the first day of work for Carlor Coker, the junior bookkeeper. The secretary to the managing director received the letter from me, signed the forwarding order, immediately opened it, and read it in my presence. She asked me to wait as she took the letter into her boss's office.

Moments later, she returned to tell me to go to the Labor Department for my clearance. I went to the Labor Department and delivered Mr. Dawh's letter and waited. In the reception was his nephew who took the aptitude test, also waiting to see his uncle. His secretary took the letter into his office and came back out with my clearance signed and stamped by him. I don't think that he even read the letter I delivered to him. When his secretary handed me the clearance, I kissed it and walked away to complete the rest of the process.

On my way I had nothing but praises for God for yet enabling me to cross this huddle. The devil wanted to steal my blessing, but he got a solid kick in the butt, but who knows where and when next he was preparing to attack me because if you were me, born in Kissy Mess-Mess, you should be expecting an attack just when and where you least expected. I completed the rest of the requirements and turned everything over to the Personnel Department that afternoon.

The employment process was completed, and I was scheduled to report to Mr. Peter Buggie at the Accounts Department to start work on Wednesday, the day that was the deadline for me to complete the process or lose the job.

On Tuesday night when it was announced at the prayer meeting at the church that I was going to start working the next day, it was a rejoicing scene as the prayer women praised God with songs of thanksgiving African-worship style with drums beating as we all danced to the victory rhythm over the devil. I was taken to one of the women's house where I chose clothes to suit my first work wardrobe from her used-clothes collection.

On Wednesday morning before leaving for work, I looked at myself in the mirror, but the reflection wasn't me. Whosoever was reflected in that mirror demanded some respect with a prefix to his name, maybe something like Sir John Chea Davies II.

DYSFUNCTIONAL ONE

Firestone Plantations Company, an American-based entity, was widely known and noted not only for its exploitation of Liberian rubber but also for its ability to influence Liberian authorities and to maximize profits at the expense of its local employees and community development. According to the 1926 concession contract shamefully awarded to the company by the protectorate government of the republic at that time, the company was given concession to tap rubber on about one-third of the country's landscape at the rate of $1 an acre for ninety-nine years, ending in 2025. In addition, the company was exempted from paying taxes and 8,500 of its 10,000 original laborers were forced as slaves to work on its plantation in compliance to a clause that the company introduced. Consideration for growth or upgrade of community development standards were underrated, while conditions that might trigger future increase in the price the company should pay per acre were ignored even though the so-called developed countries would frequently dictate and influence increase in the value of rubber and a variety of rubber products on the world market.

At the time of my employment in early 1977, FPCO had about forty thousand employees and was deemed to have exploited hundreds of billions of dollars through its PIP (profit improvement programs) and other exploitative systems at the expense of the country. The company utilized and benefited enormously from forced labor under protection of the government from 1926 to 1962, when forced labor was abolished. Some laborers were paid as little as ten cents a day for decades till the abolishment of forced labor as a result of ILO intervention. All the various grades of rubber processed were exported to the United States without any industries in Liberia to produce products using rubber as raw materials. When I was employed, about 95 percent of the company's forty thousand employees were Liberians, mostly laborers or tappers engaged in hard labor, tapping and physically carrying on their shoulders, latex weighing between fifty to a hundred pounds from rubber plantation to various terminals and making less than a hundred dollars a month, while the other 2 percent of its employees were foreign expatriates most of whom are from the United States making over a thousand dollars a month. The company's monthly payables, including its payroll, were under twelve million dollars.

Computers and accounting software were not popular then, so most of the accounting was done manually with calculators. EDP payroll spreadsheet system was in use, but about 97 percent of employees did not have bank accounts so the department had to pay employees with cash twice a month. Workloads at various sections of the accounting department were routinely heavier than the accounting staffs assigned can handle in a timely fashion since most part of the data-processing mechanism depended on manual inputs. For these reasons, there were always some overlapping tasks across the various sections at the department for which accounting staffs were assigned on overtime basis in order to meet deadlines, whether it be for handling payroll for the forty thousand employees paid biweekly or for monthly closing of the world's largest rubber plantation books. Monthly financial statements were to be completed and transmitted to the company's headquarters in Akron, in the United States not later than the seventh of the succeeding month. These routines posed challenges for working longer hours under pressure to meet deadlines.

According to my immediate supervisor, Mr. K. Richards, I learned the job faster than anyone he ever taught. He had served the company then for more than twenty-five years and had suppressed many of those he was supposed to train who could have taken over the position after him since the company's retirement policy matured after an employee served for twenty-five years. Like many who reached the retirement age, he was selfish and tried every trick in the book to prevent me from acquiring the required skills since I was next on the line for his position. But he was wrong, for I had picked up the entire accounting system and can do any of the jobs in various sections, plus I was the fastest with the desk calculators in the entire Accounting Department.

DYSFUNCTIONAL ONE

Peter Burgie noticed that and began to allow me to do overtime during monthly closing, assisting with the closing process despite K. Richard's protest. K. Richard was typical of many African leaders who try everything to either change the Constitution just to extend their stay in power or desired to stay in the position to cover wrongdoings. After my probation, the company confirmed my appointment and assigned me a house.

Although my salary was $325 a month, which was quite a bit of money for me, I found a way to beat the system and started making between $2,000 to $5,000 a month. Some of the vendors that FPCO dealt with needed their payments long before the thirty to sixty days term of payment that it took to received payments, and they needed an inside man to make that happen for them, and I was that insider whom no one never detected, from my supervisor to the chief accountant and his assistant. My role was to backdate the data on the books to match a new backdated invoice that suppliers would provide me in order to show that their payment was matured. I would switch and replace the original invoices with the new backdated ones, get approval, and get Mr. Clinton, the check preparer, to prepare the supplier's check, which was easy to pass approval because the backdated invoice would show maturity and the data that I have already manipulated would support payment maturity. The obligations were genuine only that the suppliers got paid long before payments were matured, and I got a cut for making it happen.

It all started one day when a desperate Lebanese merchant came into Accounts Payable to beg for a payment that was forty days premature. He had a shipment that was accumulating storage charges down the port that he needed funds to clear, but he was not successful, so he left. After work that same day, I went to the supermarket to get groceries and met him there discussing with the management.

On the parking lot he was there by his car when I came out, and he recognized me and expressed his disappointment over the denial of his payment. So I said I might be able to help him out next time, but all he needed to do was to provide a backdated copy of the invoice with the exact supplies. I said I could not help him with the current invoice because it was already known. He offered me a percentage if I was able to help him in this way in the future. Then I helped him the first time with a forty thousand payment just within a week of his company's supply, and he gave me $2,000. Then he became my endorser with the other suppliers that he was acquainted with, and we were now in business. All he had to do was to let businesses know that he can get them their future payments now and collect from them a backdated invoice and turn that over to me. In a day or two, their checks were mailed to them, and he would come over to my house with my share. I didn't care how much he collected from his fellow vendors for the relief services I was providing them as long as I get the $500 cut for every $10,000 invoice value as agreed, so our relationship went on smoothly for a while.

Six months down the road the superintendent for Marshall Territory came to my office to transact business and told me about Princer's condition. Princer was in a relationship with one of the superintendent's daughters. I was compelled then to go see him and break the ice between us; after which I began supporting him monthly. My newfound brother George and his family were well taken care of, and so were many others, including my aunt down Gibraltar in Monrovia.

It was at the same Harbel Supermarket that I met my first girlfriend in Monrovia, Liberia, Kolue Cyrus. I was young, twenty-three, and transformed beyond recognition for so many who knew me before. I could not keep a bank account, or else I will be exposed or questioned as to where I was getting all that money from. My house was well furnished, and I had a lot of friends and entertained them too. On some weekends, I would buy air tickets for some of my friends and myself to fly to neighboring countries to watch soccer matches, which I was very fond of, and I would return early enough for work.

DYSFUNCTIONAL ONE

The money was flowing, and I was overwhelmed and misguided in my use of it. One thing was very clear with me was that I was never going to be a Jacksony; in other words, I was never a womanizer simply because I did not know how to love two women at the same time, so my girlfriend was just enough for me.

Princer was different, he was a Jacksony, and that did not sit well with me, for there were just too many women and therefore too many issues, complaints, maneuvers, alibis, and cover-ups that I was forced to involve with, and that mostly placed me in an embarrassing position.

FPCO was a different kind of company in a broader sense. Living and working on the plantation was like being shut off from the outside world with that annoying and unpleasant smell of raw rubber twenty-four hours a day. I sometimes wondered how some people got used to that smell, living in that environment for decades especially in the early-morning hours when doors are opened to that inescapable thick smell of latex rushing through nostrils straight into the head, which felt like sniffing snuff. The company built shags for labors to live in and bungalows and single-family homes for other administrative staffs, and rental for these housing units are embedded but concealed in employees' pay arrangements, so it appeared as if the company was doing its employees a favor by providing them free housing. There was a community school, a clinic, recreational centers, clubhouses, and electric supply provided and operated by the company. There was a departmental soccer league in which I participated, and there were leagues in other types of sports. There was only one chess player I knew in the plantation, and that was the chief accountant, D. R. L. Williams, a British national, but he had no time to play, so we talk chess history and sometimes reference a particular world-class games. He had a wooden chess set that he gave up to one of our colleagues, A. S. Cole, who had expressed interest in learning the game, and once in a while Cole and I would play for fun.

In a company the size of FPCO, diversity along ethnic, cultural, and political lines incites tolerance and exposes people to a variety of cultures, homogeneous groups, etcetera. Soon money, friends, and partying took over my life, and my religious participation reduced. I started mingling with the elite and was initiated in the local United Brotherhood Fellowship (UBF), a Masonic society recognized and respected by the upper class, and people like Joe Dawh and others who were viewed as obnoxious became my Masonic brother, and we began to forge a relationship. By the end of 1977, my name was a household name in the Harbel and Smell-No-Taste areas.

Chapter 15

I entered 1978 big in grand style with about $25,000 in hundred-dollar bills hidden in my attic plus a couple of thousands more handy. There was always a chartered vehicle to take me around. Across from neighboring Sierra Leone and within Liberia, request for assistance from friends and relatives came flying in at me, and because of my generous heart or because I wanted to make a point that, after all, I have risen above perceptions, I catered to many requests and helped so many in need. Even Mum was sending messages asking for assistance and advising me to keep up the good name she was hearing about me—the "good-for-nothing son" as she called me many times in the past. I was given VIP treatments whenever I was in the company of relatives or friends. I was now in position where people were confiding in me, sharing their deepest personal problems with me, or asking my advice. As a person with a compassionate heart, I catered to almost everyone who asked favor of me without any form of discrimination whatsoever.

One day in the month of March 1978, few of my colleagues and I were strolling to a nearby restaurant for lunch when three younger men approached me to ask for a room to live in. They were students from Booker Washington Institute in Kakata who were to start a three-month internship with the company, and they needed a place to stay. Someone told them to contact me because I was alone in my house with my two dogs, (Romeo and Juliet). They showed me their internship admittance letter on the street, and I immediately gave them a duplicate key to my house and directed them which room in my house they can have.

The students were surprised, and so were my colleagues. Everyone, including the students, said that they never thought I would have reacted so quickly to their request, and my colleagues simply said they would not have decided the way I did. But that was one of the differences between them and me. Most likely, they all grew under parental care with affection and never once experienced homelessness, let alone extreme hunger. Before the students left us, I offered them something to eat, and they were even more grateful. Over lunch we got to know one another a little bit more.

An overwhelming number of FPCO employees did not have any bank account back then, so salaries were paid by cash money stuffed in envelopes, and there were nothing like direct deposits in the Liberian banking system, so the few employees who had bank accounts had to pick up their paychecks to do whatever they wanted to do with it. The only bank in Harbel to serve the company and its foreign employees was the US-based Chase Manhattan Bank. There the company would withdraw hundreds of thousands of dollars in various denominations to meet its biweekly payrolls. These amounts were kept in a vault at the administrative building where the Account Department was situated.

Every other week the payroll accountant would withdraw from the bank, which was about a quarter of a mile away from the administrative building, hundreds of thousands of dollars in various denominations, placed in wooden boxes with metal locks. The boxes would then be transported, accompanied to the vault by plant protection officers. There were no machines to check money at the time, so most of the accounting staff, including myself, would have to work in the bank to assist with manual counting of money under the watchful eyes of the company's plant protection officers. The size of the vault at our office was probably fifty by thirty feet, and it usually contained cash money up to a million dollar in several of the boxes. The combination to the vault was top secret known only by three people: the managing director, the chief accountant, and his assistant.

In order to pay biweekly wages and salaries, a number of accounting staff had to assist the Payroll Department. Tons of payroll spreadsheets were lined up with envelopes bearing employees' names and amounts corresponding to the name and amount on the spreadsheets. Designated staffs at each table would then be given a spreadsheet, the envelopes matching the spreadsheet and the exact money denomination to stuff the exact individual employee's wages inside the envelopes accordingly. There were two things I hated during my work with FPCO. One was the thick rubber smell in the morning when I opened my door, and the other was the smell from stack of dollar bills inside the Chase Manhattan Bank. Even though I hated the smell from the money, I love looking at it, and I sometimes wondered if such piles of money would just magically stockpile in my house, how lovely that would be. Although this was just a joke that most of the accounting staff shared whenever we are assigned to work in the bank, it was becoming real to me personally. I really wanted to see a room in my house full of dollars from the floor to ceiling as in the bank. After all, FPCO deserved to be taught a lesson, and every Liberian deserves to get their share of the pie that was still being stolen from them through the Firestone Concession Agreement of 1026. The Americo-Congo legislature that introduced and approved the concession bill then together with Mr. Harvey Firestone robbed the entire country and deprived generations unborn from the benefits of its resources. The concession bill awarded Firestone one million acres of land or an area equal to 4 percent of Liberia's territory for ninety-nine years at the rate of $1 an acre. The bill also granted the American-backed company exemption from paying present and future taxes to the Liberian people during the life of the concession agreement while every businesses in America pays taxes, and, to put the icing on the cake, the then protectorate Liberian government granted Harvey Firestone condition to provide and maintain adequate labor supply; hence, the Liberia army was used to force the recruitment of tens of thousands of the indigenous as slaves to work for the company from 1926 until 1961 when the Portuguese government filed a forced labor case against the Liberian government with the International Labor Organization (ILO). Sadly two of the senators who introduced the Firestone Concession Bill at the Liberian Senate and lobbied for its approval were hired by Harvey Firestone as his company's lawyer; one of them was Arthur Barclay, former president of the republic, and the other was then senator William Tubman, who later became president of the republic as well; an odd coincidence. Both lobbied for the bill to pass, backed and supported by the incumbent president of the republic, President Charles King. The approval of the bill was a home run that Harvey Firestone himself referred to as "the greatest concession of its kind ever made in history."

Could this be a coincidence that three presidents in time—past, present, and future—would support and lobby for such a bill that was doomed to grossly disadvantaged the country for a century? Liberian politics then was grossly evolved around American interest, so it was no coincidence that those who took the oath to serve, preserve, and protect the constitution of Liberian and its resources would resolve to betray the oath to benefit America and them. Like in many slave situations, many lives were lost as some of the indigenous resisted the forced labor recruitment clause in the bill, giving assurances that the government would provide labor to work the plantations.

My dad was twelve years old then in 1926 when his parents joined the resistance group of indigenous who fled from the Firestone forced labor recruitment as well as the shipment of forced labor to the Spanish island of Fernando Poo, which the King administration was engaged in. My great-grandfather and some of Dad's cousins and uncles were captured then and forced to work on rubber plantations, and some of them were shipped to the island of Fernando Poo, and they never again united with their families or heard of again.

Later as a result of the League of Nations' findings, known as the Christy Report, President Charles King, resigned from the presidency in 1930 just when the House of Representatives began impeachment proceedings to uproot him from office for Liberia's involvement in the scandal, but it was not until 1961 before the practice of forced labor recruitment was outlawed when ILO was investigating allegations of forced labor recruitment practiced in

Liberia. The ILO investigation was prompted by the Portuguese government in retaliation for Liberia's staunched opposition to colonialism while under the same breath encouraged and practice an element of slavery, forced labor. Many of my colleagues believed that because the company was an American company, its security systems were sophisticated and impenetrable. But that was not true as far as I was concerned, for I was already the highest-paid staff on the plantation, at least so I thought, and nobody knew except my Lebanese partner.

As a young man making so much money than I can handle, there were no planning for my future besides the corresponding courses I was taking from London Educational Association and Metropolitan College. I have always believed I would never fall or run out of money anymore in my life. I was no longer attending church as I used to, but I was partying more and passing time at high costs. I spent weekends with my girlfriend at Ducor Palace Hotel or Ambassador Hotel in Monrovia, eating, drinking, entertaining friends, and at times playing chess games mainly with foreigners. My wardrobe was exquisite, and so was my girlfriend, who was envied by many of her peers.

On July 22, 1978, I celebrated my twenty-fourth birthday at the Kru governor's house at Point Four in Monrovia. It was a spectacular event for me and to many. I told the governor to pass the word around and invited as many people as possible. The fact that I had not celebrated my birthday since I was eight years old made things looked like I was making up for all those years lost. I spent about $3,000, which was a hefty amount of money for a typical twenty-four-year old. But my birthday was only a prelude to the execution of my biggest plan then. The company imported a giant Chubb Vault Door from the United States and brought their expert to replace their vault door with a giant steel door containing multiple combinations. It appeared as though they knew I was there and wanted to make sure that the company's main vault door was made of multiple layers of steel with multiple combinations to secure the hundreds of thousands of dollars that was always kept in that vault.

But while they were preparing this high-powered security measure, I was also preparing a simpler form of countersecurity measure to get my share of the pie. The massive steel door arrived at the Freeport of Monrovia on a Saturday and was delivered the following Wednesday. The two Chubb experts flew in from the United States on Tuesday, and on Thursday the installation job was completed around 2:00 p.m. From ten feet away, I was in my office when the work was going on, and all I needed was the code to all the combinations on that door. I had bought a couple of carbonated writing pads that artists used for sketching for the purpose of deluding the experts and set two of the pads with ballpoint pens on the two nearby tables where the experts had some of their tools and some materials.

Like a fish, they took the bait and started writing code after code as they tested to open and close the vault door several times. When they were done, one of the experts who wrote the codes simply cut off the top page and placed the pad and the pen back on the table. I immediately dialed Mr. Clinton's extension, and his phone rang continuously because he was not behind his desk. They had removed all staff away from the area where the vault door was located for security purposes and to give the experts more room to do their work. From my office, I could see clearly that Mr. Clinton, whose desk was close to the vault, was not at his desk. Keeping my phone hand piece opened, I walked over to answer Mr. Clinton's still-ringing phone. I pulled up the receiver to my ear and pretended like I was talking to someone while beckoning to one of the experts, who passed me the pad to write a message for Mr. Clinton. The man was generous and helpful to pass the pad to me, and I tore off the first two pages containing the impressions of their writings, placed the pad and pen back on the nearby desk, thanked the expert who smiled back at me as I walked passed him back to my office.

DYSFUNCTIONAL ONE

Moments later the chief accountant and his assistant came in, and again the expert wrote the codes using the pad, and both of them tested the door. When they were done, they too tore off the page containing the codes and took their copy, and the blessed pad was placed back on the desk as the experts packed up their tools, cleaned up the place, and left. Then I politely walked to the area near the vault and picked up all of my pads and pen placed in strategic places and put them in my bag.

At home that night, I went on the drawing board and sketched the impressions on the papers and arrived at the same characters that made up the codes to the combinations of the vault; the Davies concession bill was born and doomed to be introduced on July 28, 1978—the day that over half a million dollars was expected to be sitting in boxes in the vault.

Chapter 16

On Saturday July 22, 1978, I purchased a toolbox containing various sizes of screwdrivers, pliers, and cutters down Monrovia while I was preparing to celebrate my birthday. The wooden boxes in the vault had hinges on the rear part and giant steel locks at the front. I did not need the keys to the boxes, only the right screwdriver to unscrew the hinges at the back, and it would open. There are three screws on each one of the two hinges, which I estimated could take up to two minutes to unscrew all six screws per box.

July 28 was perfect timing for the operation because it was the last weekend for closing the company books for the month so that overtime as an alibi was justified; on the other hand, the biweekly payroll was due the coming week, so there were many accounting tasks that some of the department staffs would be working long hours on Friday, even on Saturday and Sunday.

In my planning, the operation was to involve what I called an "open risk," meaning that it should be done while other staffs were still around at their desks working, and I was not to be the last man working to leave the building. During the week of my birthday, I was part of the designated team to count and pack about eight hundred thousand dollars of the company's money at the bank and placed the money in various denominations in the boxes before the plant protection officers transported them to the vault at company's head office.

While we were counting and verifying money at the bank, I marked the boxes according to their denominations. The boxes containing hundred-dollar bills and fifty-dollar bills were marked with red ink, the one with twenty dollar-bills I marked with blue ink, and the ones with ten-, five-, and one-dollar bills I mark with black ink. Those boxes containing coins were left unmarked. This was necessary so as not to waste time with boxes containing smaller denominations as those smaller denominations were forbidden in what I termed the Davies Concession Bill, mimicking the Firestone Concession Bill of 1962.

There were three accounting clerks whose desks were in the room where entrance to the vault was situated. One of them, Mr. Clinton, the check writer, did not work overtime. The other, Mr. Fambuleh, usually left for Kakata on weekends to spend time with his girlfriend who lived there. The only obstacle was Mr. Cole, who happened to be a workaholic, but I had something for him. He loved hanging out with me once in a while, so I invited him to hang out with me on Friday evening, but when he said he too had a date in Kakata so he would not be working overtime on Friday, I looked up to the heavens and sent my thanks.

The next obstacles were officers of the Plant Protection Department, whose duty was to secure the building and particularly the vault twenty four hours round the clock. Their main post in the building was the first office at the entrance of the building where they would come from to patrol offices and around the building every fifteen minutes. So if I were to realize a successful operation or pass the Davies concession bill on Friday, July 28, 1978, as planned, I must be precise in timing and crafty in dislodging and deluding the company's plant protection systems.

On Friday, I took an excuse from work in the morning and went to the clinic for dysentery. The doctor prescribed medication, which I never took since I was not sick but just wanted to build up alibi.

At 4:00 p.m. after work, I went to the supermarket and bought groceries and placed them in two large paper bags and took a taxi back to the office to work overtime. When I got off the taxi with the two large paper bags in my hand, I walked toward the security post and deliberately stumbled, throwing everything in both bags on the ground: bread, cracker biscuits, butter, chocolates, candies, packs of tea, coffee, cocoa, etcetera—all scattered everywhere on the ground. I sat there holding my foot and laughing at myself, and the three officers present came over to lift me up, helped to pick and pack the groceries into the bags, and then I went to my office.

Moments later two of the officers patrolled the offices, and when they reached me, we laughed, and they wanted to know if I was fine, and I said my left foot was sprained. Then I said that I would, in fact, be leaving soon if the pain would not subside.

As soon as they walked through the door, I started the operation. Some of the accounting staffs were in the back office, and I could hear them chatting. No one was within sight of the area where the vault was situated. I put on my glove, walked to the vault, and began applying the codes, which were already memorized. Then I heard the first click after applying the first code. I applied the second code, and the second click registered, and I pulled the handle toward me, and the heavy vault door opened. I quickly went inside and pulled one of the boxes marked with the red ink and placed it under Mr. Fambuleh's desk, and then I went back in and pulled two other boxes with blue ink. Those officers who packed the boxes inside the vault unknowingly placed my favorite red-marked boxes at the back, which might take me more time than planned to reach them, for I would have to remove boxes after boxes to reach them. So I quickly decided to take the other boxes marked with blue ink since that meant they contained twenty-dollar bills, and I left the ones marked black because they either contained ten-, five-, or one-dollar bills. I placed all of the boxes under the same desk, and then I closed the vault door. Then I took out the exact screwdriver and unscrewed the boxes and placed their contents into the grocery bags, which I had emptied, and put two packs of cracker biscuits on top.

It was now about nine minutes into the operations. I looked around, and I could still hear the other staffs in the back office chatting and their desk calculators roaring. I closed the boxes and placed them back into the vault and then locked the door. Then I took off my gloves and put them, along with the screws that came from the boxes, into my jacket pocket. I locked the screwdriver in my drawer together with the rest of the groceries. I would have time to take care of those on Monday.

Exactly fifteen minutes later, the security officers came around patrolling, and one of them asked how I was feeling, and I said that I was leaving because of the pain on my left leg. I called out to the staff at the back, and a few of them came over and heard from the security that I fell and sprained my ankle, so one of them offered to drop me at the marketplace with their car so I can take a taxi from there to go home.

Moments later, with my two grocery bags in hand—bread and biscuits visible on top of each—I walked slowly past the sympathetic plant protection officers and entered the vehicle that took me to the market.

The Davies concession bill had been approved, but not with all the desired conditions. Only one of the red-marked boxes was within easy reach. However, one condition that concession growing out of the Firestone effect had in common in Liberia was exemption from present and future taxes, so there were no tax liens on the content in my grocery bags, present and future.

At the Harbel Market, I bought a travel bag in which I placed the two paper bags, and then I chartered a taxi to take me wherever I wanted to go for the rest of the evening at $5 an hour. There was one thing missing in my planning, which was very significant. What next after the Davies concession is passed? What was I going to do with the money, and where was I going to keep it? Or how, when, and where would I use it? I was now stuck with whether I should just go home to think about it; after all, no one is going to know that the money is missing from the vault until maybe midweek to the next weekend. Certainly I was not going to join the money with some $35,000 or so that I already had hidden at my attic, which no one knew about or would be looking for. Suddenly the question with what to do right now began to weigh in on me, and it occurred to me that the only person I could talk to was Princer. He was brave, calculating, and we have many things like this in common, and he used to be the brain to so many deals we had pulled when we were struggling after Dad left, plus he was my blood brother from the same parents. Maybe the money could change our relationship and bring us closer together, which was something I have always wanted. We could set up our own business or travel to some Western country and put ourselves in great universities. But I was seriously mistaken and wrong.

So I went to Smell-No-Taste to find Princer, but he was gone to Monrovia with some woman to spend the weekend there. Since my girlfriend usually spent the weekend at my place, I decided to go home and asked her to accompany me to Monrovia to spend the weekend there as well, away from the smell of rubber, but my objective was to find Princer. I could not confine or rely on George, for he was not like Princer and me. He was soft and a submissive type to the status quo, scared and contented with the $150 a month that FPCO paid him, and has established his loyalty for a long time. Princer and I shared the same childhood, and there was a special bond that binds us even though we don't get along well. He was also smart as I was and apparently matured than I was at the time. He had accreditation from the police academy and served the government as a customs officer at the RIA, entering a variety of deals and receiving bribes, so he was the right closest person that I could relate to under the circumstances. Besides, he was connected in the community, knowing so many big sharks.

So I picked up my girlfriend, and we went to Monrovia and put up at Carlton Hotel on Broad Street. Near the hotel was a store where I bought a briefcase to pack the morney in. I had checked it overnight in the restroom while Kolue was asleep and was disappointed that the Davies concession bill was not approved in its entirety. The amount was $86,700, which was a substantial amount of money at the time. It would have taken me approximately twenty-two years to make that amount of money from my current salary of $325 a month.

DYSFUNCTIONAL ONE

The next morning we went around in another chartered taxi in search of Princer, and when we could not find him, we went to Gibraltar town and left word for him to meet me at the hotel if at all he comes around. When Princer could not show up on Sunday and it was getting too late for us to return since Kolue was supposed to go back to her parents' house to prepare for school the next morning while I was supposed to be at work, I became worried by the minute, and finally before we left the hotel, we returned to Gibraltar town where I decided to leave the briefcase there with one of my cousins at my aunt's house to turn it over to Princer. I had reset a new combination on the briefcase and locked it also with the key and went away with it. Then Kolue and I went back to Harbel.

On our way we stopped at Smell-No-Taste, but Princer was not yet back. The next morning I went to work, and during the course of the day I took care of things like the screwdriver and the groceries.

That evening after work, I met Princer at my house, and we spoke in my bedroom. Then he drove in his Isuzu to Gibraltar town in Monrovia to pick up the briefcase, and once he got it, I never again laid eyes on neither the briefcase nor its content till today. Princer came back and confirmed that he got it and everything was under control. I loved my brother then and now, and I trusted his judgment, but little did I know in my slightest imagination that he would have double-crossed me and disappeared, never to face me again for over thirty-five years. The name of the town where he lived, Smell-No-Taste, was not justified in my mind until I realized that the money that I smelled was never for me to taste.

Chapter 17

On Wednesday that week, the chief accountant and paymaster went to the vault with a number of security personnel and started pulling out box after box to stuff employees' cash in payroll envelopes. By Friday afternoon, it became clear to them that something had happened. According to their tally, three boxes containing the sum of $86,700 had mysteriously vanished without a trace, and according to the evidence, only one of the three people who knew the combination to the vault could have done this; nobody else. There was only one person in the company who knew both combinations, and that was the managing director. The chief accountant, his assistant, and the payroll accountant only had one set of the combination, and neither of them could open the vault without the managing director or his assistant applying the other combination. Therefore investigators believed that the vault, which happened to be twice the size of any of the vaults at the National Bank of Liberia, was even more secured to the extent that it was impossible for any of the ordinary employees to open and enter it. Especially so that the security measures and procedures where such that it was not possible that it would have been left opened by all means because there were five personnel from three different departments responsible to be present when it was being opened, and they were to make sure it was physically locked, logging their respective records of each activities, acknowledging their presence and participation. Those personnel were representatives from the office of the managing director, two from the Account Department (payroll accountant and chief accountant or his assistant) and the chief of Plant Protection Department.

Furthermore, the vault is checked every fifteen minutes by plant protection officers twenty-four hours round the clock. All these departments' logs recorded that they fully participated and physically made sure that twenty-five boxes containing $800,000 were placed into the vault on Tuesday and Thursday, July 25 and 27, 1978, and they all physically turned the bolt on the vault door to make sure it was locked.

Thereafter, for three days during the next week, August 2 to August 4, the same procedure had been applied to take boxes after boxes for payroll purposes till Friday when three of the boxes were reportedly discovered inside the vault, broken into with their contents mysteriously vanished. The Plant Protection Department could not crack the case or solve the puzzle since they also are subjected to investigation because it was their job to make sure that money were transported, placed inside the vault, and then to ascertain and verify that the vault's door was locked at all times even during their patrol.

On Saturday morning, the company officials met and formed a scenario that the boxes could have been mistakenly left outside the vault, and any of the accounting staff could have committed the crime, so the failed Plant Protection Department decided to interrogate all staff.

Although it was not a working day, they knew where we all lived, so they rounded us up, and we were taken to the PPD headquarters for a very long and boring interrogation that ruined everyone's weekend. On Saturday August 5, 1978, the national police at the RIA got involved, and the matter was placed into their hands for investigation. The managing director and staffs concerned who had access to both combinations of the vault had to assist the investigation by way of their statements and through interrogation like everyone else. But they were allowed to walk away.

The chief accountant and his assistant who could not open the vault because they only had one section of the combination also gave their statements and were released. The payroll accountant, like the chief accountant and his assistant who also had one set of the combination and could not open the vault without the managing director or his assistant, was detained in custody, simply because of the color of his skin; he was a Liberian, black and a member of the indigenous.

During interrogation, both the chief accountant and assistant chief accountant in response to an hypothetical question on who they think among the staff could pull this perfect crime off, they both selected the same name: John C. Davies. They were asked why, and their answers were also the same: They thought that I was brilliant and smarter, above average, than anybody else in the department. Based on their suppositions, I was arrested, interrogated, and detained in the same cell as the payroll accountant.

My girlfriend heard that I was being detained, so she went to informed George and Princer. By Monday morning the news media picked up the story and exploded it beyond proportion, and the whole country was glued to the radio, and newspapers subsequently followed the case.

On that same morning, Princer came to see me and inquired from investigators why I was being detained, and he found out that besides rumors about my lifestyle before the crime, there was nothing of substance but assumption to tie me to it. He argued with investigators and threatened to fight back if I was not released, claiming violation of my constitutional rights for being detained for over forty-eight hours. A theory was developed by investigators to the effect that the three boxes containing the missing money may had been inadvertently left outside of the vault, which means that it could have been within reach of any of the staff of the department. But there were so many things wrong with that theory; the boxes that were allegedly tampered with were all found inside the vault, and all those responsible testified to it. Therefore the theory could not hold because if the three boxes were inadvertently left out of the vault, then the question on how the empty boxes got into the vault and were found there left another puzzle.

On the other hand, according to the records, those three boxes did not come in the same day. The amount of $800,000 was counted at the bank and bought into the company's vault on two separate days, Tuesday, July 25, 1978, and Thursday, July 27, 1978 of the week in question. One of the boxes was recorded as brought in on Tuesday, and the other two were brought in Thursday. How would all of the staff and officers concerned make the same mistakes twice in two days and their individual records matched? Showing that those boxes were placed in the vault was another thing that was wrong with the theory. In order to pin me to any of the theories, one must be able to prove that the managing director and I are the only two people in the company who had the full combinations to the vault and can open it without assistance from anyone else.

Several scenarios and theories were formed, but it still bore down to three key objects: the vault, the combinations, and the boxes. Investigators cracked their brains and used all their techniques in the book, but there was nothing they could do to crack the case.

As for the Plant Protection Department, it was sleeplessness as the entire department, including their chiefs and officers, combed area after area in the surroundings and followed leads after leads to no avail.

Before all these, on Tuesday, August 1, 1978, Princer had visited me to discuss how to proceed and conduct ourselves when things blew up. We agreed that there was a need for us to pretend that we do not get along well with each other, which were true, and many could testify to it. Then we talked about any money I may have with me, so I released all the moneys in the attic to him, which could have been about $40,000. It made sense at the time that if that kind of money was found in my attic, it could have led investigators to pin the crime on me.

But there was something else Princer was working on ever since he laid his hands on the first big money from Gibraltar town. He was being assisted by his girlfriend's father to process travel documents and visas for him and for the man's four children: two daughters and two brothers along with a grandchild that was supposedly Princer's child by his girlfriend. They were slated to leave the country on August 10 for the United States, and I had no way of knowing what was going on on the outside since I was being detained only on the presumption that I was smart. If Mr. Williams of the CCC in Freetown heard that I was being detained on this basis, surely he would have conceded on the theory and added insult to injuries already being carried out. When Princer visited me at the RIA police station, he assured me of legal protection so that my constitutional rights would be respected, and I was stunned on Tuesday morning when I was taken from the cell to meet my legal counsel inside the office of the commander of police. I thought for a moment that this must be the company's lawyer, but I was wrong; he was hired by Princer to represent me. He was the senior senator for Grand Bassa County at the national legislature and legal counsel for True Wig Party, the ruling party of the government of Liberia and the president's private lawyer.

Counselor Joseph Findley was big name in Liberian politics and a tycoon in the legal arena. When he said he was there to represent me and wanted me to sign some papers to empower him as my lawyer, my jaw dropped. Princer had always referred to me as a small boy, and in most cases he meant and bragged about his age, his connections, and in other cases it was just a display of arrogance for which he was known.

As I was being led back into the cell, I thought, after all, that Princer was really not a small boy like me. Senator Findley was a big potato, a man of flamboyance and style. His elegance and perfume smell dominated the commander's office, and the mere fact that he was there for me changed the way and manner in which I was treated thereafter.

After Senator Findley assured me of his best representation and left, the police commander looked at me, and he said under his breath to his colleagues in the room that he can bet his head off that I knew something about the missing money; otherwise, a man like Findley would not leave his responsibilities at the Liberian Senate or at the TWP office or at his own private law firm where other attorneys who work for him could have been assigned to the case to travel from Monrovia to introduced himself as legal representative on my behalf. Then he shook his head continuously and said, "It is over; this case is over once Findley is in it." He then turned his attention to me and asked how much I paid Findley to represent me. I said with a smile that he was my uncle and everyone laughed. "Something must have moved a man like that to leave all his busy activities to come here just to announce his representation of you."

At 1:00 p.m. that day, the commander received instructions from the director of police to transfer me to Monrovia immediately. I was transferred to police headquarters in Monrovia where a writ of habeas corpus was already served on the police director to produce me in court the following day to show why I was being detained. The next day I was release by court order when the police department could not provide any reason why I was being detained.

Korlue, Princer, and a host of people from the Kru tribe were in the courtroom when the judge ordered my release, and there was this victory noise when I appeared outside the courtroom. Many of the people who attended my birthday party, many of whom did not know me personally, showed up to support me. I was taken to a hotel where I spent the night. There was an appointment to meet with Senator Findley, August 10, 1978. The meeting was about what to expect from the company, the police, and from prosecutors in the days ahead.

Also, Princer had paid a few people through the Kru governor to pose bail for me if there was any indictment in the future. After the meeting where Counselor Findley assured me of his representation to the very end, Princer informed me of a party that we were to attend at Logan town at one of our cousins' house in the evenings. Little did I know that the party was meant to dislodge me, while he and his girlfriend with three of his in-laws and the girlfriend's child take off on Pan Am at 10:00 p.m. for the United States. When he came to meet me in the hotel that evening before we went to the party, he presented me with a key to a new Isuzu sedan, which he bought that same day for $4,000 from Chiri Brothers, where he worked as storekeeper in 1971. He had purchased his first car from there long before he was fired from the customs.

That evening we dined together at a local restaurant, and he suggested that we all drive in his old vehicle to the party, so we left the new vehicle at the hotel parking. He had assured me that all purchases were in his name, and no one will question things that he bought and gave his younger brother to use. All that made sense, and we went to the party together. We had planned to meet in a secluded place to talk about all the money and plan our next move.

We arrived at cousin Mary's house at 7:00 p.m., where I thought the occasion was her birthday celebration, but it was a Princer's sponsored sendoff party, and it appeared as though Mary was a coconspirator. About an hour later, Princer disappeared, and I thought he was somewhere around maybe chatting with friends. I had Mary and few others engaging me and my girlfriend in various conversations. At 9:15 p.m., I went in the backyard to use the restroom, and it was occupied by a group of women, one of whom happens to be Mary's best friend. They engaged me in conversation, and Mary's best friend, thinking that I was part of Princer's entourage, released the hint by accusing me to be secretive and leaving for the United States that night.

I then started to look for Princer but was told that he was talking with one of his old girlfriends. But I was a bit worried, so I confronted Mary and asked her to be straight with me, and she finally told me the truth but said that Princer told her that my flight was later that same night and that he just did not want to be seen with me leaving with him together. She said that she had been keeping his briefcase containing his travel document, and then she handed me the key to his car, which, according to her, he instructed her to release to me after 11:00 p.m.

With Korlue sitting in the front passenger seat, I took Princer's car and drove to RIA in record speed, but I was a few minutes late. Pan Am flight was already in the air. I went over to some of the airport staff who knew him, and they confirmed he and some of his in-laws were on the flight. A staff showed me copy of their manifest, and when I saw Princer's name, I became dizzy, and my feet actually refused to move. For a moment the world around me disappeared, and I struggled real hard to put myself together. I found myself leaning for support on a railing at the balcony, and I heard faint voices asking repeatedly, "Are you all right?"

I was ushered down the stairs by two airport staffs who insisted to help me if I tell them what the problem was. They took me over to the car, and by this time, Korlue, who never had a chance to say a word since we were halfway to RIA, stepped out of the car to assist me from their hands. I was put into the driving seat of the car, and I lay my head on the steering wheel.

I heard Korlue telling them that I would be fine. "He had a terrible headache this morning, it was worse than that, but he would be fine," she said.

One of the men uttered something about safe driving, and she replied, "I won't let him drive, we would just sit in the car for a while, and if we need help, I will call you guys."

Not still getting myself together, I sat there with my head on the steering wheel, sobbing, and she entered the vehicle. Sitting on the passenger side and squeezing her fist into my flesh, she asked, "Princer has traveled out of the country, right?"

I did not answer, and she said, "I knew it, Chris—I knew it. It is like monkey work and bamboo draw," she said almost underneath her breath.

Those words cut through my heart like butchery, and for a moment I thought about committing suicide. We sat in the car in silence for about any hour thinking.

And then Korlue broke the silence. "What are we doing here? Let us go and see what he left behind in his room. Maybe he left you a message or a lead."

This idea put a little life into my exhausted brain, and I turned the ignition and drove to Smell-No-Taste where we spent the night in his room. I had his car parked exactly where he used to park near his in-laws' house. I did this for security purposes because cars are frequently broken into especially at night. We walked over to his house, which was just about thirty to forty yards away, and when I opened his room, it was scattered. He had given away most of his belongings. We searched the place and found nothing interesting. By the time we were done, it was around 4:00 a.m. We were exhausted and sleepy, so we slept there in his room until, say, after 9:00 a.m.

When we were ready to leave, I went over to his in-laws' place to get the car, but to my surprise, all four tires were severely cut with a sharp instrument, leaving the car sitting literally on the rims. This, I believed, was a message from his girlfriend's parents to never come near them. We had to buy new tires and had a mechanic put them on and never again interacted with those heartless but shameless folks. The old folks were spying from their kitchen window when the tires were being fixed.

They aided my brother to double-cross me and take their children to the United States at my expense and to my distress, and here they were being so cruel, rude, and provocative toward me and causing me more pain.

I drove away and picked up Korlue, and then we went over to Herbel, Firestone. On our way I bought a few bottles of brandy with some marijuana. I also bought a gross of Benson & Hedges cigarette. Korlue had never seen me smoking before, but she was not surprised that I was buying all these. She knew that I was in a different place and needed help. She said later that what she saw in my eyes at that moment in my life troubled her, and she knew I was going to hurt myself. She was hurt and in a state of shock as much as I was. But she told me upfront that I do not need drugs and alcohol as a solution, for they would take me deeply into depression and ruin my life more quickly than I can imagine. She said that we were in this together, and she would be by my side to the very end. She said that she did not love me for money and that she would rather have me sober and focused than to see me intoxicating myself, which would lead to ruin and would not help me in any way whatsoever, but I did not listen.

Actually, I had stopped smoking cigarette long before I started working on the ship because it was making me weak. It was Princer who introduced me to marijuana smoking, but I knew it was not good for me because it slows me down and deluded my concentration, and I could tell because of my inability to execute strategies in chess game compared when I was not under the influence. In other words, my ability to lose my trend of thoughts when executing a strategy left me vulnerable to my opponents. Therefore in my consciousness, I knew alcohol and drugs with cigarettes were not the way out of the heaviest blow I had received at that point in my life. Yet I resorted to all of them very heavily as pressure mounted from all angle around me, and Korlue was severely hurt by my actions.

Chapter 18

There was an eviction order signed by Joe Dawh pasted on the front door of my house, allowing me seven days to vacate company's property effective August 14, 1978. A termination letter was placed on the table in the sitting room. Officers from Plant Protection Department had searched my house without warrant and interrogated the three students who lived with me. They got nothing from their search and interrogations to support the assumptions that the boxes containing the money were inadvertently left out of the vault, and somehow the empty boxes were placed into the vault at subsequent dates unnoticed. The fact that I was released sent the entire Firestone community into a frenzy of debates. Some declared that with that kind of money in my hand, along with Counselor Findley in my corner, the entire judicial system can be bought, and elbows bent.

I moved to a small section of Smell-No-Taste known as Millionaire Quarters, and Korlue also moved in with me. She had been expelled from the Firestone community school because she was registered under my auspices while living with her parents. I employed two drivers and made both vehicles taxicabs to bring in income. Despite her protest and constant appeal to me, I smoked and drank a lot hoping that my frustrations would go away, but it deepened, plus it was an invitation to health problems.

Korlue was a very strong girl, and I really do not know what I would have done without her love and support at the time. In my predicament, I dropped out of the advance courses I was taking with the Metropolitan College and the London Educational Association. It was difficult to deal with the general public as almost everyone knew me, eyes would be on me anywhere I went, and I could almost feel the gossips around me. I was hoping Princer would come to his senses sooner or later to establish contact with me, but my hope rested in limbo up to the publication of this book thirty-five years later. There were some things that he did to protect me before he fled to the United States, but all those would backfire, leaving me open to confrontation from various people.

Princer and Counselor Findley had anticipated my indictment, and so he had consulted with the Kru governor, who in turn acquired other people's properties to put in place for me a quarter of a million dollar bond any time the need arose. In order to have this done, these properties must be free and clear of all taxes owed the government of Liberia, so Princer spent about $1,200 to pay property taxes owed and promised to pay all seven of the people's concerned fees ranging from $300 to $500 each for posing their properties to obtain the bond in my behalf.

After Princer left, the Kru governor, who himself was an attorney at law and was uncomfortable about Counselor Findley's retainer over him, needed a piece of the pie. He recalled the role played in my employment and felt betrayed that Counselor Findley was selected over him, to which I played no role. Furthermore, he knew how much money I spent on my birthday, and he was damn sure that big-time lawyers like Counselor Findley must have been well paid to represent me. Apparently the governor and all of the other sureties, Mary included, believed that my brother and his girlfriend and several of his in-laws had traveled to the United States under my sponsorship and that I was also in control over everything. It became extremely difficult for me to put up a poker face while deep inside me, depression, eruptions, and emotion were tearing me apart.

Often, people would ask me about Princer, and I had to say nice things about him. How could I tell anyone anything negative about him when they asked questions like how he was doing in the United States, what state he was in, and how he was adjusting to the weather there. And in some cases, they would be sending their greetings and love to him through me when next I spoke with him. A host of people had no idea what was going on in the inside, and I dared not share the predicaments and complications that were killing me inside. As for my sureties, Mary being one of them, the math was easy: if I can afford to pay property taxes on their various properties to qualify them to post bond on my behalf when the time comes, and if I could afford to retain a big-time lawyer like Findley and to sponsor my brother and five others, including his girlfriend to the United States, then chances are that the FPCO accusation was true; I was definitely perceived a rich guy, just laying low and playing the innocent card. If only they knew what I was going through, I have no idea how each of them would have reacted. I actually do not know what to do with myself. If I looked someone in the eye and tell them that I did not have any money or I was innocent of the FPCO allegaions, I felt within myself that I was insulting their intelligence. But in reality, there were no evidence, physical or circumstantial, tying me to any crime other than the wild guesses of the department leaders that I was the only person who fits the profile and therefore should not be underestimated outside of the other responsible management staff. Every personal assets I owned after the crime were property of Princer and nothing is wrong with a brother leaving his belongings in the care of his brother or nothing is wrong with a brother hiring a lawyer for his brother or financing the cost for a bond for his brother, especially so where that brother was not an employee of FPCO nor was he near the crime scene or accused of any crime. Even the PFCO security records showed that I was never in the office alone at any time before, during, and after the crime, though they could not specifically tell when the crime was committed. The Davies concession was after all a perfect bill.

On one hand, if I should attend to everybody's request for money, then I would run out of money in a short while, and I would have nothing left to live the pathetic life I was living. On the other hand, I could not tell people that Princer double-crossed me; then it would call for more details leading into the FPCO accusation. So I have to make a face for each person I met, which was a difficult thing to do, carrying multiple faces to suit each need. People knew

I had two taxis running, and the conflicting rumors about me and my brother were out there. Somehow I survived the harassments from sureties and others, including the Kru governor, for a couple of months, but the pressure kept mounting, and I needed a way out. Counselor Findley made sure he got an agreement signed by each one of the sureties before their respective property taxes were paid, and in the agreement they were tied and consented to using their respective properties to post bond for me in the case *Republic of Liberia vs John Christian Chea Davies, II*, until the case is concluded. They tendered their deeds and signed the understanding, which was notarized as the law required. But the bond was not yet posted because there was no indictment. So when the sureties met and decided to approach me for the money that Prince promised to pay them as fees, I consulted with Counselor Findley, and he made things clear for me.

News about my so-called fortune had reached Freetown and became household talk there. Soon my younger sister, Victoria, came with her one-year-old son to Liberia to live with me. I learned from her that Magnoose was admitted at Laka Hospital, suffering from tuberculosis and that Princer was in contact with Mum. The news about Magnoose devastated me beyond words, so I decided to go to Freetown to rescue him and to see Mum; maybe she might be able to talk some sense into her boy, Princer, but I was wrong. Mum was prepared to craftily take a treacherous role in the entire affairs.

I flew to Freetown in February 1979, and I was surprised how popular I had become. I met with Mum, and when we settled down to talk about the incident, she told me not to say too much, for she have heard the entire story. How Princer treated me was wrong, and she was prepared to correct that. She expressed in strong words her disappointment at Princer's behavior as an elder brother. She said that ever since she heard the story from one of our cousins from Liberia, she spoke with Princer once when he telephoned her from the United States. She had admonished him to send me enough money to take care of myself or to arrange for me to join him in the

United States. She swore that if he would not do what she asked of him, then she was going to will her house to me to compensate me for what she called "a great loss and betrayal."

I did not believe that she would will her house over to me nor am I interested either, especially because I already knew what lay ahead with all those many children she had with different fathers, there is bound to be fighting over that property in the future, and I do not want to be a part of it. But for some reason, I believed her that she was going to get Prince rto reconsider his position and do something about me. She even promised to give me his contact immediately after he released it to her. I then informed her about my intention to transfer Magnoose from Laka Hospital to Liberia where there was a better facility for tuberculosis.

Long before I came to Liberia to live, there was all sort of troubling rumors in Freetown about Laka Hospital that scared the devil out of people, and since it was known for quarantining patients for a long time and curing rates of patients there was said to be at its lowest at the time, I was afraid the Magnoose might never come out well sooner.

Sierra Leone was being transformed from a country that cares about the well-being of its citizens and communities to a governance of "get rich fast" at the expense and to the detriment of the masses. The country was revving downhill fast enough economically, socially, and morally to the extent that downtrends were being felt in many ways by its people, and a place like Laka was not a safe haven for sick people from the lower class who could not afford to finance the cost of their cure.

Magnoose did not have any travel documents, and he did not have a clue that I was in Freetown. The last time I heard from him was on my early days in Firestone; he was doing well trying to own and run his own auto repairs garage. I had written back to him and encouraged him to keep it up and then shared the exciting news of my graduation from Lincoln Secretariat Institute and my new job. Later I had planned a surprise for him to help him own and operate a garage.

I called and spoke with one of the administrators about transferring a patient from their institution to another institution in another country, and he explained some difficulties based on assumptions since there was no president. We agreed, however, that if I have a passport, visa, and ticket for the patient plus something to bribe two others in authority there, they would let me walk away with him. An acceptance letter from the institution where the patient would be transferred was also necessary, so I spent three extra days working to get all these.

Through a friend in Monrovia, I got a fax sent from one of the hospitals in Liberia to Laka Hospital, accepting the transfer, and, with a little cash to bribe my way through, I had his passport done and obtained a visa from the Liberian Embassy. Then I bought a ticket for him, and he was released. We flew to Liberia where I had him admitted at the hospital in ELWA.

It turned out that his diagnosis was totally wrong; he was suffering from pneumonia and not tuberculosis. A couple of weeks later, his health improved, and he was discharged from the hospital; then I took him home to live with me at Millionaire Quarters in Smell-No-Taste. Magnoose confided in me and disclosed that Mum and Princer were in close contact with each other, so I should not believe a word that she told me about him.

By May 1979, my relationship with the Kru governor and some of the sureties was at its lowest culminating into one threat after another. It turned out that all the sureties, including cousin Mary, wanted to see me indicted so that their fees become mature according to the agreement. It was like having a bounty over my head. On the other hand, if I should be indicted and don't have up to $3,000 to pay them, then they might withdraw their properties, which means that I might remain in custody until the case was decided by the court. There were so many angles to the case and so many interests: Counselor Findley wanted prosecutors to go ahead with the indictment. He was planning a half-million-dollar damage lawsuit against the company. Since he was friendly with prosecutors, he tried to influence my indictment, but the company's private lawyers predicted the outcome of the case in my favor since there was no evidence order than the assumption theory, which was doomed to be thrown out of the window.

I was fed up being in the middle of all the pulling and pushing and maneuvering and politicking, and I just needed some space, so I convinced Korlue that we should take a vacation to Freetown, leaving Magnoose and Victoria to take care of our home and the taxis. What I did not tell her was the fact that I was going there to monitor Mum in order to trail Princer.

Chapter 19

We were barely in Freetown for a month when Magnoose, who was in close contact with us, informed me that I was going to be indicted. We were planning our return when suddenly, two CID agents from Liberia were sent to Freetown to have me repatriated. I was arrested and detained for two days at the Sierra Leonean CID, and on the third day, I was released to the Liberian agents and repatriated to Liberia.

We flew to Monrovia on a Saturday, and I was detained at the CID headquarters at Mamba Point. The *Liberian Age* published my repatriation and characterized it as extradition in their Monday publication. On Tuesday I was taken to court where all parties were present, including my lawyer. I entered a plea of not guilty, and the judge ruled that I remained in custody until a two hundred thousand dollars bond was posed. I had a two-hundred-and-fifty-thousand dollar bond already waiting, which my lawyer quickly processed to meet all the legal formalities, and I was released on bond the next day. Then my sureties pursued me to pay their fees, or they would withdraw their properties, which would have resulted to revocation of the bond. I then sold one of the taxis to settle with everyone, and we were all fine in the meantime while I waited for the case to be docketed for trial.

Meanwhile, I had to rebut the *Liberian Age* publication in three other newspapers in an article entitled "Why Me?" It was a very strong defense to the charges levied against me. In November 1979, Counselor Findley requested a trial, and when the court called the case for trial, the prosecution filed a motion saying that the case was not docketed for that term of court and that they were not ready. Counselor Findley countered their motion and won. He argued that there were no rules extended within our jurisdiction that forbids the hearing of cases not specifically docketed, and that once charged and indicted, it is the right of defendants to ask for disposition of the case brought against them, especially in this case where there has been sufficient time over a year ago when his client was framed, wrongfully dismissed from his job, his premises searched without a warrant, unlawfully detained by the company's plant protection department, and repatriated from Sierra Leone while vacationing, only for the prosecution to appear and to say that the case was not docketed, hence, they are not ready? The court overruled the prosecution's motion and ruled that the case be heard.

The prosecution then requested for a two-day postponement to have some of their witnesses ready, and Counselor Findley did not challenge them, so the court ruled postponement of the case for the following week, granting the prosecution more days to locate and prepare their witnesses as requested.

The following week when the case was called for hearing, the prosecution took the stand and entered a plea of nolle prosequi in favor of the defendant for lack of evidence to prosecute the case. This brought the case to an end in my favor, and I was then acquitted and discharged by the court from all charges, and behold, it was my turn to attack. But first, I needed to enjoy my newfound freedom, bringing me one step closer to normality once again—a relief off the burden that weighed me down for a long time.

Liberian politics was taking a new but interesting turn at the time. Things were shifting from a one party state of affairs to multiparty state of affairs. Several oppositions had emerged as the United States's support of the Tolbert regime was becoming problematic, leading to the notorious April 14, 1979, riot in capital city of Monrovia, which was believed to have been instigated by scarcity of the U.S.-produced PL480 parboil rice known locally as 'pusawa.'" At the advent of fierce political rivalry and decline in US relations, the ruling True Wig Party was facing increasing challenges and threats of uprisings.

DYSFUNCTIONAL ONE

Counselor Findley, the legal counsel for the True Wig Party, became very occupied, especially so that the party's convention was coming up. After I was acquitted, Counselor Findley and I forged a friendship, and I was privileged to hanging out with him, which put me in the position to meet so many of the prominent figures in Liberian politics. I had the opportunity to travel with him one day to Grand Bassa County, where he represented LAMCO, one of the biggest companies in the country, in another case. We used his official Senate-assigned car.

By the time we were halfway to Bassa County, he had fired two drivers. The first driver almost caused an accident just few miles from Paynesville, and he asked him to stop at a nearby garage where he hired another driver and sent the first driver back to Monrovia. I think the second driver was disoriented and shocked at getting to drive the flamboyant and prominent lawyer and senator, so he was nervous and drove very slow to the annoyance of his new boss, who claimed he was getting late for his courtroom appearance. After he fired the second driver in Kakata, I volunteered to drive the senator for the rest of the trip, and he was very pleased with my driving, complimenting me as a cautious driver.

From that day onward, our friendship culminated to me driving him around as I waited for the half-a-million-dollar lawsuit against FPCO. This new role led me to meet people of prominence especially during the True Wig Party convention. Two weeks before the convention, the first Liberian Open National Chess Championships organized by the Ministry of Sports in collaboration of the University of Liberia took place on the premises of the university. That was the first chess tournament that I participated in and won. That brought my name into another sphere for recognition order than the FPCO case.

Counselor Findley became very proud of me then, and he would introduce me to others as a client of multiple talents, which was understandable between us. We were prepared to file the damages case against FPCO on April 16, 1980. I was asked by Counselor Findley to assist Counselor Benson, the barrister at Findley Law Firm, in preparing the damage case. Counselor Benson completed his work, and the file was turned over to Counselor Findley for his review. He then picked the filing date for April 16, 1980, but little did anyone of us know that there was an impending coup d'état to take place on April 12, 1980, which ousted the True Wig Party from power.

I was spending more of my time in Monrovia at one of my in-laws' house near the national police headquarters. In the early morning hours of April 12, 1980, I was awoken at about two thirty by sounds from heavy machine-gun firings. When I came to my senses, I noticed that every occupants of the house had been up long enough. I came in to the sitting room to join the other tenants who looked very scared.

"What is happening?" I asked.

"We don't know, but there is shootings going on, and it seemed to be going on at the Executive Mansion," one of the tenants replied.

I slightly opened the back door and peeped just a few inches to figure out the direction of the heavy gunfire sounds were coming from. Indeed it was apparent that the shootings were at the Executive Mansion, which was just about three hundred yards away from where we were. There was definitely something terrifying going on at the official residence of the president of the republic. People close by were up from bed, scared but packing up bags in readiness to fleeing if the situation calls for running. There was no more sleeping for anybody that night, but as darkness was transforming into light, the situation was becoming clear.

The nation's major radio station, ELBC, is usually closed at midnight and open at 5:00 a.m., but on this morning, it started with the usual national anthem followed by military musical tunes, which was unusual. At around 6:00 a.m. the religious Christian radio station, ELWA, began broadcasting, but strangely it was only playing military music as well.

DYSFUNCTIONAL ONE

A few minutes after 6:00 a.m., we heard voices outside, and suddenly when we opened the front door to peep, we found a group of policemen begging our neighbors for any type of plain clothes to change their uniforms. Some of them had already taken off their uniforms in a bid to disguise themselves as civilians. One of our neighbors who also was a policeman was spotted in civilian clothing and giving his colleagues civilian clothes to wear.

A woman tenant from our house went over to get information on what was happening. When she returned, scared, she told us what she have heard. I was frozen when she broke the news that the president of the Republic, Dr. William R. Tolbert, had been assassinated, and the True Wig Party government toppled. I felt like using the restroom instantly when I heard it. My stomach somersaulted, and my blood circulated to higher levels. I felt at that moment as if the whole world crumbled on me. Not only that these events significantly affected relations with Counselor Findley on whom I depended for the pending claim against FPCO, but also the fact that my association with him, driving around in his senate-assigned vehicle, had exposed me to be seen as member of the elite that was now doomed to be put to hell even before the dust settled.

At about seven thirty that faithful morning of April 12, 1980, the nervous but terribly shaky voice of Master Sergeant Samuel K. Doe announced on the nation's ELBC radio, with the help of henchmen in the background whispering word for word, that he and sixteen others toppled the government of Dr. William R. Tolbert and that all deposed government officials should turn themselves in at the Barclays Training Center, failure to which would lead to serious consequences.

Upon hearing this announcement, the city exploded with unprecedented excitement, and crowds of people took to the street chanting redemption songs. Lyrics of one of such songs ran like this: "Native woman born soldier, Congo woman born thief." This outburst came from the deep-rooted grudges that some sector of the aborigine had accumulated for decades against the Americo Congo elites, extrinsically motivated and incited.

As sons of the indigenous, Master Sergeant Samuel K. Doe and his colleagues were viewed as redeemers and heroes. When he announced the military takeover that morning, an overwhelming crowd from all sixteen ethnic groups took to the streets fishing out all the Congo people that they knew holding high positions in the defunct True Wig Party government. It was a wonder that two days later, Counselor Findley was still at his Sinkor resident untouched. So many Congo people with few of their loyal indigenous supporters were humiliated, beaten up, incarcerated, or killed. Many others fled the country or went in hiding for a while.

On the third day, I was at the Findleys' residence when the military came to arrest him. I joined his family in prayer in one of the rooms, while military men waited in the sitting room and surrounded their home. When he was being taken away, like Simon Peter following behind his master, I followed, driving an old Renault car own by one of his sons. He was taken to the BTC military base, where few days later thirteen of the leading government officials from the deposed True Wig Party government were speedily tried, convicted, and executed by firing squad in what was believed to be one of Africa's most gruesome executions. All thirteen men were tied to thirteen poles about three yards apart from each other, while trigger-happy military men used their M16 assault weapons and emptied their magazines on bodies. It was hard to believe these things were happening in Liberia.

Counselor Findley and others were tried, found guilty of whatever charges levied on them, and sentenced to prison terms ranging from one to five years. He served a year at Belleyalah, the maximum-security prison situated on an island. Since his office was ransacked, no one from his scattered staff and family member were able to find my file. So I had to start afresh to file the claim against FPCO through another law firm before the one year statute of limitation expired.

The first lawyer who represented me in the claim was Counselor Eddie S. Watson. He wrote the company, giving them the chance to address settlement out of court, and the company through their legal counsel, J. P. Bracewell, replied, asking for a little time for them to meet and decide with their legal team. But it was apparent that Bracewell was stalling the process so that the statute of limitation runs out and I have no legal claim.

While waiting, J. P. Bracewell invited me to meet with him secretly without my legal counsel. I could not at the time, and I insisted that my lawyer be present, but he called off the meeting and said that their legal team would get back to us.

While waiting for this opportunity, Counselor Watson lost his life mysteriously. Rumor had it that some client of his set him up in a bizarre incident, and he was killed. I ended alone again, and since the statute of limitation was running out, I contacted and struck a deal with Flomo, Williams & Agbagi Law Firm, who filed the damaged case against the company on my behalf.

Chapter 20

Before the military coup d'état on April 12, 1980, the only vehicle we were surviving on had a major mechanical problem that Magnoose could not fix without the required parts, and there was no more money to buy the parts needed, so the vehicle was wrecked.

Victore then traveled back to Freetown leaving her son, Victory, with me. It happened that Princer had arranged for her to join him in the United States, and she and Mum were keeping it as secret from me. Before she left for Freetown, she gave birth to her second boy whom she had by another friend of mine—an affair that did not sit well with me when I learned she was dating this friend of mine.

After the coup d'état, my life became awkward and messy to a point that Korlue could not put up with me anymore, for I was into marijuana, cigarettes, and alcohol. Counselor Findley, who filled in the blanks in my life and kept things working for me, was no longer there. And within a few months from the coup d'état, I become completely broke, homeless, depressed, and frustrated. After she dumped me, I was left alone with my nephew Victor, who was only three years old at the time. I had been taking care of him ever since he was a year old and we were very fond of each other, so that gave me hope to stay alive. I have always loved children and related with them well, and sometimes I feel like one too, and I think children related to that mode as well. He was the only precious being I now have on my side after all was lost, and I felt obligated to protect and care for him despite my plight and state of mind.

I had a casual family friend on Benson Street with whom I would spend the nights while I roam the streets till dawn. I was hoping that the FPCO claim would have materialized sooner than later, but when my new lawyer mysteriously died after the progress he made for an out-of-court settlement, I was left wondering if I should meet with J. P. Bracewell to strike a deal. So I called him, and on the phone he told me to come up to Harbel for us to talk face-to-face, but this was something I was never going to do because I was scared. The second time we spoke, he insinuated that they were considering a $5,000 settlement and nothing more. At this juncture, I struck a deal with Flomo, William & Agbagi Law Firm in which the firm agreed to take 40 percent of whatever the final settlement amount would be.

I often thought about Korlue and wondered if she felt the same way about me. It was her elder sister who influenced her to walk away when her family tried but failed to stop me from my drinking and drugging habits. I could not have traded her for anything in the world, and I was hoping that if the claim went through, I would win her back and give up these habits. I knew that my habits and the rate at which I was at them would have landed me in early grave, and I realized how much pain and embarrassments I was causing the few people who really loved and cared about me, but I was helpless and lacked the volition to stop and deal with the shame and degradations I caused on myself and to take corrective actions to put my life back in order.

In the fall of 1980, the Ministry of Sports announced the registration for the upcoming Open National Chess Championships under the sponsorship of INTRUSTCO, a foreign bank located on Broad Street. As the current champion, I had to prepare myself not only to defend the title but also to improve my appearance, my deteriorating image, and to regain and elevate my self-esteem. The announcement talked some sense into me as my name was in the news, and questions and doubts on how prepared I was to defend the title was being talked about around town. This ignited something inside me, and I thought that after all, there were some things that nobody can take away from me but me. I began to reverse my lifestyle, which was not an easy task, but once my mind was made up and I could see myself clearly how useful I was to others who believed in me and my obligation not to let them down, I knew that I had to throw away the self-pity sentiments and make use of the real me.

Before I was eight years old, I had promised to become a lawyer and a musician.

Where was it now? I asked myself.

When I started playing chess and reading more about the game, I promised myself that I would not be a walkover for anyone in the world of chess at any level. Obviously, taking drugs or getting high and drinking liquor excessively was like a vehicle that lost control on the highway but has not yet crashed, but if the driver can take back control, stabilize the vehicle, and drive safely to his destination, it would be a notable feat. I was not going to allow my destiny to be crashed at that point, but rather I was going to show resilience, determination, and resolve in my commitment to overcome my bad habits and to pursue my dreams and to excel.

The line was drawn, and I was back in control of myself. The head of my family friend on Benson Street where Victor would spend the night happened to be one of my chess fans who one day asked how prepared I was, and I was able to confined in him about my condition. I was afraid to open up to him since he was the deputy director of the national police force. So I told him a made-up story about a false accusation that led to my losing my job and eventually I became broke and homeless, so he and his wife, Agnes, began to cater to some of my needs. He linked me on to the new director of the national police force, Sam A. Massaquoi, who was also one of my fans, and he, in turn, offered me to help his children with their homework for a stipend. So I started teaching at his home at Matadi Estate, and before long some of the councilmen in the new military government began contracting me to teach their children.

In a couple of months, I had about thirty children, all of whom began to excel in their various schools, for which their parents offered me various favors in addition to the fees they were already paying me.

In February 1981, I defended my championship and retained the Open National Chess Championship 1981 title, which earned me more fame and friendship because there were more foreigners than in the previous 1980 event. In this event, some of the players were from embassies, companies, and banks around the country. It was a Russian and I who entered the finals, and most people thought he would beat me because of his long chess background, but when I beat him four games straight from the total of six games in the championship phase, it was like an assurance that my life was getting back on track.

I received a formal invitation to spend weekends at an INTRUSCO bank residence near the beach in Sinkor, Monrovia, where some foreign expatriates and investors from the United States and Europe spent weekends playing chess. On my first weekend, I played and defeated several opponents, including Alexander Baisden, president of INTRUSCO bank.

Baisden, who happened to be a generous American from Sun City, Arizona, dropped me off on Monday morning in front of the bank and handed me an envelope containing fresh, crispy notes that reminded me of my heydays. I now had a place to spend my weekends, from Friday evenings to Monday mornings; there was always plenty of food, plenty to drink, plenty of cigarettes and cigars, and plenty of guest rooms. But I had suspended myself from cigarette, alcohol, and marijuana, and life was getting better once again.

In June 1981, Victoria returned from Freetown, took Victor away from me without saying thank you or without giving my nephew and me the opportunity to say good-bye, and she sent him by someone else to Mum in Freetown while she took off from RIA for the United States to join Princer without telling me or even saying good-bye to me. They both would never care to send Magnoose or me a postcard for decades to come. Their contact information in the United States were top secret in the family; no one was allowed to share them with either Magnoose or me, so we carried on with our lives, and they carried on with theirs, with Mum in the center of it all, manipulating things and destroying relationships among the four Davies children and having her other children interfering and playing along accordingly.

Not long after Victoria left for the United States, the Reverend Sylvanusy Paynee Jacksony abandoned the church he helped to polarized and escaped the troubles he caused many members of his congregation. He traveled to the United States with his wife and settled down there. He left behind unhealed wounds with families torn apart. Rumor had it that many of the women in the congregation that he had affairs with were ganging up against him, and some of the husbands and fiancées involved and some of the children he bore with these women were agonized, traumatized, and despaired. Although DNA was not part of the culture and norm in African settings at the time, some people have a way of determining biological male parents especially with the Kru tribal clan that would invoke certain traditional ritual to make this determination. Besides that, the pastor had a strong gene and some of the child that he secretly fathered resembled him considerably, so many of the family he tempered with knows by looking at a child borne. A Jacksony was easy to tell even though in some cases some families would prefer to conceal things and try to avoid the stigma that is already their burden. An example of these plights is the case of the Thompson family who are staunch members of the church even before Jacksony dreamt of pastoring it. The man, Mr. Forh Thompson, was a well-known and reputable pharmacist and sadly a very close friend of the pastor. His daughter, Herberto Thomson, lived in his household and completed high school with his name, but the stigma was still there and finally Mrs. Thompson confessed her affairs with the pastor and that resulted amongst other things to the changing of their daughter's name from Herberto Thompson to Herberto Jacksony. Herberto attended the same high school that my wife attended and knew her as a Thompson. Later, in 1990 when my wife witnessed both Princes and Herberto acknowledging each other as blood sisters, it was nothing but a shocker.

DYSFUNCTIONAL ONE

About a year or two after the disgraced Reverend Jacksony fled with his wife to live in the United States to start life afresh, he filed derivative proceedings with the INS to bring his last daughter, Glorie, whom he and Mum bore in their last adulterous affairs after he was married to his current wife, ordained and commissioned to pastor the church. This did not sit well with their first two girls, Princes and Sylvia, who felt they should have been a part of the derivative package. Princes was already a school dropout because he had refused to support her after she slapped and whipped the devil in him from the pulpit in open church before the congregation when he was delivering his Easter sermon. After that incident, their relationship became deranged, and he vowed then to disown her and to have nothing to do with her "in this world and the next." Sylvia was still attending high school and her dad promised to bring her over to join him in the United States after her graduation. Princes then became extremely angry with her dad and dangerously jealous of her two sisters, so she joined Mum in going underworld—consulting witch doctors, practicing sorceries, dealing with and practicing voodoos for various purposes. However, over time, Glorie's traveling process matured, and Mum prepared her for her trip to the United States to join her dad, but more than that, Mum and Princes were not going to let Glorie come empty-handed without luring her to bring some juju work that she was instructed to sprinkle in strategic places inside the house and inside the pillow of her stepmother whom Mum believed to have betrayed her trust and now enjoying her lover boy. If Mrs. Jacksony is out of their way, then they can deal with the playboy himself and get him to do whatever they wanted. From Princes's perspective, no stepmother would take her dad away from her and expect a happy marriage, nor would her dad favor her younger sisters over her by bringing them to the United States, leaving her to perish in a third world country—no, that would not happen; over her dead body.

The juju dust was tied and placed inside some animal horn and then wrapped in a red and black clothing. Mum told her daughter to be careful so that no one saw or noticed the juju. When the child arrived in the United States, her dad went to the airport to receive her. While dad and daughter were waiting for her baggage to be processed before leaving the airport, the US Customs found this strange object and took her, accompanied by her dad since she was a minor, into their office for questioning. Scared and confused, the little girl could not explain or make sense to custom officers, but her dad, who himself had dealt with various forms of jujus in the past, knew exactly what he was looking at and was amazed. Custom officers politely trashed the juju. Later, when Mum called from Freetown to speak to her Glorie, a furious Reverend Jacksony rebuked her and barred her from calling his home ever again. Mum was quoted as vowing to get even with him and to teach him and his wife a lesson they would always remember.

Poor Reverend Jacksony, hearing this threat and knowing how vulnerable, he could not decide whether to pursue filing processes for Sylvia to join him in the United States. She had completed high school with excellent result and wanted to study law in the United States but that dream would be short-lived as the pastor began to show signs of favoritism toward her. Mum and Princes went underground. Princes made a vow that none of her sisters or brothers, young or old, known or to be known, would never again reunite with her father in the United States if not her. Sylvia, who was next on the line to reunite with her dad, died mysteriously.

Chapter 21

FPCO quietly settled out of court in 1983 after a series of meeting my legal counsels. The amount was a minimal $15,000. It was not what I wanted, but I had no choice. My legal interest in the claim was in jeopardy in an environment where lawyers would sell their client's interest for their own gains. Besides, I was fully back to recovering control over myself.

I had secured a job in the public accounting sector working with Gbasegee & Associates, Certified Public Accountants, and through the apprenticeship system, I became eligible for certification to provide bookkeeping and accounting services to the general public.

By 1982, chess was becoming popular in the country, and shortly after I successfully defended the National Open Chess Championship title that year, the Monrovia Chess Club was formed, and I was voted its first president. With the $9,000 that I realized from the settlement, I chased and realized my certification dream and established my own accounting firm called Davies & Associates, CPAs, in 1984.

That same year the Ministry of Sport received an invitation for Liberia's participation in Sierra Leone's first Open National Chess Championships. At the time there was no budget for chess programs at the ministry unfortunately, and efforts that the ministry made to get sponsors did not materialized so the Monrovia Chess Club sponsored me to represent Liberia in the event in which I became runner-up, losing to Dr. Sarjah Wright, who was also governor of the Bank of Sierra Leone. He was probably in his early fifties and had long years of experience in the game from the United States where he was already a thirteen-year member of the US Chess Federation. It was devastating after I lost to him in the finals. I thought that I messed up in my endgames, but I learned something about myself when he commended me for being the most tactical player he had ever played at the time and suggested that if I could be strategic or follow through a strategy at every stage of my game, especially in endgames, that would make me a formidable player.

Dr. Wright was right. Street life had shaped and impacted my mode of reasoning, and traces of these characteristics are displayed in my game: the instinct to compartmentalize objectives into bits and pieces and to plan and execute short term instead of viewing things and planning to cover the broader spectrum. For instance, if the Davies concession was planned beyond just getting the money, then it may not have gone the way it went even though it was love for family and relative that led to the decision I made at the time.

Following the Sierra Leone Open Chess Championships, I was invited by a chess group at Foray Bay University to attend an evening of chess program. At the program, many players in the group expressed their desire to play me—some enthusiastic about beating me, having heard about my chess record in Liberia.

In the spirit to promoting the game, I offered a hundred dollars prize money for anyone in the entire country, including the current open national champion, Dr. Wright, who would beat me in a set of two games. The news media then published my challenge and players came from various places across the city in a month long chess playing frenzy, which took place at Bishop House, Siaka Stevens Stadium.

During the same period, the prestigious Zone Two Soccer Tournament involving several West African countries was hosted by Sierra Leone with all the matches being played at the same stadium where Bishop House is situated. This was an exciting time with many people coming into the city from upcountry to watch the soccer matches, and I thought then that it was perfect timing to show critics in the country where I grew up literally in the streets, that I rose above their curses and degradation about my future. I enjoyed my stay, and the more that the news media reported week after week that no one was able to beat me in the challenge, the prouder I became.

DYSFUNCTIONAL ONE

On the week that I prepared to return to Liberia, Mum visited me at the hotel and wanted to talk to me about something she said was very important about my life. She convinced me with tears running down her chin that I needed spiritual fortification to be protected against evil forces that may be seeking my destruction. But she got my full attention when she mentioned that it was also for my own good, for my financial independence and stability. I was reluctant about it for a while and referenced Princer and Victoria, and I said that she failed me when she promised about three years back that she was going to have Princer reconsider me. She swore about trying to get his contact information, but Princer was unstable and that she talked him into sending me some money but that the thing they were all worried about when it comes to me was that money was not stable in my hand, and that was the reason I needed the seven-day spiritual bath to reverse whatever spell that someone may have cast upon me. She said that she had already arranged for that from the moment I visited her upon my arrival. She said it was not going to cost me any money, for she has already taken care of it for me.

At that time I had no idea that Mum was deeply into sorcery, witchcraft, and juju invocations. Convinced, I packed up my bags, checked out of the hotel, and followed Mum to the place where she claimed that I would be taken good care of, but I was being deceived and I took the bait, though I was indecisive and skeptical. We took a taxi to her house where I sorted out my stuff and left one of my bags with her. And together we took the same cab to Calaba town in the east of Freetown, a few miles from Kissy Mess-Mess.

We arrived at the spiritualist's house on a hill. Two elderly women came to the front door and let us know that their husband, Pa Bangura, went to search for herbs in nearby bushes. We were given seats at the veranda upfront, overlooking the street. We waited for over two hours, but the man did not show up, and nobody knew when he would return.

Then Mum started grumbling that she was running out of time for something else that she had to do, so she might as well just have a word with one of the man's wife, and I would stay and wait till he comes. I agreed, and she went into the house and hauled one of the man's wives to the backyard where she had a private talk with her.

When they were done talking, they came upfront at the veranda, and Mum introduced her as the eldest wife of the man that I would be waiting for and that she would introduce me to her husband when he arrives.

Mum left me with assurances that I was in good hands for the next seven days, and she would be coming back to see me before the seven days ended. The man had many clients who came in and out, and there was a periodic ringing of phone inside the house.

Few minutes after Mum left, I felt bored, and so I grabbed my portable chess set and a few recorded games and began to analyze a couple of them. While concentrating on one of the games, I noticed from the corner of my eye that someone was standing at the doorway looking at me. Thinking it was one of the women, I did not pay any attention.

After a while I decided to look in the direction, and my eyes caught a young woman standing there by the door watching me with a broom in hand. We smiled at each other; then she asked if I was playing checkers against myself. We started chatting, getting to know each other, and from time to time she would go answer the phone calls inside the house and then come back to chat with me.

This young lady, Fatmata, happened to be a niece of the spiritualist. Another two hours passed by, and Pa Bangura did not show up. Within those two hours, both of Pa Bangura's wives had come out to ask me several times over again what was my relationship with the woman who brought me there to see their husband. I told them she was my mother, but they seemed to be not at ease with my answer.

"Is she a distant relative of yours?" one of them asked at one point.

Curious about their inquiry, I asked why, but they could not say anything except look suspiciously at me and at the same time grin at each other. I had a feeling something was not right, but I had no idea what it was.

Moments later, another woman entered the house through the back door. She was wife number three, younger and fluent in Creole. She also came to have a glimpse at me. Something did not seem right, I thought. Something like an argument ensued among them, but they were speaking in Loko dialect, which was foreign to me, so I could not understand what the argument was about, but I had a strong feeling it must be concerning my mother and I.

Fatmata who could have helped me out with translation had disappeared into the backyard. I was now beginning to feel uncomfortable, suspicious, and afraid. Instinctively I decided to approach the women to ask for the restroom even though I wasn't pressed, but I just wanted to see their faces and reactions. They all went silent as I entered the sitting room. I forced a smile and asked to use the restroom, and one of them led me to the backyard where it was.

I tried to appear nice and polite when I returned to the sitting room when they all became quiet as I appeared. I asked why everyone was questioning my relationship with the woman who brought me there.

"Is something wrong?" I asked.

Everyone looked in the direction of the elder wife simply because she was the one whom Mum confined in, and they dared not say anything.

"Do you have any problem with your mother?" the elder wife asked.

"No," I said.

Then she gestured with her shoulder like something was missing, or I wasn't telling the truth. Then I said that my mother and I do not have any direct problem, but she was siding with my brother whom I had some serious problem with. That made sense to everyone of them as they exchanged gestures, and it was from that moment that I realized that Mum took me there for something else other than the protection she emphasized for me.

Then the elder wife shook her head with both hands on her chest, and her countenance was one of sorrow. She held my hand and took me in the backyard where we were alone; then she asked me to confide in her and give her details of the problem between me and my brother. This was something she needed in exchange for what I wanted to hear from her. She wanted to know why a mother would want her son to be made insane.

When I was done telling her my side of the story, she was even stunned that a mother would be engaged in sowing seeds of enmity between her own children to the extent of executing a plan to make one of her own sons insane. I was so badly shaken, and for a long time whenever I think about the entire episode, I often grasp for breath.

Mum had planned to have some spell cast on me to make me go insane so that her son Princer can be free to travel to Sierra Leone and Liberia, while I would be incapacitated to confront him. The woman then advised me not to be afraid because God had shown me a great favor, and she would like for me to meet her husband. She said that what Mum wanted would never happen, and she wanted to talk to her husband about it before I leave.

At around 6:00 p.m., an old taxicab pulled up front, and a dark elderly, one-hand man descended from the backseat. He looked tired but fearful. The driver offloaded all of the herbs tied on top of the vehicle, while the elderly man went for his wallet to pay the driver. He useed his mouth to support his one hand to remove the money from his wallet. I knew right away it must be Pa Bangura, so I went up front, greeted him, and assisted him with the herbs. Then he walked toward the house, climbing the stairs to the veranda where he asked me to put the herb on the floor. He thanked me and went inside the house.

Moments later all of the women came out of the house to get the bundles of leaves placed on a veranda floor. They took the leaves at the back of the house, and they returned into the sitting room.

Few minutes passed by, and then I heard the man speaking in Loco dialect, and then the women engaged him in orderly manner. Then suddenly the elder wife came and invited me into the house. Pa Bangura, the so-called spiritualist, looked curiously into my eyes as he asked my relationship with the woman who brought me to him. He would not believe that she was my biological mother.

"That was not what she told me about you," he said, "and I don't know who of the two of you is lying to me.

His elder wife asked me to explain what I earlier explained about my brother. In my bag was a file containing overwhelming documents, including newspapers about FPCO case, photocopies of the bill of sales for the vehicles that Princer bought with group pictures. Fortunately, Pa Bangura still has contact information of the woman who originally introduced Mum to him a few years back, and he also had contact information of a few clients whom Mum had brought to him.

While I was displaying documentary proofs of my blood relationship, he got on the phone and started talking to one of the women who knew Mum very well. When he was done talking on the phone, he took a deep breath, and his countenance, like that of his elder wife, expressed one of sorrow.

There was silence for about a minute, and then he said, "Now, what kind of a mother is this who would make up stories and set her own blood son up for something like this?"

As though his question was directed to the women, they all surged in response, and the elder wife reaffirmed her position that she spoke with me in confidence after she listened to Fatmata and I talking at the veranda; then she began to evaluate the message that Mum left for her husband.

It turned out that Mum had not seen Pa Bangura for over a year then, but she telephoned him on the week of my arrival in Freetown and informed him that I have falsified the will and testament of her deceased father and used my influence to possess properties belonging to her family in Monrovia. She said that I was an adopted child who had no blood connections whatsoever, but after her family had assisted me and I was living with her father and before he passed, I changed the document and now possessed what was her property, so she wanted some spell cast on me to make me crazy. She went on to tell Pa Bangura that she can convince and deceive me and bring me over to his place to be fixed before I leave for Liberia.

I had my hands over my face and my head bowed as I was badly shaking and sobbing. They consoled me, and when I calmed down a little, they asked what I was going to do. I said that I was going back to my mother's house to pick up my suitcase and leave the country. But the old man and his wives did not believe that, they believed that I was not going to be able to control myself, and I might cause trouble for which they would also feel guilty.

The old man said if I could trust him, I could stay with him for the next couple of days, and he would rather help me rather than hurt me. He swore over his own children that he would not do me no harm on top of the wicked ways my own family had already treated me. Another thing at stake was the fee that Mum agreed to pay over my head, which we all agreed that I should stay calm for her to make the payment in a few days. Even the elder wife cut in and said she was sure that if I were to go back to my mother's house, trouble was sure to erupt, and I also knew that even though I was fighting inside me resisting the temptation to go there and put her house on fire as an insane man, the old man's elder wife said that Mum would know right away that she, Mrs. Bangura, betrayed the confidence that Mum placed in her, and whatever happened there might bring them into it as witnesses.

I was restrained and decided to play along, so I stayed with the Banguras for more than a week.

Chapter 22

Two days into my stay at the Banguras, I made a decision to get my suitcase from Mum. This was against the advice of my host since the plan was to wait for Mum to come over to make payment within my seven days of treatment. By this time I had gained control of myself emotionally and mentally, but the idea that my suitcase was still with Mum made me jittery though it was locked by numeric code that only I knew. I convinced myself that I should put up a smile and tried to stay calm whenever we met, though I was not certain about what might happen. Besides there were items in my suitcase that I needed, so I decided first to speak to her to find out if she would be available so we can make an appointment for me to come get it.

I had prepared a lie for her just in case she asked how the seven-day spiritual treatment was going. I first thought about calling a nearby friend to her house to set the appointment for me, and then I remembered that I had the Robertson family's telephone number; they were the closest neighbors just opposite her house at 25 Berwick Street. A member of the Robertson family who received my call placed me on hold while she called Mum's name out across the street to let her know that she had a phone call. I had no idea and never had it crossed my mind that the Robertson's phone was the medium of communication between Mum and Princer.

When Mum came to the phone, she immediately pronounced Princer's pet name in Kru dialect the way that only she was entitled to.

"Guah Jugbeh" she said, which signifies her love and adoration.

In our tradition, a favorite child name is called after the parents as an expression of their love and adoration.

"Yes, Mum," I replied in Kru dialect, and she did not notice it was me. The entire act was spontaneous but divine in that Mum, as smart a woman she is, though not educated, should have known throughout our conversation that it was not her favorite son, Princer, on the phone. I waited for her to introduce a topic after we greeted each other. I could feel her confidence and a special note of excitement in her voice level.

"Your brother, John, is still around playing chess, but I have finally got him where he needed to be. When everything is done, you would be free to visit us whenever you want and to leave without any threat from him," she said.

"That is excellent," I said.

"Did you receive my last letter?" she asked.

Hoping that the cat won't be let out of the bag, I replied, "I am attending a conference in one city in Texas and also visiting some friends there. When I return home after the conference, I would have a chance to go through my mails."

I certainly did not know which state Princer lived in at the time, so I was being careful not to be specific in calling names of cities. Then I asked her to give me a heads-up on what the letter was about.

"It is about the money you promised to send last month for me to repair and renovate my kitchen and restroom," she answered.

"Okay, I get it. Just give me a few days after my return home. Then I will send it," I replied.

Changing the subject to what I am most interested in, I asked, "Is John going to have a chance to get back to Liberia when everything is done, or is he going to be wrecked in Sierra Leone?"

She laughed aloud and then said, "That would depend on where he would be when he started losing his sanity. Don't worry about him"—still she continued to laugh—"you can be rest assured that he would never be able to recognize you, let alone confront you in this world even if you were standing before him."

I struggled with my emotions and tried very hard to keep my voice steady as I listened to a mother's quest for destruction of her own son over another for the love of money. We talked about other things, and she reminded me about sending the money as soon as possible to help take care of a number of things, including the refund of Pa Bangura's fees, which she lied that she borrowed from someone else and paid.

When we hanged up, I was frozen, and my eyes glued to the phone as though I could see the reflection of her face on it. My body began to shiver as I wondered in absolute disbelief concerning these things that were unfolding right before me.

Pa Bangura was busy with a few clients, so I waited for him, and finally when he was through, I told him about my telephone conversation with my mother. He was not surprise, but he was content that I was able to confirm for myself directly from my mother's mouth the snare she had going against me for the love of money. I told him that I would like to go pick up my suitcase form her house immediately, but I think that he sensed my desire to confront my mother about her deeds, so he admonished me to be wise and advised me as follows: "God is on your side, my son. There is no doubt about this. You must not fight for yourself, but let him do the fighting for you, and let him be the judge between you and your mother. If you go there, do not say a word except that you will be taking off from my house to go back to Liberia after your treatment. Be wise and do this for the sake of your future and for the sake of my household. I shall know what to tell her one of these days when she come to see me."

That evening I chartered a taxi and went down town Freetown to pick up my suitcase. On my way, I thought about the excitements in my life from one event to another, and I marveled at the craftiness of the greatest man behind the scene who moves the chess pieces, God.

When I arrived at Mum's house, she was upstairs when she heard two of her younger daughters and youngest son ran toward me with joy to greet me, and they started telling me about everything they knew happened in my absence. One of them said Princer called today from America, and the others repeated the same as we all made our way upstairs where Mum was listening.

Mum came out of her room quickly and took a seat nearby the stairs. She had a big smile on her face as she welcomed me, and before I could say anything, she began telling me about a telephone call she got from Princer at midday.

"I was surprised that he called today," she started. "I spoke to him about you, my son—about the hardship you have been enduring ever since. I vowed to disown him if he cannot make peace with you and provide you with some money to console you or to even help you to join him in the United States. I have given him an ultimatum to get back to me on this issue as soon as possible; otherwise, I will, will my house over to you, as I have said in the past, to console you for the loss you sustained and for all the trouble you have been through as a result of his selfish actions. This time he assured me that he would get back to me soon about a package he is putting together for you."

"Very well, Mum, it looks like there is light at the end of the tunnel after all these years, and I look forward to it," I said with a smile while fighting hard to keep my calm.

"How is the treatment coming on?" she asked.

"Very well, Mum. Today is the second day of the treatment, and I got five more days to go, but I must take my suitcase with me as there are so many things that I need."

"Do you have anything specifically to tell your brother if he gets back to me soon?" she asked.

"Not really, I like the way you are handling it, and I look forward to hearing from you when I arrive in Monrovia," I said.

We agreed that maybe we would see each other if she comes up to Pa Bangura before I leave for Monrovia. I picked up my suitcase as we were talking, and I tried as much as possible to avoid looking straight into her eyes so that she doesn't read me. I thanked her for everything, and while I was saying good-bye, she stood up and came forward for a hug, and I reached out for an apologizing hug. As the children walked me to the waiting taxi upfront on the street, I noticed she was curiously looking at me from a window upstairs, and I had to play the happy card by waving to her.

DYSFUNCTIONAL ONE

Fatmata and I found common ground, and we both felt the need to console each and other. She failed the Sierra Leone Nursing School exams after her fiancé dumped their planned wedding and ended up marrying to her best friend. It happened a week before her final exams. The disappointment devastated her, and she never gained control of herself in time for the exams up till the time we met. She had no other choice but to start the three-year course over again, which was not only humiliation to her as much as it was painful for members of her family who sponsored her education.

Fatmata's failure became a talking point in the school, among her peers, and in communities. She wanted to go far away from Sierra Leone to heal and complete her course, which was her dream career, to become a registered nurse, and she saw me as the hope for her.

"I do not feel comfortable going back to that school to start over from square one with new enrollees for another three years," she told me repeatedly. She said that if there was another nursing school in the country other than one, then maybe she won't mind enrolling in the other school to pursue her dream career. Her plight was something I could relate to in many ways: it brought me back to my common entrance examination experience with Mum, and the narrative about her fiancé marrying her best friend also fitted Mum's profile with the Jacksony fiasco.

Many relatives of the Bangura family lived in single-bedroom apartments attached to the main five-bedroom house where Pa Bangura and his wife and younger children lived. Fatmata lived in one of these single-bedroom apartments. They owned and operated a small bar attached to the left side of the main house. Two of the old man's sons, Bambay and Amara, were managing the bar, and it was at the bar that Fatmata and I developed interest in each other. My take in the relationship was more about paying back the Bangura family for the kindness they showed me and also my empathy for her plights. For her, it was about coming to Liberia with me to be enrolled in the nursing school at the John F. Kennedy Medical Center to pursue her desire to become a registered nurse.

I felt her pain as she confided in me, and apart from my own situations, I felt obligated to help her realize her dream. She had now trusted me with her heart after all she has been through. She was drinking heavily each night at the bar, and I knew from experience how easily one gets hooked to drinking and drugging to the point of no return for some people, unfortunately.

Our relationship was getting stronger as days turned to weeks, and each time I planned to leave for Monrovia, she would be sad and indulged into more drinking. She wanted me to help her out of her predicament, and when I assured her that I would go ahead to arrange her schooling and then send for her, she was suspicious that she may never get to see me again if I leave for Liberia without her. It felt like she was really on the edge, and I had to do something to give her hope to fill the vacuum in her life.

News quickly spread in the community that she had someone in her life and that elevated her worries that if I left and never come back, it will only deepen her wounds and that might add to more humiliation she already suffered. I had cancelled three travel plans because she would spend the whole night crying and expressing her fears. She was a very intelligent and smart young woman, and I was pretty confident that she would have passed the nursing school exams had it not been for the disappointment that broke her heart and threw her off.

Some people in the vicinity supported her while others mocked her. One night after a tense discussion, we decided that she and I would travel together to Liberia, and I assured her that I would see to it that she enrolled in the nursing school. But there were a number of obstacles in our way. First, I was already in a relationship in Monrovia before I traveled and my girlfriend was waiting for me. Second, foreigners were not allowed at the nursing school in Liberia unless they are married to a Liberian, and finally, her family would not release her to travel with me to another country outside of traditional marriage.

DYSFUNCTIONAL ONE

So the night of our very serious talk, we agreed between us the following:

- That she was coming with me for the primary purpose of attending the nursing school at JFK;
- That we would have a traditional marriage before leaving and that she would use my surname (Davies) as my wife to enter the school;
- That I will sponsor and finance her education up to graduation; and,
- That our marriage was subject to unilateral dissolution outside of the legal divorce laws and legal processes and that either of us would be free to walk away from it with or without notice or legal recourse.

She told her family about the part that concerned them, and a traditional marriage was organized for us within a week. Mum's bounty fees over my head was generously used by Pa Bangura to help finance the quiet but befitting ceremonies, which by the way, he got Mum to attend, along with her children. He used the telephone conversation I had with Mum to convince her that she let the cat out of the bag. He told that the conversation she thought that she having with her son in America, it was me she was talking to, and it was his house phone that I used to call at the time to make arrangement to pick up my suitcase when she disclosed the true reason why she brought me there. He pretended to blame her for exposing him and his family. He told her that she was responsible for everything and that I wanted to involve the police and scandalize the issue, but it was his niece, Fatmata, who resolved and calmed things down; otherwise, they both would have been in serious trouble. According to the old man, Mum burst out and cried unstoppably when they spoke in seclusion. She expressed remorse, regretted the incident, and apologized to him for the inconveniences and embarrassment she caused his family.

I had invited some of my close friends on Berwick Street to the ceremonies, but since such ceremonies calls for the presence of families, Pa Bangura and his wives invited Mum to my annoyance. They, however, admonished me to show constrain and allow her to attend the ceremonies since God has raised me above their wicked intentions and defeated her purpose for which she brought me there.

The sight of Mum in the ceremonies made me sick to my stomach—especially seeing her faking to be nice and funny, acting jovial and having others laughing. As for Fatmata, it was one of the proudest moments in her life. The news of her marriage spread in communities to the amazement of many who thought she was never going to come out of her plights and the fact that she was taken away to another country by her husband to pursue her dream appeared like another fairy tale, giving credit to the adage that her disappointment was actually a blessing.

Two days after the marriage, I left with my new bride for the journey to Liberia in compliance to our mutual agreement.

Chapter 23

Magnoose was always there to save the day. He had moved from Millionaire Quarters in Smell-No-Taste to work with the Seventh-Day Adventist Church on Camp Johnson Road in Monrovia. Fatmata and I spend days in a motel after our arrival in Monrovia, while Magnoose got involved to allow us to stay in his one-room apartment until I have worked out a solution. It was not easy for me to be playing between two women—one knowing that we were at least a marriage couple, while the other believing that I am her husband-to-be. I certainly did not learn much from Jacksony's playbook, and at that point in my life, I had to take off my hat for him. How in the world was he able to cope with womanizing was something that wore me down in practice. My love for chess playing was used as a cover-up between the two women, but it was exhausting me by the day.

I had hoped to have Famata enrolled at the nursing school and keep her in the boarding home there, but enrollment for the year was closed, so we had to wait for the 1985 school season. However, I met in advance with the registrar to buy favor for her enrollment since there was a limited number of applicants selected from the long list of applications, and many had been on waiting list for a long time.

I secured a permanent job as general manager with Scott Brothers Incorporated, a carpentry workshop situated on UN Drive. The company was one of the few clients that I provided public accounting services before I went on the chess trip to Freetown, which turned out to be an adventure.

I managed to secure a spot for Fatmata at the school and provided all of the requirements for her course, but I was not successful in getting her to live on campus, which would have made my double life easier, but that did not work out.

About a year after she started attending the school, however, our relationship began to fade. Her jealousy was very fierce, and she told me blankly that she was in love with me and would not share me with another woman, covenants or no covenants.

In the fall of 1985, I made a choice to stick to one woman, and so I married the one I was deeply in love with after breaking up with Famata, but it was not after a fight for she would not let go of me easily. We both came to our senses thereafter and forged a friendship since she continued to school under my auspices and subsequently graduated as a registered nurse under the name Fatmata Davies.

She invited me to her graduation ceremony at the JFK Medical Center in 1987. It was an emotional moment for both of us, but she was very happy that I showed up, and I was proud of her that she finally achieved her career dream. As soon as she got off the stage with her certificate, she walked over to me in the crowd, and we hugged each other with tears flowing our cheeks. Before we let go of each other, she whispered in my ear, "Why did not you tell me you wanted kids? I would have traded this dream to get you as many as you wanted." This was in reference to the fact that my wife was pregnant with our second twin. We had the first twin—a boy and girl—in December 1986, a year after we got married. Her sense of humor resulted into our laughter as we both wiped the tears.

After graduation, Fatmata took a job with Dr. Kasas's Clinic on Randall Street, Monrovia, and she was very helpful to my family, providing most of our medications free of charge. She fell in love with someone else and informed me when they were getting married, and in 1989, she and her husband traveled abroad to live. We had dinner the day before she left, and we wished each other well, and that was the last time that we saw or spoke to each other.

In 1995, while working as general manager for Scott Brothers Inc. I rented a small office space on Broad Street to house my public accounting services under the name Davies & Associates, CPAs. Before then, I worked from home, but my clientele was building up. I needed an office space, and thereafter I employed bookkeepers and accountants to work with me as the business grow. Managing a wood and carpentry business exposed me to the politicking in the industry, and so I organized the Liberian Wood & Carpentry Industrial Association comprising of all Liberians in the wood and carpentry industry to combat foreign domination and exploitation of our forests and to urge legislature that gives preference and/or monopoly to Liberians in the industry over foreign competitors.

Most large government contracts were greedily traded for favors by government officials to foreign-owned businesses in the industry, whereas over 95 percent of the jobs were done by Liberians, either directly working for these businesses or being subcontracted to perform these large contracts. At the same time, Liberian forests were being depleted by foreign logging operations, exploiting the country's forest resources and creating deforestation, erosion, and other forms of environmental problems at the expense of the Liberian people but to the personal benefits of a few government officials and their foreign friends.

In the first largest gathering of people in the industry at the city hall of Monrovia on Capitol Hill out of which gathering the association was born, I was commended and voted secretary general of the association by an overwhelming number in attendance. The objectives of the association was accepted by a number of people in high places, but it was partly so because the country was transitioning from military rule to civilian rule, and many government officials were maneuvering for offices.

Head of state, Samuel K. Doe, had formed his own political party named the National Democratic Party of Liberia (NDPL) and together with his military comrades were in the process of transitioning their military dictatorship into a civilian government through a pseudo-democratic process so that they could continue to stay in power. Some section of the foreign stakeholders in the industry realized what the LWCA was up to, so they also started making things harder for us since they had so much money to buy favor from officials in authority. However, the military government started awarding some of government contracts to Liberians in the carpentry industry. I signed several major contracts on behalf of Scott Brothers Inc., one was to product the presidential chairs for the president, vice president, first and second ladies. The special chairs were custom designed for Liberian presidential inaugurations, built with mahogany wood with carvings depicting the national seal and other traditional leadership characters.

Mr. Daniel Scott, senior partner of the company, was the mastermind behind all of the meticulous craftsmanship and carpentry works displayed with the production to the amazement of most Liberians. The contract, however, almost landed me in trouble after their completion when I allowed my wife to sit in the first kady's chair while I sat in the president's chair for photo ops. Somehow the coordinator of the project came in at the time the photos were being taken, and he objected and later confiscated the camera along with the films for security reasons, he claimed. I pleaded that management needed to assure the quality of the products and to keep sample pictures of the finished products, but he contended that not when someone else other than the president, vice president, and the first and second ladies are sitting on them. I conceded in order to close the matter.

The contracts brought me closer to officials at the Executive Mansion and later propelled me into accepting a government assignment to serve as contractual counterpart in the office of the comptroller at the Ministry of Finance. This job entails the reparation of government monthly cash flow statements and the activities involving compilation of data exposed me to the in-depth behind-the-scene inflows and outflows of the government financing internally and externally. There was no doubt the fact that I had risen above my adversaries to the astonishment of many who had discounted me and downplayed my value in society, but interestingly, I have entered another phase in my life that I would not have achieved if I was still counting my losses and disappointments in life and indulging in self-pity, drugs, and drunkenness. I was glad that I got hold of myself, strengthened by the power of God, and did not listen to the noise at marketplaces (meaning that the negative things people think, talk, and share about me did not determine who I am or shape my destiny), and effectively using the 3P system (purpose, patience, and perseverance) I developed as a principle to living my life, the comeback kid was back in business though on a higher plane this time, but if you were born in Kissy Mess Mess as I am, you should always ask yourself : Comeback! For how long? Up until 1990, I was the best chess player in the entire country, the guy that people placed their bet on when I played important matches either in defense of the Open National Championship title, which I successfully defended up to then. I was still president of Monrovia Chess Club; contractual counterpart at the Ministry of Finance; managing director of Davies & Associates, CPAs; secretary general of the Liberian Wood & Carpentry Industrial Association; and most importantly, I was a loving father of five beautiful children and a faithful husband, at least life was good.

There was no doubt the fact that I had risen above my adversaries to the astonishment of many who had discounted me and downplayed my value in society, but interestingly, I came out of all these with an acute sense of purpose, patience, and perseverance (my triple Ps), which turned out to be the yardstick in my approach to life. My place and status in society was unique. I was the best chess player in the entire country until 1990, the guy with whom people placed their bet on when I played important games or when in a bid to defend my Open National Championship title, which I successfully defended up to then, to the envy of many other contenders and rivals, unfortunately. I was still president of Monrovia Chess Club; contractual counterpart at the Ministry of Finance; managing director of Davies & Associates, CPAs; secretary general of the Liberian Wood & Carpentry Industrial Association; and most importantly, I was a loving father of five beautiful children and a faithful husband, at least.

Chapter 24

On December 24, 1989, Davies & Associates and the Monrovia Chess Club sponsored a Christmas party that took place at Stouffer's Bar & Restaurant on Carey Street. A photographer hired for the occasion disclosed news of rebel invasion into the country, but everyone at the party downplayed the information. We have had various attempted coup d'états since April 12, 1980, some of which many believed were staged by the Doe regime itself either to frame and get rid of an opposition or someone that they feared, but not an invasion of the size and magnitude that was underway, so it was hard to believe the information. On November 12, 1985, General Thomas Quenwonkpah, who had been in exile for a while, secretly returned into the country with some mercenaries and other Liberian fighters and launched a coup d'état that eventually failed. That was the last major national disturbance we experienced so far. But we underestimated the information provided by the photographer. The National Patriotic Front of Liberia (NPFL) led by Charles Taylor, former director general of the General Service Agency in Doe's regime, was born. Accused of embezzling large sums of money from the Liberian government, Charles Taylor was facing extradition proceedings in the United States and was supposed to be in the custody of United States penitentiary in Boston, Massachusetts, pending extradition proceeding in accordance with the existing extradition treaty between the two countries. Relations between the US government and the Doe regime had gone sour and the ousting of Doe from power was already sanctioned by the White House. But it was the cock and bull story that the American government told that Charles Taylor broke jail in Boston and thereafter escape from US shores that baffled the intelligence of so many people around the world. For such a high-profile prisoner to broke jail in Boston, pass through airport authorities with so much US military hardware, arms, and ammunitions and enough money to hire mercenaries to evade his own country was certainly an organized plan showing the handprint of some authority for which the U.S. cannot escape liability. But it was the visit of a U.S. ex-president to the rebel leader during the invasion that actually deciphered the puzzle for some who could not believe the power beyond Charles Taylor's incursion. Samuel K. Doe has reached the peak of understanding realization of the politics behind the assassination of President William R. Tolbert. His days were numbered and the movement that would see that through and change the cause of history for many, citizens and foreigners alike, was doomed. We rebuked the photographer at the party and dismissed him before all of the photos we needed were taken. We continued to have fun until in the early-morning hours on Christmas Day. Later during the day, the shocking news of the rebel invasion, as told by the photographer, came hitting many of us like brick stone in the face as the BBC Focus on Africa network broke the news. The NPFL led by Charles Taylor had captured major towns, villages, and it had taken over companies, including LAMCO, a large concession company in Nimba County. They set up several command posts, checkpoints, and training grounds where some of their captives were recruited.

Over the next few months, despite the Doe government downplaying of the rebel's daily gain, the rebels continued to gain and control territories, considerably shrinking and restricting the government-controlled territories.

By July 1990, the rebels were close to the capital city, Monrovia, and threatening to take it over. Fear and panic had taken hold of citizens in the capital and nearby towns. Tons of people were fleeing during the day and overnight. For many of them it was a long walk, hundreds of miles to get to the Sierra Leone border. There were a few public transportation running in the capital, and fares had escalated beyond control as shortage of gasoline and other panic factors took their toll. There were very few Air Liberia taxis operating at Springfield Airport in the city, and the cost of hiring one tripled as the demand increased. Thousands of people spent day and night there waiting for a chance to fly out of the country.

As the price for chartering air taxis escalated by the hour, people who cannot afford the cost either sought other means, while two or three families would join resources to meet the costs of a single trip. Ironically most of the air taxis did not take more than twelve people, so when two or more families joined together to meet the cost of a one-way trip either to Freetown, Guinea, or Ivory Coast, it was with the understanding to divide the family members proportionately to match up with the plane's capacity. Therefore besides the high panic and anxiety level among passengers at the airport praying for a flight to flee the country, there were also tears of sorrow as families struggled over the ultimate decision, deciding who in their respective families should remain in the war zone and who should take the allotted slot on board the plane to leave the country. At the far end of the airfield was the government Boeing 747 jet airplane used to airlift women and children of the Krahn tribe to Zwedru, Grand Gedeh County, in the east.

Apparently, the Doe government was using the government aircraft to take care of the women and children of his Krahn ethnic group, while the rest of the other ethnic groups were left to find their way out.

Like many other families, I had spent a lot of money stocking up foodstuff and other necessities in preparation for the much-anticipated fighting for control of the capital city. Many people predicted that at the pace that the rebels had gained territory after territory, the battle for Monrovia would be no more than two weeks, but predictions were wrong. The government had stockpiled heavy arms and ammunitions and dared the rebels to take Monrovia like they did other counties. What was awaiting Monrovia was bloodbath that the country had never seen before. The government propaganda was not working anymore, and the people knew it.

Charles Taylor was not alone; evidently there was a powerful force behind him, and Doe's government was doomed to fall. The line for me was drawn, and I planned to escape with my family, but the question was how. If I were alone as I used to be, then the answer to the question would have been easier, but as a family man with five children and a six-month pregnant wife, escaping Monrovia in 1990 was one of the most troubling challenges in my life. Many of the government officials had already fled, and there were hardly any streets in the capital city where decomposed bodies or body parts were not lying. Government soldiers were busy searching for and fishing out rebel sympathizers and killing them in the city. I love everyone in my family so dearly and unconditionally that I was ready to do anything, including laying down my life for any of them. I regretted other earlier opportunities I had to flee the country that I did not make use of.

A wealthy client of Davies & Associates who also was my chess partner offered me three seats on his private flight to Ghana for me and two other members of my family, and he offered to sponsor me through to the United States while leaving the two members of my family with his in-laws in Ghana. The offer was good, but to leave the rest of my family in a war zone was troubling to me, so I turned it down.

There was no doubt that Monrovia was doomed for bloodbath as the city was gripped with fear in light of the impending threats. The rebels were being held back by government troops from entering the city just within ten miles away. What was once a lively and vibrant commercial West African city, full of live with all types of activities: school, work, business, recreation, etc., was replaced with fear, panic, and trauma as seen on the faces of its residents. The carnage that awaits it was unmistakably written in bold prints on the wall as tension mounted by the minutes.

The Americans, Liberia's long-standing sugar-ant friend, would stand by and watch it happen even though they had the power, influence, and resources to stop it from happening, but they would play passive and say that they do not meddle in Liberia's internal affairs. It was just a matter of time before the senseless killings began. Monrovia, like other parts of the country, was overcrowded with victims of displacement, starvation, rapes, and other forms of disasters—doomed for its shares in volumes of the impending carnage.

By early July 1990, missiles were being fired at various places in the capital city in addition to the frequent machine gun shootings. Regrettably, the risk for escaping the country became elevated and intense, making it difficult to execute my plan to evacuate my family. I went to Springfield early one morning to see if it were possible to charter a flight to Freetown. On my way I was shocked to see that many areas were badly destroyed and abandoned. I managed to book one of the Air Liberia miniplanes for the next day and came back home to prepare my family for the trip to the airport by foot because there was no gasoline left in the car to bring me back home from Springfield Airport.

The next morning, we finally made it at the airport where we joined other families on the waiting list for a chance to be airlifted. We waited three days at the airport before we finally got a chance with one of the only two miniplanes left. Many of the air taxis were down because of engine problems, and also at that point, pilots who left Springfield Airport refused to risk their lives to return to Liberia. Actually access to the planes were not in order of first-come first-serve basis any longer; it was by who paid or bribed the most money. The Lebanese and Indian merchants and their families had more money and could afford to pay a little more or bribe their way through so they were preferred over anybody else. When it was my family's turn to use one of the planes, the price had gone up to $3,000 dollars from $2,000. We boarded the miniplane after the usual checkups, and it taxied its way along the runway.

But instead of taking off after reaching the far end of the airstrip, it slowly made its way back to where we came from and stopped. The pilot came out and spoke with some of the men working at the airline, and we were asked to embark from the plane for a couple of minutes. After we did, the plane was pulled toward a garage for some mechanical work to be done. What was said to be a couple of minutes became four hours. The other plane had made two trips while we were still waiting. At around 2:30 p.m., one of the Air Liberia staff who knew me very well came over to my family to disclose secretly that the particular plane assigned to us was in a very bad shape and could crash any moment, and he was not sure even if the repairs being done on it would make any difference because the real technicians and mechanics had fled, and those that were working on it were a bunch of apprentices. He said one of the two engines was completely down, and the other had serious mechanical problems. Even the pilot was helping with the repairs because he also wanted to leave the country and never to return to Liberia. The company agreed that he should leave the plane at Hasting Airport in Freetown if he gets there safely for a detailed repair.

When my wife heard this, she panicked and became overwhelmed with fear, especially so because she was almost six months pregnant. She swore that no member of her family would on board that particular plane even if the repairs were done correctly. I insisted that if the repairs were satisfactorily done, we should take the risk once and for all. This brought a disagreement between us, and my mother-in-law, who during normal times was afraid to ride in a plane because she claimed that there were no streets or parking lots up in the sky where a plane would park if there were any problems, joined her daughter and insisted they were not leaving with the children.

However, we reached a compromised, and it was agreed that I would leave with our first twins, Harry and Harriette, and they would wait at the airport where a friend of mine who worked there would help them later that evening or the next morning with the other plane. I decided then to negotiate with two other families who were ready to pay me a total of $5,000 to take the risk and occupy the rest of the seats. I then left enough money with my wife to pay for the other flight. It was a tough decision to leave my pregnant wife, her mother, and three of our children at the airport, but we were left without any choice. It was risky to return home without incident, for there were many checkpoints created and soldiers on every street, requiring bribery, demanding IDs, and harassing peaceful citizens. I pleaded with my friends at the airport, many of whom assured me that they would do everything possible to make sure my wife and children travel that evening or very early in the morning.

The flight finally departed Springfield Airport at 5:30 p.m. and miraculously arrived at Hasting Airport at 6:40 p.m. There were several scary moments: thick black smoke coming from both wings of the plane that clouded our visions and several jolting moments in the air but we finally made it at Hasting Airport. When we arrived there, the pilot disclosed the danger we were in with a sinister smile and expressed his opinion that he was not going back to Liberia soon. He had agreed, however, that before we left Springfield that he was going to assist me with a communication system in Hasting to speak with my wife. He did, and we passed word that we arrived safely. We both put up at the Bintumani Hotel that night.

On our third day at the hotel, the phone in my room rang around 12:00 p.m. when I was napping. I had a sleepless night plotting my family's exit from Monrovia. They had experienced a delay that stretched their departure from Springfield Airport on the day after I left, and Eric had hooked me up with one of his friends at a communication tower at Lungi Airport. He had been helping me during late shift overnight to communicate to Springfield Airport, negotiating my family's evacuation. I had also spent some time at SLET, a telecommunication terminal down town Freetown, to get Magnoose to go to Springfield Airport to assist my family, and he actually arrived there and assumed control to ensure that my family was evacuated.

It was an exhausting evening for the twins and me as we waited at SLET to confirm that arrival of Magnoose at the airport. I picked up the receiver, and it was Eric on the line. Sensing the urgency note in his voice, I was jolted and upright on the bed.

"John, have you heard the news?" he asked.

There had been several developing news by the minute on several fronts in Liberia, so I asked, "Which one?"

DYSFUNCTIONAL ONE

"Well, I am sorry to tell you that Springfield Airport fell to the rebels this morning."

My eyes went dark, my feet weaker to stand, and my heart somersaulted. I could hear him faintly saying, "Are you there, John?" The twins were playing with their toys on the floor, but suddenly they began fading before my eyes as I lost consciousness. I came back to myself after Eric splashed cold water on my face. It was a good thing that he came into my room when I could not continue our conversation on the phone. Eric later left the country that evening.

With the influx of Liberian refugees into Sierra Leone by the tens of thousands per day since January 1990, the city of Freetown was already congested, and news of the Liberian war was the main talk around town, in households and in street corners. The news on the war front that day was worse for residence of Monrovia. The rebels were in some part of the city and in a fierce battle with government troop fighting to repel them and to regain part of the city already lost to the rebels earlier that morning. Also the government's suspicion of certain residents aiding rebels ignited mass raids in the capital, leading to many deaths, houses put on fire, women being raped, and many other forms of atrocities that had my head spinning. At various places in Freetown, Liberians in small and large groups converged to discuss the war, the faith of refugees' loiter the streets without a camp and consolidate to set up hotlines to share information.

As though I could not believe the news, I went downtown with the twin to SLET to make calls to Liberia. No one picked up the calls I placed to Springfield Airport, and Magnoose did not respond either when I called the residence at Seventh-Day Adventist Church on Camp Johnson Road where the officials resided there fled and left him as caretaker. Surprisingly my wife picked up the call that I placed home, and hearing her voice suddenly relieved me a little of the heavy burden that overwhelmed my heart, but it was just for a moment as she burst up crying on the phone to give gruesome details of the ordeal at Springfield: the missiles that were launched by both sides, the heavy gun firing and people running helter shelter and scrambling to survive. She praised Magnoose for helping out to rescue the family with exception of her mother and our oldest daughter, Elizabeth, both of whom were in the bathroom when the fighting started. Magnoose was badly wounded three places and was there at our home sleeping. They had not slept the whole night, and Magnoose's wounds were taken care of by her. The government troops repelled the rebels, but there were still sporadic firing. I encouraged her not to worry and vowed to rescue them by all means and at all cost. She expressed regret that she should not have been adamant about staying; otherwise, the entire family would not have been divided. Now she was caught up in the war zone, six months pregnant, stuck with our two-years-old twin girls, and worried about the whereabouts of our six-year-old Elizabeth and her grandmother. We spoke for about an hour, and I assured her that I would be back to get them in a few days.

"Just stay home, I will definitely come to rescue you all soon," I said, but I did not think that she believed that I would return to the war zone.

When the twins and I returned to the hotel my parents were there to see me. They have both heard about me and the twins and decided to visit me at the hotel. It was Mum who first arrived at 4:30 p.m., and when she was told that I was out, she decided to wait. About an hour later, seventy-six-year-old Dad arrived to see me and also decided to wait. He had retired from work and was living with the same woman who bore him four children. We met them both sitting far apart from each other in the reception room. Dad's head was buried in a newspaper, while Mum had her eyes fixed up the ceiling.

I invited them both for dinner, and we walked to the restaurant with them both trying to befriend the twin. They asked questions about the rest of my family, and I told them what the situation was with them. When I disclosed that I would be returning to Monrovia in a day or two to try to rescue the rest of my family, they both expressed a unified opinion, opposing the idea and showing concern for my life. After dinner, Mum said that she actually wanted to have a confidential talk with me, so we went to a secluded area in another hall, while the twins remained with Dad at the restaurant.

When we were alone, Mum quickly kneeled down and held my feet asking for my forgiveness for all that she has done to me in my life. It was a very moving and emotional scene as she admitted her wrongs and said that she wanted to do this before I left for Liberia with Fatmata and that I cannot imagine how she felt about herself all these years. She talked about how my forgiveness would help her heal the burden she has been carrying all these years, and she would like us to put every difference behind us and forge a new beginning now that I have my own family. She talked about how she wanted to be in the lives of my children to make up for all the things she had done wrong.

In our culture, kneeling before a person with your head bowed and holding on to their feet is the last resort a person uses to show how deeply sorry and regretful they are for their offence, and when that happened, they put themselves at the mercy of the one offended, and once the party who is hurt taps the back of the one asking pardon, then pardon is granted, forgiveness is given, everyone is relieved, and a the old chapter is closed. I have never known any parent to go this far— kneeling before their child feet to ask for pardon—and I certainly did not know what to do, seeing my mother with tears running profusely down her chin begging and asking me for forgiveness. How I could be so crude as not to grant her that wish? I tapped her back, and she sprang to her feet, and we hugged.

Chapter 25

For three days in a row I talked to my wife for hours along with our second set of twins and also to Magnoose, giving them hope of my coming to rescue them as if I was some sort of a hero to just enter the war zone, pick them up, and evacuate them. But my decision to go back into the war zone to plot the way out was already made. The only thing that was holding me back was the security of the children I had with me: To whom do I leave them? Certainly, I would never trust my dog with neither my mother nor dad's girlfriend. Besides,

Mum no longer had the house that her father willed to her. The bastard son she had by the policeman burned her house down to the ground one evening in 1997. He lit a candle overnight while everyone was asleep while he went in search of marijuana. The candle burned to the surface of the wooden table, and fire caught the tablecloth, spreading fire inside his room on the second floor. Inside some of the rooms on the ground floor were gallons of gasoline that some mechanic who lived there kept. The fire quickly burned through the wooden floor, and fire dropped on rubber gallons of gasoline inside one of the rooms beneath. Soon the entire two-story building was in flames that burned it down to the ground. Mum became homeless with her flock, but thanks to one of her brothers who lived in London and sublet her to live freely at his own property at 28 Berwick Street, so she was allowed to temporarily live in two of the bedrooms upstairs.

Although I had forgiven her, I had not forgotten nor did I underestimated her unpredictability. Like a soldier, I was going to war and may not return with the rest of my family, so it was important that I make a wise decision for the care of my kids. I had to leave them with someone who cared, responsible, and loving but most especially in better financial standing to adopt them in case we (the rest of our family) did not make it back.

Moreover, I needed to be able to focus on the task I had committed to myself and not worry about them once I entered the battlefield. In Liberia, my family had lived fairly, decently above the average lifestyle in Sierra Leone. My monthly income was a little over $1,500, which was a substantial amount of money compared to the average salary range in Sierra Leone. Many of the well-educated people in Sierra Leone could hardly make a hundred dollars a month, so the challenge was to leave the children to a family that could afford to protect and secure the lifestyle they were used to, where they can be comfortable rather than leaving them with a struggling family who might just use up whatever amount I may allot for the kid's welfare to their own personal use.

On the down side, the children would have to be left with a total stranger, and that was also something that worried me. They were attached to me and would surely miss me, as they had already missed the other members of our family including their daycare friends, all of whom they asked for all day long.

Somehow, a few Liberians at the hotel found out that I planned to go back to Liberia, so on my tenth day in Freetown, I was having dinner with the kids at the restaurant when a Liberian woman in her late fifties came over to my table and introduced herself as Felicia Norman, a business owner from Monrovia. She was sent by two of her friends who wanted me to do them a favor if I really was going back to Monrovia. I gave her my room number, and we set an appointment to meet the next day with her friends.

The situation in Monrovia had become unpredictable in the last two days, and time was now of the essence. The telephone lines were cut off, so no calls were going through that I knew of; hence, I was not able to make any more calls to my wife. Worse of all, no vehicles were allowed to enter the city by air, sea, and road. A buffer zone was established between government troops and the rebels. Civilians who made their way to the border withstood the risk of being killed, captured, sent back, or allowed to cross into Sierra Leone.

Early the next morning, Felicia, accompanied by two men, tapped at my room door, and I let them in. The men introduced themselves as Charles Barclay, owner of a used-car dealership in Sinkor, Monrovia, and his friend James Dorboh introduced as one of the managers at the dealership. But the two men lied; James Dorboh was not a manager at Barclay's used-car dealership. He was an ammunition procurement officer in the Doe government. He fled to Freetown following the overnight invasion of the United Nations compound in Sinkor, Monrovia, where women and children of the Geo and Manor tribes were being sheltered. Some of the women and children were captured while others who tried to flee were shot and killed massacre style. Their captive were placed in military trucks and taken behind the Executive Mansion where they were interrogated, killed, and their bullet-riddled bodies dumped at the sea. A ten-year-old boy, who was among their captives, jumped from one of the moving military trucks as it approached Capitol Hill. He was shot multiple times as the moving truck went away. The boy survived for a few hours and later died around 10:00 a.m. Before his death, he told nearby residents who went over to help him that the president, Samuel K. Doe, was also among their captors. He was wearing a military combat fatigue.

James Dorbor, a captain in the military, was among the intruders who murdered those women and children. His military ID dropped during the attack at the UN compound and was found lying in blood on the morning after the attack. It was after that incident that James Dorboh fled to Sierra Leone posing as manager of a used-car company owned by Barclay, who himself was a front for government officials in oil deals, running several gas stations in the country undercover for them. I was in Monrovia when the two incidents occurred at the church and at the UN compound. Dorboh was probably one of those who invaded the Lutheran church in Sinkor, murdering the Geo and Manor women and children.

We talked about what they wanted, and they also agreed to keep and care for my children even if I do not make it back. It was a tough thing for me to leave my children in the care of strangers, but I had no other choice. I had been hearing horrible stories from survivors of the war and a few eyewitness' accounts of events, all of which left me clenching my fist at times or leaving my head spinning. What the two men wanted me to do for them was to rescue their wives and children whom they cowardly left behind in Monrovia. I would have kicked them both out of my room if I knew who they were, but I had no idea, and I believed them. Both of them gave me details of where to find their families.

Barclay offered me to take any number of vehicles from his dealership as compensation if I can make it there and get his family. They both gave me some personal items that would make their respective families believed that they sent me. They were so friendly and encouraging as we spent that whole day talking, eating together, planning, and plotting my trip for the next day.

Felicia, who claimed to be Barclay's secretary, vowed to look after my children like hers, and both men also vowed to participate in helping to look after the children. It was a mutual understanding that I cherished since I perceived that these men, like me, cared and worried about their respective families, but at hindsight this was something I would not have subscribed to, especially entrusting my children to a group that was capable of murdering children and women. Why was it that the two men fled Monrovia without their respective families was something I did not ask them or asked myself then.

The two men chartered the vehicles that took me to the border. They accompanied me in a chattered taxi from Freetown to Kenema where we all spent the night in a hotel. Then, the next morning they accompanied me to a terminal and hired a pickup truck to take me to the border, and then they returned to Freetown.

It was raining season, and part of the unpaved roads were eroded, bumpy, and very slippery, so it took up to eight hours to reach the town of Zimmy, which is probably less than a hundred miles away from Kenema. The pickup driver was very curious to know why it was so important for me to go back to Liberia where everyone was running from. He said that there were no vehicles going in, and he did not see how I would be allowed to enter the country let alone to go to Monrovia that was over a hundred miles away from the border.

We were delayed at Zimmy, where a long line of refugees were being checked, and after they checked us, we proceeded toward the boarder. We arrived there around 9:00 p.m. The driver was exhausted to return right away, so we both slept in the vehicle till the early morning hours.

When dawn came, we noticed there were thousands of people on the Liberian side of the border waiting to be processed to leave the country. Hundred others had crossed into the Sierra Leone side but were awaiting authorities to process them. They were being guarded by the Sierra Leone military. Apparently the Sierra Leonean government had beefed up its security on their side of the boarder in the light of the growing military activities on the Liberian side. There was no one leaving the Sierra Leonean side of the border to go into Liberia.

Across the bridge on the Liberian side I could also see some vehicles on the ground probably waiting to be cleared to cross over to the Sierra Leone side. I went into the Sierra Leone Immigration booth to process my departure from Sierra Leone to Liberia, and I was resisted by one of the officers who took my passport, opened it, and asked where I was going. I told him I was going back to Liberia, and he looked at me as though I had some kind of metal derangement.

"We have not processed anyone going into Liberia for a long time. Are you in your right mind?" he asked.

One of the other officers said, "You will be killed immediately when you cross that bridge, no doubt about it, because there is nothing you can say to convince those bloodthirsty soldiers that you are not a rebel or rebel sympathizer. You should ask your fellow Liberians to tell you how many people now are slaughtered before they are even interrogated."

On that note, one of them went out of the booth and came back with a couple of Liberians who had just arrived from the Liberian side of the boarder. They looked pale, tired, and apparently staving. They were asked to tell me a little of what was going on the Liberian side where they came from. The stories were frightening, inhumane, and unbelievable, but they would just not repel me from crossing. My mind was made up to rescue my wife and children.

Based on information I gathered from there and seeing my resilience, one of the immigration officers insinuated that my best chance would be at Bombom Waterside, located a few miles away from the Manor River Bridge. He said that it might be possible there but highly risky. I thanked them and walked back to the pickup driver, who was negotiating with some refugees to take them to Kenema. He dropped the negotiation after I asked him to take me to Bombom Waterside.

We arrived there around 11:00 a.m., but there were barely any travelers, only a few soldiers and the usual authorities: customs and immigration officers that are assigned there. Everyone came out of their booths and huts upon hearing the roaring of the vehicle. By the time the pickup stopped, a crowd of curious officers were already pounding questions on what was our mission. I introduced myself and began to explain my plight and mission. The officers asked the same questions I was asked earlier at the Mano River Union Bridge: "Are you insane or losing your mind? How are you going to cross to the other side of the border?"

At Bombom Waterside there was no other road or bridges on which a vehicle can drive to either side of the border. There is a platform made of wood floating on waters without engine on which a vehicle is placed and there are chains or ropes tied on hard surfaces hanging and stretching from both sides of the border, which were pulled to move the platform to and fro. At this point the platform was stocked at the Liberian side of the border and the ropes or chain cut off. The driver of the pickup was quick to clarify that he had no intentions to take his vehicle to Liberian territories. His contract ended there, and he was going back as soon as I paid him off and released him. On the Liberian side there was no sign of life as the place looked totally deserted.

On the day I left the rest of my family at Springfield Airport in Monrovia, I started smoking cigarettes and bought a gross of Benson & Hedges at the airport. I had no idea that foreign cigarettes were prohibited in Sierra Leone, and all along no one told me I had violated any cigarette regulations. I pulled out a cigarette from the pack I had in pocket, and as I was reaching for a lighter, an officer approached me and said that he was arresting me for being in possession of a foreign cigarette on Sierra Leonean soil. I was stunned when told that only cigarettes manufactured in Sierra Leone are legally allowed for smoking in Sierra Leone. He and his colleagues took the remaining packs of cigarettes I had on me, and then I was taken into one of the booths where I was detained until their commander came to decide my fate. While waiting, the pickup driver approached me for settlement; then he left.

About an hour later, I befriended a few of the officers who engaged me in conversation. There was also a woman officer who tried to encourage me to give up my plans to rescue my wife, saying that she is also a mother and a wife, and given the situation, she would have been thankful that her husband fled that deadly zone with two of her children and never expected him to come back, risking his life when he should be looking after the two children who are now counting on him.

"What if you are killed?" she asked. "Who is going to take care of your children?"

The question hit me like a brick of rock as if I never asked myself the same question.

After she could not get me to change my mind, she ended up saying, "I have not seen or heard of any man or woman going back into an active war zone empty-handed to rescue their spouse. I think your wife is the luckiest woman in the whole world, and the two of you are a testimony of modern-day Romeo and Juliet."

We all laughed at her humor, and I enriched her humor by pulling and waving a white handkerchief my Dad gave me to use on my way into Liberia to wave at armed men, indicating I am peaceful or I surrender. They all laughed even more loudly as they mocked me, saying that this was not the 1940s and that these bloodthirsty rebels and government soldiers does not recognize or understand the meaning of white or any color flag waving nor are they governed or respect international laws.

We chatted for a while until moments later their commander came, passed judgment over me, and I was fined a thousand Leone for each stick of cigarette. Since there are twenty sticks of cigarettes in a pack and I carried several packs with me, they took away from me two hundred dollars. After the commander received the amount, he then asked me for details why I needed to be in Monrovia. He seems to be suggesting that I was using the story of family as a pretext to go in. In order to convince him that I was not a rebel or dealing with any rebels, I pulled out several photos of my family and several Liberian newspaper articles carrying my family's pictures. These convinced all of them, and they all began looking into my situation more deeply, some suggesting that it would be good to return to take care of my children and pray for the best of the other members of my family stranded in the war. The commander recounted that the government of Liberia has closed their side of the border, and so there are no vehicles or people being processed from the Sierra Leonean side to go to Liberia at the moment.

"Even if you were to get on the other side of the border, how would you make it when there are no vehicles and the first village is miles away. Don't you think you could languish and maybe attacked by animals, and no one would never know anything about you, while your wife would also be thinking that you are out there taking care of her children?" he admonished. He then gave me back a few packs of my cigarette while he held on to the others.

A few moments later, they all gathered and shared the cigarettes and the money they have collected. Some of them were smoking and comparing the taste with locally produced cigarettes. Interestingly the woman officer came over to me and sat near me. Putting her arm on my shoulder as if to console me, she said that she knew someone who could likely help me, but that person was about five miles away. She said he was a fisherman who usually supplied them with fishes.

"He has a canoe that could be used to cross the river even though I do not guarantee that he would," she said.

To get to where the fisherman lives, I had to buy fuel for another man who owned a motorcycle to go get him. At about 3:00 p.m., the motorcycle man returned with the fisherman who looked half-drunk. The officer who was sent for him and I went to a secluded place under a tree to talk. The unbearable smell of palm wine was upon his breath each time he opened up his mouth to speak. The officer introduced the topic by telling the fisherman about my plight. Then she asked if he could take me with his canoe to cross the river to the Liberian side for a fee.

It was at this instant that the fisherman who looked half-drunk showed some soberness. His eyes widened as he looked straight into the officer's eyes. As if he did not understand what he heard, he asked, "Do you mean that I should take this man across to the Liberian side with my canoe?"

The officer quickly explained that I was going to pay him in US dollars just to drop me off and return. The man protested that no matter what currency he was going to be paid with and no matter how much money I was willing to pay, he would rather stay poor and enjoy his life than to get rich and lose his life. In strong words the man protested and declined any offer. The woman turned to me and began to say that this was all she can do having seen my perseverance and dedication toward my family.

Before she could say anything further, I interrupted her and then turned to the man, looking him straight in the eyes and asked him, "What if I buy your canoe with US dollars and paddle my way across without you?"

He hesitated and said nothing. There was a pause; then I cut in again, suggesting that even though I would have bought the canoe, it was still his property because I was going to anchor it just where I can use it on my return if I came back this way or it would be there for him to pick it up any time he wanted.

Then he hesitated again for a few second and asked, "How much do you want to pay for it?"

"Three hundred dollars US," I said.

His eyes widened and immediately accepted the deal. The officer threw in some words, and then we shook hands, and the deal was sealed.

Chapter 26

After we sealed the canoe deal, the fisherman and I rode together with the motorcyclist back to his village where the canoe was anchored. When we arrived I paid off the motorcyclist, and he returned to Bombom Waterside. The fisherman then took me to his hut and introduced me to his family. He took me to meet with his partner, who supposedly had a lien on the canoe.

We met his partner at a palm wine shop with other group of men drinking and listening to news about the war on radio. Among them were few Liberians who also escaped from the war. Musa, as the fisherman was called, introduced me to some of the Liberians, and soon most of them learned that I was returning to Liberia to rescue my family. One of them offered me a glass of palm wine, which I accepted.

The owner of the shop called me over to confirm my returning to Liberia. Suddenly he asked me to do him a favor. One of his friends, also a Liberian lodging with him, bought some vehicle parts for his cousin who lived in a village seven miles from the border in Liberia. Since the vehicle parts were purchased a week ago, they have no idea how to send it over to him because the relative who should have returned to deliver the parts had no way to return to the village in Liberia.

Suddenly I find myself in the midst of people who are interested in my returning to Liberia, many of whom were familiar with the terrains on both sides of the border. The Liberian who had the parts brought it and wrote down all the information about his cousin whose name was Joe. He told me that Joe, his cousin, was a taxi driver who was planning to use the vehicle to drive down to Bong Mining Company in Bomi Hills located about thirty miles from Monrovia to pick up his wife, two children, and his aging mother to bring them to this village until the war is over. They began to show me how to navigate my way in the bush road to get to Joe's village. There were too many tutorials about the safer bush road safer and what to look for as landmarks to get me where I should go, and at some point I became confused. So I wrote down a number of instructions and sketches to help with my navigation.

About an hour later, a few men followed me down the wharf where the canoe was anchored on a muddy surface. All my life, this was the first time I paid for something before I set my eyes on it. The canoe was not even worth $50. It was very old, and its wooden edges were rotten, and there were quite a number of splits and holes on it.

At five twenty that evening, I started paddling my newly purchased canoe from the village near the bank of the river that divided the two countries. As I paddled my way to the other side, I thought for a moment that under normal circumstances, I would not invest a dollar in a canoe like that. Maybe if I had seen it in advance, I might not have offered $300 to buy it, but it was doing the job—taking me across and maybe bring my family back, God willing. I recited the Psalms 23 and 121, which I know by heart, and prayed to make my mission successful.

It took about forty minutes to get on the Liberian side of the border, about twenty minutes more than what Musa suggested. Suddenly, near my destination I saw something floating on the waters. As I approached, it became clear that it was the body of a woman. Her face was badly damaged, and she looked pregnant. Not far from her was another body of a little child, maybe two or three years old. A sudden fear engulfed me, and I started shaking so badly that the canoe made a U-turn before I found my bearing again.

When I finally reached the bank of the waters, I realized that the soil was muddy, so I was unable to pull the canoe out of the waters. It was like quicksand. I had to roll up my trousers and took off my shoes and socks and put them in my bag. I took three of the planks used inside the canoe for bench to facilitate me walk on the sinking mud by laying one plank and standing on it and then laying the next one couple of feet ahead and jump on it and then the next to get me on hard surface.

Carrying the rope that anchored the canoe I tied it to the nearest solid surface, and it took me some time to find my bearing. Before I started my journey into the bush, I noticed some impressions in the mud that looked like animal footprints with curling impressions.

I was going to settle down, check how much money I have left, eat something, and read my instructions and sketches before continuing the journey, but the impressions I saw on the muddy grounds definitely told me that there must be some kind of animals nearby. All along I made sure that the money I was carrying was separated in bits and pieces and hidden in various places—different places inside and under my bag, in the bag wheels, and in about five different places on me.

I had a reserved $1,000 wrapped in a plastic smartly sandwiched in a tuna fish sandwich I was carrying. Even the securities who searched me at the Mano River Union Bridge and at Bombom Waterside where I was arrested and detained did not find the large sum of money on me. I was traveling with approximately five thousand US dollars in various denominations but mostly in hundreds and fifties. As a principle before I attempted to pay anyone, I would first give the impression that I was very pressed to use the restroom with the idea to ease myself. I would then take out approximately the amount needed and transfer it to my pocket. My gut instinct told me I was in an alligator or crocodile territories, so I quickly looked at my instructions and immediately began to walk in a narrow footpath in the bushes that led me to nowhere until darkness consumed my world.

I assumed that I was not anywhere near any town or village as yet. To prove this I climbed a tree say about thirty yards above the surface and looked around me as far as my eyes could see, and I actually did not see anything showing humans activities or any signs of life. While up the tree, I wondered how far I would have to go in this wilderness before I get to the first village, and I also wondered if turning on the torchlight I carries would be to my advantage or disadvantage.

Suddenly while on the tree, I heard a very powerful cry of an animal. It was so loud that I imagine it was coming from beneath the tree I had just climbed. I stayed still for a moment, and the cry repeated, but this time it was not close, and minutes later I heard the same cry again but farther. At this point I decided to stay up the tree, so I stayed there till daylight.

The art of spending the night on a tree that was not prepared for sleeping was a challenge that lived on me forever. The night was crudely boring, mentally draining, physically painful, and emotionally torturing. It was a long and cold night, and in a way the experience helped to strengthen me for the mission and helped me build up patience as a virtue to endure and to overcome. Sporadically, there were queer sounds like groaning, barkings, squeaking, and finally toward the early morning hours, the reward I got from spending the night on a tree was the clear but beautiful tweeting from the early birds, an assurance that the long night was reaching its end.

I found a branch on the tree where I sat with my back resting on another branch. There was not enough room to accommodate my feet to stretch them, so for most part throughout the night they were hanging. At times I felt my feet, back, neck, and sides cramping. There was another reachable branch where I would move to, to sit and stretch my feet, but my buttocks hurt and sore because the surface was very rough and uncomfortable, so I switched places every now and then.

Despite all these odd challenges, there were several blessings that made the night outstanding and encouraging. There was no rain that night, and the moonlight was helpful, for I never had to turn on my torchlight. I imagined what it would look like if the dark clouds swallowed the moon, and in the midst of the darkness rain started pouring down, but that never happened. Another thing that did not happen, which I thought was a miracle, was the fact that the tree and other trees around me were engulfed with black ants, which I did not notice until during the early hours when the sun began to rise. They were all over and under the trees, on the ground, and to a large extent on the narrow foot parts. It puzzled me to think that they were there when I climbed the tree and spent about ten hours up there without a single sting from any. There was no way to avoid them, but somehow I managed to descend from the tree, and without stopping I ran with aching legs along the narrow parts until they were out of sight.

The walk was a long one. Even though my body ached and I needed rest, I walked miles just to come out of the bushes to a dusty road. I have no idea how many miles I walked nor did I remember how many times I recited the Psalm 23 as I went along, but once I reached the narrow, dusty road, I felt relieved. I looked at my sketches and notes to figure out which way to go, but nothing made sense to me since there were no landmarks. The name of the road where I found myself was not known. There was a rock on the opposite side of the road where I decided to sit a little and to eat snacks. I was already running out of drinking water. As I was eating, I realized there were tire tracks on some parts of the dusty road, and that was encouraging at least.

Suddenly my eyes caught a faded signpost nailed to a tree near the bush road I came from. It read, "Beware of Dangerous Animals." I crossed over to read the faded prints, and immediately I strapped my bag and began jogging. At around eleven o'clock that fateful morning, I reached the first village, but it was deserted. Miraculously, the map sketch began to make sense to me; the name of the deserted village matched the third village on my sketch, which told me that I was within reach of the village where Joe lived. On my way I wondered what if Joe's village was also deserted and there was no one to talk to.

Shortly before twelve noon, I spotted the first human. She was an elderly woman picking herbs on the side of the road. As soon as she saw me she started running into the bushes. Once she was running, I stopped jogging because I figured she might have been frightened by seeing an unexpected human. I wanted to go after her, but I had no idea what would have happened if she started calling for help, thinking that I was after her.

So I walked until I passed the part of the bush where she entered, and then I started jogging again until I came to the village where Joe lived. There was a courtyard hut where villagers settled their disputes. I sat down in front of it trying to catch my breath and to rest a little before I would start my enquiry of Joe.

Moments later two elderly men came from the bush road behind the courtyard with their palm wine jugs hanging on their shoulders. I went over to them and greeted them, and I asked for Joe. They sat their jugs down as they curiously questioned me and my motive. They concluded that there was no Joe living in their village, and they walked away.

I was wondering if I was in the wrong village when suddenly two younger men came by, one carrying wood on his head and the other some farm products. One of the two young men was related to Joe and his cousin who gave me the parts for Joe's vehicle. Soon the men were satisfied with me, and they asked that I walk with them to where Joe lived.

I felt relieved when I saw a yellow Datsun Nissan sedan parked in the front yard where Joe lived. The men tapped on his door, but there was no response. A neighbor said he was around this morning, but he thought he had gone in search for parts for his vehicle to a nearby town. The two young men left me and went away, and I sat at Joe's doorsteps feeling frustrated that Joe might not be back soon, or he may have given up waiting for his cousin and decided to find another means to go to Bomi Hills where his family lived.

While sitting with my head bowed, the neighbor who said Joe was not around came to interrogate me. After we chatted and I called the name of Joe's cousin who sent me and I took out the vehicle parts for Joe's vehicle—spark plugs and contact breaker—his eyes brightened, and he asked me to wait for him. Moments later he came back with a man in his early thirties. He was Joe. Apparently the men who first met me were suspicious of me, and so they went to inform

Joe to hide himself for fear that I may have been sent to harm him. Joe then was hiding at his neighbor's place just before the two young men led me to his place.

Finally I met with Joe who hugged me with his gallant physique and confessed that he was hiding when they told him about me. We laughed about it, and I gave him the vehicle parts. Joe's gratitude for the delivery of his vehicle parts was expressed in a variety of outstanding ways with a joyful heart.

I was feeling feverish, exhausted, and hungry, but after Joe made me a hot bath that I needed, he provided me some cooked food, some herbal drink that energized me, and he allowed me to rest on his bed, while he started working on his vehicle. My snoring must have removed the paint on the walls in the small room as napping turned into the real deep sleep—the sleep I lost overnight. I was awoken hours later by the roaring of a car engine. At least, my trip to Monrovia was promising.

Chapter 27

Joe got his car fixed, but he could not fix the electrical system well enough to get the headlights working properly. He was testing the vehicle around the block when I stepped out of the room to join the rest of the guys helping with the repairs and others who just sat there making jokes. One of them asked how I made it to reach their village, and they all keenly listened as I told my story on how I was able to cross that uncontrolled part of the border. I was interrupted several times as they wanted me to know that part of the route I took was created by smugglers and hunters. They were thrilled with fear when they heard where I passed the night. Some of them told stories of dangerous encounters with reptiles: crocodiles, alligators, and serpents that are in that part of the border where I landed the canoe and the bushes where I spent the night. Their stories sent chills waives up my spine, almost paralyzing me. I do not know how I would have attempted to use that route if I was told in advance of the danger in it.

I learned then that Musa and others were reptile hunters who usually ply the area in groups to hunt, especially reptiles that are delicacies in the area. Besides the danger of reptile encounters, there were several traps set by hunters in the areas. Had it not been for the parts and note sent by Joe's cousin to deliver to him, no one would have believed that I passed through those areas in the night for that matter. For them it was not believable that any human would be in that area all by themselves overnight.

Joe returned with a smile on his face and asked if I was ready for our trip that night. He had told me that he would not go to Monrovia for obvious reasons, but he can drop me off at the final checkpoint to branch off toward Bomi Hills, or I could go to Bomi Hills with him and see if I could find transportation from there to Monrovia.

Moments later, Joe packed a few items, and after some emotional farewell talk with friends and relatives, we set off for the journey at 6:30 p.m. He was already prepared for the trip; he had a full tank of gasoline and two five-gallon containers full in the car boot to refill his tank if we ran out. I sat in the front passenger sit as we started off toward what was going to be a challenging task undertaken by two men whose parts crossed in unity with a single goal to rescue those who are dearest to them, the family.

Thankfully there were only sporadic rebel activities in Cape Mount County in the northwestern parts of the country at that time. We barely covered ten miles of the journey before dark clouds began to cover the sky. As darkness engulfed us, I asked Joe to switch on the headlights, but he instead turned on the emergency lights, yet the moonlight made the road visible. Interestingly, we drove for close to two hours without seeing a single vehicle either coming or going, which to me highlighted the danger of our journey.

I was stunned when Joe disclosed that the vehicle's headlights were not working but only the emergency lights, which he had on. I panicked a little but saw that the moonlight and the emergency light work well for us especially so that some parts of the paved road had blinkers that helped keeping us right on the road.

We probably drove for two and a half hours before one vehicle came from the opposite direction. I guess the occupants of that vehicle were scared as we were. We were just within reach of the Bomi Hills' interception when suddenly we came to a checkpoint at a little town called Gbahn. As we approached the village, Joe murmured something and stepped on the break so hard that the vehicle came to an abrupt stop.

Simultaneously, there were commanding voices everywhere yielding, "halt!" The windows were opened, and I looked through my side and realized that military men were pointing their AK-45s at us. They had set a road block or checkpoint at the mouth of the town, and they were everywhere—hanging on trees and lying in the bushes—and a few of them came surrounding the vehicle.

It all happened so fast that my only reaction was to put both hands through my window at the same time shouting repeatedly, "We are civilians, and we are unarmed."

"Get out of the car now!" yielded many of the commanding voices.

Together Joe and I got out and placed out hands above our heads. On the right side of the road was where they built a small command post with sticks and covered with palm straws. With a couple of gun butt slamming on our shoulders and backs, we were taken in it and set on the floor to sit while they pounded questions: who we are, where we were from, where we were heading to, etcetera. It was a chaotic scene with more than ten of them asking different questions at the same time, and we were confused as to whose question to answer first.

While trying to answer their questions, others were accusing us as being on recognizance mission for Charles Taylor's NPLF rebel group. Joe seemed sucked and muted by the accusation; then I realized that something had to be said in defense of their accusations. So I spoke for us both. I first of all thanked the men for protecting the best interest of our country, and I applauded them for a job well done, but I told them, "With all due respect, we are not rebels, and I can prove it to you all that we are ordinary citizens."

I already learned that when rebels met civilians, they accused them of being supporters or sympathizers of the Doe government, while on the other hand, government troops would accuse civilians that they were rebels or rebel sympathizers, vice visa.

Three months earlier, in April before things started happening in the city, I was among three others—including General Ibrahim Bambagida, president of the Republic of Nigeria, who happened to be a good friend of President Samuel Doe—to be honored for chess promotion on the continent of Africa. The event, which was widely publicized, was attended by a few members of the government, including Sports Ministry officials, few members of the diplomatic core, including staffs of the Nigerian Embassy who received their president's Certificate of Honor. Before the event that took place at Stouffer's Bar & Restaurant on Carey Street, I had solicited a letter of invitation from a chess association in Sierra Leone, which I displayed to reporters, setting up an alibi for my leaving the country. The letter was published along with the honoring event. I had all those newspapers in my bag plus I had my government job ID also, so I asked one of the soldiers to bring my bag, and I will prove that I was just returning into the country from a conference in Sierra Leone. I said as a patriotic citizen I was simply returning back home, and the soldiers at the border many of whom knew me assisted me and allowed Joe to take me to Monrovia since he was on his way to join his family in Bomi Hills.

One of them read out loud some of the newspapers and a few others among them recognized me from my chess record. I recognized the name of the soldier that their commander sent to get my bag as a member of the Kru tribe. Upon his return with my bag, I started speaking in Kru to him and tried to relax as I spoke. After they checked my ID and passport, the soldier I spoke to in Kru then responded to me and encouraged me not to worry. He said that some of his colleagues already knew me and recognized me as the national chess champion. I thanked him in Kru dialect.

The commander instructed that they gave me back my all my documents, and he asked what I brought from Freetown to present them for their bravery. I had $200 in my upper pocket, which I gave him, and then he turned to Joe and asked why his vehicle was without lights, and I said yes, the lights gave up on us on the way, and there was nothing Joe and I can do until we arrived in Monrovia. At this point he said that he did not think that it was safe for us to continue with our journey without lights, so he would detain us until daylight before we would be allowed to proceed.

While we still sat on the ground waiting for the next instructions on where they want Joe to park the vehicle until daylight, then came three military trucks led by a jeep, all loaded with soldiers from the opposite direction in a convoy. All the trucks and the jeep signaled their headlights multiple times, and the commander who was interrogating us called out to his men and told them that they have to show the approaching platoon that they are doing their duties well. Their attention shifted away from us, and they spread themselves across the street, some climbing trees and others lying flat in the bushes, while a couple of them stood in the middle of the road with their weapons pointed to the direction of the upcoming convoy. They all yield out like they did to us: "Halt! Identify yourself."

Then a member of the convoy yielded back some numbers and a few words, and there was couple of shots fired in the air; then the gate was opened for their convoy to drive through. As all the vehicles in the convoy passed through, their convoy stopped. All of the soldiers descended their vehicles, and together the host soldiers and the ones from the convoy began to sing and dance, jubilating and sporadically shooting in the air. The lyric of their song was very scary. It goes like this: "We are blood drinkers, and we would suck life from flesh and bones."

Fear engulfed and overwhelmed Joe and me. After a while they settled down and began to discuss among themselves. Joe asked me what I was thinking, and I said that I was scared to death. He nodded, agreeing that he too was scared as I was. We do not know what these men would do to us, but we both knew that lives mean nothing to them, and they can turn the table on us any moment.

On our far right about fifteen yards away was a house with lights on and the door was half-opened. I had been seeing soldiers going in and coming out of the house with drinks in hand, and it looked like drinks were being sold their. I picked up my bag and told Joe I was going to check it out and get something for us to drink. We were both in panic, and I was doing this absolutely out of fear.

I walked straight to the house hoping that nobody spotted me or call me back. When I reached the house, I pushed the door slightly open and walked in. There were military men inside seating down drinking beer and watching the news on national television. On the right were two long freezers and crate piles of beer, stout, and soft drinks. Sitting by the freezers were an elderly couple probably in their midseventies. Some of the men watching TV wore military uniforms, while others had their uniform pants and boots on with civilian shirts. I forced a smile as curious eyes began to check me out.

Trying to sound casual, I asked the old woman how much were the drinks being sold for, and she told me. The price of beer quadrupled, but who cares about that at this time when you find yourself among men who were blood drinkers delighted to suck life from flesh and bones. Out of fear and thinking that eyes were still on me instead of the TV, I asked if there was enough drink to serve everyone there. This caught the attention of the old woman's spouse.

"Yes, Chief," the old man said in a shaky voice, "we have enough for several rounds too."

There was laughter, and I turned around to face the men and to share a joke. The old man's respect of me was probably out of fear, but it helped presented me as a VIP or maybe someone he already knew, and almost immediately one of the men offered me his seat, while he pulled one of the empty crates for himself to sit on. Without any hesitation two of the men reached out to one of the freezers and began pulling drinks for the others to make good of my offer. News on the TV was very interesting, so everyone watched as they drank. I wished that this atmosphere would stay just like that till daylight, but I knew deep inside me that when the soldiers out there settled down after their counterpart left, I might be called back out there. If that did not happen, the television station would close at twelve midnight as usual or if the old folks decided to go to sleep, what would become of me?

I thought about Joe. He was still sitting out there waiting and scared. His vehicle was out there, and they may want him to park it somewhere, or it may just be a wise thing to be there waiting for their instruction—I had no idea. The vehicle was his livelihood and the only useful asset he had to evacuate his family. It was a little over eleven o'clock, and I was worried what would happen, especially after hearing on the news that the rebels had put a time table to capturing Bong Mining Company, which means that Bomi Hills where Joe's family lived and other adjacent towns, including the town of Gbahn where we were, could be battle ground any moment. If the rebels would attack the place tonight, Joe and I would be dead meat without question.

Suddenly an idea came up, and I had to act before it was too late. So I stood up and asked the old man to use their restroom. He directed me to go down the corridor outside the back door and make a left turn, and I would see the restroom. I followed the direction, and at the door I pretended that the handle to the door was not turning just to get an opportunity for a one-on-one talk with him.

When he came close to the backdoor where I was standing, I asked him in a low voice, "Can you do me a favor, sir?"

He nodded and walked outdoor with me. I told him that I was traveling to Monrovia from a conference in Sierra Leone, but the taxi I was traveling in had electrical problem, so the soldiers out there were holding us up until daylight before we would be allowed to proceed since the vehicle lights' were not working. For this reason I asked that I spend the night on his couch. The first thing he said was that he thought all along that I was a part of the military men or one of their commanders. He said his family was also in the same predicament and that he and his wife were only waiting for their grandson to return from Monrovia where they sent him to get funds from their bank account for them to leave the country. Their family had lived in Gbahn for forty years farming, but they now felt besieged, and they are very old to run away with their grandson and without any money to survive on. He said that as soon as their grandson would return tomorrow or the day after, they would be leaving for Freetown, Sierra Leone.

"Let us see what my wife thinks about your request and I would let you know," he concluded.

He returned, and I used the restroom and came back to my seat. A few moments after I was seated, I heard the roaring of the military trucks, and I knew without a doubt that the soldiers in the convoy were leaving or continuing their journey. Moments later I heard the commander interrogating Joe about someone that they claimed was found dead on the middle of the road from the direction that we came from. I heard Joe pleading that he never hit anyone and that they can ask me. Then the commander asked for me, and he told them where I was, so the commander instructed KokoWleh, the same soldier who was sent to get my bag to get me.

Although I was sitting in that house looking at the TV, my ears were out there listening through the half-open door. My stomach somersaulted as the sound of Koko Wleh's boot struck closer to the door. As soon as he entered, I asked in Kru dialect if his commander and the men out there would like to drink something. He nodded, and together we took two crates of beer and six bottles of Guinness stout for his comrades.

As we stepped out of the door, KokoWleh confined in me that his bosses want to seize Joe's vehicle, so if they asked me to validate any accusations against him I should do so, so that I would not be detained, and I would be free to leave in the morning. I knew immediately what he meant, but I did not know if I would ever forgive myself if I should lie on Joe just to free myself. We distributed the drinks, and there were more soldiers without any, so I promised to get them some drinks later after I attended to the commander's call.

Then the commander thanked me for the drink and said that he has a question for me and that I should be straight with him.

"Do you remember that the car you were in as passenger hit someone or something that you may have thought was an animal on the road while it was coming this direction without lights?"

I said no; the car did not hit anything or any person. One of them said that I should think well, and I said I was sure that it must have been some other vehicle and not Joe's vehicle. At that point the commander said in a commanding voice that he was asking me the question one more time and that I better tell him the right answers, or I would be sorry for it. I was shaking, and I peed a little in my pants, but I repeated what I have said that I did not see Joe hit any object, and that was the truth, and I swore to it. Then the commander said that he got a radio call from his colleagues who just went the opposite direction where we came from that a man was knocked down and killed by a vehicle, and as far as he was concerned, we were the only people who came in with a vehicle without lights, so Joe was responsible. He said they were going to turn Joe over to the authorities in the morning and that I should give them my address in Monrovia in case Joe needed me as a witness.

KokoWleh walked me back to the house with two of his colleagues to get the drinks. On our way to the house, Kokowleh said to me in Kru dialect that I messed up after he had told me what to do to save myself. He said that I took a big risk that could have cost me my life because he already told me that they were seizing Joe's car to use it for military errand in the area.

After the two soldiers took the drinks for their comrades, KokoWleh stayed with me, and we chatted in Kru as though we knew each other a long time ago. At twelve midnight when the television station closed, all the soldiers left me sitting there, and as soon as they were all gone, the old folks locked their front door and began to tell me stories of the fearful things they had seen and heard since the soldiers made a checkpoint near their farmhouse. I told them about Joe and the false accusations they had levied on him in order to take his vehicle from him. The old man said he was not surprised because his family also felt like being hostaged by the government troops ever since they created a checkpoint in front of their home. He explained that the soldiers took and ate their farm produces and beverages whenever they wanted without paying for them. We chatted for about twenty minutes, and then the old man led me to their grandson's room at the back of the house to pass the night there.

When we entered the room, he shut the door behind him and lowered his voice when he asked how I was going to Monrovia the next day if they took Joe's vehicle from him. It was as though he was reading my mind, for I had been thinking how I was going to leave Gbahn to go to Monrovia in the morning. From the side of the house, we peered to see if Joe and his vehicle were within sight, but they were not. As the old man was leaving, I wished him good night, but he replied, "I don't remember when last I had one.

Chapter 28

It was one the longest but scary nights of my life that I will never forget. Throughout, there were sporadic gun firings. I had to stuff pieces of cloth in my ear to reduce the terrible sounds, which sometimes came close and closer like some of the shootings were coming from inside the room. It was not only a sleepless night but also a restless one indeed.

I was almost dosing off around 3:30 a.m. when I heard voices in the distance. I recognized Joe's voice like he was crying and begging. I cringed to the floor where I lay down on blankets, praying that the voice I just heard would not be Joe's, but it was hard for me to assume it wasn't Joe crying and begging for his life.

I heard a voice saying in the distance, "Come on! Don't waste my time, I have to carry out orders, don't beg me, let's go, keep moving!"

I closed my eyes when I heard the distant gunshots that followed after the voices faded away. Somehow I fell asleep and had a terrible dream. In the dream, I was lying down on a bed, and a white snake came from underneath the bed slowly trying to bite my hand hanging over the edge. There was a knock to the door, and I was awoken from the dream, sweating profusely and scared to death.

The old woman was at the door to speak to me. It was exactly 5:33 a.m., and I was scared to open the door. Then I recognized her voice and opened up moments later. She said there was good and bad news, but I told her not to say the bad news because I knew what it was. She took a deep breath, paused, and removed her glasses as she wiped tears off her face. And then she asked how many children were there in my family, how many months was my wife in her pregnancy, and how far was my house from Duala Market in Monrovia. I gave her the distance. Then she disclosed to me that a truck was coming in thirty minutes to pick up farm produce for Duala Market, but besides the driver, only women were allowed to ride the truck from four different farms.

"Would you mind dressing like a woman to join the other women to go to Duala this morning?" she asked out of the blue.

I hesitated only because I was not sure I heard her. "Of course, I do not mind appearing like a woman if that would get me to Monrovia," I said enthusiastically.

"Okay, my husband and I would have a word with the women when they get here," she said.

After she left, I went into the outside bathroom to wash my face and brush my teeth. At 6:05 a.m. a green Toyota truck arrived with three women, the driver, and his apprentice. A small warehouse half-filled with farm produce in bags was opened, and the driver and his apprentice began uploading the half-full truck. The women were called indoors, and after a few minutes I was called in where I displayed photos of my family and newspaper publications, all of which made my story believable.

When everyone was in agreement, the old woman brought me an African cotton dress, which fit me well. I quickly shaved, and my face was powdered and my bra stuffed with paper towels. A pair of clipper earring and head tie completed the feminine look except that none of the female shoe fit, so the old woman gave me her bedroom slippers and a scarf that I used to cover my chin and neck. I was to pretend pregnant, sick, and needed medical attention, and I lay down on produce.

There were five checkpoints from Gbahn to Duala in Monrovia. I was told that the women and most of the soldiers at all five checkpoints knew each other and had fostered some sort of friendly relationship so the women would handle them as we go, but the only one that they were critical of was the Virginia checkpoint, where the guards there were somehow difficult to deal with. It turned out that the Virginia checkpoint was the easiest that morning. The guards were busy interrogating a group of travelers on the opposite side of the road, and the only guard who checked us was a friend of the women. The only thing he did to me after he was told that I was sick, pregnant, and was being taken to the hospital was to squeeze my butt and throw rude paradoxical jokes at me, something along the lines like, "Women who ate too much are bound to have their belly full."

We arrived at Duala Market at 9:45 a.m., and I went into a nearby restroom and transformed myself into my normal self. I thanked the women and left. The streets were clear with only few people walking them and only few cars plying them. There were checkpoints everywhere with soldiers manning them. I walked from Duala to Rally Time Market where the house my family lived in was located.

I arrived home a little after midday and tapped at the main gate several times. Lucia, the housemaid, and Coucou, the nanny, were home with my wife. They spied to see who it was, and when Lucia recognized it was me, she screamed my name loud and came running to open the main gate. They all hugged me as I entered the yard, and the two-year-old twins, Shirley and Gracious, were excited to see me once again. The looks on everyone's faces was nothing short of perplexity, doubt, and confusion if indeed it was me. My wife struggled to catch her breath and stumbled over words in trying to ascertain if it was really me.

"For God's sake, how did you get here?" she asked.

"Sorry, baby," I replied, "there is no time to read the book before it is written, it is time to pack up, and get ready to leave Liberia for a long time."

We went inside, and I briefly told her where I left our twin children in Freetown and the tasks and challenges ahead of us. Telling her everything I went through from the border and the experience they had been through at Springfield Airport might frighten her and make it harder for me to get her cooperation, so it was best to say very little. Even though I was physically there, it was hard for her to come to reality of my being there. She momentarily would bury her head in her hands, wondering how on earth I made it there. Apparently, she did not believe I would have come in to help with the evacuation of the rest of the family. Sadly, traces of her mother and our oldest daughter, Elizabeth, showed that they drifted beyond rebel lines, and unfortunately no civilian would survive in the buffer zone created between the government troop and the rebels.

On the other hand, there were no leads on what county, city, or village they may be, or no one was even sure that they were still alive. My brother, Magnoose, came in about an hour later, and together he and I left to find the Barclays and Dorbors. Barclay's family was quite easy to find, and once I presented his letter and the ring he gave me, his family believed me without a doubt, and they took me to his used-car dealership lot to choose the kind of vehicles that would be appropriate for our trip to Sierra Leone. I choose two buses: one Nissan and the other a VW. One of Barclay's gas stations was not far away from the dealership where we went next to fill up both vehicles with gas plus a few more containers.

I asked Magnoose to take the VW minibus to my house and to have all the passenger seats removed. I then drove the other bus to find the Dorbor family. I was told that they moved out of the address that was given me when I arrived there. Further enquiry on where they moved was difficult to obtain. However, I persisted, and my efforts paid off. I got a lead to where they moved to, but when I arrived at this new place, I was told that they only spent a couple of days and moved out. The owner of the house took me inside the empty house to make his point. The only clue I got from there led me to one of their relatives leaving nearby.

This relative of theirs was very suspicious of me. She asked all types of questions, which was normal at the time as people needed to be afraid of the finger-pointings that were going on, the raidings, and killings. However, she became convinced that I was not harmful, and she got into the bus with me and took me finally where the Dorbor family moved. They had moved to a remote area off Garnerville Road.

When we arrived there, the Dorbors had most of their household stuff outdoors as though they had just been transported to a new home. They were about twenty of them: wife and four children, sisters, cousins, nephews, and nieces. I was introduced by this relative who took me there, and I did not think Mrs. Dorboh was happy with her for revealing where they lived.

Mrs. Dorboh claimed that it was queer and almost impossible for anyone to come into the country, so she was skeptical that I claimed to have been sent by her husband to rescue their family. I turned over the letter her husband wrote to her, and I also provided her with a picture of their family that her husband carried in his wallet, which he gave me. She took them into the house and called all members of their family, and after a while she came out relieved and convinced. She asked me a couple of questions about her husband, and then she wanted to know when we are travelling. When I told her the next day, she protested that all nineteen members in her family did not have any traveling documents, and that was a problem because it may take a couple of days to process them because of the high demand. I assured her that I can have all done before noon the next day because of my connection with the director of passport at the Foreign Affairs Ministry.

So I asked Mrs. Dorboh to make passport-size photos available for everyone and deliver them to me first thing in the morning with a list of their particulars. I gave her my address and directed that we should meet at my house no later than 12:30 p.m. the next day to plan the trip. On that note, I said good-bye and drove to Barnesville in search of Jallah, a member of the Monrovia Chess Club who worked at the Passport Office at the Ministry of Foreign Affairs.

Luckily, Jallah was home making a lot of money fixing Laissez-passer for people who were trying to leave the country. We arranged everything, and he assured me that once he received the photos and list of particulars, he can have all done within an hour.

Early the next day two of the Dorbor sons delivered all of the photos together with their particulars, and we drove over to Jallah's house where I left one of them to wait for all of the nineteen Laissez-passers.

The other Dorbor son could drive, so I took him with me back to Barclay's dealership, and we choose a smaller vehicle to help carry some of the people in our entourage. I had the seats in the VW bus taken out and loaded it with my personal items like a freezer full of foodstuff, a forty-inch television, two VCR sets and other related appliances, suitcases packed with personal effects, and a lot of other foodstuff and medications.

Magnoose claimed that the pastors at Seventh-Day Adventist church entrusted him with church properties, and he wanted to be faithful to the church, so he would rather stay in Monrovia until the war ended. He would also take care of my home and most especially keep an eye out there for six-year-old Elizabeth and my mother-in-law, who were believed to have escaped with others in the direction of Paynesville, now a rebel territory.

Only one Dorbor son could drive, so Magnoose helped me hire a licensed driver who agreed to drive one of the buses for $500 up to Kenema in Sierra Leone. This driver demanded 50 percent down payment upfront before the trip, and that was taken care of. There was a total of twenty-seven people in the rescue pack: eighteen of Dorbor's family, four of Barclay's, and five of mine, including Coucou, our housekeeper, whose elder sister begged that we carry her along with us since both of their parents and other relatives were killed in the interior of the country during the early days of the invasion. There were about seven little children and two pregnant women in the entourage. We agreed to hit the road at 2:00 p.m. the following day, so I called a meeting for all concerned at my house at 12:30 p.m. to discuss traveling game plans.

Everyone arrived at my house long before 12:30 p.m. except for the two Dorbor sons. The one with the smaller car left to pick up the other who waited for the Laissez-passers and never came back on time. The two had gone to see their girlfriends and to ride around with them while we were waiting for them before orientation for our trip. At take-off time they were still not yet arrived. We waited another fifteen minutes, but they did not show up, so we decided to leave.

DYSFUNCTIONAL ONE

On our way Mrs. Dorbor pleaded that we go find her sons. We wasted another hour looking for these teenagers, and when we could not find them, we decided to start the journey. What we did not realized at the time was that the teenagers returned to my house shortly after we left and, they thought that we had left them behind, so they decided to get on the journey to the border.

During the hour we spent driving around looking for them at places that their mother thought they might be, they had already gone past two checkpoints: the OAU checkpoint and the checkpoint at Clay junction. At these checkpoints they told militants on guard that they were a part of our convoy heading for Freetown, Sierra Leone, but that we went ahead of them, and they were trying to catch up with us. They managed to get away with that at the first checkpoint, but when they arrived at Clay, the militants there told them that no such description of the convoy they were talking about had passed their checkpoint within the hour, so they decided to return to the city to find us. According to them, they concluded that we may have gone to Jallah's house to find them since that was the last place they were to be to collect their family Laissez-passers.

On their way back to town they met us at Virginia and joined our convoy. We stopped to talk to them. A furious Mrs. Dorbor descended the bus to chastise her boys. I briefly highlighted what we had agreed upon as our game plan for the evacuation trip: rule number one was that I was the spokesperson for the evacuees unless it was necessary for anyone in the convoy to speak for themselves, rule number two was that no one was to voice out to any militants at checkpoints that we were going to Sierra Leone whether that militant was a friend or relative, rule number three, we can only say we are going to Freetown, Sierra Leone, when we are at the border. If asked, we were to say that we are going to Cape Mount County.

The idea was that militants felt somehow betrayed when citizens were leaving them in the heat of the war, and so they tend to treat people oddly, critical of them, and often extort valuable items from them and harassed them in a variety of ways, sometimes subjecting them to inhumane conditions before they would let them go if they were lucky.

But the idea that we were just leaving Monrovia to go to another county within the country was reasonably understandable and acceptable. During the meeting at my house I had given everyone many advices and information on how to talk to the militants or rebels, whichever we encountered on our journey. But now these teenagers went ahead of us and disclosed to the militants at the first and second checkpoints about our convoy heading for Freetown. Worst, when they joined us, they did not say a word where they came from and what they said to the militants about us nor did they even mention that they produced their own Laissez-passers to the militants at both checkpoints, showing that they were going to Freetown, Sierra Leone.

Chapter 29

As fate would have it at the first checkpoint, a friend of mine named Prince Toe who heads the youth wing of Samuel Doe's NDPL was present when we arrived there, so he helped me out, and we passed without incident.

But when we arrived at Clay checkpoint, the militants there ordered every one of the vehicles for inspection. As we descended the vehicles, one of them asked where we were heading. Not having any idea that the Dorbor boys had been here and telecasted our destination as Sierra Leone, and, worse of all displayed the Laissez-passers of their family members, I replied, "Cape Mount County."

One militant barked at me: "Liar." Pointing to the two teenagers, he said, "These two were just here looking for all of you, and they produced a bunch of Laissez-passers for the rest of you running away to Sierra Leone, and now you are saying we are stupid militants that you can just lie your way through, eh, Mr. Smart?" He sent speckles of spit on my face as he dangled his head at me, his nose almost touching mine.

At that point I tried to polish things by saying that we are not just going right away to Freetown. I said that we were going to Cape Mount County for a couple of days before leaving for Freetown, but I do not think I sounded convincing even to myself. They now asked that we produce travelling documents and offload everything in the vehicles for inspection. The move was to cause us undue burden, to waste our time, and to harass us and hold us in bondage until we bribe them whatever they demanded. We started offloading everything, which was laborious and time consuming, so I went over to their commander and asked for mercy, pledging that we can do something to save us the time and labor.

"Fart and let me smell," he said, which meant "show me your offer."

I offered a hundred dollars, but he wanted two instead. I gave him the amount, and we were allowed to put everything that was being offloaded back in the vehicles. But as we were parking suitcases that were already opened, my wife called my attention to one of the Dorbor suitcases containing gun magazines that the militants missed while checking inside that particular suitcases. By this time we had been detained for about an hour, and we were all tensed and frightened. The children were crying for food, and some of them needed cleanup as well. In the suitcases were a couple of magazines featuring various types of guns, ammunitions, and other instructional materials. On the cover pages of two of the magazines were the images of grenades and RPG. My wife pinched me when she saw them, and my stomach somersaulted at the sight of those magazines. They actually sent chilling vibes creeping up my spine. Luckily the militant that was searching that particular suitcase did not notice the magazines; instead, he dipped his hand below and pulled the contents beneath. He was seen pulling other stuff over the magazines as he dipped his hand underneath, and my wife kept quiet until when we were hurriedly trying to reload our luggage.

Suddenly most of the militants that were either questioning members of our convoy or helping to check content of luggage began running into the bushes, and the next thing that happened was even crazier. Instantly another group of militants in different uniforms appeared Rambo style with green leaves tied on their heads and their faces painted with much darker colors—guns in hand pointed at us and chains of ammunitions weighing down their shoulders.

Till this day I cannot tell how it happened, those militants were all over the place, on trees on both sides of the road covering about a hundred yards. We were all frozen like statutes until one of them with a commanding voice asked one of the militants who was there earlier, "What are these people doing here?"

The militant fumbled in answering, and one of the Rambo-style militant turned to the commander and said, "These vehicles look good for military operations, Chief."

The chief then inspected the vehicles, while we waited in panicking silence. When he was done, he acknowledged that they were indeed good for military use, and then he looked in our direction and asked us to leave immediately without the vehicles. I appealed to him to reconsider the children and pregnant women, and I said that there was no problem with him taking at least one of the vehicles.

"Because of the children, you guys choose one of the buses you would like to take with you and leave the other for us, and you have only one minute to do so. This place is declared a battle ground as I speak at this very moment, and it is my mandate to keep it so, and I would not hesitate to clean it up starting from you all because no civilians should be here right now." He shot in the air as he spoke.

Panic grabbed everyone, and they scrambled into the Nissan bus and into the small car in a matter of seconds and drove away, leaving me behind just as I went into the VW bus to grab my bag containing our travel documents and some of the children's foodstuff. By the time I got out of the vehicle, my evacuees were all gone, and I was left standing in the midst of fearful combatants, some shooting in the air.

As if they did not know that I was there, the commander yelled at me, "O! I see, you are the hero, still here defying my orders, right?"

I said, "No, Chief, I want to make sure you don't get stuck with this particular vehicle because there is a secret to it that you needed to know; otherwise, you might not be able to use it any time soon, and besides I would have been gone with the keys as well."

At this time all fears in me vanished, and what was left of me was a bold, brave man facing a fatal situation in which calmness was absolutely a valuable option for the best outcome. In chess games, there is always a good, better, and best move as well as bad, worse, or worst move. They took Joe's car from him and took his life also. I was not going to let them do the same thing to me. They must know that this vehicle means nothing to me and that I have abundant of them, and, in fact, I am willing to let them have as many vehicles as they wanted from my used-car lot.

"You know, Chief," I said, "we don't know each other well, but this is an opportunity for us to foster friendship, especially when you said these vehicles were good for military operations, you touched my heart, and I just felt guilty that you guys deserve more vehicles when my partner and I have so many of them sitting down at the our dealership without being used when our country needs them for our own security."

He looked at me less intense as before, and I knew he was interested when he asked the question I expected he would ask: "You are some kind of used-car importer or something like that?"

"Well, I work for the government, I work harder to put the country on the world chess map, and I and my business partner, Barclay, and I import used cars and run a few gas stations as well," I said.

His next question was along tribal lines—the usual tribal background check that automatically align or divide Liberians upon meeting. Besides, there were four tribes paired equally and fighting against one another: the Geo and Manor tribes versus the Mandingos and Samuel Doe's Krahn tribe. But when he heard that I belonged to the Kru tribe from Sinoe County, he spoke the broken Kru he knew, and I responded appropriately. Then he called one of his men who had mechanical skills to work with me to show the problems on the VW, and the militant went with me where I showed him pretty much nothing because I knew nothing about the vehicle, but I just made up stories of defect opening the hood, and he too was excited as I explained. Then I finally turned over the key to the commander with a hundred-dollar note and promised him that when all these is over, he should visit me at the dealership to collect a car of his choice, to which he said that he hope I wasn't just saying it to free myself now and when he would come there someday, I should not pretend that I do not know him. Of course I swore that I needed him now and then to foster a lasting friendship. He nodded, and we shook hands, and he ordered his men to let me go and not to be harassed. Then he turned to me and with a smile.

He said, "You are free to go but do not run, just walk normally and do not look back."

This was a single moment in my life unlike any other where I cannot find words to define fear. I was the only civilian surrounded by well-armed militants who disguised their faces, spreading on both sides of the road in bushes and on trees, and I had to walk normally in their sight for a distance of a hundred and fifty yards. That short distance was the longest walk of my life. Every step I took increased the weight my feet could carry. I was an open target to over two hundred militants, any of whom could take a shot at me any moment, and the instruction that continued to echo itself as I struggled along the way was "do not run or look back, just walk normally."

As I walked, militants shouted at me from both sides of the road, but I could hear the voice of their commander, saying, "Just keep going, do not answer to anyone."

The convoy of two vehicles was another fifty yards away waiting for me after I made the turn on the main road. By the time I reached the two vehicles, I was soaked with sweat, and I realized that I did pee in my pant. There was no space for me, so I just gave someone my bag and stood at the doorway. No one said anything, the only sound was from the children in the vehicle, especially my two-year-old twin daughters who wanted me to take them, but I was helpless, weak, and there was no way for me to reach them since I was hanging on the step of the Nissan bus. The vehicles pulled away toward our next checkpoint, Gbahn, where Joe was killed.

Chapter 30

We arrived at Gbahn around 6:45 p.m. and went through the checkpoint procedures. There were not many militants there at the time. While we were still going through the procedures, I went to see the old folks who lodged me just two nights before. I tapped at the half-opened door, and they invited me in. They were alone sitting side by side, and the house was quiet. They jumped to their feet when they recognized me, and I told them that my family and relatives were outdoors going through checkup. They were glad and amazed that I was able to reach my family and within two days I carried on with my mission to rescue them just as I said I would. They were so excited that they generously gave us two crates of soft drinks free of charge and allowed some of my evacuees to use their restroom. The old folks said that they were very proud of me and that they wish their son was like me, but he left in the early days of the war, leaving his teenage son with them. They also gave me some foodstuff enough for dinner for everyone, but they advised me to move on and not to stay around before all the militants gathered in the next hour or so.

We discussed Joe, and they confirmed he was shot and killed at the creek across the road, and his taxicab was now being used by the militants. The old folks heard and watched him beg for his life as they carried him across the road toward the creek. Then they heard three gunshots after which he ceased begging in the darkness of the night. Moments later we left Gbahn to continue our journey to the border.

About ten miles away from Gbahn, the women complained that they were afraid to travel in the dark, and I was also afraid. Besides, there was an extended danger in arriving at the boarder during the night when all official activities were closed and spending the night there was not a good idea, so we decided to stop at one of the nearest villages to spend the night. So we stopped at a village that seemed to have been abandoned by most of its inhabitants. Some Good Samaritan helped us to occupy one of the abandoned houses to pass the night. We had planned to start the journey early the next morning, but when we were awakened in the morning and were ready to leave, the Nissan bus and the hired driver disappeared. We thought that he was somewhere in the village, so we waited, but he was nowhere to be found, and we waited thinking that he would show up, but we were waiting in vain till twelve noon; then we realized our innermost fears that he took advantage of our vulnerability and ran away with the Nissan bus. We were now left with the Toyota Grown sedan, which can only take five people. The driver had insisted that he would sleep in the bus, but now we know that he had other selfish motives, maybe growing out of fear or maybe he was attacked overnight, and the vehicle taken away from him. Now we were stuck in a remote village with no clothing, no food, and no medication for anyone, and we have approximately seventy miles to get to the border. Before noon two of the teenagers and I used the smaller car to follow the tracks of the bus, and we traced it branching off a dusty road leading on to nowhere that we could identify.

We drove another five miles on that road following the tracks but to no avail. It was a gas-wasting exercise that could leave us totally stranded without any transportation means if we run out of gas. It was a good thing that we refueled the car and the bus the night before we went to bed. During the night my wife and I had secretly discussed our suspicion of the Dorbors because of the weapon catalog they carried in one of their suitcases. That alone would have cost our lives if militants find that on civilians. Now that we were stuck, we had a meeting to discuss what can be done. There were only three choices to make: The obvious one was to stay in this strange village until whatever happen happened. The second was to start walking toward the boarder, which might take several days. And the third was to go back to the militants who seized the VW minibus and make an offer that would make them release the vehicle to us.

When it came to the last option, no one wanted to put their life on the line to go back there, but everyone resolved that it would be the best option. It turned out that everyone depended on me for leadership—to make the calls and to implement them at the same time; after all, I made a commitment to evacuate them. The irony at this point was that there were only two drivers left in the group: one of the Dorbor boys and me. So to go back to the militants at Clay with a proposition to borrow the seized VW bus to transport everyone to the border and to return the bus to the militants was something that was beyond my wildest comprehension. How does one go back to those vicious beasts who kill people for fun and put one's life at risk once more? But the alternative to this question was even more gruesome; it means having my six months pregnant wife and two-year-old twin girls walk over seventy miles to the border without enough food, water, medication, and other necessities on roads that could be dangerous.

So I finally decided to go back to negotiate with the commandant at Clay checkpoint to allow me to use the VW bus. My plan was not to let him know that we lost the other bus as that would be leading him to follow the same trend in whatever way he chooses. The plan was to ask him to give me at least two of his men who can drive to transport the things that were already inside the vehicle to the border, and they would return with the two buses that we were traveling with because some border authorities refused to allow us to cross over to Sierra Leone with the buses. I was going to let their commander know that I would rather leave all two buses in their hand if they were willing to drop off the luggage inside at the border.

So the driver son of Dorbor and I took off to go back to Clay checkpoint, but when we arrived at Gbahn, my plan changed a little. There were four militants on guard there, and one of them was my tribal brother, Kokowleh. He was excited to see me, and I also played excited. I talked to him about the vehicle that was seized and acquainted him with my plans to get the items delivered at the border and to have both vehicles returned to the militants at Clay checkpoint. I offered him a hundred US dollars if he could help me pull that off, and again he became excited and willing to go with me. He joined us in the car, and we drove to clay where we met the commander there, sleeping in the bushes at the back of the command post, and the VW bus was still packed where we left it.

Before Kokowleh joined us, I had acquainted Dorbor's son with my plans and asked him to keep quiet during negotiations and not to say a word about losing the Nissan bus or about anything I say whether true or false.

We arrived at Clay checkpoint, and Kokowleh was recognized by his colleagues there, who welcomed him warmly. The militants claimed that the commander was asleep and should not be disturbed unless it was urgent. Kokowleh lied that his commander sent him and that it was urgent, so they led him to where their commander was sleeping. When he was awoken, they called us into the bush where he was. Kokowleh told him that his commander was asking favor of him, and then he paused and ask us to explain what the favor was.

Now the ball was in my court. "Chief," I said, forcing a smile, "you know that you are my prospective partner in business, so you should be my partner in helping me solve some problems here. Everyone in our group, including the children and two pregnant women, are starving and also very sick and all of the foodstuff, medication, and other necessary items are in the VW vehicle, and I know that you are not interested in these items. All I am asking at this point is for you to give me one or two of your guys who can drive to transport the luggage in the vehicle to the border and bring back the vehicle to you. The other reason why we need another driver is that some individuals in authority at the border would not allow the Nissan bus to cross over to the Sierra Leonean side, and I would rather leave both buses with you or with the commander at Gbahn who have been nice to me than to let others just take them away like that." I paused and watched him give my proposition a thought.

Then he turned to Kokowleh and asked if there was no driver at their checkpoint at Gbahn. Kokowleh said he was not sure, and there was another long pause while we waited. He then called one of his bodyguards to get the same militant whom I showed the vehicle to the day before, and he in turn got another militant whom he claimed could also operate a vehicle. The two militants had their mandate to transport the luggage to the border, offload, and return the vehicle plus the Nissan bus to their commander at Clay. They were instructed to put on civilian clothes for precaution, which they did, and the two of them drove behind us in the VW bus, while I drove the sedan from Clay to the village where the evacuees rested. When we arrived at Gbahn, Kokowleh was paid and dropped off but not before he threw in some good words on my behalf to his colleagues, who were accompanying me with the impression of bringing back the two buses to their commander.

Moments before we took off from Gbahn, a familiar taxicab came from the opposite direction with two militants in it. Kokowleh and I exchanged glance, and he surged. Without any doubt, I recognized the taxicab and as the militants in it descended. Kokowleh beckoned for me to leave, so I drove off, and the VW bus followed. The taxicab that just arrived happened to be Joe's, which was now being used by the commander of this checkpoint.

A few minutes after 3:00 p.m., we arrived at the village to the jubilation of the evacuees, most of whom were standing outside of the farmhouse. Apparently the roaring of the vehicle engines brought them to their feet as we approached the house. I offered each of the two militants dressed in civilian clothing with their handgun hidden under their jackets, a hundred dollars each to make two trips to the border: first trip with some of the evacuees and the other trip with the personal effects. They were so excited that they did not ask more questions about the Nissan bus. Once I told them that the gasoline consumption of the VW bus was economical compared to the Nissan and that it was already at the border parked in a safe place, they were happy about the money. We offloaded the items in the bus at the village and left them in the farmhouse and then have everyone on board. The pregnant women and children in the sedan driven by Dorbor's son and I drove the bus with the two militants in the front seats, and the rest of the evacuees squatted in the back without any seats. It took approximately an hour and fifteen minutes to get to the boarder. Once we were there and everyone descended, the militants wanted to collect the money and for me to show them where the other vehicle was, and they promised that they would go back to the village and return with all the personal effects. I told them that the Nissan bus is across the road in the village there, safely parked because the authorities here at the border wanted to seize it, so they should go get all our personal effects, and when they return, I would take them where the Nissan was and hand the key over and also show them a road to detour the border guards who are interested in the vehicle. It seemed to me that they were being suspicious, so I gave them a hundred US dollars and said that was fair enough because I have no guarantee in the first place that after I give them the two buses and the total amount that they would even come back with our personal effects. They agreed and promised to return in two hours.

After they left, we joined the long queue of runaways to be processed, and fortunately we were done before they arrived, but before we crossed over, we arranged with a custom broker name Mansaray, who had a lawn-mowing tractor with wagon attached to it, and was transporting baggage for evacuees or potential refugees from the Liberian side of the border to the Sierra Leonean side. He had good rapport with the military at the border and was making a lot of money helping to transport personal effects of runaways who could afford to pay him. I described the VW that was coming with our properties and wrote a note for our "militant friends," which I left with Mansaray to deliver for us.

Because Mansaray was skeptical, he invited two of his friends, one a militant and the other a customs officer, to witness the arrangement for fear that something illegal may be found among our personal effects. For fear of not knowing what might happened, I did not give them any information about the issues between our group and the two militants concerning the VW bus other than they were friends assisting to drop off our personal effects. As a broker, Mansaray handled the clearing of luggage for a fee and shared his earnings with customs officers and with the military security at the border. He charged five hundred Liberian dollars, and I advanced him 50 percent and promised to pay the balance when he delivered our luggage.

The deal was sealed, and Mansaray assured us that all of our personal effects would be delivered to us on the Sierra Leonean side as long as the vehicle I described came with it and they were all cleared by customs. We crossed over to the Sierra Leone side ten minutes before the Liberian border closure for the day at 7:00 p.m., but the Sierra Leonean side of the border was officially closed at 6:00 p.m. Mr. Mansaray did not cross over to the Sierra Leonean side that night, and we had no idea whether he received the items or not.

When we walked over the Manor River Bridge to the Sierra Leonean side of the boarder, the authorities there had closed the processing of refugees for the day, and so we had to pass the night outdoors in a swampy area where we were barricaded with other newly arrived refugees. There was no electricity or lights of any kind, so the whole place was dark, and we did not realize where we were till dawn. The night was cold, restless, and longer. It was a shame that Sierra Leone and the United Nations High Commission for Refugees were not prepared to receive the hundreds of thousands of refugees fleeing the carnage from Liberia into Sierra Leone.

It was fair to say that everyone who crossed over to the Sierra Leone side was on their own without any assistance. The wounded, the exhausted, the traumatized, the hungry, the pregnant women, the young and the old—all came from the fire into the frying pan. Most of the refugees who passed the night outdoors were welcomed on the Sierra Leonean side of the border by giant swamp mosquitoes in the dark. The parasites may be less dangerous compared to the vicious and ruthless trigger-happy militants on the shores of Liberia, but as bloodsuckers, it was paradoxical to the system that the Sierra Leone border officers and security would display in welcoming their uninvited guests. They would drain pockets and seize valuable items from refugees especially those who crossed the border without documentation.

Chapter 31

We were barricaded in a swampy area infested with mosquitoes on the Sierra Leonean side of the border, where we restlessly passed the night, tormented probably by the most resilient mosquitoes the world has ever known. Like others in our group, my wife and I, in turn, used a piece of cloth to fend them away in the dark to protect our family, but yet everyone that night donated their blood willingly or unwillingly to these parasites.

At dawn, when the place swept into view, evidence of its disgusting smell were around us—piles of human fesses, dead animals, and sewer water slowly running in a pile of nasty mud. Border operations started at 8:00 a.m., and we went ahead to be the first group of refugees to be processed by the Sierra Leonean authorities. We won the sympathy of the ordinary Sierra Leoneans petty traders who came out in the early morning fog to sell various types of food stuffs to the refugees in distress, but the authorities at the border were exactly likened to the tormenting swamp mosquitoes—doing everything to extort money or to extract valuable items from refugees before processing them.

The officers who repelled me from entering Liberia and refused to process my exit from Sierra Leone just a couple of days earlier remembered me, and they were all astonished and puzzled how I was able to bypass them to finally rescue and evacuate three families (twenty-seven people) from Monrovia. They applauded me and gathered themselves around me in astonishment as I explained my adventures. Yet during processing, these very officers still extorted money from each one of my evacuees and made entry process even harder for those refugees who could not afford to tip them. Thereafter, we waited for Mansaray, who made his first trip around 9:30 a.m. with someone else's luggage. He told us that our personal effects were received last night and would be delivered next after customs inspection. He confirmed that the green VW bus was still around, which means those two militants fell for the promises I made to them; they were still out there waiting to get the other bus and a couple of hundred dollars from me that they did not deserve. The note that I addressed to them, which Mansaray hand-delivered to them before they offload our luggage, read:

Dear friends, I am sorry that the border is close for the day, and I had to find shelter for the little children, so some of my relatives who were already processed crossed over to the Sierra Leone side of the border to spend the night in a shelter. A few others and I are passing the night at a friend's house in a nearby village where the Nissan is packed. Please offload and release our luggage to the bearer of this note, Mr. Mansaray, a customs broker, for the inspection process and keep the VW bus till we meet in the morning. You may want to find a place where you can pass the night, maybe in the vehicle after you offloaded it to create room for yourselves, and we can all meet here tomorrow morning between 10:00 a.m. to 11:00 a.m. I will come with the Nissan bus and give you guys the money that I promised, and you will be on your way. Once again, thanks for your help and friendship and please give my warmest regards to your commander upon your return. See you in the morning. Warmest personal regards, John Davies (KMA).

KMA actually meant "kiss my ass." When Mr. Mansaray read the note and asked what that meant, I simply said it was the business name of my dealership. Shortly before 11:00 a.m., Mansaray returned with our luggage and collected his balance fees. He also confirmed that the VW bus was still around, so I gave him another note to deliver to the military security at the Liberian side of the border. In the note, I wrote that the VW was my property, but the two men who were using it now stole it from us under gunpoint and promised to shoot and kill all of us if we dared tell anyone about it.

"I have no problem if the militants at the border take it from them and use it for their operations at the border," I told Mr. Mansaray, who took the note with him and delivered to the Liberian soldiers at the end of Mano River Bridge.

Later that afternoon, Mr. Mansaray reported that the vehicle was taken away from the men, and he did not know what became of them after they put up some resistance and were taken to the security post behind the administrative building where people who were captured were arbitrarily tried, executed, and dumped into the river. If they were freed, my prayer was that they walk back the long journey to Clay where they came from. We had quite a number of luggage: one deep freezer, three VCRs, three television sets, musical sets and speakers, suitcases, medications, and a lot of foodstuff. The Dorbors added some of their own stuff to ours as well.

The customs officers on the Sierra Leonean side were unreasonably assessing and levying excess duty charges on every item we brought with us in a bid to have some of the items forfeited to them. The charges were so exorbitant that I ended up relinquishing the freezer to them in order to free the other items. The important thing for all of us was to get out of harm's way, as none of the material things compare to our lives.

Once we were done with the authorities at the border, we were now left with new challenges. We only had the sedan vehicle left to move around with but not outside the villages near the border because of road conditions in these parts of Sierra Leone. Many of the roads were eroded and badly damaged during the rainy season; therefore only pickups and large trucks plied the roads, and since there were no passengers going to Liberia, hardly any commercial vehicle came to the border. Hence, hundreds of thousands of refugees who made it into Sierra Leone through the Manor River Bridge had to walk long distances to get to smaller towns where they can find transportation to get to bigger towns like Kenema, Bo, or to the capital, Freetown.

We soon realized that we were stranded. Because of the size and composition of our group and the stressful experience we have had, we needed a motel or a home to live in until we can find way to be transported to cities and towns away from the boarder. With the help of some sympathizers, we rented a furnished five-bedroom house in one of the villages near the border, and everyone had a place to live at least while we wait for opportunity to be transported to Freetown.

On the third day a Liberian named Peter who resided in the United States flew to Sierra Leone and came to Kenema, where he rented a minibus that he drove to the border to pick his family that he had earlier arranged to meet there. When he arrived he spent that day looking and asking for his family, but no one knew anything about them. After the authorities checked their records and could not find names of his family in the registry, he was referred to me by some of the Sierra Leonean officers so I can share my experience with him and to give him tips since he was contemplating to go into Liberia to check for the members of his family. I found it ridiculous that I was perceived to be a special rescue consultant. When I told the man what happened to Joe and to his vehicle and what happened to us and the loss of two buses that resulted to our being stranded at the border, I saw fear in his eyes.

That night, he slept in his vehicle, and the next day I talked to him about using his minibus to take some of my evacuees to Freetown while I was going to stay at the border keeping any eye for his family, and I was going to have his family stay with me until he return. I offered to pay him, and he agreed not for the money but for his empathy of our plights. His vehicle can only take ten passengers, so I asked him to take my pregnant wife and twin daughters along with their nanny along with Mrs. Dorbor and two of her younger children and three of the Barclays. He accepted the offer and proposed a price, which was agreed to be split among all three families.

I provided them with the address of the guesthouse at King Town in Freetown where Barclay and Dorbor lived and asked my wife to book two rooms for our family at the same guesthouse. I was confident that when the two men received members of their families, they would be grateful for what I have done for them by helping my family with lodging and other needs until my arrival in Freetown. But the two men were like wolves in sheep clothing. It took the minibus two days to arrive in Freetown because the roads were very bad.

When they arrived at the King Town Guesthouse in Freetown, both men warmly welcomed their families and left my exhausted family, especially my six months pregnant wife who became ill from the trip, to wander about booking the two rooms. Our first twin, whom I left with the men to care for, were looking very filthy, dehydrated, and neglected.

My wife cried at the sight of both Harry and Harriette, and other guests living at the guesthouse expressed their concern that the children were frequently left alone loitering in hallways and on the yard unattended and unsupervised. Evidently, the children never took a shower from the day I left them to the day their mother returned.

It was Peter, the driver, who assisted my family to rent a single room at the guesthouse and to help my family to settle down. When it came to his fees, my wife provided our portion of the charges while James Dorbor claimed that my wife should be responsible to pay the entire charges because he never asked me to go to Liberia to rescue all his extended relatives, causing his wife to spend the only four thousand Liberian dollars (approximately eight hundred US dollars) on the other members of his extended family by paying for travel documents and all the other cost associated with their travelling. He claimed that all he asked of me was to help rescue his wife and two younger children, so he is not responsible for additional costs.

Peter, who declared how grateful he would have been for the sacrifices I made in rescuing the evacuees if his family was included, rebuked James Dorbor and an altercation ensued between them which prompted Peter to involve the police. Soon thereafter, other Liberians who knew about the true identity of James Dorbor and the reasons why he fled from Liberia without his family revealed the story of his involvement in the two massacres at the United Nations Compound and at the Lutheran Church in Monrovia. This exposition infuriated Peter who regretted the trip he made by driving members of our families to Freetown. My wife explained to him that we don't know any of the two families in Liberia and that I was only helping them on humanitarian grounds when they approached me in Freetown for help. The appearance of our twin children left in their care was another evidence that convinced Peter and everyone present that these two men were heartless.

It was only at this point that it made sense why James Dorbor fled Liberia, leaving his family behind and why his family was moving from one place to another in Monrovia because they were afraid of the militants from the Geo and Manor tribes who were looking for his family in revenge of the UN and Lutheran church incidents. I had no idea this was the kind of people I risked my life and the lives of members of my family for. When Peter returned to the border, he was not the same gentleman character I thought he was when we first met. I was not only sick to my stomach, but I was also paralyzed for a moment when he explained who the Dorbors were and his encounter with them in Freetown.

In retrospect, I began to reason why the Dorbors were unstable and moving from one place to another, and that also accounted for the ammunition catalogue they carried with them. When I heard all these things, my motivation to respond to the needs of the other members of his relative faded, and I decided to stop spending to feed them and care for them. Even Peter refused to take any of the other members of the Dorbors on the second trip that took me to join my family in Freetown. Peter commended me and expressed his appreciation for what I have done. He, however, wished it was his family I had rescued instead of the Dorbors and the Barclays. The reward, he said, would have been priceless.

The following day when James Dorbor heard about my arrival in Freetown, he paid me a visit not to thank me for rescuing his family and relatives but to query why I had to increase his burden by bringing so many members of his family and relatives and to demand monies that his wife spent to shoulder expense for what he called "people he did not ask me to rescue." He claimed that he only was interested in his wife and two younger children, and so the other extended members of his family were my responsibility because he never asked me to bring them; therefore, whatever expenses we incurred for them should be proportionately shouldered by me. I was already sick, exhausted, and weary and this man's response to the kindness and love I showed his family totally left my brain paralyzed. I was speechless and unable to rationalize the reasons of the man who a little over a week earlier knelt to my feet with tears in his eyes appealing to me to do all that I can to rescue his family. However, after I factored in the things I heard about him being one of those militants who massacred the Geo and Manor women and children at the United Nations compound and at the Lutheran church in Monrovia, I realized this man's sense of judgment, morality, and honor was impaired.

Chapter 32

Every member of my family including the nanny became ill, especially my pregnant wife, whose condition was assessed as critical. She was later admitted at a private hospital at Jumbo Kenyatta Road. Although I was already ill prior to my arrival in Freetown, I had to stay put since I was the only source of strength for my family in particular and for the group I rescued. After the two days rough journey to Freetown, my body crashed and symptoms of malaria also took its toll on me. In the midst of all these, a family feud had erupted between the Dorbors and my family. They had fabricated a story that Mrs. Dorbor handed me the sum of $4,000 (Liberian dollars) on Sierra Leonean soil for safekeeping and that I was refusing to give it back to her. The story was fabricated to show that a crime was committed within the jurisdiction of Sierra Leone. They had the support of a prominent Sierra Leonean who Dorbor had befriended to help them present the fabrication to the police, and I was invited to answer to their allegations and to be detained without any investigation. I had to post bond to be released. The matter was litigated at the circuit court in Freetown. The Dorbors could not get any of their own relatives, not even their own sons to testify to their fabrications against me. Some members of their relatives who had arrived in Freetown decided to stand witness on my behalf, stating that they can never repay me for what I have done for them. The fact that the amount that they accused me of refusing to release to them included amounts spent on Liberian soil (like the laissez passé they would have acquired in Liberia before traveling) established the fact that the amount was not given to me in Sierra Leone. The court ruled in my favor, acquitting me of all charges and the judge specifically delivered some harsh words in his ruling against the Dorbor family, referring to them as the most ingrate he had come across in his thirty years career as a judge. The court computed all spending we made in Liberia and Sierra Leone; from the nineteen laissez passers to the briberies and tips we paid out to militants to the clearing of our personal effects from customs including housing cost at the village, food and transportation from the border to Freetown, all summed up to US$2,150. Ms. Dorbor was asked if that amount could worth her life or anyone in her family, and she was silenced. She was asked how much money she left Liberia with, and she said it was $4,000 (Liberian dollars). She was asked if it was my responsibility to shoulder the total cost for their rescue and travel, and she said that she does not know; but she was responsible for five people in her family and that she was entitled to get back half the amount $4,000 Liberian dollars she gave me at the border. When asked how she arrived at getting back half the amount, she replied that the total amount should have been divided by twenty-seven people so that each person paid the sum of $80 approximately. She was asked if there was any agreement between us that I should spend and shoulder all the cost in Liberia and to be refunded. She said I chose to spend for all without any agreement. My lawyer asked, "Why then would you give Mr. Davies your money for safe keeping on the shores of Sierra Leone, your destination, and not in Liberia where you needed it most. And since there was no prior mutual agreement according to you, why do you now sue for half the amount and not all the amount you gave him for safe keeping?" To these, she had no clear answer. The trial was exhausting; and it contributed to draining my family down physically, mentally, emotionally, and financially.

My wife had suffered severe complications with her pregnancy and was still hospitalized throughout August 1990, and the children's nanny had sustained a leg wound during the first scuffle in Clay, and she was also sick. I had to care for the children while taking care of everything else as well as running errands between hospital and courthouse and to meet other basic needs. I never really had the time and resources to go after the Dorbors after I was acquitted as many people urged. I spent more time with my family until my wife was discharged from the hospital on that fateful day in September when news of President Samuel Doe's capture by Prince Johnson's faction of the NPFL exploded in the news. By early October 1990, we had little money left to pay our bills for five days at the guest house, and we were evicted from there. The eviction was another wrong that our family suffered in the blood-sucking system we find ourselves in. The owner of the guest house, Charlie Whitfield, ordered his employees to pack up some of our belongings and put them on the street corner because we owed him five days rental at Le.1,000 (US$3) per day. I took my wife to follow up with her treatment at the hospital on that day. We went along with the children and their nanny in order to complete registration with the UNHCR after my wife's treatment. Upon our return that evening, our belongings were on the street corner, and we were not allowed to enter the building. Some of our valuables were seized by him for the total of US$15 we owed. We were not summoned by the court or given any court order; it was only the management of the guest house who executed the eviction in our absence and seized whatever property they wanted. There was nothing we could do to bring Charlie Whitfield or anyone to justice because of the way the blood-sucking system was structured; if you can't buy justice or, in other words, if one had no money to bribe and tip every step of the way, they would only be wasting their time and energy and ironically setting up the pace for someone else to get bribed at the expense of their rights; to put it flatly, poor people in Sierra Leone then had no rights. The ordinary people around at the time urged us to involve the police, and we did, but it was a waste of time for us and an opportunity for the police to make money from Charlie Whitfield at our expense. When push came to shove, Charlie Whitfield went into hiding and was said to have traveled to Europe and that was where and how the case ended. We lost items valued over a thousand US dollars because we owed US$15. Even the police officer that was instructed by his boss to take down our statement demanded money from us for what he referred to as cost for "paper and pen" to write the statement and transport fare for him to reach the guest house management. Living life in that system was like living in an endless nightmare—it replicated the metaphor of the swamp mosquitoes, sucking blood no matter from who or under what circumstances. There was no protection for refugees only money protects one's interest, nothing else.

News reached my mother that my family was homeless, and she came and extended invitation for my family to stay with her. I was skeptical at first because of past experience. It was not the best decision for me, but I had no immediate solution to the problem. My gut instinct tells me that with her there was more and more trouble ahead. She and her children had been visiting us at the guest house frequently, and she had been playing the nice card so well to the extent that my wife felt that this could not be the same woman that Magnoose and I talked about in Monrovia or that she had realized her mistakes and have changed her wicked ways maybe for the sake of her grandchildren. However, we accepted the offer to live with her at 28 Berwick Street. Few days later, my wife gave birth to Jacqueline, the sixth child in the family.

The house is a two-story building, about nine hundred square feet with three bedrooms and two parlors upstairs. The smaller parlor is exclusively attached to the master bedroom, which she offered my family of eight to live in. One of the three bedrooms was rented out to someone else and that leaves Mum and her family of seven (the two Jacksony girls, Princes and Sylvia; the two Davis girls, Joliette and Patent; and Ambray, the policeman's son; and my nephew, Victor. By this time there were so many dramatic events that transpired behind me while I was living in Liberia, which Mum had instructed her children to keep secret from me just like they all did hiding the addresses of Princer and Victoria from me for a decade. There were tons of conflicts they had against some people in the neighborhood and in various communities, and indeed, there were issues that divided them just as there were other issues that united them. Princes and Mum had involved themselves with sorcery, practicing witchcraft, and dealing with mediums and with necromancers. Many people in the community knew about their dealings and feared both of them, especially so they were bold and defying. For example: Mum had seduced another man known only as Devil who abandoned his wife and children and was now hanging out with her. Devil, a retired seafarer, abandoned his family, sold his house, leaving his family including himself homeless while he used the proceeds to hang out with Mum in bars, partying until he went broke and eventually hit rock bottom, a place he never recovered from until his death and burial as a pauper years later. Princes had slapped and beaten up her pastor dad in open church and the church congregation was so deeply polarized in many ways just as the Rev. Jacksony structured it before he left to live in the United States. Some of the women he seduced and their friends and supporters had formed themselves into groups, and there were always some kind of incidents amongst them long after Jackie-boy— as he was affectionately known among them—left. Mum had also physically engaged Mrs. Davis (the widow of Mr. Lawrenczo Davis) in a fight at the church during Mr. Davis's funeral service. She demanded that her two daughters she had by him, Joliette and Patent, must be recognized as the deceased children before his remains left the church for burial. The police next block came in to quiet things down before the funeral procession left the church and the incident made headlines in local newspapers in the city. These and many more incidents, which were gossips in various quarters, were kept secret from my family so we had no idea that we had fallen into the ridicule and degradation surrounding Mum's and her household, most especially we did not know the danger around us from people who were also trying to get even with her for various reasons.

Sylvia was already a high school graduate and was working harder for admittance into law school at Foray Bay College. She had a job at one of the local hotels trying to raise fund to finance her dream. She was also trying to get her dad, Rev. Jacksony, in the United States to support her; but her sister Princes, being jealous, had already vowed that Rev. Jacksony would never succeed by putting her two younger sisters in front of her or over her. Joliette, Patent, Ambray, and Victor were also attending school. My wife, who is gifted in interpreting dreams, soon began to sense some weird differences. Mum was always with an issue and on a daily basis consulting mediums. She soon found out that my wife had a special gift in dream interpretation, so she began to share her dreams on a regular basis and my wife would interpret them most of the time to Mum's dismay and annoyance.

Every two weeks, the UNHCR would supply refugees' ration, and whenever we collected ours, we would share it with Mum as well. The United Methodist Church also assisted some refugees for a while, and my family qualified for financial assistance on a monthly basis. We shared with Mum in return for lodging our family whenever we got these assistances, but it appeared as though Mum had anticipated these refugee benefits as her reason for lodging our family. There would be an issue if for a good cause we delayed in sharing any of these with her. Few members of the Monrovia Chess Club (MCC) who fled the Liberian war often visited me to play chess at the veranda, but Princes and Mum did not like that especially, so if the ration and cash assistance are delayed or reduced, they would be pretty nasty with my visitors as much as with my wife and children. Mum was caught redhanded one day telling my children to get the f*** from her face while she was eating. My wife and I were held up at the hospital where we took Jacqueline for treatment much longer than expected and just as we arrived home unnoticed we ran into the scene and witnessed Mum using profanities to drive the hungry children away from her as she ate. I was not surprised, but my wife was disappointed and disoriented. Generally in African cultures, it would be a terrible thing to see a grandmother eating and driving her hungry grandchildren away from her with insults. My grandmother, Mum's mother, never once did such a thing to any child while she was eating, let alone her own grandchildren. She would rather stave than to eat without offering a hungry child around her. In contrast, her daughter, Mum, was heartless, wickedly mean, and selfish.

Chapter 33

Joseph DeShields was working at JFK Medical Hospital in Monrovia before the war, and he also was a member of Monrovia Chess Club. During the finals of the 1988 Liberian National Open Chess Championship Tournament at the YMCA in Monrovia, Joseph was my sparring partner and was in my corner when I defeated the German expatriate whom many thought was going to break my winning streak to the title. While in exile in Sierra Leone, we connected and our friendship became stronger especially after we jointly struck a deal with another Liberian named Vinicius Hodges who currently is said to be a member of the Liberian Legislature. Vinicius sold us his defective 1982 Ford Club Wagon that was impounded by the court in Freetown for reasons unknown to both Joseph and I. At the time, Vinicius was forfeiting the vehicle if it were not redeemed within a short period of time he had left. He then met with us and proposed that if we paid the debt he owed and redeemed the vehicle, he would then relinquish it to us for US $300, which was better for him than forfeiting it to the government.

Joseph and I felt it would be a good idea to jointly raise the funds needed to buy the vehicle outright so that we could run it commercially in order to sustain our respective families. Joseph had his five-year-old son Eric with him together with his girlfriend, and they were living with a Sierra Leonean family at Wellington Street in Freetown. During this time, refugees who had caring relatives abroad were likely to be giving some sort of lodging by a Sierra Leonean family in anticipation for some fees in support. Based on the terms agreed, we paid the amount need thereby redeeming the vehicle, and we then advanced Vinicius the amount of US $150 and made stipulations to pay the balance in a few weeks' time. To raise my share of the fund, I sold some personal properties and took loans from a distant relative of my wife while Joseph got assistance from his relatives living in the United States. After we made the required payment and the vehicle was released to us, we towed it to a local garage for repairs where we finally realized there was more repairs needed than what Vinicius initially told us. We did not have any money left to pay for repair cost, so we struck a deal with the garage owner to extend us a credit with the labor cost while we went about hustling for the required parts for the repairs. We borrowed US $100 from Mr. Raleigh Seekie, former assistant minister of Finance in the Doe government who fled the war and was living in Freetown.

The growing need for public commercial transportation services in the country could not be overemphasized, so our investment plan was worthy, but what we did not know about and never considered in our planning including repayment schedules we committed to was the fact that the playing grounds for people and business in Sierra Leone was not level. There were hardly any protection for businesses, and the adverse effect of black marketing in the country's economy was staggering. Those in authority connived with powerful people and business in creating artificial scarcity and by hoarding essential commodities including gasoline, which was needed in order to operate our vehicle commercially. The state of economy was a complete mess especially when it comes to availability and distribution of essential services and goods. It was so much of a mess that the average citizen preferred the living standards of refugees to theirs simply because of the little food supply that refugees received from UNHCR. Even rice as a staple food for the masses was also black-marketed. Instead of the government putting regulations in place and enforcing them for the sake of protecting the economy and the poor masses, its officials were individually involved in all manner of the black marketing scheme and protective of it at the expense of the poor. If there were any regulations to protect commercial activities, banking, and other financial investments, they were just for the books. After the vehicle was completely repaired, the hustle

DYSFUNCTIONAL ONE

for gasoline frustrated Joe and I as our vehicle was sadly parked 90 percent of the time. Many gas stations were without gasoline, and the few that has any were rationing it to two gallons per vehicle. The number of vehicles that queued at various gas stations for days before getting their ration of fuel was countless. But if an official of government or their contacts wanted a full tank in any vehicle, that vehicle would be allowed to jump the queue and served before those who waited days on end. Under the same breath, some privileged individuals hauled gasoline in tanks and stored in their yard for private use while other sold theirs at exorbitant prices. This puts us in a precarious position where we could not meet any of our scheduled payments to our creditors in a timely fashion: the installment payments to the garage for labor cost, the repayment to Mr. Seekie, the balance payment we owed on the vehicle, and other miscellaneous bills associated with its repairs. It was while we were experiencing this stressful situation that Mum convinced me that a man named Pa Willie on Sanders Street can be of help to our project through prayers. She said this man was a prayer warrior, and I do not know what I was thinking to have yielded to her proposition to have me and my wife taken to this man for prayers. We followed her to Pa Willie one evening for prayer and the result was disastrous. There were a handful of people we met there sitting in his sitting room waiting for prayers. Like a medical doctor, Pa Willie would call candidates one by one into a small room where the prayer is held. When it was my turn, Mum introduced me as her son and Pa Willie standing at the room doorway said a few words of admiration about Mum's children and then I was invited into the room alone without my wife. There was an altar with lighted candles on it. I was asked to kneel down with eyes closed in front of it while Pa Willie read scriptures with his hands placed on my head. Mum had impressed on us that this man was so powerful that his prayers were like magic, forcing the hand of God to react as quickly as possible. I yielded to Pa Willie's instructions to kneel before the altar with my eyes closed, and while Pa Willie was still praying, he ordered me to keep kneeling with my eyes close and my mouth open to take the Holy Communion. But I realized that the room became darker. Pa Willie had turned off all of the candles in the room and was forcing me to open my mouth to partake of a communion I could not see. A liquid from a goblet touched my lip and a little drop into my mouth as I forced my eyes opened, held and removed his hand off my head, spit off the liquid on the floor, and then I stood up and began groping backward in the dark to find the door. I opened it, walked out, and asked my wife to leave with me immediately. Mum came to the room door as Pa Willie was coming after me protesting. Mum then enquired what went wrong. Pa Willie explained as other candidates watched my wife and I walked away. Mum came after us to convince me that everything was genuine, but my wife and I just walked away while Mum returned to Pa Willie.

That night was the beginning of a very long and painful stomachache for me. I stayed up most of the night shitting my guts out. Each time I used the bathroom, I suffered excruciating pain in my belly and in my rectum. It seemed like humorous, which I had suffered years before, but the pain was different this time. I cried all night. Even the tenants living beneath our room were concerned and at some point during the night they came to see what was happening to me; but on the same floor with me, Mum could not come to see me. Instead she told generic stories about humorous the next morning. She claimed that she suffered humorous when she was pregnant with me and after she delivered me it went away and then I got it since, insinuating, that it was pretty generic. My health deteriorated over the next few days, but I had no choice but to drive the vehicle to make a few trips since Joseph could not drive and our problems were mounting. Creditors were mounting pressure, and our respective family needs were rising. Some of our creditors were threatening to seize the vehicle if they do not get paid, and at the same time, Jacqueline's health was deteriorating as well. These were real tormenting times in my life. I watched members of my family starve, including the baby, without any help. The ration from UNHCR was already not enough for our family, yet we had to share it with Mum in order to pay our dues for staying there. It turned out however that Mum had plotted to eliminate my friend Joseph and me so she can take over our vehicle.

Joseph and I went on a trip to Waterloo Town a week after my experience with Pa Willie and the vehicle broke down there, and we were stranded for three days. We could not diagnose the problem, nor did we have the resource to fix it or to tow it. We were stranded for three days. Miraculously on the third day, a sergeant in the military named I. S. Mansaray came to our rescue. He had been traveling to and fro nearby Benguima Military Barracks where he lived and was curious of our vehicle parking on the main road, so he decided to check it out. I was in serious abdominal pain and resting after Joseph administered some pain killers. Sergeant Mansaray enquired who we were and what the problem was. Joseph explained our situation, and the sergeant became compassionate and invited us to his house at the military barracks for dinner. It turned out that the sergeant was a mechanic, specialized in heavy-duty vehicles. At his house, he introduced us to his wife and children, and we ate dinner with his family. He allowed us to sleep in his seating room, and the next day, he towed our vehicle to a military garage at the barracks and had it repaired free of charge, but once the vehicle was repaired and ready to be used, we realized that we had little gasoline left in it, and we had no money. I. S., as he was affectionately called in the barracks, amazingly decided to strike a deal with us that puts his twenty-five years in the military at risk. His boss had traveled to Europe on vacation and had left a drum of gasoline in I. S.'s care until his return. I. S. was not sure when his boss would return, but he thought maybe in two weeks time. So he decided to loan us half a drum of the gasoline, and he asked that we go to the diamond areas in Kono District where transportation generates more revenues instead of running in the city where there are lot of competition and gasoline is a serious problem. The deal was for us to run the vehicle for a week in Kono District and generate more money and return to pay him so that he can replace the gasoline he loaned us. We could not go back to Freetown to see our families before taking off for the trip to Kono District because instinctively we knew that our creditors, who had been harassing us, would be waiting since we were not seen for a couple of days; and everyone was concerned about what was going on with us. On the other hand, we missed our families for several days and now leaving for this long trip without any contact with them was painful, especially so that we had left them with little or nothing to live on. We had given I. S. our addresses in Freetown with names of our respective family members before leaving. It was interesting to find someone after all who believed in us and entrusted us and that feeling was reassuring and encouraging. It took us two days before we arrived in Kono District. We arrived in the night and indeed we made more money for the first time since we got the vehicle. We passed the night in the vehicle at the general park in Koidu City, but I could not sleep because my health had badly deteriorated. All along I suffered severe abdominal pain, and even the pain killers I was using were no longer effective. The next morning, Joseph found some other drugs for me, but my health continued to deteriorate. We had loaded the vehicle to transport some traders to another town about two hundred miles away, but after the first five miles, I could no longer drive. Since Joseph does not drive, we ended up off-loading the vehicle and some of the passengers became angry with us. Since I could not drive any farther, we parked in a nearby village. One of the passengers realized the problem and decided to help me by contacting someone whom he knew in the village. I was then taken to a house where I spent the next two days waiting to die as my health continued to decline and none of the painkillers meant anything anymore, and Joseph became frustrated over the situation decided to drink the local palm wine and became drunk. We both wished we had not committed to do business in this type of environment, and we thought probably the best thing would be to get rid of the vehicle if we can find a buyer and then go back to Freetown.

On the second day, I became weaker, restless, and lay on the floor of the village hut, fighting for my life. A well-dressed figure of a man appeared in the hut, but my eyes were blurred and my voice was already hoarse because I cried throughout the night struggling with the pain in my stomach and rectum. Joseph had gone to see if he could hire a driver to run our vehicle. The man who I could hardly recognize was Mr. Raleigh Seekie, who had loaned us an amount equivalent to a $100 for repair of our vehicle. He grabbed me by my shirt as I lay in pain on the floor, and he demanded that I pay him his $100 immediately or he was dragging me to the police. I never knew that Raleigh would be that heartless, cruel, and wicked after he chased us and found our location and witnessed the situation with us firsthand. He stepped on my head on the floor and demanded the money or the key to the vehicle. I struggled to free my head. Joseph came just in time to explain our situation, but he would not listen and so the vehicle key was turned over to him. He went away to take the vehicle; but unfortunately for him, the vehicle would not start. I had always disconnected some wires from the engine each time I parked it. This was a way to make it harder for rouges who might attempt to steal the vehicle. If we were sleeping in the vehicle, I would not disconnect the wires just in case we needed to use it in an emergency. When Raleigh could not move the vehicle, he came back about an hour later with two policemen, and I was forcefully taken to a nearby police station. The chief police officer at the police station happened to be the elder brother of the Rev. S. P. Jacksony who immediately befriended Raleigh when he heard I was the one involved. Even though the matter is not a police case, but as fate would have it, I had become a subject to another Jacksony once more and only God must send an angel to deliver me from the hands of these men who took the law in their hands to increase my pain and sufferings by dumping me into a cell where I passed the night struggling without any help. My stomach somersaulted, and I almost passed out when I recognized the CPO as the other Jacksony who lived at Clark Street in Freetown. He ordered my detention without any investigation and I was locked up in a cell immediately. He took Raleigh home with him that evening while I slept in the cell. Inmates in the cell enquired of me about my pain and why I was there. I struggled to explain the situation, and they were all stunned and annoyed that the police would detain me for owing someone. They said it was a civil case, but they believe that there was something more to it than that. One of the inmates related to a politician on the district board then directed Joseph to request his intervention. The politician and his brother, Sorie Fofanah, who owned an auto mechanic garage, took interest in the vehicle, and instantly decided to pay Raleigh off thereby placing a lean on the vehicle. I knew then that we had a bigger problem on hand because politicians are excessively powerful and feared. They control the police and they are the law; whatever they want goes. They have paid Raleigh off not because they want to help us but because they wanted the vehicle for themselves. The two brothers who lived in a bigger town in the district decided to tow our vehicle to Sorrie Fofanah's garage while Joseph and I were left at the small village. They gave their addresses and assured us that when I feel better, we should come so we can negotiate how they can get there hundred dollars back.

There were only few huts in the village where they left me, and both Joseph and I were strangers. We knew no one there except for the owner of the hut that one of the passengers had asked to help us. The Fofanah brothers spoke with a woman said to be a witch doctor to help look after me but only God knew what this woman was supposed to do to me. My condition continued to deteriorate as she administered more and more herbal medicine the more I became helpless. Then Joseph left the next day to the big town to meet with the Fofanahs to update them about my situation and asked for help to transfer me to a hospital. I almost passed out when he came back to inform me that our vehicle had been repainted to a blue color vehicle and our service name on it which read REFUGE'S CAGE was removed and replaced with the name SORRIE FOFANAH'S

DYSFUNCTIONAL ONE

TRANSPORT. A driver was assigned by Mr. Fofanah, and the vehicle was now running. By this time, abdominal pain had overwhelmed me to the point where I could not stand up. I had to crawl to go use the bathroom, and I would cry like a baby. Joseph had used some of the money we made to buy food stuff for us and some painkillers for me. The situation was as such that Joseph was exhausted, and I was afraid for his safety. Since the Fofanahs have seized our vehicle, they must be sure that sooner or later I would be dead and Joseph, who is new in Sierra Leone especially in that part of the country where there are hardly any Liberians, could be in trouble. A week passed by, and I was convinced that my end day was at hand, especially when I think of the sufferings that my family could be enduring since I left nothing for them. On the tenth day before noon, I was lying on the bare floor inside the hut crying when I heard a knock at the door. It was I. S. Mansaray in military uniform. He had traveled over four hundred miles in search of us, and the drivers union at the general park where we dropped off our passengers upon our arrival in Koidu, the capital of Kono District, disclosed to him their version of our plight and finally led him to the village where I was stranded. For a moment, I thought this was the end of me. Raleigh Seekie pursued me, and when he found me in the condition I was in, he instead aggravated my injuries and suffering and left me to die. The Fofanah brothers resolved my debt to him, and they took our vehicle, leaving me in a remote village to die. *This is it*, I thought to myself, *I. S. would just put the nail to my coffin*. I could not look into his eyes for I felt guilty and was ashamed that the trust and confidence he placed in me had been betrayed. But I. S. was the Good Samaritan in this situation. He knelt down and held my head up, and he looked around the small muddy room and the herbs that the witch doctor was feeding me with. He then lifted me to sit up with by back against the wall and began smelling the herbs. "These herbs will help to kill you faster," he said as he gathered them all and trashed them in the nearby bush. He lifted me up and put me in his military vehicle and drove me out of the village. As we entered a bigger town, he stopped at a clinic where I was attended to by a registered nurse. Few hours later, I felt much better after certain medicines were administered with a much stronger painkiller. Then he disclosed news of my family's condition. He had visited them in search of Joseph and I and was compelled to provide food to last them for a couple of days, and he then promised them that he was going all out to find us because we breached the arrangement to replace the gasoline he loaned us. But he was convinced that something must have happened after talking to my wife who told him that there was no way I could have been gone this long without any communication to them. He said that my newborn baby was very ill and the other children were starving including my wife. My temperature went up again when he told me about the condition of my family, but after he revealed that he had to do something for them to help them out, I became overwhelmed with emotion and cried to show appreciation for his kindness. He eventually took my wife and baby Jacqueline to the hospital and gave my wife some money to buy food and medication. Upon hearing this, I wept uncontrollably. Later we drove to the general park in Koidu to find Joseph, and together all three of us went to the Fofanahs.

Chapter 34

The presence of I. S. in our meeting with the Fofanahs made a big difference. However, the Fofanahs cleverly put up the face like they were sympathetic of our situation and only wanted to help us. We realized that we were in a predicament. We could not repay them for what they were claiming that they had spent in order to redeem our vehicle from them. So they decided to pay I. S. for the gasoline he loaned us and then they gave him additional Le.20,000 (approximately US$30) to deliver to our families in Freetown. They offered to keep us in one of their guestrooms and promised to help me with the needed medical treatment and to turn the vehicle back to us after they collect all of the money they spent on our behalf from its operation. We agreed on a two weeks' timeline beginning the day they took possession of the vehicle for them to operate it and collect all of their money and turn the vehicle back to us. They claimed that some repair work was done by them in order to get the vehicle operating again. They also claimed money they paid to the witch doctor who was treating me, but I. S. rejected that treatment and warned never to continue with it. Before I. S. left for Freetown, he had a confidential discussion with Joseph and me in which he highlighted his fear and skepticism of the intention of the Fofanahs concerning the vehicle. He said if he had the total amount they were claiming, he would have released the vehicle from them, but he was also in a bad situation concerning the gasoline that he loaned us since his boss returned, and there is an impending inventory to be conducted at the barracks garage the next day. But he was sure that the Fofanahs would use their power and influence in the district to keep our vehicle as theirs and we should do everything possible to hold on to our vehicle. An additional three weeks went by after I. S. left, and we saw our vehicle being operated, leaving in the early morning hours and returning in the evening with the new driver reporting directly to Sorie Fofanah. I was getting weaker by the day as my health never seemed to have improved, and I was afraid that the Fofanahs could secretly kill me and get rid of Joseph who seemed to be a lesser threat to them.

Frustration led Joseph and I to argue frequently about what we could do to get out of the plight we found ourselves in. Soon, relations between us began to deteriorate as we argued about little things. He blamed me for not moving fast enough, which gave Fofanah the leverage to hold us hostage, and I blamed him for not knowing how to operate a vehicle and for his drinking habit. Each day that passed by without any clear vision about our fate unbearably increased our stress levels. I knew that if my health was good enough, the Fofanahs would wake up one morning to find the vehicle no more. For days we would not speak to each other even though we live in the same guest room and share the same bed provided us by Fofanah. The only thing we had in common was the chess game on the center table in the room. Although I would not see him make his move, I will make mine any time I found out that he made his. In a queer way, the last completed game we played depicted the complexity of the situation we were faced with, and by the time that particular game ended in a stalemate, I knew that we were in much serious problem than we imagined. Our dilemma was in a way a blessing in disguise. In spite of all what we were going through and the issues that divided us, something divinely mysterious was going on in Freetown for which we should be thankful that we were not there. Mum and Princes had planned to eliminate Joseph and I in order to take possession of the vehicle, but neither Joseph nor I knew about this plan. Probably, if we were in Freetown at this time, both of us would have lost our lives mysteriously. I knew what I was going through was not ordinary, and I suspected that the liquid that Pa Willie administered must have been a lethal liquid, but I had no way of proving it for sure, and I blamed myself for being so stupid to have trusted Mum. While we were so far away in Kono District, Mum tried to convince my wife that Joseph was the cause of my illness. She told her that Joseph was involved with some kind of sorcery that aimed at eliminating me so that he can take over and exercise full control of the vehicle that we jointly owned. She brought in a man simply known as Gbashey, who is said to be another witch doctor, and together they claimed to have found out that Joseph was the cause for my illness and that if my wife did not act to stop Joseph, she would be a widow soon and stuck with six little children to care for. They brought in some fictitious items already prepared and tied in black, white, and red cloth with an egg and tried to persuade her to perform certain ceremony in the early morning hours in the middle of the street. She was instructed to be naked when performing the ceremony and to call Joseph's name seven times. She was to bring back the cloth after scattering the items in it and spread it on the ground for Joseph to step or sit on it anytime he visited our family. She was told that after that ritual, Joseph would have seven days to live on earth. My wife refused to accept the items and to perform the action that she was instructed to do, and my mum became angry with her. She had tried to convince her that if anything should happen to me then she would be responsible because it was clear that Joseph was trying to get rid of me.

My grandmother passed away while we were stranded in Kono District and during I. S.'s visit to my family before he pursued us in Kono District; he knew about it, but he could not disclose it to me then.

About sixty days into our ordeal in Kono District, Joseph and I returned to Freetown in a cargo truck loaded with live stocks: cows, goats, sheep, and chickens. It was an awfully painful trip for me. My condition was at its worst. I could barely stand up by myself without someone holding on to me or without a walking stick. Joseph had insisted that the Fofanahs pay us an agreed amount for the vehicle, which was a good idea, but Sorie Fofanah would not yield to that. In a bid to get rid of us, Fofanah provided us with some money, about Le.25,000 each to go back to our families. He said he would be sending us some money later from the revenues generated from the vehicle. The amount he provided us was just enough for transportation to reach us in Freetown. It was a tough situation for us to go back to our families after eight weeks without any money. So we went over to the drivers' union for help. They linked us with this truck loaded with animals heading for Freetown. Since we needed to save the money we had for our families, we agreed to ride free with the animal truck. This turned out to be the most painful ride of my life. We squatted through the first three hundred miles, which took approximately eight to ten hours. Most of the animals were hungry and tied. They cried all the way through and so did I. I guess the animal cry overshadowed mine. The truck driver along with his two apprentices decided to spend the night in a small town. Since they were not responsible for providing us sleeping place, they left us to sleep with the animals in the truck. I slept on top of the truck where few animals were tied. Inside the truck was messy and the strong smell of animal feces was overwhelming. Joseph, for his part, had a bottle of gin to neutralize the unbearable smell. We arrived in Freetown the next day in the night and both of us went our separate ways; he went home to his son and girlfriend; and I literally crawled home to my wife, five children, and the nanny with the sad news that we lost the vehicle. That night, my wife told me everything that went on while I was away. When she relayed the socking news concerning Joseph's involvement with my illness and about Mum's intention to harm him, my blood pressure reached record high. Joseph had promised me upon our arrival in Freetown that in two days time, he would be coming to see me to strategize and decide a plan to retrieve our vehicle from the Fofanahs or to get them to pay for it. Mum came over to me to inquire about the vehicle, and she confirmed what she wanted my wife to do and expressed her anger that she (my wife) refused to do it. She assured us that she was going to do it if we can tell her when next Joseph would be coming to spend the day with us. Though I did not trust Mum, I was confused and terribly shocked over the fact that my friend may also lose his life under the pretext that Mum was acting to protect me from harm for that old vehicle. As I lay in pain during the early morning hours, contemplating on all of the issues, it doomed on me that my life was also at risk and that I had to do something to stop Joseph from coming over to Mum's house, and I had to do it fast. I awoke my wife and told her my theory of what Mum may have planned along with her daughter Princes. Now we could not tell Joseph what was going on because we were still confused and not sure how he would take it and what would happen to us and our innocent children if Mum found out that we exposed her plan to him. Joseph had insinuated that he thinks I was trying to double-cross him with whatever proceeds the Fofanahs may pay for the vehicle, so in my mind, I am thinking that if my wife and I disclosed this to him, he might think that was my new plan to keep him away from me so that he will not know anything about the negotiations between the Fofanahs and me for the vehicle.

On the other hand, if Mum was right that Joseph was doing something to me in order to get rid of me for the vehicle, then what would happen if I drop dead now that the vehicle was in the hands of others and Joseph needed me to retrieve it or get paid for it? I told my wife that we had to stop them both and neutralize this senseless saga. "How?" she asked me in the slightly dark room. I told her that I would make a case against Joseph at the police station in the morning, and he would be arrested for the Le.2,000 that I asked him to deliver to her when we were stranded at Waterloo before I. S. came to our aid. This would shock him and damage our friendship, and he would never come back here again. Mum would find out that we broke up for other reasons order than what she might be thinking. She would also be given the impression that I would be going back up to Kono District when I feel better to get the vehicle down here. This plan worked perfectly well for everyone. Joseph was arrested the next day by the police, detained and released on the same day as there was no substance in the complaint I filed against him. He was surprised and shocked that I would do a thing like that, which instantly soiled our friendship and kept him away. In retaliation, he led Vinicius Hodges to Kono District to face the Fofanahs with threat to repossess the vehicle if the balance we owed on it was not paid. These events ate me up inside till this day when I think of it because Joseph was such a nice person and a good friend to me overall, and he never deserved it. For me to have taken the line of action I took was troubling, and I have no excuses for that but I was cornered, exhausted from the illness and did not fully understood the weight and dimensions of my actions. Till this day my wife and I remember this moment with nothing but regret because we were both convinced then that Joseph was in no way responsible for my illness nor was he interested in attempting to cheat me in any way whatsoever. It was Mum who planned to get rid of both of us in order to take control of the vehicle. With Joseph and me out of the way, my poor wife and children would have been no match against the mystery and power of Mum and her daughter Princes.

Chapter 35

It was a hot April morning in 1991. I lay helplessly on the room floor struggling and coaxing the excruciating abdominal pain that has routinely hunted and pinned me down since my daring encounter with Pa Willie. The pain had intensely sharpened, sending burning sensation sporadically in various parts of my body. It was like a bunch of hot needles piercing my rectum continuously, igniting electric shock up my spine. I was thinking seriously of suicide for a remedy but the thought of leaving my wife and children in such terrible poverty at the mercy of the most formidable foes in my life—my cruel and heartless mother and her gang of bastards—fueled my will to hang on. If I committed suicide, only God knows what would become of my family. We had reached rock bottom; we lost the vehicle I invested my last valuables on and were engulfed with debts with no means to pay back. My movement was limited since I was seriously ill, bewitched, broken with no income, and indeed, hopeless. Tension was building around my family as Princes and Ambray supported by Mum were out making trouble with my wife and children. Mum, at this point, had been expressing hatred for my family in many ways, especially my wife who, through her gift in interpreting dreams, was seen as a bone of contention for her. Mum had asked that we start paying rent in cash for the space she allowed my family to live in, instead of the usual food supplies. Because I could not meet the cash payment on time, she and her children were taking it on my family. As I lay in pain, I heard commotion downstairs in the yard. They had ganged up on my wife; I managed to drag myself down the stairs to take her away from them, but they included me. I got punched, and they threw stones and other objects at us. Our children began crying and running helter-skelter. They were beating up the children too. Somehow I got hold of an iron that was set up to press cloths.

There was fire coal in it. I picked it up by the handle and slanted it on the head of Ambrey. A piece of skin peeled off, exposing his skull as blood came shooting out. The iron swung open, sending tiny bits of red-hot charcoal burning flesh as some screamed for help. Tension mounted and somehow I became strengthened to fight for my family. Mum went upstairs into our room and began throwing my family belongings into the street, and she ordered the whipping of my children too. The gang did just that. I managed to get my half-naked family out of the house with exception of seven-month-old Jacqueline who was asleep in the room. They picked her up and laid her on the sidewalk. Bystanders on the street rushed to aid and protect the deeply agonizing and traumatized children. The street was now crowded while the gang gathered on the porch overlooking the street and throwing curses down at us. Soon the news of the saga reached my mother-in-law who came over with the local load carrier (omolankey), and my family was taken away to squat with a family of six (husband, wife, and four children) living in a one-bedroom apartment on Kroo Town Road. I had no one to take me in, so I was sleeping on the porch of a casual friend on Robert Street. A few days later, Ambrey came with a police in search of me. He had filed an assault charge against me at the Adelaide Street Police Station where his dad was commanding officer in the 1980s before he took up a national security appointment in Liberia. Officers who were under his father's command decided to have me arrested and charged. There was no mention in their findings that Mum and her adult children started the fight; there was no mention of the beating that my wife and children took from their hands and no mention of the damages to our personal effects and of the punches and beating I received. Strangely, the report simply stated that I stole items belonging to them, and when they approached me to produce the items that I have stolen, I used the iron that I was using to press my cloths and strike Ambray on the head. The police started looking for me, and Ambray led two police officers days later to a house on Jones Street where I usually go to play chess. They met me over a chessboard

DYSFUNCTIONAL ONE

playing with Dr. Willie Pratt, a respected high school principal who was knowledgeable of the situation my family was experiencing. He told the police to go back to the station and tell their boss that he (Dr. Willie Pratt) was interested in the matter and that he will present me to the police station that very evening. The officers went away and later Dr. Pratt went to the police station alone and took care of the situation.

That weekend, I went to Waterloo Refugee Camp to collect my family's monthly food supply. I returned with a 50 lb. bag of rice, a gallon of oil, and few pounds of beans, corn meal, and bulgur. I carried these items on my head for a few miles, and just as I arrived at the drop-off place where my family squatted, there was awaiting me news of Jacqueline's hospitalization at Dr. Cole's Clinic on Edward Street. Exhausted and tired, I sat down to rest. The rest of the children were happy to see me and so was I. As I settled down to play with them, I noticed that my wife and Jacqueline were not around. Our host then approached me and informed me that Jacqueline was passed out and was rushed to Dr. Cole's Clinic. I took a deep breath and closed my eyes for a moment to exert and control my emotions and the pain I was feeling as blood came shooting up my head. By now my exhaustion and the slight abdominal pain that I suffered every step on the way coupled with the hunger I felt had instantly disappeared replaced by a torturing fear about what might have happened to my little girl. The only food I ate that morning was offered by a Good Samaritan. Earlier that morning on my way to Camp Waterloo for the food I needed help from a commercial bus driver at the terminal on Ford Street. I had no money to pay the fares to and fro the twenty miles journey. Fortunately, the first driver I approached was eating breakfast, and upon understanding my situation, he offered me to join him to eat breakfast first before the ride. I was touched by his act of compassion, and I was overwhelmed with emotion when the driver who goes by name of Balla, offer to bring me back to the terminal after I received the food stuff and offered future free rides anytime in I needed it. This was an answered prayer; a great relief as commuting to Camp Waterloo for various reasons was a real problem for which we were missing out on a lot of services for refugees. I could not hide my emotions as tears ran down my cheeks as I ate breakfast with Balla. The only burden I had left is the total of four miles I would have to walk with the food stuff on my head from Camp Waterloo to Waterloo Village where the Waterloo Bus Terminal is located and the other distance I would have to cover in Freetown from the terminal to Kroo Town Road where my family squatted. I ran to Dr. Cole Clinic and found my wife and mother-in-law seating outside of the clinic crying. "What happened" I asked as I tried to catch my breath. "Jacqueline had a convulsion, and she is in coma right now. They are not sure if she would make it," my wife said in a cold, sharp, but shaky voice. My feet almost crumbled, and my eyes went darker and almost everything became blurred as I struggled to keep my feet strong.

They disclosed that Dr. Cole had a policy that is unfavorable to our situation: strictly no refugees are treated at his clinic without referral from the United Nations High Commission for Refugees (UNHCR) unless that refugee can make down payment for services. It was a good thing that my wife informed me about this policy before I went inside the clinic to see Jacqueline and to have a word with the doctor in charge. When Jacqueline was rushed to the clinic in a lifesaving emergency, questions about her status and the financial standing of her parents were not asked. The process to save the child's life and to stabilize her started before her mother was asked to make advance payment. At that point, she disclosed that her family was under refugee status. The doctor threatened to cease the lifesaving process if there was no down payment or guarantee from the UNHCR in an hour. My wife assured them that her husband was in good standing and would take care of that as soon as he arrives. That was a smart thing to do then. She managed the situation up to my arrival, and it was time for me to take things from there upon my arrival. It is good to know that I have a wife who believes in me as empty and broken as I was. I first struggled to calm myself down and then I put up a poker face and quietly walked into the clinic and then I introduced myself and asked to see the child first. The child was lying on a bed unconscious with a couple of drips and other wires plugged into her nose, mouth, and other body parts. After that the senior nurse and I settled down to talk. She explained the policy to me and why they had such policy. She said that a pregnant refugee woman was rushed to their clinic during the early days of the war when the influx of Liberia refugees in Sierra Leon began. The clinic provided the required medical service and had this woman delivered her twin. They forward the bill to the UNHCR but the high commissioner refused to honor it on the basis that UNHCR did not initiate the referral even though the woman's refugee status was acknowledged. I know better that UNCHR would not do anything different in my situation, so I was not going to be standing there like a pathetic fool pleading for them not to pull the plug under my child. I forced a smile immediately and asked that we keep UNHCR out of this. "How much down payment are you asking for?" I asked, keeping my poker face. Her face brightened and she went in the next room to hang heads with the doctor. Moments later she returned with an invoice on which an initial down payment in the amount of Le.150,000 (approximately $400) was stipulated. I was prepared for this. "This is a hundred dollar less than our monthly support from my siblings in the United States," I muttered almost underneath my breath but made sure she heard that. "Can you guys give me a week to make that payment?" I asked, and not giving her any time to response, I said: "I would have to inform my brothers and sisters in the United States about the emergency and it might take a couple of days to collect the money in full from them," I pleaded. This of course was just desperate lies to buy time in order for me to get the UNHCR involved. I don't even know which state in the United States my brothers and sisters lived in nor have they ever contacted me since they traveled to the United States. But she bought my proposition and decided to go in to talk to Dr. Cole. I offered to tip her if she worked things out for me, and she fell for it. She came closer to me and lowered her voice so that no one overheard what she was about to say. She was going to convince Dr. Cole to work out a payment plan, and she would throw in a few favorable words for me for an exception to the policy. Moments later, she returned from the doctor's office to ask if I have any guarantees—any valuable items, jewelries, etc.—that the doctor would hold on to in place of the down payment until it is made at the appointed time. I was taking off my wedding band when she held my hand and looked over her shoulder making sure no one heard as she whispered, "You don't have to do that. Get something else, like your passport. Liberian passports are valuable items these days." I agreed and sent my wife to get my passport, which I tendered to the clinic. For the next five days, Jacqueline was in coma. I hardly left the clinic without making sure someone from our family was near her bedside. Throughout those five days I slept on a couch in the waiting room at the clinic at night, and I was able to forge a friendly relationship with some of the nurses and the janitor. Some of them would pray for my girl and offer words of encouragement. During my first night on the couch, I looked back at the events of the day that started with a driver's divine act of compassion toward me and by evening time I gained favor with a nurse on my side to save my six-month-old daughter's life, and finally, I was sleeping on a couch with soft cushion and not on the wooden bench on the pouch of a casual friend. I was thankful for all the events for the day, and I thought about the passport as well; it has been rumored that Liberian passports became valuable assets for many other nationalities trying to obtain visa to European countries and to the United States. Little did I know that my passport would become a lifesaver.

Chapter 36

Waterloo Refugee Camp (WRC) is situated roughly two miles away from the general marketplace in Waterloo. At the marketplace, there is a parking lot used for public transportation terminal where passengers usually board vehicles travelling to other parts of the country. Vehicles carrying farm products and other merchandises are frequently plying to and fro this terminal. The village is some twenty miles away from the capital city, Freetown. There were few commercial transportation plying the route from Waterloo Village to Freetown, and there were fewer passenger transportation plying the route from Waterloo Village to nearby villages and the refugee camp. Most refugees walked the two miles distance to and fro the camp and the Waterloo marketplace or to nearby villages since transportation was scarce, and in most cases, fares for transportation were a problem for many. The airstrip and surrounding lands had been abandoned since the late 1940s. Trees and thick bushes had covered the reptile-infested lands, which became home for scorpions, ants, and all types of snakes. Some of the trees there, however, bear fruits like mango, apples, oranges, palm nuts, etc. In early 1991, the government of Sierra Leone provided this long abandoned air strip to the United Nations High Commission for Refugees (UNHCR) for settlement of Liberian refugees. UNHCR then named the area Waterloo Refugee Camp and announced that all Liberian refugees should proceed to make this long abandoned air strip their new home "as is." Refugees were told they would no longer receive benefits or services anywhere else in and around the capital city except at this new site. Truckloads of refugees were transported to the site and forced to clean up the bushes to make the place habitable. They were given shovels, rakes, cutlasses, and tarpaulins; and it took days, weeks, and months for the refugees to build their tents and huts for shelter.

While these tasks were in progress most refugees lived and slept on the runway and in other open areas until their respective individual shelters were completed. In fact, tarpaulins for roofing were not issued until individual shelter reached roof level and inspected. If a tent or hut was not yet at roof level, the owner or owners would not receive roofing material. Materials such as bricks, sticks, rocks, ropes and etc., were produced of manufactured by refugees themselves. Bricks were made from dirt dug out from the ground mixed with gravel and water to make mortar. Water was fetched from nearby rivers around the camp and sometimes the frequent pouring of rain helped to reduce the strain and labor to fetch water. It was a very stressful living condition and the tasks to building shelters were exhaustive for the majority of the refugees; many were weary, sickly, and some even died in the process. UNHCR officials and the government agency officials entrusted with resources for the welfare and care of refugees took the responsibility as opportunity to enrich themselves while using the refugees in a number game to muster as much aids that they can get that would eventually go to the benefit of the officials for the most part. Therefore, all sort of stupid policies and procedures were formulated and imposed on the refugee in a bid to create and to maintain a stressful culture especially when it comes to delivering services and benefits. Several tents were built on both sides of the half-mile-long airstrips by the exhausted and traumatized refugees. Some who could not overcome the frequently changing and complicated policies to receive tarpaulin to cover their household extracted palm straws and other bush materials to manufacture their own roofing as the authorities sold most of the tarpaulins to vendors in and around Freetown. Rumor even spread that in order to justify funding provided for construction of the camp, the UNHCR staff, along with their governmental counterpart, even took photographs of the Kissy Police Barracks and used those photographs to donors to portray as the camp they built for Liberian refugees at Waterloo. Contract agreements were entered into with a quick-fixed architectural consulting and construction firm portrayed as builders of the camp when indeed it was the refugees who cleaned up the bushes and all of the messes therein and provided most of the materials to build their own tents and huts. The quick-fixed firm was linked to one of the UNHCR staff who was later recalled and transferred after the deals leaked out and was published in the *Liberty Now* newspaper, one of the popular newspapers in the country. In fact, two of the so-called consultants who sadly happened to be Nigerian nationals roamed around the camp for a couple of weeks claiming to be inspecting the buildings while at the same time taking advantage of and seducing vulnerable refugee women in the camp. The authorities however overlooked the fact that there existed at the time a regulation prohibiting consulting firms from performing both architectural and construction services for the same project at the same time. But these were just the beginning of a series of nonstop patterns of corruption to come for a long time. Within two years of the establishment of the camp, various types of bold-faced corruption that was deeply seated in the core of the country governance became aligned with all facets of refugee subsistence and benefits. The icing on the cake was sexual abuses of vulnerable refugee girls and women by the so-called officials amidst the variety of scandalous maneuvers aiming at using refugees as numbers to make the cases to donors for more and more aids. Corruption in Camp Waterloo and how those in authority get more benefits over the refugees was now the talk around town.

In 1992, the *Liberty Press* newspaper published an article entitled "Refugee Camp on Fire," denouncing and exposing massive corruption within various refugee subsistence programs. The camp itself, in the early days, was a death trap, totally unfit for human living. During raining season it transformed into a nasty swamp infested with mosquitoes, causing and spreading malaria epidemic for its inhabitants while reptiles hunting frogs, lizards, and other preys unfortunately pose serious encounters occasionally with humans. On a few occasions, refugee farmers plowing the earth dug out objects believed to be explosives and in one scary moment an unexpected explosion not only confirmed that but sent waves of shuck and panic in the camp sending everyone within proximity, running helter-skelter. During dry season, the camp was frequently clouded with red dust especially on windy days. Inhaling particles of the red dust was inescapable. In addition to these environmental conditions are the frequent challenges that the human habitats faced while living side by side poisonous ants, scorpions, and snakes that mainly stings and bites during darkness. Shelters at the camp were built on both sides of the runway while the runway itself was left opened. These shelters were plotted and grouped by areas labeled Section A–Z. There were no toilets, no electricity. Water from nearby river was supplied through water tanks installed at a hundred yards apart on both sides of the runway. The authorities selected a refugee from each of the twenty-six sections to serve as head of their respective sections. These section heads are directly accountable to a refugee committee, which comprised of UNHCR handpicked refugees whose loyalty to protecting the interest of the authorities order than representing the best interest of the majority was the very platform for its existence. Each member of the refugee committee was committed to betrayal of their fellow refugees in return for a little more special treatment. The overwhelming majority of members comprising of the refugee executive committee were from the Krahn tribe who considered themselves as the main victims of the Liberian war since leadership and administration of government fell into their hands when Samuel Doe came to power in April 1980. Although all of the ethnic groups were victims of the Liberian war, suffered equally across the board, yet people of the Krahn tribe living in the camp considered themselves as suffered the most, therefore, must be benefit the most over others. Somehow they regrouped in the camp and took leadership positions over all the other tribes that were also equally affected by the wars. This was however not surprising to many refugees at the time since a lot of Krahn rebel fighters under United Liberation Movement for Democracy in Liberia (ULIMO) were contracted by the military government of Sierra Leone in the fight against the Revolutionary United Front (RUF). The majority of the section heads at the camp and members of the Refugee Executive Committee (REC), known as protectorate of the authorities, were of the Krahn tribe that the authorities handpicked over the rest of the refugees to serve as the voice and representative for the refugees at the camp. This structure coupled with many unfair treatments suffered by the majority of the refugees led to the polarization of the camp. Later in 1992, following protests and demonstrations for upgrade of social services to address deplorable conditions in the camp, a clinic and a primary school were built. Though the operation and administration of both clinic and school were far below national or international standards, they appeased and quieted down sentiment of uprising that brewed amongst the majority of refugees, many of whom were cognizant of the fact that they were being used as numbers to only benefit members of the authorities. Hour of operation at the clinic was from 8:00 a.m. to 5:00 p.m. Mondays through Fridays. There were no medical services during weekends. A doctor who lived in Freetown was contracted with three nurses who the authorities transported to and fro the camp during these weekdays. Emergency cases after 5:00 p.m. during week days and those that occurred on weekends were not provided for, and they were expected to be on hold until the next working day if the patient survived. Also at school, all of the teachers were refugees, many of whom were not trained teachers, but they were paid $10 each per month along with the trained teachers. Construction costs of both clinic and school together with their various administrative and operational costs were astronomically higher on paper compared to the reality as experienced. A nongovernment organization (NGO) known as Cause Canada was contracted by UNHCR to assist with tallying, receiving, storing, and distribution of supplies. From time to time, the refugee executive committee would be called upon to assist Cause Canada with performing any of its activities. Some of the activities that member of the REC would assist Cause Canada with were mainly population censuses, distribution of food and other materials. From the standpoint of intelligence, the camp literally symbolized an allegory or dystopia of George Orwell's "Animal Farm" published in England in 1945. Although census shows about thirty thousand refugees on the UNHCR record, there were far less that amount of refugee actually living in the camp. Not only that many Liberians who fled the Liberian war did not register as refugee in Freetown, but some of them just transited while many others lived on their own with help from relatives and friends abroad. But numbers were advantageous for the authorities because it beefed up the volume and makes the case for receiving sizable returns on behalf of the refugees. When the order forcing refugees to come make the camp their home was issued, many of those who turned up to register at the camp and to build tents were those who had nowhere else to turn. Some showed up but were not physically fit to build their own tents while others paid their fellow refugees to construct tents for them. Others just simply registered under existing tents but were actually not living in the camp because of its deplorable living conditions. On days when monthly food supply or materials were issued or when certain benefits or events were mandatory, the camp would be crowded as refugees plus nonrefugees who also registered as refugees would show up to benefit. At the same time all manner of merchants and petty traders would emerge to buy stuff from the refugees. The total of refugees who actually lived in the camp could be under three thousand. My family was one of those registered under another refugee's shelter at the camp in the early days when it was established. After we hit rock bottom with no money left and no valuables left to sell, we folded and went to the camp to live there. We suffered a series of unlawful evictions eventually resulting to homelessness. In the fall of 1991, two weeks after Jacqueline was discharged from hospital, I took my family over to the camp, reregistered, and built our own unit at Section T, labeled T-12. While Jacqueline was in coma for five days at Dr. Cole's clinic, I pleaded with the UNHCR authorities for help, but to no avail, and the only way we could get help was to show proof of living in the camp. To begin living at Camp Waterloo with my wife and five children in a tent with no bed or beddings, no restroom, no kitchen, and no room for recreation for the children with little food to take us through a month was a challenge. We joined the many traumatized and grieving families; some single parents, orphans living in deplorable conditions that I can only describe as naked and destitute humans living and surviving life in a jungle. Truly, it seemed and felt like we had reached our waterloos.

Chapter 37

Corruption was decentralized at all levels of refugee resource management; from those at the top of the management pyramid down to those at the floor level, they all benefited immorally from resources designated for refugees. There were no effective or efficient internal control systems as those who were responsible to design and install one knew exactly how to create loopholes or to elevate the level of risks for fraud. Everything to do with resources was tied up to some cooked policy, regulations, rules, or arbitrary actions that deprived the rightful beneficiaries from benefiting. From population census to acquisition, delivery, storage, and distribution of supplies and services, the refugee community was constantly scammed.

According to many studies and established trends from recognized institutions around the world, Sierra Leone was measured at lowest point demographically amongst other nations in morale, economy, social welfare, etc., since mid '70s when poor governance and lack of good leadership led the country to its decline in good standings. Not even the office of the president or the justice system or law enforcement agencies would have made any difference to protect the living standards of refugees in a society where greed and selfishness in leadership has not only succeeded in creating mass poverty but created a culture infested with a catchphrase meant for justification and tolerance of immorality, expressed in colloquial as: "who-sei den tie cow, na dae e for eat," interpreted in English as "everything that is within reach (not earned) is for grab." In other words, since the income of the majority of the people cannot match with the cost of living and with living conditions in the society (and even more so that the leaders are grabbing wealth for themselves, their families, and friends), the rest of the masses can grab anything within their reach if they can. In general, this culture became acceptable in the society and set the pace for people, especially at places of work to steal, cheat, deceive, lie, or undermine somebody else or a good system to enrich themselves from whatever position they held or any responsibility assigned to them. The corrupt culture became so popular that if you are an honest person and you conducted yourself based on honest principles in the discharge of your duties and you have little or nothing when you retired or fired, you became a laughingstock to most people in the society, especially if one was placed in high position of trust in government, and at the end of their tenure or at some point during their service, they did not have riches for themselves to do things like—sponsoring their children abroad for education, constructed or own properties at home or abroad, riding fancy and expensive cars, owned stakes in some type of businesses, or having some hefty foreign bank account—then they were tabooed as outcast, labeled as unserious with a counter catchphrase in colloquial saying: "e nor cam for betteh." The roots of this type of culture deepened and spread like the tentacles of octopus to the extent that new generations accepted it as justified living conditions. By 1990 when Liberians were in distress and needed help from their neighbors, unfortunately, the mass population of Sierra Leone was already suffering severely from the very core of a corrupt system. Though the ordinary Sierra Leonean would have liked to help their Liberian neighbors in meaningful ways as many of them wished, it was difficult for them to do so. Instead the tables were turned on the refugees who became vulnerable to the system and were helplessly victimized in many ways.

In 1990, when Liberians began to seek refuge into Sierra Leone, there were hardly any middle class in the Sierra Leone economy. It would be fair to say that the rich were probably less than 5 percent while the rest of the population watched their lifestyle and living conditions slowly but painfully dissipated, leading the masses into abject poverty. As cost of living skyrocketed while government employees' paychecks are delinquent, say four to six months behind, it became harder for people to survive in the economic system. Even an honest monthly income earned from any government jobs or jobs in the private sector cannot cover average monthly living expenses for a family without acquiring subsidy from other sources. This is where the catchphrase system kicks in: "who-sei den tie cow, na dae e for eat." How would government employees and their families survive several months without being paid was never a serious concern to those in authority as long as their individual scheming projects were flourishing uninterrupted. These trends led those have-nots to submit directly or indirectly to the spells of those haves in order to get crumps from them personally to survive on, and as such, the haves see themselves as genuine providers of subsistence for interest groups and therefore deserve praises and adorations for their benevolence gestures. As corruption in high places continue to be a pride in the eyes of the people and acceptable by society, it goes without saying that fear became an added feat to those in power to the extent that the people dare not confront their leaders in any shape of form, instead the culture of adorations and admirations that fans generally display for their favorite sport clubs and players who plays for those clubs are the same that the ordinary poor people holds for the rich, the elite, and the powerful who are treated ironically as celebrities. People often gather in street corners like fans to praise, compare, and argue about them and about the exquisite luxury cars they imported into the country or the fabulous house they just built for a mistress or the schools that their children are attending abroad—things like that. Refugees were not spared in this environment. UNHCR Staff and their governmental counterparts, staff of the local Red Cross, staff of Causes Canada, and sadly the members of the Refugee Executive Committee quickly adjusted to norms to the fullest extent. Refugee became mere numbers used in variable bids to solicit supports or to justify budgetary allocations, which ended up privately benefiting the authorities and their families and friends. In cases where ordinary citizens undertook the responsibility to lodge refugees in their homes, the motive was obvious; generally it was in return for a portion of the refugees' monthly rations, and in other cases, it would be in return for a piece of whatever support that comes from relatives of the refugees living abroad. The resettlement program for refugees was the most cherished amongst the number of entitlements to refugees. It was the one thing that ensured durable solution to their problems. Resettlement programs are meant to resettle refugees in Europe, Canada, and the United States where better living conditions, protection, and opportunities for rebuilding broken lives are affordable and to some extent guaranteed. Resettlement to some extent is a win-win situation for refugees and most of the countries that offers it. On the one hand, some of these countries are seeking to beef up their human resource pools for jobs that their own citizens considers degrading and would not do, while on the other hand, refugees are delighted to be resettled in a country where life is good, human rights are respected, at least, and countless opportunities for excelling and building their lives are possible. It does not matter if a refugee was a medical doctor or some other professional in his own country and now would became a janitor, cleaning toilets in some European country as long he is no longer a refugee in a so-called third-world country and left all the hustling and bustling behind. At the expense of Liberian refugees in Sierra Leone, resettlement programs became the most lucrative for the authorities and were sold at secret auctions where highest bidders snatched the opportunity away from deserving refugees. The major players in this scheme were the staffs and contractors of the UNHCR and their governmental counterparts. Those programs in which a genuine relative of a particular refugee family living abroad filed to resettle their refugee relatives are different and untouchable even though nothing prevents nonrefugee relatives living abroad from faking as refugee relatives just to set the basis for these types of schemes. But when it comes to the other program category where countries' annual intake quotas are left solely in the hands of UNHCR, the fate of the actual refugees hanged in limbo as these types of programs were auctioned, sold for the most part. There were just too many schemes going on and too many people hustling to benefit from each category of the refugee resettlement programs. With respect to food stuff and other materials designated for refugees, many times these changed hands with merchants who bought them by truckloads and sometimes a better quality rice or goods are exchange for low-quality products before handed over to the refugees. At one time the whole month food supply for refugees disappeared, and there was no food supply for that month. Many other times the monthly rations were reduced because part of the foodstuff were sold or stolen. At one time, truckloads containing foodstuff reported to be on the way to the camp disappeared while refugees queued up under the hot weather waiting endlessly to receive supply that never reached them. The Refugee Executive Committee that was supposed to represent the best interest of their fellow refugees, unfortunately, served as front for the UNHCR and stood prepared to sign any document confirming that refugees did received their supplies and that the services at the camp were satisfactory. If visitors or inspectors came from Geneva or elsewhere to visit the camp, the Executive Committee was prepped by UNHCR staffs to make representations as though all was well. By 1993, the majority of refugees at the camp became fed up as the boldface and defying acts of corruptions and abuses mounted and the need for improvement in the system became necessary. So a few brave refugees in the camp headed by me mobilized to make constitutional the refugee representation system in the camp; hence, a referendum was constructed to the effect and put to the refugees in the camp to create an electorate system wherein the general refugees would participate in a democratic electoral process to elect committee members with a one-year term for all serving on this committee under the constitution. The referendum was subscribed to by two-third of the refugees living in the camp with exception of those scary elements who were skeptical that things might backfire and they would be marginalized and punished for their participation in what was described as potential uprising. However, the authorities used all type of scare tactics to quash our new movement known simple as Concerned Refugees. In one desperate attempt to scare off the movement, the authorities brought military presence in the camp and circulated flyers banning any act of politics inside the camp until further notice. But the opposition movement was already born, alive and few of us as leaders decided to meet elsewhere outside of the camp to plan and strategize. Armed with a draft constitution together with the referendum that called for the constitution, we petitioned the Waterloo Township leaders for recognition to our cause and after a while we won their recognition and the Concern Refugees petitioned UNHCR along with the government counterpart to have them recognized the majority voice in the camp, but they both jointly declared that in order for them to address the petition, the current Refugee Committee must sign off on the petition, but that was never going to happen. It was meant for delaying the constitutional process. There were a lot at stake and many secrets that the authorities would not dare allow new persons like me to get fingers on; secrets that these committee members were seating on and doing everything to conceal from the rest of the refugee community. One of these secrets was to do with the Refugee Burial Fund, which only the committee members and the authorities knew about and benefited from. When a registered refugee dies—as was the case at the camp where hundreds died from malaria, snake bites, scorpion stings, mal-nourishment, cholera and many other man-made causes—the Refugee Executive Committee would pretend to show their sympathy toward the family of the deceased and then collect the information of the dead for registration purposes in order to obtain death certificate on behalf of the family. The death certificate is then presented to the UNHCR office to start the process for obtaining an allotment from the burial fund, which checks were never delivered to the deceased family nor does the family knew that such fund existed. The deal was arranged as such that checks were made in the name of a committee member acting for the family or relative of the dead. When the committee received the check, they would cash it and share the amount amongst themselves and never disclose or deliver it to the family member or relatives of the dead. This was happening until in September 1993 when my dad passed, and I was desperately trying to raise fund to bury him. I obtained the death certificate and attached copy to a letter I wrote to the British High Commission in Freetown to be transmitted to the British Ex-servicemen League in London for help since my dad was once a high-ranking officer in the British Royal Navy (623) and had fought for the British during the Second World War. The British High Commissioner then forwarded my request to the Ex-Servicemen League in England, and two days later, I received a response to my request. The British Ex-Servicemen League does not have funding for burial of ex-servicemen, but they would assist the widow and minor children of the deceased. Attached to the response was reference to UN policy on the death of a registered refugee. Armed with the information, I went to the UNHCR Office that same day and met one on one with the United Nations high commissioner for refugees, Mr. Godfred Sabiti. Mr. Sabiti and Mrs. Thomas, the protection officer, tried to convince me to channel my request through the Refugee Executive Committee at the camp. First of all I don't get along with any of the members in that committee and, secondly, time was of the essence to me as my father's remains were at a funeral home in Freetown and would not be touched until I can make a part payment of the charges. I earlier had a family meeting with my mother, stepmother, and other family members concerning fund-raising for my dad's burial. The only money I had was turned over to my mother three days earlier to make the advance payment to the funeral home. She had announced during the meeting that my brother Princer in the United States had said that he care less and would not be contributing anything. She also said that my younger sister Victoria, also in the United States, sent word that she was not working so she would not be contributing anything as well. Unfortunately, it was not true as Victoria sent $1,000, which she instructed Mum to turn over to me, but she concealed it and converted it to her personal use and also held on to the amount I contributed instead of making the initial payment to the funeral home. At the time I had no information about all these, but I was resilient and I was going to stay in Freetown for a few days to take care of business. I couldn't afford to go back to Waterloo just to meet committee members to turn over a death certificate that I have already obtained.

I waited a long time at the UNHCR office, and seeing my resilience, Commissioner Sabiti finally decided to address my emergency. First thing I got from him as I entered his office was an accusation. "You are John Davies, the troublemaker at that camp, right?" he asked.

"That's why we have you as the trouble fixer, Mr. Sabiti," I replied as I pulled a chair he pointed me to.

"What else can I do for you?" he asked. "I have a lot to do so make it snappy," he snapped.

"So do I, Mr. Commissioner," I said. I told him about the loss of my dad again and what I am doing to raise fund to bury him and insisted on getting help from the burial fund for his burial.

"Have you spoken to the executive committee?" he asked. Continuing, he added: "These types of matters are channeled through them, and they present UNHCR with all the information on which we pay out a check to the deceased family." I explained that I cannot go to the camp for a few days until I take care of arrangements in Freetown, etc., and then I threw in something along the lines that the British High Commissioner was interested to know what the UNHCR would do about his funeral and that he might get a call from the British High Commissioner's office. Commissioner Sabiti immediately changed his position and requested the protection office at his office to provide me with the relevant forms for processing of a check. In turn, she assigned another staff to assist me with the paperwork, which was done in a short period of time. The staff handed me a ledger book for me to make sure the information recorded about my dad was correct. On the cover of the book marked in bold ink: "Refugee Burial Fund Register 1993 C." I briefly looked over some of the information in the register and what I saw struck me beyond belief. Flipping through the pages, I noticed three signatures in it which means that only three people were signing receipt of all the checks as relatives. I struggled to control my emotions over what my eyes was seeing and managed to forced a smile as I asked the staff to make a photocopy of the Le.50,000 check he handed me. When that was done, I asked the staff for a copy of the page in the ledger where my dad's information is recorded, and to my surprise, he did that just a few seconds before Commissioner Sabiti's Special Assistance entered the room. I gently thanked them for the check and closed the door behind me with a smile. Down the hallway, I stopped, peeped into the commissioner's office, and waved goodbye. The document highlighted two other deaths recorded the week before, and I was pretty sure that the relatives of the two deceased persons whose names appeared on the record did not get the checks. and it was so when I enquired that both families were astonished. Although I did not know exactly how many pages contained in the Refugee Burial Fund Register, but I knew it was not the first register for that year, 1993. Obviously, there were hundreds of deaths during the year 1990 and each year thereafter up to 1993 and beyond. It was also clear that each page recorded a total of fifteen names in the following format: item number, name of deceased, date of birth, date of death, death certificate reference number, check number, recipients. My deceased father's information was exactly listed as item 623 in the register, a number which left me dumbfounded as it was coincidentally dad's service number in the British Royal Navy as well. For his naval number to correspond to his name in the registry send waves of something mysterious in my head. Since that number was by far more than the number of refugee deaths at Camp Waterloo that year, my initial thought was that the number must be accumulated death that occurred since 1990 when Liberian refugees started entering Sierra Leone. One other thing that rings a bell from the photocopy of the page I obtained was that under the recipients' column only one signature shows recipient of checks issued for item 621 and 622. The matter was temporarily put to rest until weeks after my father's burial.

DYSFUNCTIONAL ONE

I first had separate chats with the widow of deceased number 621 and the relatives of decease number 622. In both cases, I just asked the question in a way that these families do not think that they were entitled to burial assistance even though they were. I asked if they received any assistance in cash from any organization, including churches or UNHCR for burial of their love ones, and they answered in the negative. This was good for the safety of my own family as disclosing my findings to those mourning the loss of their love ones might stir up serious uncontrollable anger, and the perpetrators of such a disgusting scam, unfortunately, could also do anything to cover up their dirty dealings. There were so many issues on the ground that the Concern Refugee Group, led by me and others, were fighting to make right; and this new discovery added to the corruption list was just something that may distract everything else and put the camp on fire once more. However, as instructed by the UNHCR protection officer, I paid the secretary of the Refugees Executive Committee a visit at the camp and provided him a copy of my deceased father's death certificate for update of their records, and I also informed him that I have already collected burial assistance from the UNHCR office in Freetown. Then I asked how come there were over six hundred death cases on the UNHCR files for this year alone when we do not have that many deaths in the camp. I guess he was surprised by my question and so he began stammering, blinking his eyes multiple times while trying to avoid mine. He stated that the record covered refugee death in the entire country and not just death that occurred in the camp or in Freetown. "This makes sense to me now," I said with a smile to put him at ease, trying not to give away anything. It was a good thing that I did not give him a copy of the register I got from the UNHCR office nor mentioned it; otherwise he would have suspected that I have more information that only members of the committee shared with their counterpart. Further investigation into this scandal revealed that ULIMO rebels who died in combat were also classified as refugees, and the burial fund was tapped into on their behalf. Any issues concerning ULIMO mercenaries were critical at the time. They were being disarmed and dissociated from the military junta that contracted them to fight alongside against RUF because of their involvement in havocs in interior parts of the country—havocs like unnecessary killings of villagers, looting and raping for which they were known to the embarrassment of the military junta which eventually blamed. ULIMO comprised of remnant of the deposed Liberian army that exiled in Sierra Leone after the capture and mutilation of the Liberian president, Samuel K. Doe. They are predominantly of the Krahn tribe with one objective to take power in Liberia by the gun and not through a democratic process. They were already furious about the capture and death of Samuel K. Doe, and they believed that they could conquer both Charles Taylor's NDFL and Prince Johnson's INDFL to take over Liberia or control some of its territories. Some of their leaders resided at Camp Waterloo posing as refugees and were overwhelmingly supported by the REC as well. After they were disarmed and discharged, a large number of them were brought into Camp Waterloo in truckloads to live there, to the anger of the majority of refugees residing there. The Concerned Refugee issued a protest to the UNHCR and the government to have the combatants separate from the refugees and to provide rehabilitation programs for them. Crime rates in the camp increased in a matter of hours after they were dumped and abandoned there by the junta. UNHCR was forced to talk the military junta government into addressing this serious issue, which did not only increase crime rate in the camp but also poses serious threat to public peace. Three months later the combatants were separated from the refugee community but not before the increased crime rates at the camp had badly ruined so many helpless but innocent people. Even after the combatants were removed from the camp and resettled at another camp about ten miles away, their intimidating presence at WRC was still felt as they visited their relatives and friends there frequently. This issue was already fresh on the ground when the burial fund scandal was discovered and after thorough investigation and sufficient proof that that was the case, the Concern Refugee

Group decided to make an announcement in the camp, distributed flyers informing everyone that burial assistance is an entitlement for all, and advised how to go about it to receive their checks in the event of death of a loved one.

A week later, we lost a teacher in the camp who was ill for a long time. His widow came to me to walk her through the process, and after she got her check, only then the camp was convinced that the announcement was real. There was no attempt made to expose the burial fund scandal nor did the allocation of the fund to nonregistered refugees like ULIMO fighters stopped, but what was guaranteed was the fact that Concern Refugee Group made sure that every legitimate refugee was informed that such funding existed to assist when the need arose.

Chapter 38

In mid-1994, the National Bank of Sierra Leone liquidated the International Bank for Trade and Industry (IBTI) after it was declared insolvent due to a number of corrupt practices that rendered it bankrupted. The bank's inability to effectively and efficiently discharge its obligations to its customers. IBTI was literarily being operated as piggy bank for a Lebanese tycoon known as Jemil Sahid who established it. I was contracted by the governor of the National Bank of Sierra Leone to join a team of auditors assigned to execute the liquidation process, and my task was specifically to audit the bank's fixed assets and report to the governor who heads the team. Jamil Sahid was known to most Sierra Leoneans as the richest Lebanese businessmen in the country, notorious for buying out politicians and manipulating them as he wanted and exploiting the country's economy to his advantage and tilting systems, rules, and regulations to suit his empire while enriching himself and his cronies in the Lebanese community. He bribed politicians, law makers and law enforcers who are willing to sell out their country for personal gains at the expense of the welfare of the ordinary citizens and their country. There was rumor that a fishing company he owned had exclusive rights over all shrimps in Sierra Leone waters by regulation over local fishermen whose catch were considered unauthorized and illegal.

By early 1994, IBTI began to show signs of not being able to honor customers' demand, and by midyear the situation became worse as more and more customers find it harder to withdraw their funds. The bank then began stalling and rationing customers' withdrawal and so majority of its customers also began withholding their deposits or diverting it to other banks as fear gripped majority of the general public. Rumors of the bank operating below central bank standards began to spread and finally exploded, sending shock waves and panicking its customer in particular. It was at this juncture that the Nation Bank of Sierra Leone stepped in to shut it down.

By this time, Jamil, who had absconded the country after a failed coup plot he engineered to overthrow the military junta government, was living in exile in England. My engagement with this contract slows down the Concern Refugee Group's activities at Camp Waterloo. I had to stay in Freetown during weekdays and on weekends I traveled to the camp to spend time with my family. The job required long tedious hours, and it was risky and dangerous because though Jamil was out of the country, his presence was still there and very much felt among the few staff that were retained to assist auditors through the liquidation process. The bank's workforce was downsized so only a few staff retained to assist with the process. There were no doubt that these staffs were either puppets of Jamil or that they were afraid of him so there were several attempts by them to help conceal bogus transactions and make things difficult for our team. On the other hand, there was suspicion mounting amongst members of the liquidation team, which did not surprise me since we were all in to put the final nail on the coffin in fulfillment of the doctrine: "who-sei den tie cow, na dae e for eat."

It was not surprising to me when an elderly woman who was not a part of our team nor a member of the bank staff visited me overnight at my lodging place in Freetown to propose an offer. On the day before, I had uncovered a scheming in which the bank periodically disburse funds for bogus machineries and equipment purchases on behalf of one of its customers who happened to be an accomplice in the transactions. The fraud was also extended to periodic disbursements of funds to a maintenance company for bogus maintenance contracts on the machinery and equipment, which never existed. The investigation established evidence linking a local maintenance contractor and a local representative of a bogus oversea machinery dealer in cohort with senior bank officers defrauding the bank hundreds of thousands of dollars over a period of eight years.

The woman was probably in her late fifties with light skin, about 5'6" tall, and had a bulky figure. There was something sinister about her grins and smiles that made me feel uneasy. She knew everything about the liquidation process, and she was well informed about the daily status reports, and she knew all the important players by name. In concluding her short commentary which was precise, sharp, and to the point, she said, "This is a dog-eat-dog business that no one man or group of men can change overnight, so take what you are offered and do what we are asking and keep your contract or refuse what we are offering and be kicked out of the contract no later than tomorrow morning. It is that simple," she said with a smile. She knew some personal things about me, including my chess playing relationship with the governor; she knew my bank account number with the Sierra Leone Commercial Bank (SLCB) on Siaka Stevens Street. She also knew exactly the balance on the account, which was less than Le.20,000. She knew about my family and about Waterloo Refugee Camp where I lived. She also knew about the small poultry and pig farm my family was engaged with at the camp. Like a frozen deer on the middle of the road stocked at high beam flashing lights, I watched her slowly walk away after a consensus was reached with me agreeing to cover up my findings in return for a slightly hefty bank balance by midday. She patted my cheeks before leaving and whispered in my ear: "Good boy," she said and then she picked up her handbag and slowly walked away. The deal was for me not to include in my report the two types of scheming that were uncovered. In other words, I was to ignore any material misstatements in the financial statements as far as fixed assets are concern, to verify the assertions and sign off on the fix assets audit as though I physically checked all of the assets with their serial numbers on records that they existed and all applicable depreciation provisions over the years were justified.

She was sure no one would countercheck my work, and even if it were counterchecked, I had nothing to worry about because everything was under control. It was a sleepless night for me after she left. Emotions were high and confusing. I had never experienced my manhood so belittled by the presence and authoritative assertions and command of a woman. I struggled between mixed emotions and periodically though of fighting back by doing the right thing for the sake of my pride, my manhood, to show her how tough a man I can be, but then fear kicked in as I considered the consequences of disobedience to a woman of her stature. I thought about the material benefit I hope to gain from the entire audit: a total of Le.120,000 in three months and the thought of being Le.3,000,000 rich in a few hours sent chills up my spine. Before dawn, all factors under the circumstance were weighted and my decision was not only reached but justified. I was not going to play the fool again like I did in the audit of the Sierra Leone Cocoa & Coffee Production Corporation in 1991 when I stumbled upon and reported significant discrepancies and the next day my assignment was abruptly cut off, and I was assigned by the subcontractor to take inventory of a small beer and wine bar on Pademba Road.

By noon the next day, I strolled to the SLCB to check on my account and indeed the amount had been deposited. I withdrew Le.200,000, and I went to one of the high-class restaurants in town for lunch. As I returned to my IBTI office, feeling confident as a newly initiated Jamil puppet, I wondered which of my colleagues, superiors, or staffs of the bank knew what I know or how much do they know that I don't know. I also thought about the woman. How many of my colleagues have she visited? Will we even know each other?

At the IBTI that fateful afternoon, I met a refugee fellow that my wife had sent to me with an urgent message. There was a grave matter at Camp Waterloo that demanded immediate actions. Cause Canada had distributed contaminated chocolates and biscuits that were declared not good for human consumption by custom officers and food specialist at the quay. The consignment of chocolates and biscuits were donated to our refugee community from the Netherlands a few months earlier, and it was designated to be shared amongst the children in the camp. Inscribed on the container was the wording: "Not for sale," as if the donors knew the opposite. Yet more than half of the container was sold to petty traders by the authorities. Then the news media probed into the matter and published a story about refugee biscuits marked "not for sale" on the general market. The authorities then stopped the sales of the rest of the products but still kept it while waiting for another opportunity to put the rest on the market. The products, which were near expiration when they first arrived, were kept for two more months and never supplied to the children at the camp. The expired product became infested with maggots and other incepts. The port authorities found out that the container containing the products was still at the port a month later and inspectors declared the product unsafe for human consumption. UNHCR was called upon to come get the cargo and trash it. But instead, Cause Canada picked up the rotten products and transported it to the camp. Then they used a substance named Sheltox—an insecticide used to kill mosquitoes, roaches, flies etc.—to spray the product, killing all the maggot and infected insects. And when that exercise was completed, Cause Canada then distributed the poisonous and contaminated products to the children and some older folks in the camp. One of the laborers working at the warehouse where the Sheltox was used showed his resentment and displayed the empty cans and boxes of the insecticide to some of the refugees and encouraged them to trash their share, but he was quickly caught by Cause Canada Staff who chastised him. The smell from the products was awful and disgusting as the messenger pulled a little of it from a pack to show me. Some of the kids in the camp began eating almost immediately when they received their share and some of the older folks decided to sell their family share to some petty traders who usually come to the camp on supply days to buy products from the refugees. The camp became divided over the product distribution, and soon a group of refugees went over to my tent to look for me and at that point my wife became concerned and decided to send someone to Freetown with some of the products to show me. There was nothing I could do to stop the distribution of the products or to stop these poor, hungry children in the camp from eating or selling them to petty traders since I was about twenty miles away. I took immediate leave from my contract and went to the camp in a chartered taxi. The laborer told me where the Sheltox boxes and empty containers were trashed. I verified it and then used a microphone to announce in the camp from section A–Z calling on all those who received the deadly supply to either trash it or return it back. But for the most part, my plea fell on deaf ears as many already ate some of their share or sold it to petty traders from neighboring villages. Within twenty-four hours, the camp began to experience massive cholera outbreak and in the surrounding villages too where petty traders lived. The epidemic was later used by UNHCR to justify the use of emergency medical funds most of which without question went into private pockets as usual.

This incident was the final wake-up call that led me to reorganize and legalize the Concern Refugee Group under a new name called AccordOne. It was then registered as a nongovernmental organization (NGO) and qualified to address and participate in issues of refugee concern, to hold press conference, and to attend joint meeting of NGOs among other rights and privileges. At the NGO level, one assumes the rights and privileges to meet any of the parties dealing with refugees to raise issues and to discuss them, to oppose and expose deeds, to effect policies and procedures, and to speak against those policies and procedures and regulations that could pose hardship on refugees or deprived them of their rights. In order to accomplish this, I had to engage the involvement of prominent Liberians who were not refugees but were living, working, respected, and influential one way or the other in the Sierra Leonean society including a Mr. Donald Redd who is an American doing business in the country.

The Liberians that were involved with this venture were Dr. Isaac Roland, who was then a lecturer at Milton Margai Teachers' College; Mrs. Welma Redd, a former Miss Liberia and newscaster who was then a staff of Mano River Union in Freetown (a joint venture corporative involving three neighboring countries: Liberia, Guinea, and Sierra Leon); and other prominent Liberians.

Since it was founded pursuant to the "Friendly Societies Ordinance of 1924," AccordOne automatically assumed the rights and privileges to operate as a legal NGO and listed as member of the NGO Coalition Conference. After AccordOne was formed, I rented a small office space at 13 Lifefoot Boston Street where the organization carried on its operations and employed a few staff. Because all of the prominent individuals involved were very busy people, the administration and operations of the organization were under my leadership as chairman. As a new NGO, our organization and officers were to be introduced to the Joint NGO Coalition Conference in their next upcoming meeting schedule to take place at the Youyi Building at Brookfields. Chaired by the chairman designate of the government agency, the conference was to be attended by a cross session of NGOs represented by their leaders. Commissioner Sabiti and senior officers of the UNHCR including the Cause Canada officials would all be taken by surprise by the introduction of the newest member of the coalition.

Chapter 39

The Joint NGO Coalition Conference took place once each month at designated locations in the Freetown area. During the early '90s, the coalition goal focused on the welfare of Liberian refugees; but in the fall of 1993, their scope widened in order to accommodate and address the growing number of displaced Sierra Leones fleeing the invasion of their villages and towns by ULIMO and RUF. Tens of thousands of civilians caught in the fighting had made their way into the capital city. At the advent of this massive influx of displaced civilians, the need to address the social and psychological problems that came with it stretched to areas such as shelters, foodstuffs, medical, sanitation, and to other services. These goals and the activities that came with them had to be effectively and efficiently coordinated, hence, the upcoming agenda to the conference brought more challenges to the table than usual and indeed the offspring of a new organization willing to be a part of the solution, offering a helping hand to the limited resources, was welcomed by the coalition at foresight. These type of conferences also allowed participants the opportunity to get to know each other and help everyone, including the leadership, to weigh and analyze the insatiable needs and to coordinate allocation of available resources where most needed. Business was called to order by the military chairman of the conference and following introduction of the agenda and reading of minutes of the last meeting the chair announced the emergence of AccordOne and read the list of its officers. When my name was pronounced by the chair, I did not think that he expected the same person that had been earlier branded to him as the troublemaker at Camp Waterloo. As I stood from my seat facing the chair amidst the applauding, it felt like a novice politician making his debut, his first formal public debut. The chair did not hide his surprise and so did UNHCR Commissioner Godfred Sabiti and many of their colleagues present. It was a spectacular scene. The applauding went slowly cold, and the air in the hall became intense. I caught a number of them exchanging glances and Mrs. Thomas seating close to her boss put her hand over her mouth with her eyes wide open; I guess she was wondering if she was dreaming. The applauding picked up again as Dr. Roland stood up, clashed his palms against each other as hard as he could. The applauding picked up and continued longer than I imagined, and I continued to bow as I looked around with a fake smile. For a moment I prayed that the applauding continued without ending to allow my frozen brain to defrost. Too many eyes were on me, and I was nervous to the point where I lost the brief introductory speech I had rehearsed and mastered the day before. Even those in the audience who had no idea who I was smelled something in the air. After the place became quiet and the chairman seem confused with his perhaps perplex stare at me, I took the opportunity to make a short statement indicating the core objective of my organization and introducing its officers. I then thanked the members of the coalition for all their past efforts and for welcoming my organization's membership. In conclusion, I pledged my organization's determination to work harmoniously with members of the coalition. There was another round of applause as I took my seat. After the conference, we were surrounded by supposedly well-wishers, some of whom wanted to know more about our organization and where we get funding from, etc.

The meeting lasted four hours and much of what Dr. Roland and I did was to listen and take notes. We had flyers on the table at the entrance, but it was not enough. As we walked out of the hall into the corridor, a small group of participants gathered there were apparently discussing about AccordOne. They were sort of reading and analyzing our flyer, and upon seeing us, someone called out my name, and we began shaking hands with them. Mrs. Thomas stretched her hand and so did the commissioner who pulled my hand tightly closer to himself, looking into my eyes with a rather sinister smile on his face, sarcastically asking questions after questions with his native Uganda accent and under the breath answering his own questions as he asked them. "What's this AccordOne thing about? Is it another Refugee Executive Committee? Or is it another effort to abort or replace it?" I leaned forward very close to him and looked over my shoulder as if I don't want others to hear what I was going to say. "Yes, Commissioner, you almost got it right. This is the independent check and balance arm of the Refugee Executive Committee. It is here to play a small role that is doomed to make the bigger differences in the affairs concerning refugees," I said. He let go his grip and pulled himself back, and we both exchange sarcastic grins as we eyed each other. We all walked out of the building together where their fancy vehicles were parked, engine roaring with drivers waiting behind wheels for them while Dr. Rolland and me walked to the street sidewalk to catch a Poda Poda (public bus). As the commissioner and his entourage drove passed us, they waved with provoking smiles. Dr. Rolland and me exchanged glances and laughed out loud. Our organization was young, underfunded, and could not afford a vehicle; but one thing was clear and understandable: it was a formidable force, forcing a change in the dynamics and the major players sensed that, and indeed, in the eyes of the refugee community, the birth of a brave voice for the voiceless was born. It felt like game was on.

Chapter 40

CTO King III arrived in Freetown in the fall of 1994 to join his wife who had just been accredited with the highest United Nation job in the country. As resident representative to Sierra Leone, the Uganda national would be the first female to hold the highest office a woman could possible hope for in a male-dominated environment. Although this may have humiliated Sabiti a little, but somehow he managed to find courage with the fact that they are both Ugandans. Yes, somehow Kofi Anna's head may have been brewed in an African pot to have a Ugandan pair heading two of his organization's agencies in an African nation. It was interesting to see a woman holding such prestigious portfolio and by all accounts her proud husband, CTO, as he is affectionately called, born with the silver spoon in his mouth, made a perfect combination as he enjoys the dignity, privilege, favor, and admiration that comes with the office. As a grandson of a former president of the Republic of Liberia, fame, money, flamboyance, and aristocracy are nothing new to CTO. A tall handsome figure, CTO inherited several real estate properties in Liberia from his wealthy family line. He owned and operated several businesses in Liberia, mostly some type of financial service entities prior to the war. He is known to attempting to set up some type of financial service company in every country he stepped foot in even if he was just in transit. Now that he has accompanied his wife to base in Freetown, it was befitting of CTO to attempt to set up a financial service company named Sierra Leone Financial Services LTD to serve as a subsidiary to his African Financial Services (AFS) in Baltimore, Maryland.

To set this entity up, CTO needed an assistant, and this is where I came in. As fate would have it, my IBTI contract expired just in time for me to transition into the new contract to research and assist in the formation of the Sierra Leone Financial Services LTD (SLFS). Coincidentally, my half-sister from dad's former marriage, Shirley Davies, was the CPA for CTO's African Financial Services in Baltimore. Both Mr. and Mrs. King were astonished to learn that Shirley, their accountant in the United States, is my half-sister. My relationship with the couple began to grow as they entrusted me with personal tasks that I was willing to perform for them outside of the SLFS contract especially when they were traveling abroad for conferences or for vacations. I happened to be in the company of the couple one evening at their Cape Sierra Hotel Suite shortly before the couple moved into their official Congo Cross Resident when Commissioner Sabiti and other dignitaries paid a visit, and I was privileged to have socialized together in the circle. Both Sabiti and I hid our differences and at one point I noticed the commissioner became erratic in his response to a question concerning Waterloo Refugee Camp. I guess he was embarrassed with my presence, so he stammered his way through it as he eyed me from the corner of his eyes.

Whenever the Kings traveled abroad, a fleet of official United Nations vehicles would be available for my use to accomplish various tasks. Oftentimes, I would select one of best to drive around town, and at some other times, I would drive slowly on the airstrip at the refugee camp and let as many people catch a glimpse of me as that sent different messages to different sects of the refugee community, leaving them puzzled as to how come I was driving around with Commissioner Sabiti's bosses vehicles. Before my contract with AFS ended, CTO and I had reviewed the possibility of serving as agent for a Canadian immigration firm that was processing Canadian immigration applications. The Canadian firm was looking for middleman services to help compile the application of applicants in Sierra Leone and facilitate the application process. A minimum fee would be paid by the applicants to the middleman followed by commission from the Canadian firm base on success cases. AFS or SLFS are both not registered to perform these types of services to serve as agent for the Canada firm but AccordOne is. CTO wanted AccordOne to assume the position but insisted on signing a contract with my organization for a higher percentage of the proceeds from these services because it was through his connections that the need for the service was revealed. AccordOne was a befitting organization for the program because it was registered to assist refugees and displace persons in various ways including assisting with resettlement programs. It was difficult to negotiate the percentage with CTO for the referral because it seem like he wanted control of the proceeds, and he would handout as little as 15 percent to my organization. The firm in Canada needed to move forward with the agreement while CTO was busy holding everyone up as he hired someone else to set up a new nonprofit organization to take up the agreement even though he had originally forwarded AccordOne initially to the firm. The only source of funding AccordOne depended upon was the small poultry and pig firm project that my family ran in the camp and whatever money left off the IBTI bribery and contract and the SLFS contract.

In February 1995, the SLFS contract ended, and I switched on to work on an agricultural loan I had applied for from Yoni Rural Bank I audited in the fall of 1992. By early April 1995, the farm project acquired the loan of Le.5,000,000 for expansion of my family's farm project at Camp Waterloo. Unfortunately, a large part of this loan spent on feeds and other farm products and materials would end up in the hands of RUF rebels who evaded and capture Waterloo Refugee Camp on April 21, just a few days following the approval and acquisition of the loan. The AccordOne operational costs were putting a toll on my family's farm resources, and I was beginning to consider other avenues including the CTO proposal.

Chapter 41

A couple of days following my acquisition of the agricultural loan rumors began circulating in the camp that RUF was within reach of the camp. The sources of this particular rumor was ULIMO ex-fighters whom themselves had been terrorizing some of the refugees in the camp. Many thought they were coming up with their usual tactics in order to create panic so that they use the opportunity to steal properties of those fleeing. I happen to be one of those who never believed in the rumor. On April 15, 1995, the unthinkable happened. My wife left the camp for Freetown that fateful morning to pick up a truckload of feed we had paid for the day before. A week earlier we were buying and receiving farm products and material for the expansion project for which we acquired the loan. At about 4:00 p.m., I was cooking dinner outdoors right in front of our hut and two of our children, eight-year-old Harry and Harriette (twins), were running errant for me within the camp. Shirley was using the bathroom at the back of the hut while her twin partner, Gracious and Jacqueline, were helping me out with the cooking. The two kids were playing around and having fun when suddenly we started hearing loud noises in and around the camp and then people started running helter-skelter in the camp, some crying out loud as they ran. The three guys who help out with our farm work sprung from nowhere with members of their families running as fast as they could. They called out at me to gather my family and leave the camp immediately, and before I could figure out what was going on, they disappeared into the bushes. Someone else on the run yield out: "Mr. Davies, gather your family and leave now. RUF rebels has entered our camp." There were two carpenters I hired to do extension work on the farm; these two came running pass me leaving all their tools behind. My niece had just arrived from the river where she had gone to do the laundry. She was hanging up the cloths under the sun to dry. Gunshots took over the camp from the far end of the camp where section A begins. By this time I am in total shock and unprepared for action, but I could not leave without my children. More people kept running past my way and I headed toward where Harry and Harriette should be at either Section G or I. They had gone to collect debts from two people who owed us at Section I and G respectively. Shirley returned from the bathroom to join us before I left. Every one of my household at the point became frightened. I don't remember what I said to Nancy, one of our domestic workers who usually called me Uncle, as I ran down the footpath behind the hut to find Harry and Harriette, but that was the last time I saw her alive. I barely covered fifty yards when I saw the two kids running toward me. I took a deep breath of relief and together we ran back to the hut to get the others, but they were not where I had left them moments ago. The sound of shootings was getting closer and closer, and the impact of bullets can be heard hitting hard surfaces. I ran into the house and picked up a shirt and my business bag and found the children hiding inside. I gathered them for us to leave, but it was too late. In rushing, I fell and badly cut my right knee open. An old wound that was stitched long years ago and healed is widely open again, and my foot paralyzed momentarily; I could barely move it. I thought that we could run across the runway toward the bush road leading to Waterloo Village, but bullets were flying all over the place; no doubt that RUF presence is taking shape in the Camp Waterloo. Confused and panic, I gathered the remnant of my family back into the house. Like many of the refugees, we had demolished our palm straw tent in 1992 and built a mud house, and in 1993, I had demolished the mud house and built a two-bedroom concrete house plastered with cement with wooden doors and windows. Bullets hit the house while we were inside, and I laid everyone on the floor and placed baggage on top of us. We heard footsteps and heavy gun firing, and it seem Camp Waterloo has become battleground for the military government and RUF fighters. Finally, RUF took over the camp after the battle that left many dead including camp securities. The RUF fighters began their search of every home in the camp making sure everything is under their control. Their gun firing becomes sporadic after 7:00 p.m. I could hear distant sounds of breaking, which tells me that homes were being broken in to. They might probably not reach my unit soon enough before darkness at which time I intend to escape via the bush with my children. How dangerous that would be in going through the dark reptile-and-scorpion-infested bushes with five children to make this escape would be a challenge. But what choice do I have? RUF has a pattern of hacking off the arms of their captives mercilessly from newborn babies to any age group and to see them hacking off the hands of five children of mine would be over my dead body for I do not think I could witness such savagery in the face of my unfliching love for children, let alone mine that I love so dearly. Suddenly it dawn on me that Nancy is not with us in the house and none of the children could account for her. She must have run off after I left to find Harry and Harriette. As we lay in the dark, hungry, panicky, shaky, and worried about the worst that might happen to us in this situation and about my wife and how she would take the news. I reached for my portable radio and used the headphone to listen to the local news and BBC Africa. The military spokesperson on the local news downplayed the falling of Waterloo to RUF rebels and called it propaganda even in the face of credible references—the people who fled nearby villages, trekking several miles toward the capital with their baggage. Though foreign media were reporting the capture of villages around the Waterloo area, yet the military government spokesperson being interviewed on the local news bended on deception and insisted that those who fled were cowards, which made some of us who did not have a chance to flee look like heroes. Another media report claimed that the camp had fallen to the rebels so easily without much resistance from the government troop. The military spokesman denied the capturing of the camp and claimed that the camp is a UN grounds and would not be attacked or taken over by neither sides. As I lay there on the floor I think about how happy Commissioner Sabati and his staff would be to collect buried fund for all of those who might have lost their lives. The thought of him collecting mine felt creepy. Later, I froze as I listened to reporters pounding questions at him and fewer other Liberian refugees. He would not say the camp was taken over by RUF for that would conflict the position of the government. The reporter said that they had confirmed report that all the refugees were on the street except for the dead yet he denied. Moments later, excerpt of the interview of some group of refugees was aired. One refugee quoting another said that they are pretty sure the securities at the gate were ambushed and killed and few of the refugees who could not escape got shot. He said that there were some refugees who could not be rescued neither helped with the wounds they received from gunshots. Upon hearing the refugee's account, a chill crept up my spine, sending my whole body paralyzed. Before 8:00 p.m. the camp turned dark and relatively quiet except for sporadic gun firings. For about half an hour, we have not heard any close gunshot, but suddenly the sounds of dogs barking and fighting came close as though they were in the house with us. My first thought was that they may have been fighting over mating because this is usually the main cause of dog fighting in the camp. It turned out that the dogs were fighting over the food that I was cooking outdoor. Suddenly a close gunshot and the sound of pandemonium among the dogs as they fled and louder desperate dog cries and then footsteps of humans coming closer and then voices and laughter. RUF was near our doorsteps and indeed on our porch. Then a loud bang sound next door at my immediate neighbor's house. Someone was breaking their door. The Flomos had taken to their heels on the first call. In fact the man ran away without any shirt on and his wife held her slippers in hands as she followed him, and they both joined the first group of escapees. The next house would be ours, I convinced myself, and my heart pounded so loud that I could hear it. I held on to my children on the floor, and I died a little. This is the most dangerous moment of my life.

DYSFUNCTIONAL ONE

If I should die, I must make my children run into the bushes while I sacrifice myself, I thought. But how was that going to happen, I had no idea. I whispered to them that we are going to be attacked, but they should not worry and be calm. "Get ready to run as fast as you can into the bushes and stay there until we get help," I whispered. One of them asked if I would run with them, and I promised to do everything to make them safe. The youngest, five-years-old Jacqueline, asked if she should join in running in the dark into the bushes and why we had to run. I explained about how these wicked men attacked other places and people and how people run for their lives. She recalled the many happy ending stories I have told them at bedtime and the pranks that I would call magic, like the tricks I played to make candies appeared and disappeared; so she whispered that I should make magic so we can disappear and that they can't find us. I smiled at how serious she sounded but too paralyzed to think of any solution at the moment. A voice in the outside asked in the local language if everything was all right and the response was not heard, but I surmised then that they were finished with my neighbor, and we were next any moment. Then something was said and then loud laughter and then a bang; the first attempt to break our front door. I little while before then I wished I could grab a bucket full of fresh stinking human feces from the back yard or the mess from the pig pen and scatter it on the porch and on the walls in the seating room and hoping that the smell would repel intruders, but all of those thought going through my head required time which was not on our side. Like in a chess games, if the element of time is not on your side, then value of the other elements may diminish. We are at the verge of being checkmated and the best move here seem to honorably resign if there are no zugzwang options. But our opponent in this situation does not have any decency nor the discipline and certainly without principles. They are cannibals and at all times drugged, drunk, unreasonable, trigger happy, and ruthless. Not even dogs are spared by these ruthless bastards. The second bang at the door swung it wide open and panic and fear took its toll.

JOHN DAVIES

One child yield and another and another as frozen as I became I just lay there on the floor looking into the powerful torch lights as their arrays pierce everywhere followed by commanding voices ordering everyone to walk outside with their hands on their head. We were terribly scared, and I just found myself surrounded by the kids while the younger one, Jacqueline, curled herself into my sore lap and the others tightened their grip of me. It all happened so fast and as the last warning came to proceed outside or face the consequences, the fear that once engulfed me just disappeared, and slowly with hands on my head I led my children to face our captors.

Chapter 42

I don't know who among the five rebels present slammed me with the introductory slap across my face, but it sure felt like it was delivered from a mighty but seniority hand. When the slap landed, I saw a flash of daylight as I fell on my knees. The gunshot that followed left me completely paralyzed momentarily. The children went into frenzy, and they were quieted down with a couple of slaps and all of them place in the far corner of the porch. The beating then continued for a little while and then one of them asked, "Who else is hiding in there?" And I replied no one else. At that point the interrogation began, and they wanted to know who I was and what my motive for staying is when everyone else fled and the children too had to answer a few question while crying and pleading for them to stop beating up their dad. Bleeding from several wounds I sustained plus swelling on my head and shoulders as a result of kicks and gun-butt beating, I sat on the ground while they asked the questions. Out of the blue, I asked that they listen to me if they really want to know why I am still in this camp. "I know that this would sound strange to you guys, but I was waiting for your coming since I believed your presence would end the fear and maltreatment my family has been suffering in the hands of corrupt government officials and the UNHCR staff who squander almost everything that is our benefits. Two weeks ago your coming was rumored and if I considered you guys an enemy, I would have packed up my family and my business and leave the camp but instead I decided to get more farm products and feeds to keep livestock going for you as my contribution toward the fight to overthrow this corrupt military government."

"Are you not a ULIMO fighter or sponsor?" one of them asked.

"No way," I snapped. I explained that I wrote the petition that removed ULIMO fighters that were dumped here in this camp. I spoke of the major troubles ordinary people are going through in this camp and how I provided an alternative way of fighting for justice and equality and how each time the government would stand in the way to bring us back to square one. One of them was beginning to be convinced and the others wanted my fate to be decided by their commander. They asked about my poultry and the pig farm, which I was sure they would be interested in, and I also mentioned that we have a warehouse full of feed for the livestock in the capital city where my wife went to pick up a few products. By this time all five of them are halfway into the zugzwang position being created. One of them splashed some water on my face from a small bucket of water that sat on the railing. It felt better. "So you want to join us, is that what you are saying?" he asked. With a smile on my face, I said, "I am already a part of you because the same thing that motivates you motivates me and the same end result you want is what I want and that is why I am not your enemy nor are you my enemy, but instead we share a common goal, but we now need to build trust and I am sure that I can play an important role and be a trusted partner. Why would I put the most important things in my life on the line if I did not have any faith in RUF? My children and my life and all that I have?" I asked.

There was quietness while minds work and then the senior guy said. "We would take you to spend the night with us and your children would stay right here by themselves until tomorrow. Your faith would be in the hands of our commander. There is no guarantee of safety for you or for your children as things can change any time. We are at war." Moments later another group from Section Z came and reported their mission and together we all walked down to the clinic that is now their base in the camp. The thought of leaving my children behind paralyzed me every step on the way and that was the longest night of my life. "Where is the poultry farm located?" they asked. I pointed to the barns at the back of the building and hesitated as I saw one flashlight rested on a dead dog that has been shot. It was the dog that they shot earlier. I agreed to show them around the farm in the morning during daylight. At their base they decided to have me tied up for the night because they claimed that they have not trusted me yet and that they may have an assignment for me in the morning to prove if I should be trusted, but for security, they would have me tied up till tomorrow. "We don't have any cell of jailhouse to keep you, but we would do what we do to everyone else until we trust you are a part of us. Right now our commander is not here to decide you and your children's fate, and you should be thankful that head is still seating on your shoulder and your children are not yet meat for the vultures."

My feet were bound and my hands also bound behind my back and then they threw me under one of the clinic bed and promised that they would patrol the camp and check on my children and warned that I do not try anything funny. There was a shot fired every hour for reasons I cannot tell. Throughout the night, I thought about my children's safety, and I think about what they would have me do in the morning. I hope it was not any stupid thing like having me shot any of my children to prove my bond with the RUF or raping any one of them or some crazy stuff. I thought about my wife in light of the invasion and how she must be tortured not knowing what had happened to her husband and children, her family. What if anything happened to us by tomorrow? How would she take it? Would she even sleep this night? If so, how and where? Before daylight, I fell asleep.

Chapter 43

My wife was on her way with the truckload of feeds and other farm supplies when she was stopped at a new checkpoint created by the military government troop blockading people leaving Freetown in search for family members in Waterloo and surrounding villages. The new checkpoint was just a few miles from a small town called Jua about five miles away from Waterloo. She was shocked to see a lot of people queued up at that checkpoint and no vehicle or people were allowed to go toward Waterloo. Only people and vehicles coming into Freetown were allowed after thorough search by military officers. She encountered hundreds of distressed but exhausted refugees at the checkpoint who had fled from the camp. News of the attack on the camp terrified her very badly, and she immediately began enquiring specifically about her family. However many of the refugees she initially spoke with gave vague accounts of the attack, and no one could provide specifics about her family's fate except for few who remembered calling out to me to flee with the children. She refused to return to Freetown but waited by the hour at the checkpoint as more and more refugees arrived there. There she was until nighttime when the military officers processing escapees suspended their work to continue the next day, keeping the queue stagnant until daylight. However, escapees who had cash and were ready to bribe their way were selected, processed throughout the night, but the checkpoint was officially closed. She passed the night in the front seat of the truck a few yards away from the checkpoint and periodically would enquire of new arrivals about her family. Early the next morning, she met with a few refugees who simply insinuated that they are not sure if there was any time left for me and the children to make the escape. By noon she received an eye witness account of her family that aggravated her fears. One witness recalled that he was in a group escaping when he saw me searching for some of the children, suggesting that I should have joined them and saved some of the children that was with me then and leave the others for it would have been better to get some of the children alive than to lose all of them. These observations threw my wife over the limit and she began crying and worrying. News of fierce fighting between RUF fighters and government troops in and around Waterloo including the camp and another large town name Foremile, spread like wildfire as escapees from these areas shared their stories at the checkpoint. The government-controlled radio station also confirmed the news of the fighting but denied that these areas fell to RUF rebels. The government spokesman continued to deny it, but they had denied all along about towns and villages in the providences that the rebels took over. It was the same situation in Liberia in 1990 up to September when President Samuel K. Doe was captured by INDFL rebels led by Prince Johnson. The government had used state media to deceive and lie about territories lost to rebel fighters. Another refugee woman who was one of the last escapees arrived at the checkpoint and reported that one person from their group was shot in the camp while they were escaping and that person did not make it so he was left on the way to die. They then told my wife that the children and I could have been killed as well in the camp. She told my wife that she was sure that a bullet caught me and I fell over and then the children came running up to me but she was far away from the children to help save them so she fled. This is where my wife loses control of herself and before the end of the day the story of the killing of a refugee man and his five children had circulated all over Freetown. She was devastated and insisted on coming to the camp amidst the fighting that was going on but the military officers at the checkpoint would not allow anyone to go through what they had declared to be buffer zone between them and the rebels. At the camp I was awaken by various sounds of never-ending gunshots and explosions. No one was in the clinic where they had me tied up. The government troop made a daring attempt that morning to take back Waterloo and the surrounding villages, but they were met with stiff resistance and repelled. At around midday, I got my first relief from the terrible shape I was in having lost a good amount of blood, enduring terrible pain everywhere in my body, and the agony and emotions of not knowing my children's fate. Two of the rebels came in and untied me and provided me with water to wash my face and my wounds and to drink. They then took me to the camp administrative office which now happens to be annexed to their command post. There, a lot of them converged, and I was given two tasks that they argue about as to which one of them I should do first. One task was for me to start digging a mass grave and to assist in the collection of dead bodies in the camp to bury them. The next job was for me to go across the main road toward Benguima Military Barracks that is about a mile away from the camp and come back to report whatever I see or observe. If I did not show up in about an hour or so then my children would be meat for the vultures. They disagreed on which of these tasks first I should do because some think that if I got shot and killed while spying then the collection of the dead in the camp would be their assignment while the others felt that it was important to make sure that the barracks was abandoned as reported. While they were discussing, one of their vehicles drove into the camp with about six women and few bags of vegetables and other foodstuff. Then someone asked if they should get chicken and a pig from my farm to prepare food for them. At this, I took a deep breath of relief as I quickly consented because it would mean the opportunity to see my kids. It was hard for me to figure out who amongst them was actually in control because they were indecisive, argumentative, and noisy. Finally an overriding order came from inside the office where it is agreed that they get about fifty chickens and two pigs from my farm for the women to prepare. I rode in the back of the pickup with two others. It was a great relief to see my kids again, and they too were very glad to see me. They had prepared scrabble eggs for themselves, and they shared some of it with me, and I was able to use my first-aid kit to take care of some of the wounds on my children and on various part of my body. I took the four rebels to the farm where the rebels brutally killed fifty chickens by holding them by the head and swinging them around, twisting their necks until they are broken and then throwing them in the back of the pickup. It was heartbreaking for me, but I try as much as possible to remain friendly. When they were done loading the pickup, I offered a bag of rice and a few bottles of local-made gin called ormolay and convinced them that I need to stay to feed the livestock and to take care of the children before coming to base. They decided that two of the rebel stayed with me to "protect me" while the other two returned to their base. I knew that "protect me" meant to keep eye on me, but I would not have attempted any escape without knowing the positions of all of the other rebels that are spread in and around the camp even if I was left alone with the children because I noticed when we were coming that they had more men spread out in the camp from the beginning to the end of the airstrip. As we are walking toward the parked pickup with bottles of gin in my hands and the other two rebels struggling with the bag of rice to jump over the three feet wide gutter, few of their colleagues approached them asking to have them transport some items that they got from residents of the camp who fled. As they chat it was disclosed that three bodies were lying along the way toward Section Z. This news discouraged me since I was the guy responsible for collection of dead bodies. After the pickup left the two who were supposed to be keeping watch on me entered a long chat with the others while I was inside the house encouraging my already traumatized children who wanted to know where their mother and Nancy was also if we were leaving the camp and when. "If we try to leave now and they capture us, then they will surely kill us, so our best chance is to keep being friendly with them while I try to find a way out," I encouraged my kids. I thought about their mother. If she was here they would have kill me a long time ago. As a general rule, they don't keep husbands and wives captives at the same time. Mostly it would be the men that would be killed. The women are raped and/or held as sex slaves. It was a good thing afterward that my wife was away when they took over the camp. We could hear the men laughing outdoor and later they called out my name in a friendly manner asking if I still have some more gin to give their friends. With a good smile, I welcomed the idea and provided them with one more bottle of gin. To continue building a zugzwang, I implied that if only we could find ways to bring in the truckload of goods that my wife went to pick up from Freetown we would have a lot of alcohol to drink, weeds and cigarettes to smoke, and more feeds for the livestock; and I can tell from the look on their faces that they too wished how great it would be to have these items in the camp. Impressed, one of them referred to me as a little tycoon in the camp. "You are running your own farm and at the same time supplying and circulating much needed drugs," he said. "Wow, I like that," exclaimed another. While they were drinking, I was in the back feeding the livestock when I heard the roaring of engine. It was the pickup, and it stopped in front of my house again. This time they were 3 strange men inside. They called me out and as I stepped out in the open facing the side of the pickup, two of the men jumped out from the back of the pickup and pointed their AK-47 straight at me. Blood shot straight up my head as I stood frozen, peeing a little in my pants, and my heart stopped as my feet crumbled underneath me. The cup of water I was holding slipped from my hand and fell as I struggled to stand upright. "Ha, ha, ha," they laughed out loud as they lowered their weapons away from me. "Are you afraid to die, Davies?" one of them snapped. I stood muted and don't know if I have any more smile left in me to complement this kind of joke. "Do you have shovels, diggers, and wheelbarrows?" asked the other. I nodded. "Well get them into the pickup and join us. We are going to dig a mass grave to bury the dead before bodies began to decompose. Okay?" "Sure," I said after taking a deep breath. One of them picked up the cup that fell from me and tapped me on the shoulder. "Dying by the bullet is easy and quick, Davies. When it happens, you will love it. It is better than being ill and in pain, taken to hospital, and doctors keep injecting you or sometimes operating on you and in the end you die. We are here to provide the shortcut to all these kind of pain and suffering," he added. We all laughed though my laughter was actually a struggle to suppress the agony I felt as I still struggle to find calm within. After I loaded the equipment for the job, we drove away with the last bottle of gin to help inspire the mass grave digging.

Chapter 44

We drove to the back of their command post where the camp cemetery is located and the two rebels, who were assigned to help me dig the grave, only sat, smoked some weed, drank, chatted, and laughed out loud. I probably started digging around noon, and I dug for hours without ceasing. There was no direct pressure on me because for the most part I was left alone while my two masters found cool shades under a tree to rest, but I needed to get this over with and be with my children, so I continued until a sizable four feet mass grave was completed. Also they were talking about some of their activities, how they took over some of the villages and towns and some of the events they thought was funny that made them happier. I felt that if I stopped to rest they might suspect that I am listening, so I kept digging. They talked about how they would have attacked the camp about a week earlier but for some change in planning and condemned one of their commanders who handled everything with iron hand without any consideration and made everything hard for everybody. The camp they concluded was not a refugee camp but rather a ULIMO base; those ULIMO fighters that they must flushed out at all cost. The camp, they said, is strategic to marshalling their men for the "do or die battle" to take over Freetown, the capital city. Part of the area that they had me digging had human bones and at one point I called their attention to it. I was scared, but they were not. One of them picked up a large piece of human bone and claimed he was going to make a locket of it to tie around his neck. I was exhausted, hungry, and frightened, but I dug on until my hands started bleeding. While I was busy with this task, some of the rebels who earlier begged me for a bottle of gin went back behind me to my house, intimidated and harassed the children, and ransacked the place in search for alcohol and any valuable items they could lay their hands on including the little money I have to start life with if we ever made an escape. The children were extremely terrified especially so that they were told that I was digging a grave for my family to rest in peace together ever after. Not knowing what was happening at my home worried me and I was wary and needed rest but frightened to suggest that. Surprisingly, one of them commended me for a job well done and called the task off to be continued the following day. We all thought that this task was halfway to its completion and that it should be completed by noon the next day if we start early enough. When we arrived at the command post, they were using the camp security tent as a kitchen, and the women were cooking and singing and making jokes while some of the rebels laughed. The elderly man who was with the group when we were captured the day before was there, and he commended me after the other two reported the job I have done. He assured me that their commander would be in by tomorrow, and he would throw in some good words for me. I asked if I would be allowed to go be with my children and take care of the livestock, and he said there was no problem so long that I do not try anything stupid. The pickup was not available so he asked that the two escorted me home. They walked me back to my house and waited on till I completed feeding the livestock and provided them water for the evening then they advised me not to leave my house for I could be shot. They would check on me while patrolling and finally pick me early in the morning to complete the job.

The walk to my house took about twenty minutes because I was exhausted. My feet felt weaker as the wound to my right knee hurt badly at each step; the wound on my head hurt as well and the peeling inside both palms also hurt from digging the mass grave. When we arrived, we found out that some of their men ransacked my house and took away a lot of items that I could not account for at the time. The children had cried until their throat hoarse. This infuriated the two who radioed their command base and informed them of what had happened. The rebels who earlier asked me for the gin were recalled from their post and made to report at their command post immediately, and I was asked to make a list of items that were missing from my house. But this was a conflicting situation that I never wanted to drag anywhere. I do not trust any of these guys nor am I interested in pursuing any issue order than finding a way out of this mess so I said that I would have the list ready by tomorrow morning. The two rebels warned again that I should not step out of the house and that they would check on me overnight. I agreed and they left. As the kids and I were trying to figure out the items taken, my heart froze as I became aware that my radio tape recorder set was among the items taken. I began perspiring profusely, and my heartbeat arose to a level where I could hear it. It was not for the set but for the cassette that was in it. It contained about forty-five minutes of recording of the activities on the night of our capture. I had pressed the recording button to record any encounter hoping that the recordings might give an account of our final moments. The recording button was pushed on moments before our home was attacked the night before. Although I had no chance to listen to the cassette, which had the original Bob Marley "Survival" collection of songs on it, it must have been erased and replaced with recordings of the rebel intrusion of my house the night before. It may be the single most item that could send me and the kids to the grave indeed for I can find no reasonable explanation to appease my captors as to why I recorded the event of my capture. On the other hand, they may not be interested in any explanation or excuses but they might just take any actions because they might think I had set them up, betrayed them. I should have removed the cassette from the recorder, but I had not thought of it all along. If those who ransacked my house did so without any order from their command post and it was a secret to them, then they might not expose the cassette. I took a shower in the house and cooked some food on the stove and ate dinner with the children. On several occasions we heard footsteps and twice my name was called and a voice would say we are just checking and the footsteps would fade away. It was after 8:00 a.m., and I was in a deep sleep because I stayed up most part of the night trying to figure a way out of what seem like a dead end or maybe "interference" as would be defined in chess populace. If I was alone, this episode would have been closed this very night because I would escape but for the children. The only option I am left with is to make no list and to say nothing was missing from my house. If those who took my stuff realized that they have nothing to worry about because I lost nothing then they would need to keep this to themselves. I jumped out of bed as the children woke me up. "There is a knock on the door," they said. But I was too tired and almost went back to sleep. I stumbled toward the door and opened it. The two had come to pick me up to go complete the digging task. "What happened to your colleagues who intruded my house yesterday?" I asked.

"They said that they were just checking on the children and never took anything from your house," one of them responded. Then he asked for a list of all that they took from me. I said nothing. They were only looking for something to drink, gin, and my children were scared. We then left to complete the digging and before midday the task of digging was completed, and we now have the other phase of the task to complete, the collection and burial of dead bodies.

Chapter 45

I wish I never had to dig a mass grave, but I had no choice. I told the kids what was going to happen, and they had also told me what one of the intruder told them, that I was digging a grave where they would bury all of us including the dogs that they shot in the camp. I told them that it was not true. "They were just scaring you kids," I said.

Long before midday, the task of removing the dead began. The first three were rebels who died during the fight with the government troop the day before. I used a wheelbarrow, and my two rebel helpers helped to put the bodies in the wheelbarrow, and I pushed it all the way to the cemetery and dumped the bodies in the grave. When I was taking the first body, I noticed he was a tiny man, maybe in his early forties. The bullet caught him in the back of his neck. As I pushed this little bastard to his final resting place, I wondered how many people he may have killed or the carnages he may have participated in, and I wished his soul the longest punishment in hell. Along the way, the wheelbarrow wheel hit a rooted tree stump, and I struggled to keep the body from tumbling over, but the body tilted and it seem he was smiling—or was that the expression on his face when he passed? But it felt like he heard me cursing and wishing him hell under my breath. His fellow rebels standing at their command post bowed as I passed by them struggling with the wheelbarrow. They never joined the procession. I was the only one taking this man I do not know from Adam to his grave. They do not even have the dignity to honor a falling comrade, and that shows how uncultured and ungrateful these savages are.

The other two helpers were waiting for me at the spot where their second falling comrade lay so they would help load his body in the wheelbarrow upon my return. At the grave site, I pushed the wheelbarrow upward and threw the son of a bitch over to have him rolled into the grave, but his body fell off and rested at the edge of the grave. He fell forward with his face to the ground and part of his body still on the edge of the wheelbarrow and his dirty black ass like that of a monkey's ass projected as part of his balls hanged between his legs. The bastard died not wearing underwear, I observed. I could bet my life this ruthless spinster had not taken a bath for a very long time before the bullet that ended his savagery on planet earth.

As I tried to pull the wheelbarrow underneath his body, I noticed he had a secret pocket on the big black belt around his pants. The belt had a zip, and there was the impression of something. I hesitated for a moment and then decided to unzip it. The object in it was tied in a dirty stinky cloth. Curious, I painfully loosened the knot to open it, and the hair on my skin rose at the sight of what I was looking at. My hand began to shiver at the sight of the objects, which are unmistakably sizable pieces of gems—diamonds! I quickly looked around to make sure no one was looking then I tied up the cloth again and quickly went by a nearby tree and buried the cloth there. I returned and spoke words of blessing upon this fine man and gently pushed him into the grave. I prayed that his stay in hell would be temporary. In his lifetime, he may not have accomplished anything good, but in death, this man, whatever his name was, have done the right thing by delivering diamonds that he may have killed others for to the rightful owner.

Since his colleagues were not present nor interested in delivering an eulogy at his funeral and I happen to be the only one present to convey his mortal body unto the ground, I therefore should not let him be interned without eulogizing him at least for his accomplishment in death; therefore, by the power invested in me, I conveyed the mortal body of John Doe to the ground and spoke peace unto his soul, God willing. Before I pushed him down into the pit for a crash, I thought about further search of pockets, perhaps one never know what the dead have to offer, but instead I found tobacco, snuff, cola nuts, and a piece of paper with a female name and address on it. After that was done, I gently kicked the little man, committing him into the ground along with his tobacco, snuff, and cola nuts. Then I vowed to myself that from then onward, the dead bodies of RUF and/or military fighter that I am chanced to process for burial *must* be thoroughly searched, and if there is need to perform autopsy in order to satisfy my curiosity, so be it.

My zeal and enthusiasm for the job increased to the commendation of all those concerned. It appeared as though the other dead bodies were searched by their colleagues. It was even possible that John Doe was searched but his secret wallet was missed. When we were done with four rebel bodies, we now proceeded to get the ones that were near the footpath from the bush road in Section Z. Pushing the wheelbarrow past the command post, I noticed there were a number of vehicles there: Jeeps, Land Rovers, and a couple of sedans, and a truck; and there were more rebels. Many of them were neatly dressed in different combat uniform, presumably bodyguards, and heavily armed. The atmosphere and dynamics had totally changed, and the place became quieter. Even the guys who were getting comfortable with me kept their distance and calm. Suddenly I was pulled over and approached by two curious new guys in uniform, wanting to know who I was, what I was doing in the camp, and what I was doing with the wheelbarrow. I tried to relax and to stay calm while trying to explain myself to them, but I wasn't getting anywhere for as far as they were concern, I did not belong there. They wanted to know who assigned me to do the jobs I told them about, and since I do not have names, I looked around for the two guys I worked with, and they were nowhere around. The others who had been commending me for my hard work seem scared to come forward to rescue me. I decided to describe the elderly who seemed to be holding high rank and one of my interrogators called the name of a coronel and I said, "Yes, that's him." One of them went into the crowded command base and moments later came back with the coronel, and it felt relieving that my description fit the right one, but my troubles with this new group were just beginning.

The coronel asked if I was done with the tasks, and I said that there were three more bodies near Section Z where the other two were waiting for me to come with the wheelbarrow. He called out for the driver of one of the pickup to take me with one of the two that were interrogating me to join the others and pick up the other dead bodies for burial instead of using the wheelbarrow. The coronel ordered that after we were done, they should bring me to him to complete an unfinished business.

My mind switched on to the Bob Marley cassette. Did they listen to it? Did the guys who intruded my house and took my stuff confessed to it? I declared nothing missing this morning, and the coronel assured me that no one would harass my children again. If they had listened to the tape, then I was done. We then drove past my house toward Section Z, and there were five of the rebels including my two helpers, and we walked over to where the first body was. It was a man in civilian cloth I could not recognize. I had to pick leaves and spread them in the pickup before we placed his body in it. Then we drove farther up the road to pick up the next body. As we approached the next dead body that they said was a woman, I imagine it could be someone I knew who lived in the camp. To the suck of my life, the dead body they had referred to as a woman was my niece, Nancy. Blood come shooting up my head, and I almost dropped and I shouted her name, "Nancy! Oh my god!" Everyone noticed my anger and my agony, and they asked, "Do you know her? Is she a relative?" Like Peter denied Christ, I denied Nancy being my relative and branded her as the daughter of one of the suppressors at the camp, who worked with the greedy government officials and stole every benefits belonging to us in the camp. I said I wished he was the one here dead than his poor little daughter, and then I forced a smile to suppress the combination of agony and betrayal I felt. I thought Nancy escaped with the last group of escapees. Maybe she needed my help before she died, and I knew not. How can I explain this to the children and how can I live life, if I survive this, and carry this horrible moment and the agony that comes with it?

We picked up her body and placed her in the pickup. She was shot on her left upper leg and lost considerable amount of blood. For a moment, I wish I could lay hands on a weapon that I could use to shoot and kill all of these heartless bastards around me. I thought about the children, and along the way to pick up the next dead body and for the rest of the day, I struggled to remain calm, to keep a smiling face. The thought of Nancy's body in the same pickup with her killers and me together, coupled with the fact that she was going to be buried with these bustards, sent sad but burning sensations up my spine.

After the bodies were place in the pit, the men ordered that the pit should remain open as there was room for more dead bodies. They then took me over to the base where there was already a debate in progress as to my fate and the fate of my children. The rebel commandant, as I understood, rejected my reason for remaining in the camp and ordered my children to be brought to their command post. His second in command then ordered me tied up and held in custody for further interrogation. Those rebels that I thought were getting comfortable with me showed me their double face as they grabbed me and lifted me up and my hands locked elbow to elbow behind my back and tied. I was then carried to the far end behind the camp warehouse, and I was shocked to find three other people there tied up waiting for their judgment to decide their fate. I cried out loud begging for my life, and when they brought my children, and I heard the chaotic pandemonium and the threat to have their arms hacked off and hearing the children crying and beginning for them to be left alone, my heart erupted and I passed out.

Chapter 46

"If I was already dead, then why should I resurrect to the same situation and the same state of mind?" This was my first thought after I was revived and water dripped from my body. I managed to sit on the ground; my eyes blurred as I struggled to see the people standing in a circle around me. I could hear voices but don't know what to make of them. I was no longer tied, but at least I remembered being tied as the last thing that happened to me. In a little while my eyes began to clear, and I came back to my senses, at least making sense of what is being said around. I stood up and asked for my children. A woman pointed to the other side of the tent at the camp entrance and a few rebels held me up and help me walked toward the tent. On our way they said to me that my children and I are now free to leave the camp any time we want to and that I should thank God for my eight-year-old daughter Harriette. I am not sure that I understood what they said to me neither could I make sense of what they were saying. But as they aided me into the opened tent, my children were seating on a bench and my daughter Harriette was seating on the lap of the commandant of the rebels and the only thing he said to me was that: "You guys are free to leave the camp but my advice is that you do not use the bush roads. Use the main road, and good luck." The women who cooked for the rebels packed some fruits in a sack and gave them to me. Their eyes were full of tears as they consoled the children.

The commander asked if I would like to take stuff from my house, and I hesitated and then said it was not necessary. Two men in civilian clothes scribbling something on writing pads with camera hanging on their shoulders approached and ask how I felt as a free man now, and I said something like I thank God for the commandant's decision. Then I asked permission to go get my wheelbarrow so that

I can use it to carry some of the children and the sack of fruit. The wheelbarrow I used earlier was actually in front of the clinic where the two rebels pulled me over, but I took the opposite direction to the cemetery and quickly pulled out my dirty cloth and put it inside my underwear and I quickly walk back and pretended that I cannot find my wheelbarrow. Someone remembered seeing it near the clinic, and they went out there to get it for me. I spread a cardboard in it and set the sack of fruit in it and put my four-year-old daughter Jacqueline in it. I said thanks to everyone present, and we set off walking toward the entrance of the camp into the main road, and it still felt like their eyes were on us for a long time to come.

The distance to Freetown from the camp is twenty-two miles yet the thought of covering these mileages by foot in our broken condition seem like drinking a glass of ice-cold water to quench a thirst compared to staying in troubled Waterloo Refugee Camp. As we walked two miles into our journey, near the main intercession that branched into Waterloo Village, we began hearing distant roaring of an engine; and as we kept walking, the sound roared louder and louder until it became clear that a vehicle was approaching us from the back. Could it be the rebels coming after us? Had they found something out about us? These thoughts made me nervous until far behind us a commercial truck from up country became visible, running probably about seventy miles an hour. We shifted to the left part of the road to let it pass and after it passed us by the driver stepped on the breaks and finally stopped about twenty-five yards ahead of us. A woman stepped out from the front passenger seat, and she waved to the children to run quickly to get aboard the truck. The children ran faster while I struggled with the wheelbarrow pushing Jacqueline with the fruit. I heard her asking if we were heading for Freetown, and I yelled back: "Yes! Yes! Yes!" The children were helped on board by the apprentice, and Jacqueline and I finally got on board with the sack of fruits, leaving the wheelbarrow on the sidewalk.

DYSFUNCTIONAL ONE

The truck was half loaded with farm products: cassava, cocoa, plantains, and potatoes. We went past two checkpoints before we arrived in Freetown. The gems were already placed in an orange, which I held in my hand when we were being searched. Each child had an opened orange to eat at each checkpoint, and I had mine that was half opened. The truck's destination was at Kissy, not far away from the home of AccordOne's recently employed receptionist. We decided to go see her first; and as we approached her home, her parents were seating at the veranda. I introduced myself and the children, almost immediately they both sprung from their chairs to embrace us while they called out for their daughter. Upon laying her eyes on me, Aminata froze with her eyes wide open and both hands on her head. "There is news around town that you and the children were killed in the camp, and your wife is in terrible shape," she cried out. "This is our ghost, Aminata. We actually died there," I said, and she smiled. Her parents prepared hot bath for us and helped with painkillers and other medication to mend our wounds, and they provided food and bed for us. Before we went to bed, Harriette explained again how we were spared; it was a miracle. RUF plan to attack and take over the camp was two weeks before. They actually carried recognizance earlier in the camp but one of their commander called off the attack on the last minute because of a series of problems including the weather condition, which affected their movement and transportation of hardware and ammunition. On that day when their plan changed, they needed food for a number of their men stationed in the bushes of Fourmile. They then went over to Waterloo Village and from there on to the camp to get chicken and eggs from my farm. My wife was out and I was in Freetown. The men who sometime help with the farm work were on break and few of the rebels and their commandant insisted that they do not want to deal with an eight-year-old girl for the large quantity of farm products they wanted. Harriette, who the rebel commandant recalled was exceptionally brilliant, challenged them that she could handle any transaction even if it involved the whole farm. So the rebels decided to fool around with this little girl in a bid to confuse her with variables in the order of prices per dozen since there were three sizes of eggs (small, medium, and large) and each size carried different prices, but she calculated without any calculator and arrived at the exact total that the rebels disputed just so to have her confused, but they finally agreed with her calculation and in paying her they tried again to fool her with the currency, but she realized that the cash did not tally with the total amount for the order. Impressed, the commandant engaged her in other subjects, and Harriette was impressive with the other subjects and when it came to her favorite subject, the Holy Bible, which she had read completely from Genesis to Revelation, the commandant was blown away when she quoted chapters and verses. The rebels noticed a blackboard on the porch with chess algebraic notations. Curious, one of them refer to it as some kind of mathematical formula, but she laughed at their ignorance and explained what it was and they all thought Harriette was a genius. Before leaving, the commandant asked her name and told all the others that Harriette will become his wife when she grew up, and he would come back one day to marry her. They joked around, laughed, and he then tipped her and they left. Now, at the time I was tied and passed out behind the warehouse, the second in command sent for the children with bad intentions, but upon seeing Harriette, the commandant stopped what his men planned to do and asked Harriette to go away. But Harriette would not leave and insisted that she would not leave her dad whom her whole life depended on. They then went in a conference to discuss why her family should be treated different from others. All the other rebels who went in the camp that day for the transaction remembered Harriette and convinced the rest that we were not harmful to them. Even the women who cooked their food threw in some words indirectly for us and explained my hard work. Aminata then explained that she gave the key to the office to my wife, and she should be at the office as we speak and then she was going to pass the night there. It was a long way to the office in the heart of Freetown, and it was in the night. My body aches and the children and I needed sleep so badly so we decided we would go to the office in the morning. As we shared our stories with the Sesay family, word about our appearance at their home circulated and more and more people in the neighborhood came to see the family that was pronounced dead in the Camp Waterloo.

Chapter 47

The next morning, my wife was seating at the front of the building surrounded by sympathizers consoling her when the taxi arrived. The taxi stopped and the four kids in the back got out first. I heard someone yell and pandemonium was ignited as the crowd rushed toward the taxi. By the time I got my aching body out of the vehicle, I literally begged to stop the endless hugs that hurt so badly. My wife was ecstatic but all beaten up; she was physically faded, pale, and her eyes were swollen, her voice rough and husky. If I had access to telephone, I would have called the office where she spent the night to update her about our status and where we are. That would have saved her one more long but agonizing night. In a matter of minutes the intercession was full of people, and traffic began detouring. People love comeback stories especially so when it is like coming from the dead to life. As the news spread more and more people kept pouring to take a glimpse of us, to touch, hug or shake hands and to see if they can get a piece of the incredible story from the horse's mouth. My wife knew as much as I do that we needed medical attention, and it was so good that the curious taxi driver who had no idea whom his passengers were was standing by his car marveling over his surprised encounter. We were ushered into it and slowly the crowd made opening for the taxi to drive through. At the hospital, two of the doctors who looked after us recommended bed rest for me and wanted me admitted a few days, but I was reluctant, so they took x-rays, conducted various tests, and made prescriptions. It was agreed for me to check in the next day, and they advised that I stay in bed. How does one bed rest when homeless was a question we all wrestled with.

I needed to get some money from the bank for my family and without a checkbook to write a check, my presence was needed at the bank. After the withdrawal, we stopped by nearby stores to buy cheap cloths for our family and buy some of the prescribed drugs then found a restaurant to eat lunch. My body ached at every step I took, and my wife had to support me most of the time. She explained that she had gone to see the Kings the day before to get help finding us but they are both out of the country. As we descended the taxi at my office, two military personnel and a band of reporters were waiting for us. The military investigated anyone who survives an encounter with RUF. If hands or feet were hacked off from the encounter, then that would have been convincing and indeed a key evidence to eliminate the government suspicion of the victims; otherwise, if victims show up in one piece with all body parts intact, regardless of the circumstances, they were suspicious. Curious for our story, aggressive reporters stood in our way, throwing questions at us while the military personnel are forcing us to go with them into their vehicle. We were exhausted, weary, and wanted our family to be left alone; but since we had nowhere else to hide, it had become difficult to usher into the peace and quietness we so badly needed. I told the military personnel that we needed time to come to their base in Wilberforce because we are under medical at the moment and that the only reason we came to the office is to collect a few items. But we were told that we had no choice and must be taken whether we want to or not. A group of refugees intervened and tried to talk some sense into the military personnel, but they insisted this was the order they received from their commander. While we were at it, word came from the Refugee Executive Committee that I was needed at the American embassy. Hundreds of displaced refugees had assembled near the embassy trying to convince Washington to open up resettlement programs and to deregulate private resettlement programs so that relatives of refugees living in United States can file to bring them over to United States in relatively shorter period of time than the norm. Refugees knew that the rebels could attack Freetown anytime soon, and there is only one way out of the capital that is not under rebel control yet: Lungi Airport and the road leading from there to the Republic of Guinea.

Lungi is the only airport out from the capital, and there are two ways to it, by sea or by road. Unfortunately, part of the road leading to that airport was already in the hands of the rebels. Sadly, the UNHCR, which is the official body responsible for refugees, had taken the military government's position that the camp was safe and that refugees were just scared so they ran off without incidents and abandoned the camp. The UNHCR even insisted that my family was living peacefully and comfortably at the camp and the US embassy have no information that would dispute the official position of neither the government nor the UNHCR. These terrible lies told by officials united the refugee community, and it is believed that if the family that they used in their argument surfaced and disprove their claims, then the refugee community case would be stronger. At the UNHCR office on Wellington Street, hundreds of homeless refugees also were demonstrating and threatening to cause damages so the military government dispatched soldiers to guard the UNHCR building, their staff, and their vehicles. Upon hearing that my family has survived and escaped captivity and that we are at my office, Commissioner Sabiti and his roguish counterparts in government held an urgent meeting in which it was decided that they try to contact me and offer my family an incentive to leave the country. So the number of groups that needed a piece of me was as many and desperate, and I had no idea all these had evolved around my family.

In dealing with their double standards, the military government's theory was that if the rebels did not kill me and the children and they did not hack parts from our bodies as was their signature, then I must have joined the RUF and so I have some explaining to do. On the other hand since they have been preaching that the camp is safe and that the presence of RUF was not there then why are they suspicious that I must have joined RUF at the camp when according to them RUF is not there? The position on this chessboard was not complicated for me to make a move only that I needed to know what was going on for without an update of the situation around me in the last couple of days I would have to figure out my way as things

DYSFUNCTIONAL ONE

progress. As I was being forced to leave with the military personnel, another military vehicle came by and two other military personnel discuss in private with their comrade, and I was turned over to the new guys. They took me to the UNHCR office instead of the military base in Wilberforce. At the UNHCR office where hundreds of refugees were in the street holding banners and chanting for better attention to end their homelessness, the scene became electrified as my family descended from the military vehicle. They screamed my name and pleaded not to sell them out, and I was confused as to what was going on. I felt a bit relief that my family is brought to the UNHCR office as oppose to a military barracks where things could be more forceful, torturous, and unpleasant. It did not take long for me to put the pieces together. Moments ago I was sermon to the military barracks, and for some reason that was compromised, and I ended up at the UNHCR office, which means that something has happened between Commissioner Sabiti and government counterpart, and they may be up to something. The refugees out there are chanting for me not to sell them out and the ones that came to my office are inviting me to the embassy to confirm that the camp is not safe for them to live in. All these pieces could only mean that there was something going on; maybe a cover-up and I am supposed to be the guy everyone needed on their side at this time to lie or to tell the truth, to stand for nothing or to stand for something. To lie and stand for nothing would only mean to benefit my family alone for short term while jeopardizing the interest of hundreds of other families. Apart from that, it would also defeat the very core and pillars on which AccordOne stood, and all these people would see and brand me and my family as traitors.

At the UNHCR office, my family was taken to the office of the protection officer, Mrs. Thomas, and the two soldiers who led us in were asked to wait at the reception. Moments later the phone rang, and Mrs. Thomas said I was needed at the commissioner's office and that the rest of my family should wait in her office. She led me into the commissioner's office where two high-ranking military officers were waiting. As we entered, the three men forced a smile, and I was ushered into a seat. "You look very tired, Mr. Chairman," said the commissioner. I nodded and took my seat. One of the officers started business. "Our troops are within reach of taking over Waterloo Village and all the surrounding towns including Camp Waterloo. By early next week, we would begin evacuating people back to their respective areas where they fled from and so are the refugees. The camp, like any embassy, is considered independent ground; and it is a serious breach on the part of RUF or government troop to take fighting there, but I assure you that we are correcting this and taking over the camp. But our efforts should not be impeded by the perceptions of people. This is where you come in," he said. I said nothing and the commissioner takes off from here.

"John, we are offering you a resettlement package to resettle your family either in the United States or in Europe. It is up to you. All you need to do is to do nothing, say nothing to anyone, the press, and others would want your story in order to spread fear, and we are trying to fix things. Mrs. Thomas here would be working on your family resettlement immediately, and you would be updated regularly, and I am sure in say two to three weeks your family should be out of here." There was a pause while everyone waited for my response. I then promised not to talk to anybody, and I said that they should not rule out information that others may already have concerning my appearance after all the news about the death of my children and me. The other officer cut in and said that they do not want me to hold press conferences personally on behalf of my family nor in my capacity as chairman of AccordOne. I agreed and asked how soon they really think the camp would be restored to the refugees and our discussion around this issue gave them assurances that I was serious about their concern. They tried to assure me that it was just a matter of hours before their troops take over the camp and that they were sure to start evacuation early next week and at that point more soldiers would be assigned in and around the camp to prevent any further attacks. I was not convinced nor do I trust any of their mumbo-jumbos, but I had to let them believe that I am with them. They did not even ask what went in the camp in the last three days because they actually do not care about my family or about any of the other homeless refugee families out there. They only care about how they can manipulate the current situations to make as much money for themselves using the plights of the refugees as their front. I then impressed on them that I was supposed to be in the hospital right now as we are speaking because my condition is declared this morning as critical but because of other necessities I postponed my treatment and bed rest for this afternoon. "As long as you keep your keep quiet, John, I assure you everything would be fine, and you would not be bothered any more by us," said one of the militants. "You will not find anyone to quote me directly," I said, and the meeting was dismissed. Commissioner Sabiti offered his official car to drop off my family anywhere we needed to go. As we left the building and the crowd of helpless but frustrated refugees chanted my name, I can only think of one thing that was clear to me: no Liberian refugee in their right mind would agree to be evacuated to Camp Waterloo even if the military took it back from the rebels. Later that evening, I learned that truckloads of militants arrived at the UNHCR office to disperse the refugee demonstrators from the street. They were flogged and driven away and assured of more severe and drastic actions if they form any gathering near the UNHCR office.

Chapter 48

It had been rumored at Camp Waterloo since Godfred Sabiti took over as commissioner of UNHCR that he was once a rebel leader in his native land of Uganda sometime between 1971–1979 during the reign of Idi Amin Dada, the military dictator and third president of Uganda. If there were no truth in that rumor, it should make no difference now that it was clear that the commissioner's leadership skills and the position he took defined his compromise of moral ethics, shifting away from his utmost responsibility to protecting refugees. Instead, he chose to engage in shady deals with the military government over the interest of refugees at the time when they had nowhere turn and needed him the most. This gave credence to the rumors because any moral person who had just witnessed what hundreds of families experienced at Camp Waterloo and the surrounding villages would definitely not go the direction that the military government was advocating and neglecting the best interest of the refugees, which meant compromising their security and putting them in harm's way. Putting the refugees in harm's way in this situation could only mean for the commissioner more basis for support from international communities that eventually went into private pockets. I was not going to make any statement that would tend to infuse confidence to let refugees go back into that camp. I cannot imagine putting innocent families in that predicament let alone their innocent children. I don't think I would ever forgive myself or forget if I misled these people, and they have to go in that camp and something bad happens that would take one more life. I have reasons to want to stay in that camp but not under the current circumstances. I have my family home there that I built from scratch, which valued over Le 3,000,000. I have important documents such as marriage certificate, birth certificates, travel documents, business records, poultry and pig investments, plus construction materials and other personal asset that meant a lot to my family. But I would not go back to that camp to stay not even if the government took it back as they claim they would and surround it with military police round the clock till eternity.

After all is said and done, territories had been exchanged several times between the two warring thugs (government troops and rebels), and in these cases, innocent civilians perished and suffered. That evening at my office, a group of Liberian refugees met with me to discuss the US embassy appointment. The embassy staff do not have any proof to negate the military government and the UNHCR claims that the camp was safe for the refugees, and in their assurances to the embassy over the refugees' concern, both had used my family as an example to portray its safety. If I go with the concern group to the embassy to dispute government and UNHCR assurances, thereby making the refugees case stronger, then the question of what would happen to my family when the military government and Commissioner Sabiti finds out can only be detrimental to my family. On the other hand, there is no guarantee that a sellout cannot come from within the very Liberian refugee community as desperate refugees can do anything to gain some favor from the authorities. If I were to do this, then I would demand absolute secrecy from the group and from the embassy. I should never be quoted as direct source and only on that basis would I go to the embassy with the concern group and only on that very basis would I say anything if the embassy staff can make the same assurances not to quote me directly. After the meeting, the concern group left with the understanding that they would contact me anytime the next day to confirm the appointment with the embassy. My family passed the night at my office. We did not get the privacy we needed until after midnight. There were so many people coming to see us, some bringing stuff that we could use for beddings, etc.

The next morning was a shocker as there were newspapers carrying stories of me and my family from various sources and in some of their texts I am quoted as saying one thing or the other. Certainly the news media has caused me some trouble here, and I had to do something to repair the damage before it is too late. So I wrote a disclaimer, which I was never going to give any of them, but to cover my ass if the military government were to come after me. After that, I called Commissioner Sabiti's office to talk to him, but I was told that he had not yet arrived for work that morning, and I left a message for him to call me immediately upon his arrival. Moments later, I got a call from the protection officer, Mrs. Thomas. She wanted me to come immediately to see her; it was urgent. In a matter of minutes, I was in her office and as she dashed out the newspapers spreading them on her desk, she asked, "Have you seen the papers this morning, Mr. Davies?" I opened my bag and took out some the very papers together with my disclaimer neatly typed and addressed to each of the editors concerned. She read my disclaimer and shook her head and then asked if I have already delivered it. I said I was about to do so when her call came in. She said the commissioner was on his way and that I should wait as they have a proposal for my family. The commissioner came in and after all the newspapers and quotations were analyzed, summarized, and discussed, their proposal was put before me. My family would be divided into two groups, slotted under two separate names to travel in two weeks to a European country where we can be reunited once again as one family. I was to travel with two of my own children plus two older children with a strange woman posing as my wife but under a family name called Decker, and my real wife was to travel as a widow of another man under the family name Johnson with the rest of the other children plus one another five-year-old child. The three children and the woman posing as my wife are beneficiaries of two separate private resettlement programs. The proposition was nothing more than a demonstration of the deep-seated corrupt practices and schemes engulfing the office of the UNHCR, marketing facilities belonging to poor refugees to none-refugee bidders who paid heavily for these facilities. They were going to start sequestering my family immediately if we are ready; they would put us in Cape Sierra Hotel wherefrom our movements and activities would be restricted while paperwork for our resettlement is being speedily processed.

For me to abruptly make a decision like this, putting the fate of my family exclusively into the hands of these callously rascal manipulators was something I could not just do without consultation with my family. It also means that I would have to find people that I would delegate various responsibilities to, and I would need time to take care of my health as well. I even lied that two of my children were already hospitalized as we speak, and there was so much personal issues I have to address in a couple of days, but I would be available anytime I am needed for any aspect of the processing. Meanwhile, I would make sure that the media receive my disclaimer, and I would be back at 12:00 p.m. the next day to meet with the Decker and Johnson families whose generous resettlement programs my family is so blessed to ride on.

At my office, there was a message already from the concern refugee group stating that the meeting with the US embassy is scheduled for Tuesday the following week, which released the pressure on me and relieved me for the weekend to think things over and prepare. The next day, Friday, I met with the Decker and Johnson families at the UNHCR office, and together we had lunch with Mrs. Thomas. The meeting was short; funny but with a lot of very interesting tips that would eventually inspire me into pursuing the Canadian resettlement program that Mr. King and I had been working toward.

There were three children and a woman involved in this current UNHCR program. The woman, Teresa Decker, happened to be the mother of the youngest kid who is about five years old. The other two boys, Patrick (twelve) and Desmond (nine), were being processed to join their parents in Europe. They were not orphans as I later found out. Teresa, who would be my play wife in the deal, happened to be the younger sister to the mother of the two older kids. She is married and living in the Netherlands. During the meeting, Mrs. Thomas provided three files containing basic personal information about the characters and roles we all needed to prepare ourselves for.

"The program defines the future of your children, for the good and security of your respective families, and it requires absolute secrecy and confidentiality," she had stressed during final review of the files. After our meeting, I left the building with two files; one for my real wife and the other for me. I walked down the street about thirty yards away to wait for Teresa, my play wife, so that we can have a chat and get to know each other a little bit more. But she was not on foot as I thought; she drove a Mazda sedan, and the car faced the opposite direction from me so I walked as quickly as I could and called out her name aloud then she turned around and noticed me then patiently waited as I took baby steps to reach her. "I was trying to catch a cab, and they don't seem to come by easily around here. Can you drop me off at my office on Lightfoot Boston Streets?" I asked.

"Sure," she replied and waved Patrick, who was already sitting on the front passenger seat, moved to the backseat so I sat in the front passenger seat and then she drove off. She wanted to make a stop on Siaka Stevens Street to pick up her dress from a tailor, and she asked if I can afford the time. "Of course I have all the time in the world for my play wife," I said with a genuine smile, and she burst into laughter. I cracked more jokes like if I do not approve of the dress she wasn't going to wear for our dinner tonight, and we laughed more. I noticed the two older kids were chuckling in the backseat, and I felt the ice was broken. There was no question about the fact that she was a Sierra Leonean posing as a Liberian refugee to fit in the resettlement program. To make her more comfortable, I started speaking in Creole, and she took a keen look at me while I looked away from her. With her eyes wide opened and hand over her mouth, she asked in Creole, "So yu sef na Sierra Leonean?" meaning "You are also a Sierra Leonean?" to which I nodded with a smile, and she became as comfortable as a cushion. To gain her trust, it was time to give her something in return: "Please do not let anybody know about my nationality, not even Mrs. Thomas or any of their staff," I pleaded. "We are bound to protect each other, for if I expose you it would affect me and my family, vice versa," she affirmed. She stopped to pick up her dress while the kids and I stayed in the car. By this time the kids, who seem shy at the lunch table, had loosen up; we were able to chat, and I learned little more important things about their family. The two older kids' parents were in the Netherland, and the little kids happen to be Teresa's son. His dad left when he was a year old and married another woman. Thereafter he left with his new bride to live in London. The parents of the two brothers' have been away now for three years and Teresa, their aunt, had been taking care of them.

They lived at Congo Cross, and this would be their second attempt to leave the country to join their parents. The first was an unsuccessful student exchange program to another European country where their parents would have come to pick them up, but that did not work out until their aunt was connected with this new deal, the refugee resettlement program. Their parents send thousands of pounds sterling to pay for this program because this program would give them (the children) a secure status in the country where they are going to be resettled, and there would be a lot of programs they would be benefiting from as a refugee compared to other status. Their aunt got connected to this program through an old man who handled the programs for the UNHCR. The two older kids were giving me more details when suddenly I spotted Teresa crossing the road with her dress. I immediately interrupted the kids and asked about their school, grades, friends, and best sports, etc. By the time Teresa entered the vehicle, Desmond was naming his best friends and the fun they had playing soccer on the same team. Kids generally love to talk when they get excited and feel comfortable; and indeed, these kids, who are supposed to be my play kids, have volunteered a lot of information that had my head spinning. If only I can get Teresa to fill in the other blanks concerning the black-marketing refugee resettlement processes: how she got it, who did she approach, how much it cost, and to whom do one pay, etc., it would be helpful to know. So as she drove toward my office, I asked if we could get together to have dinner sometime this weekend and surely she accepted my proposition and the appointment set for Saturday, 6:00 p.m. at the Bristol De Paris.

Chapter 49

Friday evening was spent quietly with my family reviewing the day's activities after supper; we had taken care of our bodily injuries and dispensed medication for everyone. In reviewing the UNHCR offer, we were not excited at all, and there were so many unanswered questions and rational thoughts: (1) It was clear that they were running us out of town so that we do not expose events at the camp that might jeopardize their interest at the expense of the poor refugees. (2) We were going to lose our identity in the process and end up with two different family names. (3) How do we revert to our legitimate family name, Davies, and be legitimized wherever we are resettled? And (4) what will happen to all the relationships, documentations, and friendships we would have fostered in our new environment and who would shoulder the costs involved in legitimizing change of name, etc., if possible and if necessary. These and more questions troubled us and raised more doubt and skepticism about the offer. We slept well throughout the night till late Saturday morning and that helped in energizing minds and bodies. Later in the day, I spent a few hours reviewing the Canadian resettlement files that Mr. King and I had been working on, and I figure that AccordOne could seal the deal with Simone Immigration Firm in Canada and obtain agency license to start the process to have my family resettle in Canada. If possible, I could also process other interested refugees through the same agency and perhaps nonrefugees as well. I then began to develop strategies to have the Canadian program implemented nationwide. The timing for this was ripe, but it all depended on the concession with the firm in Canada. No matter how much it cost, I have no problem because I still have some change at the bank and, of course, the thought of appraising the diamonds frequently sent waves of excitement.

At the Bristol de Paris that evening, our grand family (Decker, Johnson, and Davies) reunion dinner conveyed with more opportunity to get to know one another. Although the likelihood of declining the UNHCR offer was being considered by my family, but the idea of staying in the deal so far to gathering more information about the scheme and its operation was helpful. One thing was clear; there is nowhere I could go to challenge this scheme without doing harm to myself or members of my family. This has been a big business in which many prominent people in the community have interest including members of the military government who also shipped their relatives abroad through this same means. Even if I was going to decline, it would be done respectfully without any effort to exposing the scheme for it was already exposed but acceptable in the society. We had dinner, and my wife took all of the children by the nearby wharf for sightseeing as planned while my play wife, Teresa, and I sipped brandy on the rocks and settled down for a serious chat. By the time my wife returned with all of the children within the hour, I have extracted a great deal of information from Teresa without her knowing since I presented myself like I already knew how things worked. I asked how much the old man charged her family for the program, and without hesitation, she told me ten thousand pound sterling is the total charge, half the amount her sister advanced with the understanding to pay the balance half immediately after all the process is completed up to medical but before orientation classes are conducted by the UNHCR staff. From experience with some of my refugee friends who were fortunate to be resettled, I already knew that orientations were the final part of the process, and they were conducted a few days before departure. She said the old man, Pa Yillah, who happened to be the connection recruiter for the UNHCR staff charged her sister twenty thousand pound sterling, but they had to negotiate to get the whole package for half that amount. She also knew some friends who paid far more amount than that for theirs for single families less than her family size. So she considered hers as a blessing. She has received her Liberian refugee IDs for her family, and they have already been photographed for their refugee passport, and the next thing in the process that they are waiting for right now is for them to receive their referral letters to the Sierra Leone immigration office for fingerprinting and to sign their UN travel documents and then the medical process. After that, her sister would be making the balance payment. She then went on to unleash what I think was a bomb, and I had trouble concealing my surprise, which she noticed. She had said that the only thing that troubled her is the fact that she had to make payment directly to Pa Yillah who is a blind man. This piece of information sent me shrinking in my chair with the expression on my face unmistakably shocking when I was supposed to play like I knew this. "Is Pa Yillah blind?" I asked before I realized myself. Without hesitation, she affirmed: "Yes, how come you don't know that? Everyone in this town knows Pa Yillah." She then narrated that he was a famous musician who sold visa of various countries to many people listing them as member of his band on tour to many countries in European and other parts of the world. During his career as a musician, he would sell visa to people who wanted to travel with his band as musicians and when they travel these people would stay while he returned. His band was connected around the world, and he got contracts and invitations for concerts, etc., and everyone know that was how he made his money until he became ill and blind then his band dissolved, but he still had strong connections in the visa business and now he was the UNHCR front for the resettlement program. He had successfully connected hundreds of families who travel and resettled in different parts of the world during his career to the time of influx of Liberian refugees into Sierra Leone. She ended up with admiration for him by saying that "He is a very smart man." I said that I have heard about him but never knew that he was blind and agreed with her that he must be more than a smart man, "a genius maybe," I mocked. And I had to suppress my emotions as I wrestled with a number of thoughts going through my head about the splendor of this perfectly crafted setup. Whosoever planned this centralization of a blind man to collect money for their scheme have perfectly put in play a perfect alibi to avoid and escape a number of legal issues. I actually had to divert the discussion to something funny in other to find some excuse for the laughter generated from these revelations. What came to mind was the old saying that "in the city of the blind, the one-eyed man is the king." But here we are in a real-life situation where in the city of fully-eyed people, the only blind man in their midst had become the king. I now see why Teresa was troubled by it because the blind man does not issue any of these people any receipts for monies received from them for resettlement packages since the deal was illegal. It was at the total risk of the buyer and the seller can deny selling anything and deny receiving any money and the fact that the agent would not be able to recognize any of his customers nor the money they claimed he received nor the people in the institution he serves as agent and of course no written contract existed between them, which placed Teresa and others who pay for this products at high risk. The buyer can even be incriminated as posing as refugee in order to benefit refugee facilities that they are not entitled to, which may lead to other charges, and if there is any trace of UNHCR acknowledgement of the individual's status as a refugee, the UNHCR staff can argue that they were deceived by the impersonation of the individual who falsified their identity and registered with them as a refugee.

Later, my wife and all the children returned, and Teresa and her family thanked us for the diner and offered next dinner would be on them. They got in their car, drove away, and I find myself dumbfounded and sleepless on a Saturday night.

Chapter 50

Anxiety overwhelmed me overnight, and after spending most part of the night strategizing how AccordOne should implement the Canadian Migration Program and designing a system for its operations nationwide, my mind had more fidgeting to do before sleep stood its ground and stole me away in the early morning hours of Sunday. There were so many time-sensitive issues I had to deal with and a lot of tough decisions to make within a relatively short period of time. By midday on Sunday after my snoring cracked the paint off the walls, I was awakened to a smell of my favorite dish. As though sleep was a part of the solution to finding answers to the issues, I can see things clearly and handle each issue independently without any interference or complications and my to-do list and approach to each issue for the week was resolved. At 5:00 a.m. on Monday, I arrived at the SLET to make a call to Canada. By 8:30, my banker wired the agency fees to the immigration firm in Canada, and at noon, I received by fax a bunch of documentation for the program including program guide and AccordOne's agency license. At 1:00 p.m., I was at the United Nations Headquarters to ask for a favor. The resident representative and her husband were still out of the country, but their staff knew me personally and some of them knew that I handle private jobs for the couple. Some of them embraced me, offering their sympathy and consoling me for the resent ordeal that had been widely publicized, and I knew any one of them would do me the favor I went there for. Lucky for me, the head driver for the resident representative who sometime drove me around on errands for the couple was available and he was willing to drive me around to handle some of my personal businesses. He then drove me in the UN1 Volvo to a meeting I had arranged with three prominent citizens: Mr. Mina, a brother of former vice president of Sierra Leone;

Ms. Jalloh, a mistress of the late President Siaka Stevens; and Mr. Harding, a former diplomat from the Ministry of Foreign Affairs. These three runs a nonprofit organization down the road from my office. I had spoken to them earlier in the morning about entering a joint venture agreement with AccordOne, a United Nations affiliate organization, to assist in the implementation of migration programs for various countries, and they were excited about the projects, most especially about the 20 percent cut from the intake that would go to them. I convinced them on the phone that it was urgent as the first phase of the projects would kick off next Monday in just seven days, and that it was someone who knew them that recommended their organization and if they do not act immediately this lucrative contract would go to other organizations that are interested in it. They were so excited that they wanted the meeting to take place earlier than 2:00 p.m., but of course, I had to prepare. I knew how greedy, crooked, and powerful these people are, most especially I now understand the layout of the playing field in this environment; it is full of pockets of rules, but all share one thing in common, they are driven and guided by one thing only: MONEY. So I had cooked up these premises that would calm them down and refrained them from even thinking that AccordOne was my own creation, or they may be tempted to high-jack the entire program from me and throw me in jail or run me out of town in a twinkle of an eye or even kill me. They were impressed to have to be contracted by a Geneva-based organization through its local agency as I emphasized. The blueprint for the tasks involved, which I needed their organization to perform, was already prepared and a tentative draft contract was also handy. Their tasks involved the interviewing of applicants in accordance with the program guidelines and categorizing them into the required groupings and also to counsel them in completion of their application requirements. AccordOne would hire customer service representatives and train them how to administer part of the process, and their NGO group would allow their facilities to be used to conduct interviews, update applicants' files in the process, and bring them to a state of completion. These completed files would then be sent over to AccordOne with the list of applicants for transmission to Canada. The application processing fee is Le.15,000 per application, and this fee is payable at the AccordOne office where several customer service clerks hired and trained would physically collect payment and have the applicant signed a Migration Application Processing Disclosure Statement (MAPDS), which I designed. This statement simply states what AccordOne obligations are as an agent for a Canadian Migration Practitioner, and it specifically states that "the payment of Le15,000 is for processing the applicant's application for the Canadian Migration Program and that it does not guarantee the approval of the applicant's application nor does it constitute all fees and/or financial obligations should the application be approved by the Canadian Immigration Authorities." On the receipt it is written at the bottom: "This fee does not qualify you for migration to any country but is for processing of your application for migration." After the fee payment is made by an applicant and the disclosure signed, his or her file is created, an application number is assigned, and a preliminary interview date and time is given together with the place for the interview. On Wednesday the training of counselors and Customer Service Representatives commenced at the AccordOne office.

Following my meeting with the Non-Profit group my UN driver drove me to the Sierra Leone Broadcasting Station (SLBS) where I submitted and paid for two weeks announcement of the program to begin on Wednesday. From SLBS we went to Tower Hill to see an artist painter and submitted my sketch for a billboard for the program. By Friday the three billboards order were completed and on Sunday night they were mounted in three strategy areas—one at the intercession of Siaka Steven Street and Wallace Johnson Street, one at the intercession of Light Foot Boston Street and Wallace Johnson Street, and the third one near the building where AccordOne office is located. When we were done with all activities, it was about 6:00 p.m. Then I tipped my UN driver and arranged with him to help me out with more errands for a few more days since his boss would not be in the country for the next ten days. I have fostered a very good relationship with him ever since I started working with his boss. He once took me to Waterloo Refugee Camp to drop off some items that I purchased for Christmas, and he was ecstatic about the fresh palm wine at the camp, which he said was not available in the capital city. Since then once in a while I would bring him a gallon of the fresh palm wine, and he had been grateful in so many ways in return when I needed transportation help. His help this day is even more gracious. He drove me wearing his official UN uniform and while my meeting was in progress; he took an order to purchase drinks and snacks, which he delivered in the conference room where the meeting was taking place, and I used the opportunity to introduce him as the chief driver for UN permanent representative to Sierra Leone. This was impressive as everyone stood up to honor him. He had a little chat with Mr. Mina in which he disclosed the number of years he had been working with the UN and every one was impressed about his dedicated services. When the meeting was done and I was being escorted by all three of my hosts, he actually opened the door for me to enter the backseat of the vehicle like a diplomat, and this brings assurances of honor. My activities for the day went on well, but there was still more work to do. The next day my UN driver friend did most of my errands. He took specimen of the receipt I designed to a printer along with the disclosure form and other document for printing. While he was gone to work on that, I joined the concern refugee committee group at the US embassy, and I did give them an overall picture of the state of the camp, which they have already read in newspapers. They assured our group that they would not quote me in their discussion with the UNHCR or with the government. Two days later, both UNHCR and the government held a joint press conference in which they conceded that the camp was in the hands of RUF rebels and that they have located a new camp for Liberian Refugees at Jua, just few miles from Freetown. Hopefully the Americans would loosen up resettlement programs for refugees who have relatives in their country wishing to file for them. This was great news and a great relief for me because I now have the choice to decline the UNHCR offer without fear of adverse consequences, and they also knew that their offer was based on selling the idea that the camp was good for habitation of the refugees…a concept in which I were to be their pawn. The only issue now is the fact that I have come to know from the insiders how refugee resettlements are managed and processed, and this would be a secret I can assure Mrs. Thomas that I would never talk about to anyone. Who knows what lies ahead since my organization is now also in the migration business.

Chapter 51

The first radio announcement about the Canadian Migration Program was aired after the seven o'clock news in the evening on Wednesday at a time when most people are expected to be at home after work. Earlier in the day, I had screened and selected sixteen casual workers out of a host of workers that the Ministry of Labor sent me upon request. The workers were divided into two groups: eight customer service representatives to receive applicants and process them through the preliminaries, including receiving application fees, and the other eight to serve as counselors to conduct interviews in accordance with the program requirement guide. For three days up to Friday, the training started at 2:00 p.m. and ended at 5:00 p.m. Training materials were provided and remained at the AccordOne office daily after each training. On Friday, the eight counselors walked with me down the road to the Jalloh Foundation to familiarize themselves with the place where they would be conducting the interviews. We were well received and the orientation went well. All the casual staff were instructed to be properly dressed on Monday; the men wearing white shirt and preferably blue-colored tie and the female white blouse and preferably blue-colored skirt. All of them were to clock in for work beginning on Monday at 8:30 a.m., and upon clocking in, would receive their respective name tag to begin. The program would be open to the public at 9:00 a.m. to 6:00 p.m. on weekdays.

Early on Wednesday, my UN drive friend drove me to a diamond broker on Kissy Street where I collected $28,000 (US dollars) for the larger of the two stones. I felt cheated when the offer was made following the appraisal process, but I was helpless in resisting it. I didn't know much about diamonds and never before sold any, and I was overwhelmed by this offer for just one of the two. The amount was beyond my expectation. I thought both gems would rip up to $15,000. I thought that this was some kind of a mistake the broker had made, and being nervous with my heart pounding, I could not wait to collect the money and run as fast as I could. The deal was through by 11:00 a.m., and before leaving, I promised the broker that we would do more business.

As I entered my UN 1 with a briefcase containing $28,000, a sudden feeling just consumed me and I really felt like a different person, someone that was no longer me. I didn't think that I could ever be able to express these feelings, but it brought me arrogance and bigotry, and I felt like an important figure with a giant mission that would impact the world. Suddenly, I realized that I had turned a millionaire according to Sierra Leone standards. I was probably worth over Le.50,000,000. I went over to my office where I stashed $25,000 and tipped off my UN 1 driver friend and dismissed him for the day.

In the same block where my office was located were money exchange depots. I quickly exchanged $1,000 for Le.800,000 and sent my wife and children to purchase cloths and other things that they needed. Near my office were several elegant stores where I bought few suits, shirts, ties, shoes, and socks. My family was at the dinner table that evening when the radio announcement about the Canadian Migration Program was aired. When AccordOne was mentioned, my heart pounded, and I became emotional. It was all like a fairy tale, and I was in the middle of it all. My wife looked straight up at me across the table, and I would never forget that look in her eyes. She was stunned and speechless. She knew about the Canadian Migration Program, but she had no idea about the planning, organizing, and implementation of it as an AccordOne project. In fact, she thought that it was some embassy, United Nations office, or some big-time NGOs that was accredited to execute such programs and not her small-time refugee husband and his small-time unknown organization. When the program was first spoken of before the camp was taken over by RUF, she was with the impression that

I would be working for the big fishes, the great Mr. King and his wife who happened to be the United Nations resident representative as they structure the entire operations. She saw me running around with UN 1, and she assumed that was the case and suddenly she was listening to the public announcement nationwide that AccordOne was accredited to process applications for the program.

We are completely two different personalities, and we both endure in variable ways to compromise our differences on a daily basis in order to keep our marriage going. I see and do things differently from her, and she gets nervous and panics frequently over little things, and she certainly has trouble taking any type of risk or handling bigger things. I am the dominating factor in our relationship because I take initiatives, I take risks, I can spend money, I make plans and implement them while she is completely opposite. We do discuss and share issues relative to our family, but we do not normally discuss in details my work or to discuss strategies. Even during normal days, if a court citation were served on us for a simple matter, my wife would use the bathroom several times longer. If we were walking on the street, my wife would change lanes if a policeman or military officer is spotted on the lane we are on, my wife would change lane. She once told me stories about her upbringing when her relatives would scare the hell out of her by using some neighbors who are in the police force to scare her many times, and she would be scared by sight of the police even if she was just walking to or from school. Because of that, she is always afraid when she sees police. Another trait is that she would jump into a frenzy and overreact at the slightest hint of any abnormalities. I remembered once in Liberia when our children were younger, we had an electrical malfunction that caused a spark of fire on the cables in a house we rented at Mamba Point in Monrovia. She ran out of the house, falling several times on the ground, without any of her children while I made sure that I went into each room where the children were and rescued them, walking calmly because the fire was not to the size that would warrant panic.

Right then as she sat across the table from me, I could see everything about her had changed from listening to the public announcement. She had entered her panicky mode once again as if the world was coming to an end, and I could tell the number of things going through her head. I was pretty sure that she would collapse if I even told her how much money one of the diamonds was sold for and that the cash was stashed right inside the chair she was seating on. Within minutes after the public announcement, the phone rang, and I saw a cup she was drinking from drop off her hand, and she ran for the bathroom. The call was from my secretary who wanted to know if I was listening to the radio. After talking, I went into the bathroom to encourage my wife that everything was fine and under control and that there was no need for panicking, but I knew I was only talking to myself.

However the road to D-day was very hectic and at least I got my lovely wife to help. Part of the monumental tasks in preparation for this big day was to make sure that the roads and partway leading to other businesses and offices was not blocked or crowed by our customers and potential customers. There were other offices in the same building where AccordOne was housed and there was a mosque upfront on the other wing. It was important to take all these into consideration to put everyone in the building and our neighbors on notice about the kind of crowd we were expecting beginning on Monday. Next, we had to fix an imaginary partway to queue into the building from the sidewalk into the building and partway to leave the building so as not to experience blockages. On Friday afternoon I struck a deal with a local security company and six officers assigned to assist with controlling partway to and fro the building. Later in the evening, I held a press conference at my office about the program and a number of reporters from various newspapers attended. Light refreshment and snack were served, and together we had a promising gathering that many of the reporters agreed we should have from time to time as the program progress. On the national news on the radio and on television the upcoming Canadian Migration Program made headline news that weekend.

On Sunday evening, the artist delivered and mounted the three billboards depicting joyful faces of travelers queuing to board a colorful aircraft marked "Canadian Migration Program." At the bottom, a pointed finger led to the inscription: "Process Your Application Here…You Can Make It Too," followed by the address and telephone number of AccordOne. The city council office charged a fee for mounting two of the billboards on the streets and that was taken care of by Thursday. That weekend, news of the program became the talk of the town in households, street corners, bars, coffee shops, and restaurant, etc. As we concluded preparation for the program and the weekend slowly faded away, drawing Monday closer, the thought that in just few hours' time the whole nation would be focusing on how AccordOne is handling this project sent waves of periodic shocks in my abdomen that made me want to join my wife in the bathroom.

Chapter 52

Monday, May 29, 1995, turned out to be D-Day. The day began with sporadic rain in the early hours, and around 5:15 a.m., the rain finally subsided. This must have been a sign of assurances from the heavens, anointing the AccordOne project, the first of its kind in the history of the country. I spent most part of the night working on controlling and directing strategies and with other preparation work. My terrified wife was also so captivated with fear and anxiety that she was awoken many times even by the slightest sound from a flipping page. Three times she abruptly jumped from her sleep to ask what I think or feel about the whole thing and if there is any way I can call it off by postponing it. She looked like a rabbit on alert near its hole. While concealing my own feelings, I assured her over and over again that I feel fantastic and that I am optimistic that the whole thing will go on well, and that she would soon get used to it. As the radio station recited the early morning public announcement and the clouds becoming clearer by the minutes, reality began to set in, raising the tension and elevating anxiety level. Each ticktock from the wall clock increased heartbeats as the hour drew near. "What is it going to be like?" was the big question that has manifested itself over and over again and refused to go away. One of the questions of concern to me, which also came up during the press conference on Friday, was whether any single nongovernmental organization is cloth with the authority to conduct this type of operation on a large scale without breaking the law or disrupting some diplomatic regulation. That aspect was researched and cleared a long time ago. AccordOne's licenses from the Sierra Leone authorities clearly states, inter alia, that the organization can assist with the migration and or resettlement of refugees and the displaced. Furthermore, the services we were about to provide was outsourced to us by a recognized and certified Canadian migration practitioner through his firm. The service itself is not a consular services or any services offered by embassies, it is nothing more than filling up a complicated application form in accordance with the required guideline and turning the applications over to the firm in Canada for processing. This can be done by any applicant but the only difference is that the firm in Canada is not accepting any applications directly from private individuals from this territory according to the existing contract between AccordOne and the firm. Any applicant who wished to do their application independently is at liberty to do so but when they file it by themselves they would be thousands of miles away from the bureaucracy and frequent changes in the immigration system in Canada and each time they want to follow up or the authorities has a query to address it would be done by mail and the postal system in Sierra Leone was perhaps one of the worst in the world. That system is grossly understaffed, which account for massive delays in mail delivery and because of economic problems with the institution being months behind with paying employees' salaries the risk of mail fraud and other problems are what an independent applicant have to put up with. Therefore, the assurances and commitment of an accredited Canadian expert, to expedite application process and to readily respond to any queries on behalf of each applicant, made a lot of sense to me and was marketable. Unfortunately for applicants, Canada does not have an embassy in Sierra Leone. The Canadian consular service covering Sierra Leone is stationed in Ghana. All these and many more factors were researched before the decision to undertake this service was reached. By 8:00 a.m., my family had prepared: children awoken, taken a bath, eaten breakfast, and dressed in new clothing. The same for my wife and I and most especially we converted the premise back to the form of an office and put all household items away. Just about then, the six security personnel I hired to help conduct the process in orderly manner and restore order if need be arrived, and we had a ten minutes orientation. One of them was assigned strictly to be with me at my office, two others to make sure that the pathway for people to leave the building after attendance was always kept open for free passage. The last three would do the same for incoming pathway, and all of them were responsible of keeping the peace and maintain cordial processing. At 8:30 all of the customer service representatives and counselors arrived and well dressed. They received and put on their respective name tags, and we all had a get a little get-to-know-each-other moment, and my wife and children were introduced. Lunch is on the organization and my wife was responsible. She also had few other refugee women to come in later to work with her to make that happen. Meanwhile there was coffee, tea, and snacks. The operations would not stop but would be slowed down as a result of staff taking turns in snacking or taking lunch. It was approaching 9:00 a.m. when my wife called me out into my office from the conference hall where I was meeting with my new staff. I went into my office to see what she was calling me about, and I noticed that look again in her eyes as she just pointed to the window. The streets were full with people to the extent that traffic was detouring, and I was totally blown away. By the time I turned around in a split second to say something to her, she rushed into the restroom and as usual I knew what that means. I immediately called all six security personnel into my office and instructed them to go out there and convince the crowd to make two queues into the building using the sidewalks and to leave the main roads so that cars can pass freely. Everyone would have a chance to process their application so there was no need to fight. At 9:00 a.m. the gate and doors to the office were opened for business. On this first day, we processed 860 applicants and collected Le.12,900,000, approximately $20,000.00. There were no major issues reported, just a little procedural adjustments and corrective actions were taken as we go. By the end of the first week, 3,917 applications had been processed bringing in a total of Le.58,755,000 approximately $95,000. Le.11,751,000 is paid out to the Jalloh Foundation for the week, and they were so happy that the three partners also became counselors in order to speed up the process.

Each of the original six counselors conducted an estimated twenty interviews per day, which gives us the capacity to interview six hundred applicants per week. The maximum time per interview is, say fifteen minutes. That first weekend, I released a public announcement aired on SLBS conveying that the organization would not be accepting any more applications after June 30, 1995, until the second week in July 1995. During the course of the week, news of the program had spread like wildfire in many quarters, and the entire refugee community became aware that I was behind the whole thing. News also reached UNHCR, and Mrs. Thomas called to speak with me about their offer. She said that from what she was hearing about my new project she did not think that I was still interested in their offer, but she wanted to hear from me. I asked for time to meet with her, and we agreed to have lunch on me the next Monday. At the same time there was a need for me to give a lending hand to my fellow Liberian refugees who had just been placed at a dilapidated wharf to leave in broken but abandoned warehouses without any roofs. So we decided and provided foodstuff to feed 1,500 of them, distributed beddings, and provided learning materials to some three hundred school children. Also, we provided medication for a few of the sick and handed first-aid kits to some five hundred families. We shouldered the medical bills for three young men in the refugee community that were seriously ill and needed operations. These events were extensively covered by the local news media, and one official of AccordOne who was once a broadcaster at the Liberian broadcasting corporation used her expertise to make a documentary for the organization. Amongst those to witness these humanitarian gestures were the Liberian ambassador to Sierra Leone, the secretary general of the Mano Union and a Liberian presidential aspirant.

Chapter 53

Mr. CTO King arrived in Freetown on Sunday, just one week after D-day and learned about the hot topics in town and that led him to attempt arranging an urgent meeting with me. His new company, Sierra Leone Financial Corporation, is also located at another wing of the building where AccordOne is housed. The crowd that he saw in the building compound and on the sidewalk on Monday morning when he arrived at his office jolted him, and he wanted to know how much money has been generated from the program, which he thought belonged to him. He wanted us to meet immediately at his office, but since my schedule was very tight, I got my secretary to return his phone call to inform him that Wednesday would be a good time, but the all-powerful King who is not used to being told no, sent back word insisting that if we do not meet before twelve noon today I would have deserved whatever comes to me. This caught my attention, and I picked up the phone to talk with him about my schedule and said I was willing and anxious to meet with him, but he insisted on me dropping everything to meet with him immediately and demanded that I should come along with a report of the program from its inception last Monday to date and then he hanged up on me. That sounded like a threat and by virtue of his status as husband to the United Nations residence representative to Sierra Leone, there is no limit to the favors this man can garner to hurt me and then grab the program from me. But what he may not have been aware of was the fact that I am also a new millionaire and in this environment where money means power, there was no limit where I can go to protect myself and indeed I am chairman for AccordOne, and I am answerable to its board, not any king. The application process continued, and I went on to take care of my scheduled activities. I knew from the beginning that I do not have to put all of the funds collected into the organization's bank account or my personal bank account, so I planned to convert a huge amount of money from Leones to US dollars and to stash it. That morning, guarded by two of my security officers, I left with a briefcase to the money exchange bureau. I walked out from the bureau with $15,000 which I carried on my person.

Later at 12:30 p.m., I arrived at the Bristol de Paris for my lunch appointment with Mrs. Thomas. We spoke about the resettlement offer, and I respectfully declined it with assurances that it would always remain confidential. I explained my current engagement and the responsibilities that come with it, and she showed understanding. I said that I would not rule out any resettlement for my family directly in my legitimate family name, and she assured that she would help process the official refugee travel document for my family, and she indeed kept her word.

Later on August 26, 1995, my wife and I finally were sent to sign and take receipt of our travel document from the Immigration Department in Freetown. At the end of our lunch, she thanked me for AccordOne support to the refugee community over the weekend and expressed sentiment of working together to improve conditions. When I returned to my office at 2:00 p.m., I met a heavily built man with a walking stick and a little boy waiting to talk to me about what the man said was very confidential matters and asking for thirty minutes of my time if I can oblige. To convince me, he said it would be highly profitable. At the same time there were urgent messages that claimed my attention. One of them was for an impromptu meeting which my secretary had set up for me to meet with one of the best law firms in the country to represent our organization and myself should King threat come to be. Following the threat from Mr. King earlier in the morning, my secretary suggested that we would need legal protection for the organization, and she was authorized to shop around for a strong attorney in the community. She finally found one and arranged for me to meet him this afternoon. The lawyer himself had called my office several times, and the secretary assured that she will set the meeting up immediately upon my arrival. So I asked this man if we can schedule the so-called confidential matters he wanted to discuss with me and he accepted, and we decided to meet at my office after working hours. It was not until he stood up and grabbed his walking stick with the little boy holding one end of it to lead him out of the office that I realized he was blind and suddenly his name, Pa Yillah, rang a bell. *This must be the UNHCR resettlement connection man*, I thought. We agreed to meet later at 7:00 p.m. that evening at my office and he left.

Attorney Urshor Williams is one of the tycoons in the city who understands both how the legal system and nonlegal systems works, and he is ready to do anything by law, by hook or by crook, to protect the interest of a rich client. He inspected AccordOne's license and the Canadian firm accreditation document for the migration program and then he said that he was prepared to protect the organization, the program, and me personally in any matter. In fact, he himself would have some relatives who might be interested in the program and would be grateful if they get special preferences.

As he inspected the documents, he asked if the applications that AccordOne has processed were for refugees or displaced. I murmured and hesitated in answering his question because I knew where he was going with it. AccordOne's license covered services to refugees and the displaced and the program it was engaged with extended to everyone without limits. As I struggled to frame my answer, the attorney interrupted me: "Whether they are refugees, displaced, or nondisplaced, it does not matter because the country is at war anyway, and everybody—even I am—displaced. I can't even go upcountry to represent my clients because they are all here living on sidewalks in the city," he concluded. We both agreed that even if the applicants were not refugees or displaced, there was no law or regulations that prevent or preclude AccordOne from processing anyone nor did the accreditation from Canada specify that. Furthermore, we are not in the business of identifying applicants. The attorney asked for Le100,000 retainer fee plus a Le.50,000 monthly legal fees. After

I made the Le.100,000 payment, the attorney provided me with what he called a strategic advice. I should write in bold letters a sign in conspicuous places at the office for all to see. The sign should read that AccordOne only process applications for refugees and the displaced. "This would not affect AccordOne's operations one bit," he said. "Everyone I know would like to leave this country under any status so that sign would make no difference to them order than protecting our organization," he concluded.

Chapter 54

Pa Yillah arrived exactly at 7:00 p.m. and waited for another thirty minutes for me to wrap things up and dismissed the rest of my staff for the day. He was then ushered into my office by his escort whom he asked to wait at the reception after taking his seat. The escort closed the door behind him, and we were left alone to discuss the very important matter that he earlier preached as being profitable for both of us. He began by stressing confidentiality about our meeting and its subject matter and then he proceeded: "For many years, I have engaged in the business of assisting people obtaining visas to travel to many countries of the world where they would settle down to improve their lives, the lives of their families, relatives, and friends right here at home. I have been following your program, and I am very proud of you, Mr. Davies. I think it might be benefiting working with your organization in processing some of my very special clients who have expressed their interest in migrating to Canada." I thanked him for the compliment and stated that the tenet of my organization is simply to assist in completing applications in accordance with the strict guidance for filing. "Beyond this," I added, "I am afraid we are powerless and without influence to do anything." He said that he understood that and few of his clients have already started the application process with us, but he is suggesting special processing preferences of his clients from the norms for a little more money. This caught my attention, and the floor was opened to hear the details of Pa Yillah's proposal.

"Instead of just processing applications, my clients are entrusting everything into my hands—everything from the beginning of application preparation, its filing, and every step on the way up to final approval and travel, just like the refugee resettlement program, and they are willing to pay big money for these services."

"What do you know about the refugee resettlement programs and its processes?" I asked, pretending not to know anything about his involvement and connections with UNHCR. The blind man removed his goggles and rolled his eyes up the ceiling, his face brightened as he giggled at my question. "Mr. Davies, I have refugee resettlement programs in the palm of my hands, and I can assure you that the highest bidder can be resettled as refugees in this town," he said.

"Does that mean that the refugee resettlement program is for sale?" I persisted. He shook his head in disappointment in a rather callous gesture indicative of saying who in this town do not know this. "It is said that what the right hand knows, the left hand should not know and what the left hand knows the right hand should not know, so I am here to work out a deal with you for my clients for the Canadian migration program. I found out that refugees stands a better chance by far to qualify for this program with less burden in the process compared to nonrefugees, so most of my clients are interested in being processed under refugee classification. But it is not what you should be concerned about because they can get authentic refugee status from the right sources, which some of them already have. I would handle the rest of the processes, and all that I need from you is to support me in verifying every step of the process for each individual program. For this you would get a fee of say twenty-five percentage of the entire processing fees received." At this point, I am still struggling with what he meant and how he was going to process these clients of his and what verification obligation I would be doing and to whom. So I enquire about all of these and in answering he shows himself as a good negotiator. He started by giving an example of the kind of money he is talking about: "We are talking thousands of US dollars here Mr. Davies and you might get between two to three thousand dollars per head. Imagine verifying the process for say twenty of my clients per month and multiply that by three thousand dollars. That's a cool sixty thousand dollars for that month."

"What am I verifying?" I asked. He paused for couple of seconds while he adjusted his goggle then leaned forward across the desk toward my face as though he could see me behind those dark shades. "All you need to verify from time to time is that I handle the full package of the Canadian migration program and that you are confident that my clients are in good hands. Always raise their confidence level about their dealings with me and that is all. You will not deal with them directly. No money will change hands from them to you nor would you discuss any money matter with them. To obtain their refugee status and to process their migration is entirely my obligation."

"It seem to me that all these could be achieved all by yourself without me, so why me?" I asked.

"Who else can be assertive, convincing, and believable than the only person that is accredited with the Canadian migration program in Sierra Leone?" he asked.

"Do I get the twenty-five percentage commission on each of your clients across the board unconditionally, and how do I know how many of them you have and how much they pay per head?" I asked.

"All of my clients would first be sent to AccordOne to start the application process up to the interview that you conducted to complete their applications. When that is done, you will send me a copy of their completed applications while you send the original to your practitioner in Canada. My contact in Canada would take it from there to expedite the process once the applications are filed. Now I would send you a list of my clients whose applications you are processing, and I will update that list on a weekly basis, and this is how you will know the number of my clients. As to how much they are paying for my services, this varies so I cannot be specific, but you will have to trust me after all. Twenty-five percentages of my minimum charges will net you $2,000, but if I get the maximum charge you will get $3,000 and that is a promise. If you want us to document this as a written understanding between us, I stand ready."

By this time, in my head, I was busy with a number of scenarios and calculating how much money I would have generated in the first month, then the next month, and the other and hopefully if the rebels do not attack the capital city soon enough to disrupt viable programs such like these, AccordOne would have become one of the most powerful NGO in the region stretching its wings across borders. "How about the clients that have already gone through the application process with us, are we going to get commission on them?" I asked. Pa Yillah smiled and stretched his hand across the table, and we tightly shook hands affirming and sealing the deal. With our hands still tightly holding, instinctively we stood up and he said in typical Creole: "Ar been don know say you na me right han man so from teday na so e go be, because wan man nor for chop everything, e go chock ham, the brade for circulate leh orda people dem sef leek han, na to so e be Mr. Davies?"

"Na so e be," I replied.

Chapter 55

At 1:00 p.m. on Tuesday, I held a revision meeting with my counselors about special preference interviewing for certain of our registered applicants. The meeting was based on the first list received early that morning from Pa Yillah delivered by his escort in a sealed envelope. I checked the records to see when all six applicants on the list were scheduled for interview, but it showed that the first interview will take place in three weeks' time and the last one will take place in seven weeks. This does not make any sense, holding up this important interest to wait for up to seven weeks when the key to making the interviews happen soonest rested in my own hands. It is only a matter of rescheduling them and having Pa Yillah notifying them that he has rescheduled their respective interviews. No one knows when Freetown would be ran over by the rebels or when it would become a battle ground where most business activities would be suspended. Two counselors were selected and entrusted with the interview of these special clients and their completed files should be on my desk immediately following completion of their applications. I would have to get Pa Yillah to contact them to come in at the rescheduled time this week for their respective interviews. I was just about to make that phone call to him when suddenly one of the security guards walked into my office to alert me of the presence of several Criminal Investigation Department (CID) personnel in the building ordering my staff to seize the application processing and asking potential applicants on both queues to return to their various homes pending an investigation into the entire program. As I walked out of my office to see what was going on, two plaincloth officers confronted me asking that I am invited by the head of CID immediately at their headquarters at Pademba Road. In the meantime, I am to instruct all my staff to seize the processing of application immediately. I inquired if there was a court order, and they said that they had no idea but was just carrying out instructions from their boss. As we were leaving the building, I noticed they were many CID personnel and some of them remained at the office to ensure that their boss's order is enforced. Those who had just enrolled into the program became concerned and potential applicants on both queues dispersed and formed pocket groups curious but unsure about what the incident might have been. Before leaving, I instructed my secretary to inform the lawyer about what was happening, and on the way, I inquired with the two escort officers what the matter was, and they could not give me any information but confirmed that the head of the CID received a couple of phone calls pressuring him to investigate the legitimacy of AccordOne's migration application processing. When we arrived, I was detained at their intake office for about an hour while waiting for their boss who was said to be in a meeting. As I waited, my mind fidgeted on several scenarios. Was the Pa Yillah visit a setup? If that was the case, then how does that incriminate me when I have not yet received any money from him or do any of the things he wanted me to do? Following the chief's meeting, I was escorted to his office where three other senior officers were waiting to interrogate me. The interrogation started with the four men trying to define me as a refugee and advancing a general notion that refugees are not supposed to initiate or implement any activities at the scale of the current activities but to confine under the wings of the UNHCR and the host country and receiving emergency services, food, medical, and shelter. To this I respectfully objected and said that I have read the Universal Declaration of Human Rights to which Sierra Leone is signatory, and I have also read the UNHCR charters and never before come across any stipulations that limited, restricted, or confined the rights of refugees in exercising their abilities to the fullest lawfully and morally. I cited examples of refugees that acclaimed prominence in host countries of asylum without such notion of hindrances, naming Madeleine Albright who is United States ambassador to the United Nations as one of my examples. Then I respectfully asked for a citation to the rules, regulations, and/or laws that they were quoting that restrict, prevent, or banned refugees from initiating, promoting, or implementing any such activities or any stipulations that layout what category or scale of activities refugees are entitled to engaged with. This made the head of the department a little angry with me. So I became quiet knowing that I have just sent the message that I was not someone that they can walk over. Then they wanted evidence to show that AccordOne is legally cloth with the authority to implement what they call "the job of an embassy." At this, I explained the services we are providing and indicated that our objectives are openly stipulated in the government-issued licenses that legalized our existence and that we also entered into a legitimate agreement with an accredited Canadian immigration practitioner to assist with the complex process of completing applications for the Canadian Migration Program.

"All of these are guarded under the watchful eyes of the organization's legal counsel, whom I am sure would have advised against our initiatives if they were against the laws of Canada or Sierra Leone," I concluded. Then came questions as to the services we are providing refugees and the displaced since our inceptions, which has no relevance to matter at issue, but I answered and gave references as to the humanitarian services we have provided the refugee community all of which I said are recognized by the UNHCR and the Coalition of Non-Governmental Organizations.

The director asked that I step out for a moment while they deliberate on the issue, and so the two officers ushered me out in the corridor. From where we stood I could faintly hear a little of what was being discussed, but the two officers have interesting observations to share with me. They disclosed that some prominent person connected with the UN office called and reported that I am conducting an illegal consular services and generating millions of Leones, but they do not think that is the case from their preliminary investigation. "You just need to find something for our chief, to befriend him, and win him over to your side so that your business can be protected henceforth," they suggested. Moments later I was called back in and this time the questions geared toward how much money has been generated so far. I said that I do not have the numbers on top of my head, and they insisted to give them a ballpark figure. Then I said maybe a million Leones or two, and one of the senior officers in the room cut his eyes at me with his face frown then he exclaimed: "Impossible! Impossible! We would like to help you out, but you are not being honest with us," he shouted at me.

I said that I am working for an organization, and to the best of my knowledge, no inventory have yet been conducted nor any report have reached me to answer all of their questions in precise terms, and beside I have no knowledge that an investigation or audit into the activities of the organization was at hand. So they sent me back to the office with the two officers escorting me to fetch the authorization documents as well as the receipt books being used or with a report of the total amount raised so far. On the way I told the two officers that I was hungry and needed to eat, so we walked past my office where pockets of crowd were still standing and waiting to see the outcome of what was happening. As we walked our way past the office, I put up a smiling face and cracked a joke that caught the officers laughing and for a moment we stopped walking and laughed out loud. All eyes were on us, and I think that helped relieve the tension that was boiling. I overheard someone saying if this program was a fake, do you think they would release him and let him walk freely without him being detained or having handcuff on him? As we reached the front of the building, I stopped and asked one of the officers to do me a favor, to go into the building to call my secretary to join us at the restaurant so that I can instruct her to get all the documents I needed. He gladly went in and the other officer and I proceeded down the road toward the restaurant.

Later, the officer and my secretary joined us at the restaurant, and I could see that they related very well. As she took her seat, she disclosed that the lawyer has sent to inquire the reason for the actions taken by CID and that he has noted the suspension of the organization's operations without a court mandate. The waitress took our orders, and while we were waiting for the food some serious discussions as to how to foil the situation and prevent any further obstructions emerged with the two officers participating as though they were members of my staff. Back at CID headquarters, the tension had reduced. Attorney Williams had intervened and spoke with the chief. He mentioned the involvement of other prominent Sierra Leoneans with the program and cited Jalloh Foundation as one organization collaborating with AccordOne and is responsible for conducting the interviews. The chief knew the individuals involved with Jalloh Foundation, and he probably realized that even if there were rules that limit refugees in Sierra Leone, those rules may not apply to me. He inspected the AccordOne's licenses and the Canadian Migration Agreement and confirmed that Attorney Williams had called him on behalf of the organization. Then he disclosed that he received several calls for various individuals including Mr. King making an issue out of the program. At this I told him that King was a disgruntled friend of mine who claimed that he should be the only one running the program here in Sierra Leone though he does not have the infrastructure yet to perform this kind of service. The atmosphere and dynamics changed, and suddenly I found myself relaxed and seating in the company of the leading officers of the Sierra Leone Criminal Investigation Department, laughing and chatting with them, and as the moment was ripe the chief asked what I can do for them. The other three officers left the room so that the chief gets his privacy and felt free to receive his "cold water."

Before leaving, each one of the other three ushered me into their respective offices to receive their own "cold water." The chief, however, instructed the two field officers to go back to my office and retrieve the others that are posted there, and if possible, let all concern know that AccordOne is cleared and operations are back in full swing. At the end of whole episode, I spent $600: $200 for the chief, $100 for each of his senior officers, and a hundred for the two field officers who escorted me. Though it was after 5:00 p.m. when

I finally returned to my office, the place was crowded. The officers told their companion and together they all spread the good news around and before long the lines were back in full swing and normal business were extended up to 8:00 p.m. in order to compensate for the patience and dedication of our clients. Though this first part of my adversary's signature plan just failed, yet the full plan was still in gear and would manifest itself on the next day, Wednesday.

Chapter 56

Nine hundred and fifteen miles away in Accra, Ghana, the Canadian high commissioner's office is alerted that AccordOne in Freetown was in the business of selling fake Canadian visas and providing consular services to thousands of civilians, refugees, and Sierra Leoneans. The information triggered an impromptu meeting of diplomats at the commissioner's office on Monday within hours of Mr. King's ultimatum and threat. In Canada, the authorities ordered an investigation into the allegations and the consul at the commissioner's office in Accra was envoy to Sierra Leone. Before departing Ghana on Tuesday for Freetown, she was assured that the assailant has been arrested and detained at the CID in Freetown awaiting her arrival. She arrived overnight and on Wednesday morning she teamed up with two lawyers and together they headed to the CID headquarters to discuss with the chief. They were disappointed that I was not being detained and found out that the allegations were false and that AccordOne is a legitimate nonprofit organization in contract with a Canadian immigration practitioner for the purpose of ensuring that applications for the Canadian Migration Program, which is opened to the general public by Canadian government are completely filled in compliance with the guidelines.

"We investigated their activities and the authority for what they are doing, and we do not find any evidence of visa transactions or any services that your consular office would provide at an embassy, so we had to let him go," the CID chief asserted. After they left the CID headquarters, Chief Dickinson called to update me about their visit and to remind me that he, Chief Dickinson, is in my corner; and he would do all that is necessary to protect me. About an hour after talking with the CID chief, my secretary informed me that I have visitors from the Canadian high commissioner's office in Ghana. A lady accompanied by two men walked into my office, and I received them well and offered light drinks which the two men received but the lady declined. The woman introduced herself as the consul from the Canadian high commissioner's office in Ghana, and she introduced the other gentlemen, one as legal counsel from her office in Ghana and the other is their legal counterpart in Sierra Leone. After the introduction and brief off-the-beat talks about population congestion in the city, I switched gears and asked what I could do for them. The lady, probably in her mid-forties and with a Sierra Leonean accent, started by asking how many application AccordOne has processed so far since the program started. I said that I do not know and asked why she wanted to know.

"Do you realize that you have gone over the top with all these thousands of applications, and you know only a few stands a chance to be approved and when that happens, they would have to be processed by my office before migrated to Canada takes place? And do you not know that you and your so-called Canadian immigration practitioners are making this a profitable business, exploiting interested applicants even though your organization is supposed to be a nonprofit entity? What are you going to do with all that money generated?"

I was confused that she asked all these questions especially about the money. I was going to ask, "Why not mind your own business?" or "Wait till approved applicants make it to your office," and "Who the hell are you to ask how we do business or what we do with our money," but somehow my diplomatic instincts kicked in, and I politely defused the tension. "Madam, I know that everything around here is eyed differently from the norm, but we are not doing this for the money as is being perceived and circulated by some people. We are a humanitarian organization, and when it comes to this program, our success lies eventually in the number of applicants that would be approved and seeing them free from this shackle of abject poverty around here would be the fulfillment of our objective. To see families escape this misery is truly our goal. If one to ten out of every one hundred applicants are approved, then our vision of success would have been priceless, not the small money we charge for helping out with this complex application processing and preparing the applicant to pass the program interview which evidently is associated with some cost for which we are charging this little fees. I am sure that you will agree with me that no organization would process the number of applications we have dealt with without incurring administrative and operational costs with a great deal of expertise inputs, staffing, stationery, mailing, etc., and you should agree with me if I say that we both have important things to do not to even mention the time and cost of traveling from Ghana to visit this issue growing out of misleading information. And I think that the only good we can make out of this meeting is to get to know each other better outside of the rumor mongering and perhaps we could turn this situation around and forge a sort of productive relationship that could be of mutual interest to us because you have come hundreds of miles away to see for yourself that such things like fake visa sales or consular services is not what we do here."

There was a momentary pause and both men looked each other in the eye and nodded toward her then she asked how I got to know about the Canadian migration program and how come the Jalloh Foundation is involved. These sounded like a King mouthpiece to me, and I was beginning to lose my patience, but I had to conceal my personal feelings and represent my organization. "As member of NGO Coalition, there is a pool of organizations we affiliate with depending on the task choice, and as you all know already the Canadian migration program is openly publicized by Canadian authorities seeking to populate territories that are less populated in their country. Now, the need for a coordinated system to help interested applicants fill in their applications in accordance with the official guideline (which changes from time to time by the way) to get them to acquire the appropriate documentations which differ from applicant to applicant and to prepare them for an interview in the event of their approval and acceptance cannot be overemphasized.

The statistics of applications that are returned back to applicants around the world for completion, attested to this need for which some immigration practitioners in Canada decided to seek partnership with befitting organizations that can help prepare these applications accordingly, hence our involvement," I said.

Continuing, I said, "This should even make embassy work easier with time savings when approved applicants are being interviewed." Turning the table on them, I asked what would be her advice or expectation moving forward now that they know that the rumors or allegations which brought them to my office are all false. I kept looking at my watch as I speak, pretending to have some scheduled businesses to take care of, and when the phone rang, I immediately knew the opportunity to wrap up this impromptu meeting was at hand, so I sprang to me feet after my telephone conversation and indicated that I was sorry, but I am late for a scheduled meeting. She said that she would have to prepare a report and might come back to see me before departing for Ghana. We shook hands, and I accompanied them all the way out to the main gate and watched them enter their vehicle and drove away. She was watching the queue of potential applicants with keen interest on her way out, and I could almost guess what was going on in her head. As soon as they drove away, I switched gear on to attending to Pa Yillah.

Chapter 57

The week passed by without any major incident except for an unwelcome visit from my mother and her brother, both of whom showed up separately on Friday. Uncle Amoso had a daughter who worked as a waitress at Art of Oak Bar & Restaurant located a block from my office. This was a local joint where regular guys meet to eat African food during the day and party all night long. By this time I had become famous in the community, and my name has fallen into gossip tracks in households, coffee shops, bars, and restaurants and the media too accounted for this. It was not a surprise to see people that I do not know either waving to me on the street or approaching me for a chat or to ask for some kind of help. The petty traders around the block and a host of refugees even named me a philanthropist. So on Thursday evening, when this waitress at the restaurant pulled up a chair at my table to start a chat with me while I was dining, my first thought was that she needed some kind of help but when she called me cousin I became curious. Then she revealed to me that she is Uncle Amoso's daughter and that her dad had been trying to reach me lately and had asked her to set up an appointment to meet with me. Like most of my relatives and friends, Uncle Amoso never helped me in any way whatsoever, not in times of need. During his hay day as a seafarer, I had to chase him many times for help but to no avail at certain point in my teens, I gave up visiting or chasing him for anything. In fact there was hardly any relationship between me and the majority of my siblings or relatives; in other words, I have been a loner all along with only my love for chess playing providing me a solace. Even in Freetown where I had so many relatives and friends hardly any one of them recognized me or offered a lending hand when I was in desperate need and when I became a poor, homeless refugee, roaming around and struggling to put roof over my family or even to stop by once in a while to show care and love for my children. All of a sudden wealth and fame is bringing many to recognize me and to identify themselves as relatives or friends. Uncle Amoso was one of the many seafarers in Sierra Leone that the broken system let down. The seafaring industry boomed long before I was born, but in recent years, greedy politicians and their cronies in high offices led the country's economy into a meltdown and the seafaring industry, like many other industries, went revving downhill into ruins affecting thousands of seafarers and their families. In the midnineties more than half of seafarers in the country were struggling to survive. Many sold every asset they had acquired during their hay days to make hands meet, so it was predictable that Uncle Amoso must have heard of his nephew's fortune and decided to make contact so as to feed on it. I told my cousin that maybe next weekend might be good time, but surprisingly early the next morning, just before 8:00 a.m., Uncle Amoso was knocking at my office door with proposal to pawn his house to me for a large amount of money. I declined that transaction for personal reasons and then offered him Le.50,000 as a gift. Few hours later, my mother showed up wanting to see me apparently to get a piece of the pie, but I anticipated this so I was not surprise because I knew her more than anyone else on earth. She can do anything for money and there is no limit to her appetite in the things she would do for money. Having disowned me and my children (her grandchildren) and threw us out in the street after ordering her diverse children to gang up and beat my wife and children at the time, we mostly need help and had nowhere else to go, now the tides have changed and she just appeared, boldfaced and shameless to identify herself as a parent who cared so as to fish some money out of me. She did not even think about my dad's funeral money that was entrusted her in September 1993, which she squandered and used for partying with her friends, causing the dead body seized by the funeral home while the funeral service was being held, congregation and pastors waiting in church for a body that was not released for burial on schedule.

DYSFUNCTIONAL ONE

While waiting at the reception in my office, she began galvanizing admiration and recognition from other visitors, introducing herself as my mother, but all that was short-lived. On my way out of the building, I stopped for a while to speak to people at the reception that came to see me and totally ignored her as she called out my name aloud multiple times. When I was done talking to those I needed to talk to, I just walked away, and she followed me still calling out my name until I crossed the street and entered a vehicle that was waiting for me. As the driver drove away, I could see her standing on the sidewalk talking with some of my visitors that were leaving the building. We never met face-to-face again until five years later in November 2000 when we met in North Carolina in the United States. Reflecting back during my haydays in Freetown in 1995, there is only one friend I could really call best and trusted. It was a stray dog, black-brown, big, and probably weighed over a hundred pound. This dog had no known owner, and it was very friendly with people. It roamed in various part of central Freetown searching for food and sometime for a place to rest. The city was crowded with so many displaced people and the homeless literally living on sidewalks. Many of these people do not like dogs, so I witnessed the dog being maltreated one day, and as it ran from up the street downward, people threw stones and other objects at it for no reason, and it cried out loud as it ran. I was on the sidewalk with my children and my heart broke to see the dog stressed out, restless, and limping as a sizable piece of rock that someone threw caught its leg. It sat in the middle of the road crying, and I left my children on the sidewalk then walked to it and began to pet it. There was a woman selling cooked food on the sidewalk. I went over to her and ordered a bowl of food for the dog and paid her for the bowl container itself because she would no longer use it to serve food for humans. The dog ate in a matter of seconds, and I knew that it was very hungry so I ordered another round for it. People thought I was crazy and don't know what to do with money to cater to the need of a stray dog. That day the dog became my faithful friend and hang out with me up to late at night. Although I do not know where it sleeps at night, it comes in the morning like an employee and wait for me at the gate, and it would never stop wagging its tail and trying to climb on me when it sees me. Just because we were friends, others around the block began to treat it nice, and no one would throw stuff at it anymore.

On the third week after D-day, I began receiving thousands of dollars from Pa Yillah for processing his clients' application. This payout was unbelievable. Our relationship became tighter as his clients kept growing. He would buy refugee identities from the refugees themselves and stock them up for his market. At this time many refugees would sell their identity card and report to UNHCR that they lost it so that a new card would be issued them. These sets of refugee identity Pa Yillah would pass on to his Canadian-inspired clients while for the refugee resettlement program, his UNHCR contacts would provide him with new refugee identity cards. Whenever any of his clients comes in to AccordOne to process their application, their interview date would be scheduled accordingly, which means that it would take over a month or two before their application would be completed. As they leave sometimes frustrated over their extended interview dates for completion of their applications, Pa Yillah would call them and tell them that he has fix things up for them to do their interview immediately. He would call me and their interview would be rescheduled and that gives them assurances that they are in good hands. The whole thing was a scam, but it looked so real the way the blind man preps his client that I almost sometimes believed it was really true, even though it wasn't.

The fact was that the refugee resettlement program was working well and many of his clients were traveling as refugees and so his reputation was unquestionable and more people came to see him. Because most of his clients were recommended or referred by other successful clients there was no questions asked or doubt cast and his business was booming. As per our understanding, the two to three thousand dollars he was to pay me was per application, but I missed the fact that he was charging per individual members in a family since any number of persons can be on a single application as family. Thus, people who are not family would put resources together to make a family in order to reduce costs. His office was always full with people transacting business. From the third week of D-day to end of July, I had received a pretty good dividend up to $40,000 from Pa Yillah for processing his clients' applications. By this time I had settled down, well known in the community, with lot of friends in higher places, and I wished there was no threat of impending war for life was good as money continued to flow in. Yes, this was my time to shine, to prove that a man's downfall is not necessarily his end as long as he keeps hope alive and keep trying.

On Liberia's Independence Day, July 26, 1995, AccordOne shouldered the cost for hosting and entertaining all Liberian refugees at the new camp with the Liberian embassy staff, including the ambassador and his family attending the ceremonies. Everyone forgot about their troubles that day, and we all had a ball. After the end of the general ceremonies at the new Jua Refugee Camp, officers of the organization along with Liberian dignitaries proceeded to the King Town Guesthouse to celebrate the rest of the day.

Chapter 58

Pastor Alfonso Collie was struggling to reestablish his small prayer group once again. The rebel attack at Camp Waterloo had scattered his small congregation and at the new emergency camp site where families were squatting in small partitions in dilapidated warehouses with no toilets, no kitchen, and no privacy; the pastor was left struggling to supplement his large family needs outside of the regular contributions from members of his prayer group. So when he was recruited by Sorie Yillah, Pa Yillah's younger brother, to represent him in the camp in buying refugee identity card from those who wish to sell theirs, the pastor saw it as another door that the good lord has opened. He, Pastor Collie and members of his small prayer group, prayed very hard for a miracle to turn around the current predicament facing the refugees and surely this must be one of the answers to their prayers. He knew that it was wrong to sell and buy identities but what other ways would the Lord answer his prayers in an environment blind to moral practices and infested in corruption? After all, the Lord promised his people that they would reap the wealth of the unrighteous and indeed his level of righteousness is paying off. The Lord did not give specifics as to how it would be done in this particular situation, but a prayerful man as he was, with power to discern, must listen and obey his inner self especially so that he was convinced that the Lord that he serves can even use the devil to make good things happen. Therefore, this was a God-sent redemption, no doubt. The refugees have lost Camp Waterloo where they developed and lived in a five-year period, and all of a sudden they lost all of it including their personal belongings too without any notice. Now, as they waited in the wilderness with broken hope and destitute, the most prayerful man in their midst had been to the mountaintop, anointed to restore hope, and all they need to do is to sell their respective identity cards through him and then apply for replacement under the pretext that their IDs were either left behind at Camp Waterloo during the attack or that it was lost. And when UNHCR reissued a new ID, they can sell it again and wait a little while to apply for the third or fourth replacement. Sorie Yillah was paying Le.40,000 per ID and then offered the pastor Le.5,000 commission on each. At the camp, the pastor passed word around and those who were interested would bring him their ID and once or twice a week he would then take the number of IDs collected to Sorie Yillah and collect the funds for the IDs plus his commission. When he returned to the camp, he would then give each of the ID owners Le.20,000 per ID as he had promised them. He would then pocket the balance Le.20,000.00 from each ID transactions in addition to his Le.5,000 commission on each. Everyone so far seemed contented and happy for the new income stream; after all, what good is an ID if the person that it identifies is staving and suffering? As for the pastor, for as long as he kept his source confidential, he would continue to be seen as the anointed one who was helping his people combat poverty. Not only that, his people would see him as a hero; the one who sought and found divine favor to supplement manna from heaven into their wilderness, but this good deed could increase his prayer group or, hopefully when things get back to normal, this great man's prayer group could transform into a great church for he has proven his holiness with strong faith and now earned the trust and admiration of his people.

At the UNHCR commissioner's office in Freetown, hundreds of refugee ID replacement applications were being processed each week, but the numbers kept growing and people who were reissued two to three weeks prior are applying again, and this gave rise to concern. A team of UNHCR staff were dispatched to the camp to investigate on the ground, and it did not take them long to find out what was going on, but the pastor was not available to throw lights on allegations that were pointing directly at him. During the influx of Liberian refugees into Sierra Leone in the early nineties, before the escalation of the Sierra Leone war, UNHCR staffs sold refugee IDs to nonrefugees for $300 minimum. Most people who obtained these ID traveled on their own to countries of choice, identified themselves there as Liberian refugees, and received refugee recognition and benefits accordingly. Others who can afford to buy both the ID and the refugee resettlement programs in Sierra Leone did just that and traveled to developed countries where all living facilities and opportunities for improvements in life are ensured. Pa Yillah was in the middle of all these, working hand in hand with the UNHCR program officer who happens to be a Nigerian.

In 2003, a terrible wave blew through the commissioner's office resulted in some undisclosed scandals and some of its staffs were relieved, transferred, or terminated. It was a known general practice inside the United Nations to conceal scandals from within and not to institute criminal charges or to pursue any such cases against one of their very own. The program officer was relieved of his post, and he immediately vanished into thin air, leaving tons of unfinished crooked businesses in the hands of the blind, Pa Yillah, who happened to be the middleman. Among the unfinished businesses was a long list of private citizens from various West African countries, some of whom traveled to Sierra Leone to buy refugee status in order to reap the benefits including resettlement into developed countries. Hundreds of thousands of dollars changed hands and some of the lucky ones traveled under the status one way or the other, but hundreds more were stranded and they knew no one else to go to for refund or for delivery of the services they paid for other than the blind man that they handed their money to without obtaining receipts. The blind man, under pressure, decided to keep the business alive as though everything was under control, but under the watchful eyes of his new partners at the commissioner's office who tried as much as possible to distance themselves from these transactions since indeed they had nothing to do with it, tension was mounting. The blind man too had his own ambitions and personal projects; construction work on his family home was on a standstill because cash flow was kind of tight. Some of his clients, at least the educated ones, suspected that something wasn't right. They had been on the waiting list for more than a year; longer than was promised and longer than they could bear, and they wanted concrete answers or their money back. Others just wanted their money back and threatened to sue, but the danger of reporting the incidents to the authorities might cause them to lose all of their money, so they decided to keep things quiet while they secretly mount pressure on the blind. There were about 223 families on the waiting list when the deposed program officer vanished, leaving behind the fate of their clients in limbo and in the hands of the blind middleman. Ironically, if any of these clients decided to crack, the whole wall will come crashing down on them and the hungry justice system will eat them up like hungry sheep in lions' den. So they are left with no option but to blindly wait in oblivion for a miracle to take place as the blind leads them and steer the ship toward its titanic fate. As time goes on, the whole episode transitioned into a somewhat pyramid scheme wherein some of the smarter clients became pitchers, soliciting and recruiting new clients to buy a package so that they (the old client) can get back some or all of their money. This scheme became very much alive while on the other hand business with the new partners in the commissioner's office was smoothly in gear. Each time one of the old clients gets part or all of their money back or taken off the list, at least two newcomers would have been enrolled. The investigation conducted into the record number of refugee ID replacement application led the staff of the commissioner's office to confirm their suspicion that the IDs were being sold. Further probe led on to Pastor Collie and during the Liberia's independent day ceremonies, rumors mongers had it that the pastor was in "hot water," a Liberian slang for being in trouble. A part of the rumors being circulated in the camp suggested that two refugees somehow bypassed the pastor and directly transacted business with Sorie Yillah in Freetown and disclosed how much money (Le.40,000) they both made on each individual ID sales, which confirmed that this amount was the standard price paid for all the others. So a week before the staff of the commissioner's office began their investigation on the ground, the rumor had circulated and some of the refugees attempted to ask the pastor, but he vehemently denied the allegation as a cheap shot on his integrity by his enemies and became less seen in public since. It did not take the staff from the commissioner's office long to gather information from disgruntled refugees that were affected and from those who knew about the deal but were afraid and unwilling to sell their IDs. All inquires overwhelmingly pointed to the pastor who was unavailable for comment so the UNHCR staff left an invitation note with his wife for him. She claimed her husband was on a revival prayer tour. He was to appear at the UNHCR office upon his return to answer these assertions which might lead to charges against him.

All these dramatic information and gossips about the incident caught my attention so during the independence celebrations in the camp, I visited Mrs. Collie to throw some light on the matter and to let her husband meet with me as soon as possible, preferably before he goes to the commissioner's office. I said that I might be able to help him, and before I left her tent I gave their three children some money along with some learning materials. Convinced that I might be of help to her husband, she confined in me and disclosed where I can find him in Freetown. The next day, I sent a messenger to the pastor's hiding place, asking him to meet me at my office at around 7:30 p.m. for a confidential talk. The pastor appeared exactly on time, and we went out for a drink and chatted for three hours. I had to conceal my emotions as he released information about the Yillahs and the predicaments they were in and about treachery of UNHCR staff and senior government officials and their involvements with refugee benefits that were being concealed. "It all bore down to the benefits. We are nothing more than numbers to them. They do not really care about us," he said at one point in our conversations. He did not deny the ID sales deals but blamed the Yillah brothers for being so greedy, and he called some Liberians as sellouts, backstabbers, and ungrateful people. "The Yillah brothers are anxious to get out of their predicaments and they are greedy. We agreed that they would only deal with me in the camp and refer any refugee directly approaching them to me. As for Liberians, whenever they see you prospering they would come with sweet talks to eat from you and then they begin to dig behind you and the next thing you know they would try to bring you down," he said. At the end of our conversation just moment before we left the bar, I asked how he intended to defuse the situation. The pastor—a tiny man about five feet ten inches tall with broad shoulders, bald head, and big eyes—paused for a while and sipped the last drip of Gordon Gin left in is glass and then looked sadly at me with those big eyes turned reddish, rubbing the middle of his bald head with his palm and said in quiet tone almost whispering: "I just don't know how." It was funny but not a laughing matter because the weight of the information he just provided me about the Yillahs and my own dealings with Pa Yillah and what it might mean if push comes to shove just weighted in on me even though the pastor had no idea about my connection with Pa Yillah. Some moments of silence passed by as our minds work then out of the blue, the frustrated pastor expressing his disappointment and broke the silence: "I don't know how, John," he repeated, "but I wish RUF rebels can just come right now and take over this corrupt city and all these BS would go away in an instant," he said jokingly as we stood up laughing our way out of the bar.

Chapter 59

I have had many long nights, and this one could not be discounted, not even the number of tequilas I had could help me sleep soundly. I was already experiencing anxiety at night, and it was more to do with the revolution around me and the money I had stashed in multiple places in and around the office building: My life had changed so rapidly, and I was struggling to handle and cope with new responsibilities, my family, and to match with my new status in society; I had money stashed in abandoned rusty water pipes in the yard, in old telephone terminal boxes; in couches, chairs, and inside unused electrical meters. AccordOne had processed a total of 3,001 applicants for the first circle and generated Le.45,015,000 plus $40,000 generated from twenty of Pa Yillah's clients. This night like many other nights, I went through imaginary drills in my head as to how to save my family with the monies I had stashed around me in the event of any occurrences resulting from either the most imminent fear of RUF attacks that the city faced or in the event that I am forced to evacuate my family for other reasons. How to conceal and travel with large piles of money without detection at checkpoints worried me all of the time even though I had thought of a few risky ways. On some sleepless nights I would ask myself if rich people sleep soundly at night or if they usually jolted from their sleep like I do to evaluate the safety of their money. There is no doubt the fact that my corroboration with Pa Yillah can be misconstrued or perceived in many ways to implicate me in whatever scheme he had going. I have smelled this since the day I agreed to process his clients and give them special services for that large sum of money. I just could not resist his proposal because of the offer, but if any scandal from his activities comes up, my enemies would surely crucify me and make things worse for me. To some extent it amazes me that a blind man can outvision and outsmart so many people with perfect eyesight, and I am puzzled as to how he became middleman for UNHCR staffs. Did they pick him, or did he sweet-talked them, which he was capable of, or did someone just put a smart team together as a way to shield themselves should things go wrong? All monies that clients pay for any of their packages are paid to the middleman in cash, strictly in foreign currencies: US dollars or British pounds, and no receipts are issued; only a journal register where names, particulars of the package bought, and the amount paid are recorded. The blind man's brother handles the journal register and oversees monetary transactions as they occurred. Even though cutoff date for the first circle of the Canadian migration application processing has been announced to the general public and the process closed, yet there was room for Pa Yillah's clients. Pastor Collie's account of the problems and challenges that the Yillahs faced was partial as he himself knew only a little.

A more in-depth account came to light from Teresa on July 29, 1995, a few days before she traveled with her family to Europe. I was in the middle of investigating the Yillahs and evaluating the existing understanding between us to see what line of action I needed to take to protect my interest when suddenly Teresa called that afternoon to say good-bye. I immediately proposed to lunch with her the next day at the Bristol de Paris, and although her schedule was tight, we spent an hour together. It turned out that her best friend was one of Pa Yillah's victims, but she retrieve half of what she paid for the resettlement program after almost two agonizing years on his waiting list. Apart from that, Teresa recalled an incident at the UNHCR office when commotions erupt when two frustrated clients confronted the new program officer and that did not go well. Those two ladies were later escorted out of the building by securities as the commissioner was quoted as saying that he would personally investigate their claims.

"It was hell broke loose, and I could relate to their frustrations because of my friend's plights, but the staff quickly cancelled all appointments that day and all visitors in the waiting room including me were asked to leave the building and to come back the next day for whatever purpose we were there for," she said. The program officer was also quoted as saying that UNHCR had nothing to do with the transactions between them and Pa Yillah and that it was bogus transactions to which the UNHCR officially had no position. They were asked to take their matter to the police. She mentioned that there were times that her friend would cry all day and sometime go on hunger strike over this issue because it was quite a substantial amount of money she put into it.

 I asked why she took the risk if she knew about her best friend's disappointment, but she said it was her sister in Europe who worked out the deal, and besides many people have benefited in the past and that her friend and others have just been unfortunate that the original program office was fired, and he disappeared with most of the money collected and he apparently never considered the other staff to comply accordingly. "This is the price they are paying now as a result of that unfortunate incident," she asserted. She acknowledged that the whole thing was like gambling and most people who entered these transactions do so secretly and would like to keep it a secretly away from their own relatives, friends, and the authorities. Teresa's friend had to join few other victims in pitching the programs to new clients in order to get back part of her money, and she was still trying to get the balance. She talked about the massive construction project that the Yillahs were putting up in Abardin, which most of his victims knew about and at one time they had to stop the construct amidst rumor of some sort from some of the victims, threatening to burn down the incomplete building to the ground if they do not get their money back. She said most of the clients knew that the absconded program officer is to be blamed for the predicament but "as a middleman who collected their payments," Pa Yillah cannot escape the victims' rage and the liabilities. By the time we were done, her narratives together with the pastor's, when pieced together had made things very clear but interesting. Shortly after Teresa traveled I was called upon by Mrs. Thomas at the UNHCR office concerning medical records I had requested for three refugees that were admitted at the Connaught Hospital under AccordOne's sponsorship. Their original medical records were left at the clinic at Camp Waterloo and the UNHCR contracted doctor had advised that the copies in his possession can only be released to the UNHCR and not directly to AccordOne so Mrs. Thomas was contacted and she was able to get the records for me. At her office we chatted on a number of fronts and just when I was about to leave, she asked that I close her office door for she had something important to discuss with me. As I closed the door and was about to take a seat, she pounded a question at me that send my heart pounding. "How well do you know Pa Yillah?" she asked. The question caught me by surprise, and I don't know if I should come up front clean and answer the question frankly or to be protective in my answer.

"Not too well," I said, followed by my question, "Why?"

"Well, Mr. Davies, there is nothing concerning refugees, their resettlement, or migration that goes on around here that is hidden from me. I have thousands of refugees on the ground interacting with our staff regularly, and we get information even when we do not ask for it," she said with a smile. "This is for your own good because you have little children, and you don't want to be caught up in a mess at this time, not after all you have been through recently," she added. My heart pounded more, and I am sure she could hear my heavy breathing once my children are highlighted. I paused for a few seconds, and as I was about to speak, she interrupted and reminded me about the CID intervention when AccordOne started the Canadian Migration Application processing. "My office was called upon, John, and if I wanted to dump you I would have done so then, but I think about what you have been through and most especially about your children," she asserted. Continuing, she dropped the bombshell: "Now we are hearing that you and Pa Yillah are executing his plans to resettle and/or to migrate nonrefugees to the United States and other European countries and extorting large sum of money from them."

This really hit me like a brick of rock, and I felt a chill creeping up my spine as I digested what was being said. Then I exclaimed, "No way." She calmed me down and asked again what my relationship with him was. I told her what Pa Yillah wanted me to do, but I could not say the truth about how much he was paying me for it. As we spoke she was looking up her computer and printing out a list of names from it. Turning over the printed sheet of paper to me, she asked if I recognized the names; and without any doubt, I recognized all of them. She then began to pass on the other printed sheets as they print from her printer. The first sheet was a summary of Pa Yillah's clients that AccordOne processed and the other sheets contain detailed particulars of each of the names on the summary sheet. Nineteen of them had family members: wives, husbands, and children to make up a total of seventy-nine people whose interest lies in limbo. "All of these are claiming Liberian citizenship and have presented themselves as Liberian refugees, but we know that they are not and the refugee's IDs they are carrying are invalid, and all these can be serious charges."

By this time I was stoned cold in the chair and muted then the next bombshell: "Now Pastor Collie was in my office yesterday, and he admitted his wrongdoings and begged for mercy. The two of you spent some time together discussing these issues a few days and from what our field staffs has gathered, John, you appear to be a big part of the Yillah scam that demine our office. Pa Yillah is a user, a con artist, who have infiltrated our office and prey on our weakness to make himself tons of money, and he thinks that he can get away with his actions without recourse. This is an enormous problem, and it is even getting more complicated than you and Pastor Collie can imagine, and it is a pity that you guys are caught in the middle of it all. Sooner or later, you guys may have to face the full weight of the law as Geneva has become involved, and they have ordered a serious investigation that would leave no stone unturned," she concluded.

I explained how I felt about his proposal when Pa Yillah approached me and that my relationship with him was nothing more than expediting his clients for an extra fee and that I am not involved in any resettlement program or migration program for the

United States and other European countries. As I viewed the list, I remembered speaking to several candidates on the list and reassured them of Pa Yillah's commitment to their course and they trusted my word as much as they believed him as doing the right things to have them migrated. What if push comes to shove and these candidates' testimonies collaborated to say that reassured them of his action, it would discredit my defense. So I sank back into the chair and in a quiet voice ask Mrs. Thomas's suggestion for a solution, any ideas or advise. She laughed out loud and said it was the same position that the pastor asked "as if to say I am some kind of damage control counselor or a crisis manager," and we laughed together but I knew deep inside that I was actually crying. "Let's go sleep on it and see if we can come up with something in a day or two, but I tell you this is tough," she concluded. I asked if she would let me have the printed copies; she said I could but to keep it confidential. Like a wet cat, I crawled out of her office.

Chapter 60

As I walked two blocks toward Connaught Hospital to drop off the medical records for the three refugees admitted there, I began to feel empty, my feet weaker at each step; the kind of feelings that come when you know the endgame is falling apart. I overheard that UNHCR inspectorate delegation arrived from their headquarters in Geneva a few days earlier, but I did not think otherwise because it sounded like the usual routine inspection. During these routine inspections, they usually speak with selected refugees about living conditions to include in their report though it made no difference year after year since the same things happened without any improvements to the living standards of refugees. But when they do speak with any refugees, word would pass around to almost every household within the refugee community. This time only rumors had circulated that they were here. It did not make sense to me at a time when refugees' living conditions were at its worst that Geneva inspectors would come into the country and did not interact with the refugees to figure out, confirm, and understand their immediate needs. I called a few staff of Cause Canada to get information and received conflicting information. Usually they also would provide some information about distribution of rations, etc., but this time they all acknowledged that a delegation from Geneva arrived during the week but they differ in opinion as to what their mission was.

All of the refugees who stopped by my office had no idea and expressed doubt if Geneva inspectors ever showed up at all. Instinctively, I decided to visit Pastor Collie at his so-called revival venue to assess the situation from his perspective. I met the pastor in a company of palm wine drinkers at a popular palm wine spot in Temgbeh Town, Brookfield. He was enjoying the cold evening wind under shade of trees, his shirt hanging on his shoulder as he swung his head to the rhythm from one of the local musical instrument played by a band of two older men who had their lips loaded with snuff. The pastor jumped to his feet when he saw me and expressed happiness. He put on his shirt, and we walked up the road to talk. He said that he was going to find me over the weekend to tip me off that my name came up several times at Mrs. Thomas's office yesterday, and he defended me over and over again that he did not think that the Yillahs had any dealings with me. Asked if he knew about any Geneva involvement into the investigation, he expressed suspicion that a middle-aged man and a woman in her thirties were present during his interview with Mrs. Thomas, and he thought they might be the Geneva base staffs spoken of.

"What did you tell them about your involvement, and what are they going to do about the whole investigation?" I asked. He said they had overwhelming evidence that he was representing the Yillahs in the buying and selling refugees' IDs so they had him write and sign a notarized statement indicating the Yillahs involvement in soliciting and buying over five hundred refugee identities from the date they approached him to the last transaction and the role that they had him play. "Why did you do such a thing when they could use it to incriminate you?" I asked. He said that they assured him that they were not after him but the "big fishes" and they offered him immunity from prosecution should the matter be turned over to the government. "What do you mean by immunity when they are not prosecutors or police or any member of the court if this matter should go that way?" I asked. He explained that after he came out clean as was agreed, they sent him in the waiting room while they hang heads to discuss his fate. When he was called back into the office, this time it was Mrs. Thomas alone, the other two were no longer there. "She offered to resettle my family someplace before the heat begins in a month or two timeframe, and I think they are going after the Yillahs big time. And things look like UNHCR local staffs are disowning their man when push has come to shove, and they are painting him as a criminal who acted on his own all these years manipulating their office," he said. "Do you know where they are taking your family?" I asked. The pastor said that Mrs. Thomas would work on it, and he would be notified the following week and thereafter his family's travel documents would be processed.

Concluding he said: "She wants me to keep this confidential so please do not let anyone know, John. You know our people will spread this like wildfire if they knew it. The only reason I am telling you this is that I know how reliable you are fighting for our cause, the tight relationship between us which is why my wife confined in you to find me here so please keep this confidential," he added. I said no one would hear it from me, not even my wife. "What do they say about me and the Yillahs because I do not even know who these Yillahs' are," I lied. He stretched his two hands toward me to emphasize his point that he told them repeatedly that he has no knowledge whatsoever of any connection between me and the Yillahs. "They do not seem to have any evidence or lead that you are engaged in the buying and selling refugees' ID," he added. I asked when last he visited his family, and he confirmed that his wife was with him earlier that day, but he would not be going back to the camp because of threats from some of the "ungrateful refugees who are claiming that I cheated them after they have benefited from the transactions. They would not even know when my family leaves the country, God willing," he concluded.

"Well, you are a very prayerful man," I said with a smile, and I added that he should not hesitate to ask if he needed anything from me for his family. Our meeting ended, and I returned with a head full of things to put on my to-do list. On top of my to-do list was exit strategy planning to evacuate my family and the next item was liquidation and consolidation of assets. AccordOne and the Canadian Migration Program had been under scrutiny for some time now, and I have no doubt that its success had ignited envy and unwarranted animosity toward me in some quarters. The CID director had mentioned that he received so many phone calls pressuring him to have me arrested; Mr. King's Sierra Leone Financial Corporation was still struggling because very few people would risk depositing or saving their money with a new business at the brink of an impending rebel invasion, and he strongly believed that I double-crossed him with the Canadian Migration Program and that he should have made the money that AccordOne made in so short a period of time. We now passed by each other without any speech, and I know that he is bitter and would do everything in his power to bring me down. Then there were others who thought AccordOne was a giant oversea entity with fabulous assets and international prestige, only to find out later that it is owned by someone like me, who they despised or who they believed to be inferior to them, notwithstanding. I have already spent tens of thousands of dollars to help others and undertook several humanitarian projects which puzzled many in the community including the UNHCR staffs as to where the funding comes from.

Like Pastor Collie insinuated, if indeed the local corrupt UNHCR staffs are under fire from Geneva then they would surely try to conceal their dirty dealings to find scapegoats and that would only mean that they would disown the Yillahs and paint them the bad guys. If the Yillahs begin to drown, chances are that they would try to cling on to anything and this is where I come in. Probably I am one of the "big fishes" that the pastor said that they were talking about. Even though the UNHCR staff had nothing on me directly, I would be a fool to stay the course and wait for them to pin the Yillahs down and eventually I be implicated by the Yillahs and put my family through hell once more. This meant that I should be planning an exit immediately and probably leave the country even before the pastor's family was shipped out. In the meantime I would keep an eye out there on him; if he disappears, then I too must disappear without delay. But there was one problem; I had pawned my family passport to Dr. Cole's Clinic during the time my daughter Jacqueline was admitted at the clinic in 1991. The next day I attempted to redeem it even though my gut feelings tell me that they had disposed of it. If I don't get it, then I will have to apply for official refugee travel documents, which mean that I would have to face Mrs. Thomas since she is responsible for that. The only trouble with that is that she could set me up very easily and sell me out so I cannot trust her entirely or rely on her. I was struggling with this when suddenly I remembered the two files she handed me earlier when she matched my family with Teresa's family under two different surnames. I reached for the files to inspect them once more and indeed the official records she had prepared with references corresponding to the logs and detailed instructions about the processing signed by her with dates of each events, including the particulars and refugee numbers assigned to Teresa's family and the other family my wife was slated to use.

Before long I formulated an approach strategy for her and so after I confirmed that Dr. Cole's Clinic had disposed of my family passport, I immediately called her and impressed on her that I had something confidential for their investigation but I would like to discuss this over lunch with her at the Bristol de Paris. She reluctantly accepted the appointment, and we set it up for the next Monday, at twelve noon.

Chapter 61

Heavy rain reigned over the weekend from Friday afternoon to Sunday night and that made living extremely difficult for the homeless and for refugee communities in and around the new temporary camp. When the heavy rain subsided on Sunday night, sporadic drizzling with thunder and lightning took over and early on Monday morning the loudest thunder and monstrous lightning struck down a number of trees in various areas and detached branches from the Cotton Tree, which has been an historic landmark located at the center of the city killing a number of vultures. Across the city three people were said to have been struck down by the lightning, which somehow caused pandemonium amongst some people misconstruing the sound of thunders and flashing of lightning for an attack on the city. Petty thieves and others took to the streets to take advantage of the situation creating wide spread panic. "The rebels are here! The rebels are here!" Early marketers, vendors, and traders ran helter-skelter and many lost their properties as they ran for their lives. The military government sent out armed troops in military trucks patrolling around the city and their movements, part of which was just a show, compounded the situation and elevated the level of fear amongst the people for a few hours. My heath pounded heavily and my stomach somersaulted as fear engulfed my family. The tension around the city resurrected the fears and trauma my family held inside, and momentarily it felt like we were back in RUF captivity at Camp Waterloo. I periodically peeped over a window to find a handful of people running or sometime with no one in view, and by 8:30 a.m. when none of my staff reported for work, things were beginning to take shape in my mind that we are yet in another phase of rebel attack. For a moment I blamed myself for not giving serious thought to securing travel documents for my family all these times when I had the resources to even buy if necessary. As tension mounted and the level of fear increased a sudden tap on the front door startled us. The look in the eyes of each member of my family asked questions that I could not find any answer for. I looked at the wall clock and it was 10:00 a.m. The radio station had not been on that morning probably because the heavy winds or lightning may have disrupted its facilities, so the lack of news also contributed to the state of the situation. The knock at the door increased and at the same time there were echo of voices from the street, which forced me to peep once more over the window to find few people standing in small groups. I recognized some of them as traders and their workers in the neighborhood chatting and laughing. I waved to them and together they started laughing at me. I guessed they saw fear in my continence, and they said everything was fine and that there were no attacks, just rumors. I took a deep breath and walked toward the main door and asked who was there and the voice of my office messenger brought assurance of relief as I quickly opened the door.

Moments later, after some jokes about the entire state of the affairs in the country and how it affected people in different ways, we restored our office and business started as usual. I called Mrs. Thomas to confirm our meeting, but I was told that she did not show up for work this day. The next day, she and I connected for lunch, and we shared our fears and our reactions of the Monday's incidents, and we talked about the rumors that took over the city like wildfire. We laughed at each other; she was so scared that not only that she did not show up for work but she did not open or leave her home the whole day, and I would not open my door when workers of my office showed up. As we finally settled for serious business I thought the opportunity was ripe to bring home my main interest even before discussing anything else. "During the situation yesterday, tension mounted in my family as fear gripped us, and I regretted turning down the resettlement you offered my family with Teresa and her family. The irony with turning down that offer is that my family did not even have any travel document to leave the country if and when the need arise, like the case yesterday. Therefore I would be grateful if you can help us with travel documents as soon as possible because nobody knows when these rebels would come attacking the city, and we would not have any travel document to take a ferry or helicopter to enter neighboring Guinea. Seriously, my wife and I looked over the two files you gave us, hoping that if push comes to shove we could use it to convince boarder authorities but that would have been a risk because our refugee IDs carries our real names while the files carried different names. It could backfire on us and we would not have any explanation for the discrepancies. So would you help us with travel documents?" I requested.

She looked puzzled and fumbled a bit as she said: "I am not sure, but I think our records shows that your family entered Sierra Leone with a Liberian passport." Continuing, she said, "I cannot provide you with a travel document without an established traveling purpose on file, and I do not have any program in mind right away. You had your chance and you blew it, so you will have to wait when I figure something out down the road because there are a lot of people on waiting list right now." I explained that our family passport remained at Camp Waterloo during the April attack then I asked: "What if I can get an official invitation letter from abroad for my family to visit Canada or some other country, and I am not asking for UNHCR sponsorship of any kind except for the travel document, would that justify the issuance of travel documents?"

Without hesitation, she acknowledged that it would do, especially if the invitation is addressed to us directly from the inviter, she added, with suggested leads as to how the invitation should be composed. Meal was served and as we began eating I thought it was time to start talking about the main purpose that she agreed to meet with me, which is to do with their investigation. I started by lowering my voice so that no one from nearby tables heard what I was about to say, which indeed caught her attention as she stopped chewing her food.

"I have been asking questions from the printout you handed me at your office last week and that led me to an individual who would like to remain anonymous. This person shared with me a file full of official UNHCR original records pertaining to various resettlement programs, records similar to the Teresa family files, dated as far back as 1993, medical record, police clearances, etc. These records had signatures of officers of the UNHCR including the commissioner, notarized documents from sponsors, with other document carrying official UNHCR seal, and etc." There was silence for a while as I watched as her continence gradually turned sore. Even I underestimated the impact of the story that I was telling. Breaking the silence, I said that most of the individuals listed in the file were duped as they never received the services that they paid tens of thousands of dollars for. I was expecting her to say something but she remained silent for another moment then I said, "Now I fully understand the reason why AccordOne's Canadian application program is targeted by the Yillahs. It is an attempt to appease their victims, to buy time and neutralize the situation." Faking a smile, I said that I wanted to thank her anyway for alerting me about the situation otherwise I would have been going on thinking that everything around me is just fine while the Jillahs continued to incriminate my organization in the schemes that they are engaged with.

"I was scared after you cautioned me at your office the other day, and so I became curious and decided to investigate why my organization is targeted and how I am being dragged into all these messes," I concluded. My guest looked around the room as she slowly chew the food already in her mouth, drank some water, and quietly leaned forward across the table and said: "For God's sake, John, this is not appropriate venue for this type of subject and conversation." I nodded and we both dogged heads into our food without saying another word until almost toward the end of our meal then she politely asked in an almost cracking voice: "Can we please talk in my car after the meal, John?"

Chapter 62

For a very long time refugee resettlement program has been in the center of a quiet scandal involving staffs of UNHCR, officials of government, and some of the wealthy elite in the community. Ironically these types of issues falling within the quiet scandal category, depending on who is connected and under what circumstances are likely adjudicated outside of the judicial system, outside of any due process, and if for any reason a particular incident became wide spread or publicized to the extent of forcing the hand of the law, then bribery, deception, and elbow bending would obviously compromise justice. Whistleblowers caught in the middle of it all would surely be exposed and left to face whatever harsh consequences since there were no protections to guarantee whistleblowers' safety, and there was no telling what could happen especially so that the culprits or perpetrators would be out there freed, powerful, and supported. For these reasons there has not been any single case completely investigated and processed through the court system but there were documentary evidences out there leaking the commission of a crime and incriminating government officials and staffs of the UNHCR, though the likelihood of court actions were almost impossible, at most, the reputation and credibility of those involve were placed on the line, when issues were publicized. Although the UNHCR did not prosecute one of their own even if there were credible evidence on hand, it would rather not keep any employee whose stains and scandals garner negative publicity that demean a branch of the United Nations. To avoid these kinds of negative images, often staffs who are implicated are reassigned, transferred to other missions in another country, or dismissed depending on the strength of their individual connections and standing within the organization.

Therefore Mrs. Thomas, who took my pranks very seriously, became apprehensive and anxious to know more and more, requesting from me names of the individuals I had spoken to and trying to get description of the actual documents in the file that I talked about. "You know my signature right, John?" she would ask many times as we talked then the second part of her question would follow: "Did you actually see my signature on any of the documents in that file?" I would say that I could not rule that out because I was not allowed more time to read through all the documents, but they were actual UNHCR documents signed by its officers and carried its stamp and seal. I said that it happened so fast and the individual was sharing contents in the file secretly to me beyond the knowledge and consent of her partner whom she claimed stole the file at Pa Yillah's office during a scuffle sometime in April, when disgruntled clients stormed his office demanding refund to their unfulfilled transactions and threatened to "burn down to the ground" an ongoing construction project he had at Brookfield. Mrs. Thomas can actually relate to some of the details here because she was aware that sometime in April, on the same day of the scuffle at the Yillahs, two disgruntled clients proceeded to the UNHCR office to meet with the new program officer and they were eventually thrown out of the building by security. "I suspect that the holders of this file may be planning extensive media coverage of their situations as a payback for their loss," I said. She asked if I was going to meet with them again anytime soon, and I said that we had no plan to meet but I might if the need arose. She then insinuated that I contact them again and review all the documents to determine if her signature was on any of the documents in the file and if possible to obtain photocopy of the file for her review. I said that it may be a tough thing to do, but I will try and let her know the status of the situation as soon as I can. Following our meeting I proceeded to SLET to make international calls to solicit an invitation letter for my family. This was the easiest thing to achieve since the country was at war and my family ordeal at the refugee camp was widely publicized plus the fact that it was not going to cost the invitee anything financially for our travel and resettlement. I succeeded in persuading an environmental group in Canada that eventually faxed an invitation letter for my family to the UNHCR.

Two days later, I got a call from Mrs. Thomas that she had received an invitation from Canada for my family, and she had begun expediting our travel documents. She asked about any progress concerning the supposed file, and I said that I was still working on it. Then she urged me to move faster because she needed to know what was in the file. I told her not to worry because I had it on my priority list. The following Monday I got another call from her again, this time I was to bring my family in for photo taking, finger printing, etc., and to obtain a police clearance as part of the prerequisite for processing and issuance of the travel documents. It turned out that while my family's travel documents were in progress, Mrs. Thomas, frustrated over the length of time I was taking in solving the mystery file concerns; worried and anxious that she might have been implicated somehow, shared my prank with some of her confidants at the UNHCR office and thereafter secret meetings with the Yillahs were held in order to ascertain the facts and to control any forthcoming damages that might surface. The Yallahs, however, denied losing any files and asserted that all sensitive records were in tack in their possession and that they never kept such records in their office but in the blind man's bedroom. On the other hand, the Yillahs would not produce any of the files in their possession because some of them contained information that could complicate things and raise the existing tension amongst staffs of the UNHCR. In a nutshell, some transactions containing in the Yillahs' business portfolios are characterized with greedy and sinister conducts that polarized the staffs with the blind man in the middle of it all; manipulating, controlling, and concealing elements to each transaction so as to protect individual interests and avoid conflicts that might otherwise erupt if staffs knew that they had been undermined in some cases or double-crossed in another, and so forth; so all that the Yillahs could say was that their records were still in tack and that they had not lost any of them. This was not good enough for Mrs. Thomas and some of her confidants so the pressure on me increased to find the people whom I claimed are holding on to a file that might cause a lot of problem. If such a file existed and the contents therein happened to be something Mrs. Thomas and her confidants could use to tarnish or incriminate some of their enemies within the organization who sidelined them and benefit from the proceeds that the Yillahs collected then why not pressurize John Davies to make this happen? As news of an unknown file that could change things for better or for worst leaks within the ranks and files in the organization, some people became nervous, anxious and curious and that puts me in the center of the gossips that goes on in their office environment. In the midst of all these, my family travel invitation and travel documents came to the limelight and soon Pa Yillah became alerted and decided to confront me, first to discuss the file that they have heard about and then about my travel plans. Two weeks before the travel documents were issued by the Sierra Leone Immigration Department pressure had mounted to the extent that I could feel the negative energy flowing from all sides of the aisle, and I was becoming scary by the moment not knowing what to expect. Mrs. Thomas was calling me three to four times a day concerning the file while on the other hand Pa Yillah returned to cancel our understanding and to persuade me to refund some of the monies he paid out to me, which he claimed were exorbitant for the service and that some of the clients had taken him to the authorities and that he is given a deadline to refund all moneys taken from his client or he and all of his culprits would suffer the consequences and that he did not want to have me implicated so it would be good for me to turn back at least $30,000.00 to save my skin. This was not a surprise to me for Mrs. Thomas had confronted me and named the exact amount of monies that Pa Yillah had paid me for processing his client's application and the only way she could have known it was either from the Yillahs directly or from the other side of the aisle but I denied that during one of our telephone conversations. Pa Yillah had been told that part of the amount paid out to me could have been used to reduce his burden and that he should get some money from me before I disappear. In another conversation I had with her, Mrs. Thomas asked me again in confidence about the exact amount that Pa Yillah paid out to me for each of the clients processed and suggested that it would actually save my name from any scandal if things get sore if I can refund back whatever the amount was. I vehemently denied receiving from Pa Yillah $2,000 per head for his client, and I even invited Mrs. Thomas or anyone interested to audit AccordOne's books to see how much money on record was received for processing their clients' applications.

On August 28, 1995 the travel documents were issued and Mrs. Thomas took possession of them. My contact from the Immigration Department tipped me off that the travel documents had been completed and picked up by Mrs. Thomas. I called to inquire about the travel documents, and she confirmed receiving them but insisted that they would be turned over to me after I provided her with a copy of the mystery file. At that point I told her that I was no longer interested in the travel documents anymore and that I was not in a hurry to travel and only wanted to have something on hand just in case the city is attacked and I needed to evacuate my family someplace else. "You can hold on to them forever Mr. Thomas", I said in my bluff. I told her that I was surprised and disappointed that she would hold on to the travel documents in bondage to get what she wanted from me after I have spent so much time and other resources and came so close to obtaining copy of the mystery file for her. I let her know that AccordOne had sufficient resources to evacuate my family plus a host of other refugee families if the need arose without UNHCR travel documents issued even though we are entitled to the documents because they are there for the use of refugees. My bluff paid off, two days later she called me to pick up the travel documents and when I insisted that I do not need them anymore and that I was not in a hurry she sent her messenger to drop them off. By this time the dynamics in the relationship between Pa Yillah and I had changed considerably. He had been chastised for dishing out all that money to me and he was in regret mode. So tension had gone higher to the extent that he convinced and assigned some of his clients and contacts to keep an eye out there on me and to alert him of my movements, so I was being watched and I knew it. In a secret meeting I had with him at my office, I argued that I was not obligated to him for I have performed my side of the understanding between us, but he insisted that the transactions were illegal and that he may be left with no choice but to implicate me when push comes to shove "soon." I then gave him the impression that my organization had put large funds into a money exchange investment for which the first quarterly dividend were due by end of September 1995 or in the first ten days in October 1995, and that if he wait at that time I might be in the position to make some refund but not in the amount of $30,000 he is asking. He asked that I make a promissory note to that effect, and I said that our understanding has been oral all along and there is no basis for a written promissory note order than oral and he took offense to that. The next day I was approached by two men who walked into my office and wanted to discuss something confidential. One of them identified himself as a nephew of Pa Yillah and claimed that he was a major in the military. They asked about the business between him and me, and I said that I was not under any obligation to disclose any information about the organization but they explained the transactions to me, and after we argued a bit, the other fellow cut in, leaned forward, and asked me these questions in a cold sinister but crack voice, "Look at me, Mr. Davies. Do you really love your family and do you love life?" I was frozen momentarily as I looked him straight in the eyes. This heavily built figure, probably in his early thirties wearing a visible military t-shirt underneath a grey shirt kept shaking his head as he speaks this time words of threats: "If we had to come back here in October because you fail to fulfill your promise to make the refund to the old man, then certainly," he paused and smiled. "You will not live to tell the story," he said and stood to his feet and they both walked away. I was speechless, paralyzed, and terrified.

DYSFUNCTIONAL ONE

A shot of brandy calmed my nerves after they left, and my first thought was to sell a few pieces of my diamond to pay back the Yillahs, but after a while, an idea came up and I dropped my first thought. News of the Kollies disappearance from the camp reached me, and I proceeded to find the pastor at his so-called revival hideout, and I was stunned that the man and his family left the country about a week earlier. Few of his palm wine drinking companions believed that he left the country with his family about a week earlier and at least one member of his prayer group later confirmed that. The news of the pastor's family travel heightened my sense of urgency to vanish, but there was so many precious items in the way: my large family was on the line, the day-to-day responsibilities running a nonprofit full time and the host of refugee affairs involved including transactions and pending provisions also were all on the line. Then there was the constant fear of the impending RUF threat to take over the city, which would no doubt be bloodier than any other battle fought by the rebels because the capital city is the last resort fortified and manned by the military government; and indeed the pressure from Mrs. Thomas and some of UNHCR staffs concerning the so-called mystery file that did not exist, the refund which I was definitely not prepared to make, all of these made life miserable and restless for me and I knew that it was just a matter of time before I find myself in some sort of scandal or legal issues. Almost two-thirds of the money I received from Pa Yillah had been used in the organization's humanitarian activities, and though I am not obligated to pay it back because that was not the original understanding, yet if he dragged me into it and made me an accomplice as he said he would, chances were that I would become a target of unknown forces from disgruntled clients whose connections may stretch from all angles and the last thing in the world I would want for my family at this time was making us a bigger target. All these culminated into an urgency that left me with no other options but to plan my family's disappearance. But this would not be an easy task as all eyes were on me.

Chapter 63

Evacuating my family from Sierra Leone was even more challenging than the three successful rescue missions I singlehandedly undertook in the heat of the Liberian war in 1990 and in 1992. Looking back, those three rescue missions seem more adventurous than the current one though they all fall within the profile of the most brutal wars ever fought in these two countries. Part of the main strategy in those first three rescue missions from Liberia were to avoid routes occupied by warring factions and since there were hundreds of thousands of people escaping, the chances of us being spotted by enemies from all sides of the aisle were narrowed. Even if my family was targeted then the number of people fleeing the conflicts would have made it difficult for any one of the warring fraction to recognize and identify us. But the current situation was different because my family was specifically targeted, being watched and sought by disgruntled people who may be related or connected to the military, probably to the rebels and definitely to people in high places. Moreover, the Waterloo Refugee Camp episode popularized us to the extent where most people would have no trouble recognizing us. Ironically, on the other hand, some of the escape routes from the capital city are feared occupied by warring factions, and I cannot risk a second encounter with the RUF. In the mist of all these factors was my edgy wife whom I dare not allowed to suspect that I was carrying a burden that could adversely affect our family, let alone to hint her about the urgent need for our family's escape or evacuation even though she knew that because of the eminent threats hanging over the city our evacuation could come anytime. Any knowledge of the current mess I was in would generate fear and puts her in the usual jittery mood, which irritates me and threw me off whenever she gets in that mood. Her reactions to every other issue would have compounded the problem and make things complicated for me. In addition she had been having frequent nightmares ever since the episode at Camp Waterloo. During times when she gets into jittery mode, she would be overprotective of her family then anxiety would kick in and a flow of unpleasant energy would be felt as we interact. There are other elements of contrast between us: I am a risk taker and fearless in confronting obstacles or finding solutions to problems while she dares not take any risk at all, and she dare not spend any money, and she gets panic too quick to handle tough problems. There are other characteristics that polarize our family: I don't need any occasion to wear new cloths or shoes while she needs an occasion to wear hers and applies the same to the children; for their part, the children would lean toward me because they can get their way easily or get whatever they wanted while she would not. If she knew anything about the current situation, she might even be shaken at the sight of any of the people who are monitoring our movement and give them something to work with. As for the children, they were beginning to live like children once again following the terrible ordeal at the camp and there was no need to put fear in them. Whenever I looked into their eyes, I am strengthened, encouraged and even more determined to make them succeed and to make life pleasant for them. For these reasons I planned to keep every member of my family out of the loop so that things looked normal while making sure that everything from planning, organizing and execution of our escape from the country remain top secret. Some of the spies are people who befriended our family and would pop in occasionally to pay a short visit or bring candies for the children and play around with them. In the early stages of my plan when I was trying to gather information, I visited a travel agent to inquire about chartering a helicopter to fly to the Republic of Guinea, but as soon as I left the travel agent office, I spotted two of the spies across the street pretending to be buying stuff from street vendors and when I walked in the opposite direction and made a turn on the next street, I noticed that one of them had crossed the road to the travel agency and the other was jogging to catch up with me but I had entered an office supplies shop and watching him looking around to see if he could find me anywhere. It was a good thing that I did not make the enquiry at the travel agency for myself or for any member of my family. My enquiry was for two officials of the Jalloh Foundation who were to attend a peace conference in Lome, Togo. I had told the agency that they would take a connecting flight from the Republic of Guinea to their destination and only needed to charter the helicopter to the Republic of Guinea. Soon after I reached my office I called the agency to inquire if someone came after me, and it was confirmed that a gentleman who claimed we were working together walked in the travel agency moments after I left and was asking questions, something along the lines of travel reservation for me but he was told that it was for two officials of the Jalloh Foundation.

That same day, in the afternoon, I took my family to the national park to buy clothes, shoes for the children and a few other items that my wife needed. While walking around we walked into the same two gentlemen again and this time they could not conceal themselves so they approached us with big smiles on their faces, and I pretended it was nice to see them. They played with the kids and offered to help us with our bags. I watched with satisfaction as my wife remained calm and normal as she cheerfully interacted with them and I played along. It was that very evening that I visualized a workable plan that would embrace everyone from Pa Yillah and his brother to all the people he set around me as spies. To execute such a plan required a lot of guts, and I have guts. That night I stayed up till dawn working on every detail of my new plan and designing documentations that I could use in the process. Early the next day before 6:00 a.m., I left my family sleeping and sneaked out, took a cab, and drove around making sure I was not being followed then I finally ended up at the office of the chief medical officer at Connaught Hospital, and I was able to meet with him directly one on one and successfully discussed his participation to examine some refugees that my organization would qualify for resettlement abroad.

At the end of our meeting we agreed that AccordOne would foot all the medical bills for each individual processed and that he, the chief himself, would get a bonus of $50 per head, but he must sign and seal each medical report and deliver to us according to our board resolution. He agreed in principle, and when he asked how many refugees I think would be processed per month, I knew exactly that he was speaking volume. No doubt he would do his part diligently with dedication and passion because the volume he was about to hear from me would motivate even the Minister of Health. "Between 100 to 250 persons per month," I said, and I watch him frozen momentarily as he calculates in his head how much money it would be, perhaps more than his annual salary. Following this meeting I proceeded to the Liberian embassy to set the pace for issuance of laissez-passer for anyone that my organization refers for resettlement purposes. The embassy staff had not been paid any salary for years since Liberia was at war so they survived by doing business in many ways outside of the norm to raise funds in order to meet personnel needs as well as office supplies etcetera. In fact rent for the embassy premises had accrued, and it was rumored that the landlords had filed eviction proceedings to vacate the embassy from their premises but for some diplomatic intervention from the government the process was being delayed. Therefore each of the embassy staff ran their own individual inside business to sustain them and to help each other.

This concept is known as Gorbachev, a Russian name that Liberians used as a slang to express the concept (chop-I-chop): meaning that money obtained from means outside of the norm should be shared or spread out to benefit others, especially those who assisted. This concept has united the staff in serving the general public not necessarily Liberians.

After I was satisfied that my contacts at the embassy got the idea and how much they would be paid for each laissez-passer issued to my clients, I moved on to the police department to arrange for fingerprinting and police clearance to be issued to clients referred by my organization. Then I went over to the UNHCR office to meet with the staff and broke the news of a private resettlement program that has be entrusted and accredited to AccordOne by a private foundation abroad for which AccordOne needed UNHCR cooperation in confirming the identity of refugees that we selected for this program. I indicated that we would provide them with official documentations about the program with an official letter from us, spelling out specific area and action for cooperation with the program. All these arrangements with exception of the meeting with UNHCR are covered with expedition incentives offered the providers.

After all these the next bold step to my plan was now to meet with Pa Yillah. So I visited his house for the first time. His brother was with him along with some family members, and they were in the middle of eating dinner when the little boy who usually accompanied him spotted me and announced my arrival with joy. They were all surprised at my unexpected visit, and they happily received me and invited me to join them at the dinner table. Without being bashful, I pulled a chair next to the blind man and whispered in his ear before taking my seat. The words I spoke to him lighten up his face and immediately called out for more food and drinks to be put on the table. We ate, drank, and chatted; and it was time to discuss the purpose of my unexpected visit. We walked over through the back of his house to where his office is, and we sat down to talk, the two brothers and me. With confidence and without any hesitation I started to roll the ball: "My organization has been commissioned to oversee selective resettlement programs under the sponsorship of an oversea charity group dedicated to assisting Liberian refugees stranded on the street of Freetown following the capture of Waterloo Refugee Camp" I said, paused and giggled while they process the information, "and guess what?" I asked, paused once more, "the frequency of this program would be on a monthly basis beginning first week in October". I said that we have been working tirelessly on accessing this program since April and finally my organization is been accredited and commissioned with exclusive rights to oversee this program.

DYSFUNCTIONAL ONE

I said that AccordOne should have acquired this right a long time ago if UNHCR had not been in the way, but thanks to an independent study of resettlement programs worldwide which found flaws, corruptions, and frauds within the UNHCR system, some sponsors are now interested in delegating the services to private nonprofit entities such as ours, so our first group of selected refugee families that are qualified would be resettled in just a matter of weeks. The government and all agencies responsible to coordinate this program are officially in gear; the Ministry of Health through the Chief Medical Officer's office would conduct and process all preliminary health screening requirements, the Ministry of Justice would do all criminal screening and provide police clearance and the Liberian embassy would provide travel documents for qualified refugees after all is done. All qualifying refugees would have to sign a work schedule agreement plus an agreement to repay the cost of their tickets after six months in their new country of resettlement" Questions were asked and I took my time to explain with confidence everything they needed to know about the program. The blind man reached for my hand and held it tightly while rolling his eyes toward the ceiling and his brother seating across the desk lean forward with hands on his chin. No doubt they have taken keen interest. There was momentary silence, then Pa Yillah took a deep breath and his brother whispered something along the lines like: 'what a wonderful God we serve' as if it was God who told them to poke their nose into refugee benefits. "What can you do for us in this situation, Mr. Davies" asked Pa Yillah. I said that was the reason why I was there to help him out with 3 families amongst the first group in order to offset the deal between us and if he is willing to deal with me in the future it would then be discussed and the fees determined then. "But I must caution you that I can only slot not more than 3 non-refugee families at a time while making sure that the rest of the other families are real refugees because the program is for us and all eyes would be on me from now on. I do not want AccordOne to look like the UNHCR resettlement saga" I concluded. The two brothers were so excited that they even disagree with each other and started arguing as to which families on their list that should be considered first in this miraculous opportunity. Before leaving I cautioned them about another point which I said was critical so they must distant themselves and keep things very confidential. The point was that the UNHCR would have only one role to play in all these and that role is to confirm the identification of qualified refugees, "But that is an area that I can handle with them if you guys would stay away and not complicate things by getting involved because they can destroy this opportunity if they find out that AccordOne is not resettling refugees alone," I warned. They both jumped to their feet and simultaneously put their index fingers on the ground and from the ground to their thongs and then stretched their hands up toward the ceiling, a customary ritual to swear and reassure that they would never do such a thing. We agreed that they should make up their mind and send me the names of three families before end of day the next day and though they wanted me to stay to drink more beer and continue to talk, I would not because I have business to take care of, so I left.

Chapter 64

That same night, I was feeling terribly awkward after breaking the news to my wife about our family resettlement opportunity to the United States, which I knew deep down in my heart, was not true. I watch how exited she became, and she wanted to talk more about the prospect of seeing our children grow in a society that provides all sort of educational opportunities, prosperity and the respect for human rights etc, but I was not incline to engage deeply with her excitement though I wished it was true, and I wished someday we could make it to the United States or some developed country if we survive the current situation to begin normal living once more.

I was busy evaluating what was accomplished that day and reviewing the plan when suddenly the phone rang and it was the Yillahs, they had agreed on their first three candidates and wanted to provide me with their particulars and they wanted to know what the next step would be. "Send them to my office tomorrow any time before 12 noon," I said and we hanged up. The three family candidates total a number of eighteen people: one family of seven, the other of six, and the other of five. I later found out deep into the process that the Yillahs had bundled two families into one for each of the three candidates but this was not something that worried me because my objective to get my family out of Sierra Leone without any obstructions was my main focus. That night I prepared documentations for the names provided and the next morning my messenger dropped off a package each for the three candidates to Mr. Molly at the post office. Mr. Molly is the postal officer responsible for dropping off refugees' mail at the UNHCR office every day, usually around 1:00 p.m. and then the UNHCR mail office would then sort out the mail and update the list of refugees to whom a mail is addressed and the list is placard on a notice board at the entrance of the building for refugees to see without entering the main offices. All mails are then turned over to the security post upfront where refugees would go to show their ID and collect the mail addressed to them. Before Waterloo Refugee Camp fell to the rebels the updated list and the mails would be brought to the camp and delivered there to make it easier for refugees since it was twenty miles away from the main office but after the rebel attack and the camp captured, refugees were scattered with many refusing to settle at the temporary camp at Jua, so the mail system changed. After that mail was hand delivered to Mr. Molly, my messenger, proceeded to deliver a sealed envelope to the Chief Medical Officer's office. In that envelope is the list of the first twenty-four people (my family included with exception of me) to be processed for medical examination. A staff of the Liberian embassy responsible for photographing that was not present when arrangements were made the day before responded to a message I left him so he came over to my office to collect fund to buy films and other necessary materials needed to take passport size photos for the Laisse Passé. Shortly before eleven O'clock, the Yillah candidates arrived, a total of eighteen people, twelve women and six men, no children. They all came into my office where I advised them about the confidentiality of the program and how they needed to distance themselves from the other candidates who are genuine refugees until the entire process is completed and they have travel and resettle in the country of resettlement. I said other refugees who are in the program might notice them or feel suspicious of them from their accent so they need not interact with any of them at any stage of the process and that I would do my best to keep and treat them separately. They all agreed and then I said that from now on I would only want to see the three family heads and not all of them at the same time and that whenever all of them are needed then their respective family head would pass word to them. At the end of the meeting I told them that their names had been sent to UNHCR that morning for verification of their identities as genuine refugees and that it would be the first step in the process. They were beginning to show signs of panicky when I said that but I assured them not to be worried about that since they already have genuine refugee IDs. Only the three family heads needed to go to the UNHCR office to see if their names are listed on the bulletin and if it is so then it means that the UNHCR has completed its identification process, and all they would have to do at that point is to go to the front desk and provide their IDs and collect their family packages and from there they can come back to my office with the packages. "It would be better to arrive there at say five to ten minutes to 4:00 p.m. when the office is about to close. At that time chances are that refugees would not be many at the building and maybe none of them may not be around," I said. I asked to inspect their refugee IDs which they obtained from the Yillahs and all looked real and genuine to me. This first step went on smoothly, and the three family head came back to see me with their respective packages. In the package was a letter addressed to AccordOne indicating that according to UNHCR record the following individuals were registered Liberian refugees and are therefore qualified for any assistance. The other documents in the package are pretty much basic documents which I extracted and customized from the original files that I received from Mrs. Thomas at the time she put me in a fixed marriage with Teresa. They were basic orientation materials for refugees who are to be resettled in a foreign country.

All three of them were so excited and thankful that they made promises as to what they would do for my family when we all travel to the United States. I told them that I was not leaving yet because I have to oversee the program but my family would be leaving with them on the first resettlement. Everyone was happy that evening, and they left to see the Yillahs to give account of all what had happened so far. Later in the night I received a call from Pa Yillah and the excitement in his voice says it all. The plan was working accordingly. The next day the three family head arrived at exactly 10:00 a.m. as instructed to receive referral for the next step, medical. They were instructed to take their families to the Chief Medical Officer's office to start the medical screening process. "My wife and children would be there to join you all in that process," I assured them. They were advised that if the medical report for anyone shows negative, then that family would not be processed any further until the health condition of the family member is cleared. They took their referral slips and in the process of two days all of them were able to undergo the necessary screening, which included blood tests, x-rays, etc., and in the end they were all given inoculations and vaccinations. I did not get all the medical result that week so I advised them to be quiet and wait for the result before the next step. Meanwhile, my family was mingling with them as they all underwent the process, and they were all showing kindness to my children particularly. I felt convicted over their kindness knowing in my heart that the entire process was a fluke.

On Monday the following week, I received all the medical reports, and I sent them to the Liberian embassy with their processing slip and everything went well then the next step was the fingerprinting and police clearance, which also went on well. After I received all the police clearances and picked up their Larissa Passé the three family heads reported to my office for signing of the contract agreement for repayment of travel expenses, etc., and a date for travelling was said to be awaiting word from abroad after tickets are purchased and flight booking including housing and other facilities at point of destination are completed, etc.

On September 28, 1995, I broke the news of the first scheduled resettlement voyage to the United States of America, for Saturday, September 30, 1995.

Chapter 65

The road leading to September 30, 1995, was full of excitements. So far, the plan had been effectively executed and all the people involved including my wife and children were confident, full of life, hope, and expectations. I would tend to think then that with assurances of coming to America people became energized and I am sure that such energy could spark life back into someone who happens to be half dead. My frequent pitching about the bogus resettlement program and intense interaction with the candidates instilled in me a belief in the plan to the extent that I felt relaxed in dealing with them; amazingly responding to complex questions without a blink which in one sense could be attributed to hallucinations on my part. Even my wife believed me so much that the looks in her eyes radiated positive energy that generated a special kind of vibrancy; a splendor complementing the sweetest atmosphere around my family, such that I had never seen or felt for a long time. It was as though we just fell in love with each other. Her frequent nightmare and signs of trauma that was seen and felt multiple times a day had gone away, at least for the time being. She was full of life and she would shower me with frequent hugs, kisses, and words of compliments that I had not received in a long time. I guess her innocence and lack of knowledge to the plan reaped the best of positive attitude out of her, and she played well in building the trust and confidence that the rest of the other candidates developed in me. Even the Yillahs hailed me as their hero and treated me specially. There were however some bittersweet moments for me when I am alone mostly at night working and everyone is asleep. It was a struggle for me because I have always been a compassionate person; therefore when thoughts of the kindness, courtesies, and positive energies I get from each of the candidates heats me including the sweet interaction with my own family and realizing that sometime on September 30, 1995, the whole jar of worms would burst open, and it would become national news and my reputation as the Good Samaritan is besmeared in the eyes of the public giving my enemies the clue they needed to scandalize and persecute me, I felt blood shooting up my head and sometimes a chill crippling up my spine. But the overriding factor that outweighed everything else was the protection of my family and the unflinching love that bonded us, something that I lost since age eight, which has come back to me in many ways. If I were alone without a family and no one to love and care about me as I used to be I would have had nothing to lose, I would stay in Freetown, stay in the system of things, and expand my agenda, make friends in higher places, manipulate my way and take advantage of the corrupt system to enrich myself materially. Maybe the only thing that would have made a difference is that social entrepreneurship spirit I had cultivated from my early hard life, which may not have allowed me to acquire and stock pile wealth while so many people struggled and perished in abject poverty. The getaway portion of my plan was crucial, and I had thought about it earlier. I rehearsed this part over and over again like the Israeli's Entebbe Raid mission to rescue their citizens held hostage by terrorist—extremists in pro-Palestinian Uganda under Field Marshall Idi Amin in June of 1976.

In my mind, this mission to get my family away from danger was like planning a high-profile escape from some prison island. No other day was suitable to execute the getaway plan order than a Saturday. The military government had put in place an ongoing curfew in the city on Saturdays from the early hours up to 10:00 a.m. The curfew was imposed on citizens compelling them to clean up their neighborhoods—streets, gutters around their homes, etc. During these curfews, vehicles are prohibited from plying the streets, all businesses or economic activities are placed on hold, people are not allowed to walk the streets unless if they were cleaning the area where they lived otherwise they would face loitering charges if caught. Truckloads of soldiers are deployed at strategic points in the city and some patrol the streets in search of violators. This was a rather bad choice of leadership and lack of vision, but since the people lived in fear, this stupid policy was reluctantly accepted without choice and therefore prevails despite its impediments and the burden placed on an already crumbling economy, imposing more hardship for the impoverished majority in the country, at least the areas controlled by the military government. The majority can hardly afford a meal a day, and they were confined for hours beyond their will and left to provide their own cleaning materials and hardware while their leaders who have squandered and stock-piled enough food, drinks, and other material wealth for themselves and their families enjoy cozy Saturday mornings and fantasized their authorities. If a leader finds that his city or country needs cleaning up, the solution was to use available resources and make allocations to the department responsible for that purpose, in this case the Ministry of Health and Sanitation, to create jobs for its struggling citizens and to equip the ministry and its workers with the necessaries to do the job eight hours a day, five days a week, and this would boost the economy one way or the other. The government can then provide dumping sites and institute sanitation regulations, empowered their enforcement in order to deter its citizens from dumping dirt all over the place. But where there is no vision but insanity, greed, and selfishness the imprint of leadership misses out on the areas that needed cleaning up the most such as: rampant corruption, gross injustice, disservices, and blatant disregard for the social welfare of the people, very poor educational provisions, and systems, broken and dilapidated infrastructures, abuse of universal rights of children, etc. Curfews should not have been remedies especially when imposed to force the people to clean up public areas that the government should be applying taxpayers' resources to clean up. However, for my getaway plan, the curfew comes favorable.

On Thursday, September 28, 1995, when I announced the voyage, a meeting was schedule for orientation the next day. During the orientation, the candidates were prepped: They were to assemble near my office at 11:00 a.m. where a hired bus would pick them up and take them to Lungi International Airport. Part of the road to go there was under rebel control so the bus would have to be ferried some part of the way to the airport. It takes the ferry about an hour from the wharf terminal in Freetown to the terminal near Lungi International Airport and it would take the bus about thirty minutes of driving to the airport. Departure schedule was set at 2:00 p.m. and processing of all of the traveling documents through immigration and other airport authorities would begin at 12:00 p.m. I would be responsible to do these processes so everyone should be confined in the bus at the parking lot until I am done then I would send my secretary to turn over each person's travel document along with their boarding passes. There should not be more than a travel bag or suitcase each per person; no one should take any items from someone else and relatives and friends wishing to accompany them from the city would not be allowed to ride the hired bus. After they received their travel documents, they would follow my secretary in a queue leading to the tarmac and avoid unnecessary talking or eye contact with anyone especially Liberian refugees. The reason for this, they were told, is to minimize chances of being noticed by someone who might know any one of them. They would have to go through customs with their baggage, and when they are done with customs, I would be standing at the immigration booth to see them through and thereafter the rest of the process would be easy as ABC, and we would all meet at the waiting room until departure time is announced. It all looked so real that even I also believed every word that I spoke and everyone seems to understand their role.

Chapter 66

Since the beginning of the civil war in Sierra Leone in 1991 up to middle part of 1995, about two million people became displaced as a direct result of attacks on a number of towns and villages throughout the country by all of warring factions involved: RUF, ULIMO, NPFL, and the national army. As these attacks caused large-scale displacement, relief workers and expatriate of nongovernmental organizations were recalled to Freetown for their own safety. The general security conditions deteriorated to the extent that private transport companies became reluctant to take contract for transporting food and other relief supplies to the eastern and southern provinces without massive military escorts. In June 1995, AccordOne contributed foodstuff and other sanitary items to a consignment pool for displaced people in the southern province who were stranded following a series of gruesome attacks. At the time I was introduced to the transportation coordinator at the Joint NGO Conference, and I met with some of his brave drivers one of whom was assigned to work with me to collect AccordOne's donations.

On a personal note, this driver shared with me stories of trips he made under heavy military escorts especially in the southern province, which he said were very dangerous. He disclosed then about areas in the northern province where private transportation was operating freely without attacks in the scale seen in the other provinces, at least at the time. Those areas he described as Lungi through Port Loko and Kambia Districts toward the Guinean border so those routes were safer. Therefore in planning my family's getaway, this information was considered, and I got updates from the transportation coordinator in a telephone conversation. I was however shocked and terrified to learn from him that the driver he assigned to me earlier along with two other laborers had been killed in an ambush while returning from delivering supplies in the southern province in mid-July. I had asked if it were possible for me to use the same driver to deliver some relief items for the children at the new refugee camp in Jua when he broke the news to me. He however agreed to assist and send me a minivan driven by another driver named Suma on the next day. Suma and I took a few learning leftover learning material to the temporary refugee camp at Jua and on the way we talked at length about the other driver whom I said was very friendly. I asked him about the deceased driver's family, and he explained how tough things were for them so I asked him to take me to see them on our way back. He was surprised when I took a hundred dollar bill and handed it to the widow and her two little children. On our way to their office in Brookfield, I asked about the danger of roads and transportation in the northwest toward the Guinean border, and he said those areas were relatively safe. Then I asked if he knew of any private transport company that operates in these areas and his eyes widened and explained that he grew up in Kambia District and most of his relatives were still living there. One of his friends from school days owned airport taxi services and lives in Lungi near the airport. I pitched about hiring a reliable vehicle to take a team of relief workers to the refugee camp in Guinea and if he can help me arrange that I would surely tip him for that. He said that was easy and that he would call his friend and introduce me at once when we arrived at their office.

By the time I was done chatting with the coordinator and thanking him for his assistance, Suma was already waiting for me in the compound with the information I needed. He has spoken with his friend and given him my telephone number and also provided me his friend's name and telephone number. On the way to my office, I stopped at Post & Telecommunications Department to verify Suma friend's telephone number to make sure it was assigned to him and not some third party. The next morning I called him and the trip was arranged to transport a few relief workers to the refugee camp in Foricariah in Guinea. His charges for the trip were less than a hundred dollars, but I offered two hundred dollars and offered to pay for all border fees and charged for the vehicle to enter the Republic of Guinea, and we agreed that the vehicle should be in excellent condition and the driver assigned must provide best service. The man was very excited and assured that he would have a Mercedes Benz ready for the relief workers on September 30. We agreed that he would receive a call at exactly 9:00 a.m. to get instruction where to pick the relief workers from in Lungi and then immediately after the curfew ceased at 10:00 a.m. the journey should begin because the relief workers are expected to be at the camp in Guinea around 4:00 p.m. He should have vehicle serviced with tank full of gas and ready to hit the roads immediately after the curfew. We reassured each other as he begged that I do not change my mind and hire someone else, and I assured him that if he does a good job this first time he would be awarded a contract to take the workers to and fro at least once each month. From the way he sounded throughout our conversation, I had a strong feeling that he regarded very highly his friend Suma's recommendation of me. After that was done, I went over to SLET to make an international call to my in-laws in Conakry, Guinea.

    My wife had relatives in Guinea who work for the government there. Her parents migrated from there and one of her cousins who spent some time with us in Liberia long before the war speaks English though not fluently. His dad was then a high-ranking member of the Guinean gendarmerie. It took me some time making enquiries to get him because I did not have his direct telephone number but with help from others I finally reached him and we spoke and understood each other and most especially he was very worried and sensitive to the urgency of my family situation as I explained. He was surprise to hear from me after news of the attack on Waterloo Refugee Camp and capture of my family reached them. So it was easier to convince him that we were still in trouble and that we would need help from their end as we are planning an escape from some of the bad guys who are still keeping eye out on us in order to do harm to us. What we needed is for them to inform the border authorities about our arrival there and to make sure we are receive and granted asylum when we get there because the Guinean border authorities has been critical of refugee influx and thoroughly screening them and sending some back from entering their country lately. The influx of refugees from both Liberia and Sierra Leone rose to an estimated two hundred thousand and causing some socio-economic problems and the Guinean authorities were worried that the wars in both countries might spill over to their territories especially so that there had been cases where rebels posed as refugees and granted asylum resulted to uproars in refugee camps and few incidents had reportedly occurred in their territories near the border with Liberia and Ivory Coast, south of Guinea. There have been several clashes in refugee camps with finger pointing to a number of rebel-turned refugees and in one of the incidents the Guinean military reinforced their security to keep the peace. These led to the Guinean authorities tightened up security on all sides of their borders with three of their neighbors: Sierra Leone, Liberia, and Ivory Coast. There are two passenger ferries operating in the ferry system, plying to and fro two terminals: Kissy Dock Yard in Freetown and Tagrin in Lungi. The two opposite terminals seem so far apart yet so close to each other for objects and movements can be clearly seen on one side from the other, vise visa. It took about an hour and fifteen minutes on average for each of the two old but exhausted ferries to cross the canal that separated the two. They are usually kept apart from each other and harbored each opposite terminals where they are retired at night after the day's last trip at 7:00 p.m. As operational procedure, both ferries are dispatched at the same time from each of the terminals so they pass each other by in the canal of the Atlantic Ocean as they head for the opposite terminals. Several trips are made daily mainly transporting vehicles plying the area, traders, farmers and products, harbor and airport workers, passengers (includes locals and people who flew into the country or about to leave the country). Because of the early Saturday curfew, the schedules for the last trip on Fridays were extended by thirty minutes. On weekdays, the ferries would start operation from 6:00 a.m. but on Saturdays when the curfew is in effect up to 10:00 a.m. the first trip begins at 11:30 a.m. So I planned to give my family a head start by spending the night in Lungi on September 29, 1995, using the last ferry that leaves Freetown Kissy Dock Yard at 7:30 p.m.

Chapter 67

During the last week in September of 1995, I had several staff and board meetings in which responsibilities were delegated for advancement of all operations and for security of all AccordOne's assets. Some critical assignments like authorization for withdrawal of funds, payroll, etc., were left open. I had given the impression that after my family leaves I will be taking my much=needed vacation by the beach at Lumley for at least a week. A special to-do list for activities on Saturday was prepared for my secretary who was assigned to accompany all of the supposedly resettlement candidates to Lungi International Airport on a hired bus. The to-do list is attached to a large envelope containing all of the travel documents and medical records, etc., for the candidates. I had purchased four suitcases for my families that were also packed with a bunch of papers and items that we no longer needed, which I also kept in her office. The assignments on the to-do list indicated that all of the candidates are to assemble at my office not later than 10:30 a.m., load their baggage including my family's four suitcases, and everyone including my secretary would board the bus. The bus would then take them to the terminal at Kissy Dock Yard and then ferried to the terminal at Tagrin and from there they would be driven to Lungi International Airport where we all will meet at the parking lot.

At the airport parking lot, I would then collect the package containing travel documents from my secretary to start the pre-travel processing and when that is done I would signal them to join me and then take things from there. Friday of course was declared half day at AccordOne and suddenly there was an impromptu sendoff party at the office that started around twelve noon. It was well attended by many uninvited guests from around the block. While we were having a good time, word spread around that my family would spend the night at Mammy Yoko Hotel and then flown by helicopter to the airport at 10:45 a.m. after the curfew, to which many applauded when I later confirmed. On purpose, I had leaked that information out knowing that it would spread. Spontaneously, one by one, some of the attendees made brief speeches while others proposed toast to the welfare and success of the Davies family while others chose to walk up to any member of the my family and express well wishes. At some point, wife and I offered words of gratitude and appreciation, and she promised to keep in touch and everything seems as real as planned. I had earlier booked a helicopter to airlift my family to the airport in the morning and made reservation for a suite to spend the night at Mammy Yoko Hotel and the manager was willing to send one of the hotel's minivan to pick my family up at the office. At 2:30 pm the hotel minivan arrived and before long everyone was bidding my family farewell with hugs, kisses, and handshakes. Volunteers then assisted us with the few bags containing items we needed and walked my family to the minivan. Surrounded by staff, family friends, and other well-wishers all of whom waived and applauded, some with tears running down their chicks while some holding back tears, the vehicle took off. It was a very emotional scene and if I had any tears to shed, I had rather saved it for the moment my family would come to know the truth.

This day, September 29, 1995, would be my family's last day in Freetown. We arrived at the hotel and settled down for a while then we ate dinner at 5:30 p.m. By this time a getaway van hired to take us to the Kissy Dock Yard Terminal was waiting at the hotel parking lot. The driver had no idea about where he was hired to take us, only me. Thirty minutes later we were done eating, and while my wife and children took the elevator upstairs, I stayed behind to talk to the front desk and later to the driver that was waiting. Then I joined my family at the suite to break the news that the helicopter was overbooked, and so we would have to be transferred to another hotel near Lungi International Airport, which means that we should be leaving now so that we do not miss the last ferry. Everyone was already excited so there was no cause of panic. We then picked up our bags and left the hotel with the key to our suite. The front desk had no idea that we were all leaving for good since we already paid for the night, and we did not checkout. We arrived at the terminal just a few minutes after seven o'clock and the driver who, for a little more money, agreed to cross over with us purchased the boarding tickets for everyone while we sit in the car waiting for the last moment to board the ferry. On the ferry, we rode first class to Targrin Terminal in Lungi that evening and slept in a motel near the airport. Early the next morning at 8:00, I sneaked out of the room leaving my wife sleeping and went over to the front desk where the only motel staff on duty was asleep in a chair. I used the phone on the counter and dialed Musa friend's number and the man was ready and waiting for this call. I then gave him the name of the motel where the décor relief workers are and asked him to call at exactly 9:00 to speak to a lady named Ramatou at Room 103. "When she comes on, just ask that you wish to speak to her husband and that it is urgent," I said. "Do not let her know why you are calling because she is favoring another private transportation company over yours for the trip and her husband, who happens to be leading the relief team, wants to honor the agreement between us," I said.

Few minutes before nine o'clock, I went into the bathroom and waited. A little while later, I heard a knock at the room door. I could hear my wife calling out to me that someone was at the door so I asked her to see who it was. Since there are no phones in the rooms at the motel, I knew that the staff would have to come knock the room door. Then I heard the door opened and my wife saying: "Yes, I am…What? Me? Okay, tell him to give me a minute." Then the sound of the door closed and my wife came straight to the bathroom and said that she had a phone call waiting at the front desk and she wonder who knew her so quick to call her. I pretended that I had no idea and urged her to go answer the call. Moments later she came back to the room to let me know that the caller needed to talk to me and that he said it was urgent. I asked who it was, and she said it was a male on the line who refused to give his name. We switched places as she walked passed me into the bathroom while I ran out to the front desk to take the call. This time I disguised my voice and confirmed the trip with the fellow on the other end, and we agreed that he would send the driver he has assigned to pick me up around 10:05 a.m. to make payment at his office before we start the journey, I went back to the room pretending to be mad and trying to look up some documents.

"What is the matter?" my wife asked several times while I kept ignoring her and pretending I was looking for some document. By this time she was concern and beginning to feel that something serious was wrong. I asked her to wait for me, and after a while, I grabbed a couple of papers and hurried back out to the front desk to make a few phone calls. This time I called the helicopter agency to reschedule my booking for Wednesday when there would have been another flight to the United States and then I called Mammy Yoko Hotel to extend my family stay to Wednesday. When I returned to the room, she was really tense and waiting to hear from me. I took a deep breath and looked straight into her eyes and said: "We have a serious setback and a change of plans. A report has been made to airport authorities that the people I processed are not refugees and a dragnet has been set for us at the airport. If they really found out that these people are not refugees, it would be serious problem for me and for AccordOne as the processing NGO."

I watched her took a deep breath, sank into a chair, and curled herself with both hands placed over her head. There was silence for a while as her countenance transformed from exuberance to traumatic and then the next thing that break the silence, she ran into the bathroom and at that point, I felt the restoration of all the negatives—the traumas, nightmares, and fright. But at this crucial time, I would have to stay strong, focused, and steadfast with the execution of the plan and make it work.

At 10:05, the vehicle arrived and a knock at the door again. I went out to meet with the driver at the reception. Then he drove me to their office, which happen to be the business owner's house. I made the payment, and he gave his driver some instructions and twenty minutes later we were back at the motel ready for the trip. With a smile on my face, I walked into the room where everyone was dressed up waiting. My wife stood up to look at me; she has a way of determining things from looking me in the eye and the examining the structuring of my face, so I conducted myself properly and accordingly. "The information is true, airport authorities have been informed that most of those being resettled are not Liberian refugees, but we have worked out a solution," I said. "We are going to bypass them and takeoff from another country where every one of you are regarded as refugees regardless of origin. Technically, these people are not Liberians, and they do not meet the definition of refugee because they are in their own country but from a third-party country view point they are qualify as refugees regardless of their nationalities. So we have all agreed to travel to Dakar, Senegal, the West African regional headquarters of UNHCR from where the resettlement trip can be possible. The others would join us there," I said. There was no argument and no sign of any suspicion from my wife, she just simply obeyed her husband who happened to be on top of his game, a man who she knew had a proven record for turning things around and who was in charge of shaping the destiny of a broken family. We placed our bags in the back hood of the Mercedes Benz, and the trip to runaway to the Republic of Guinea, which no one else knew of as yet, took off at approximately 10:45 a.m.

 This day, September 30, 1995, would be our last day on the soil of Sierra Leone if we can make it to the border fast enough and beat the chase that is bound to follow.

Chapter 68

Meanwhile in Freetown, the hired bus meant to take the resettlement candidates to the airport arrived at my office on time and so do all the candidates. Some of the candidates assisted (my secretary) Rebecca in loading my family's four suitcases. The bus made it on time at Kissy Dock Yard for the ferry departure from Freetown and, relatives, and friends who accompanied some of the candidates used private and public transportation to the terminal in Freetown. It turned out that one of the two military men who threatened me at my office about a month ago was related to one of the candidates, Miss Morgan. Another candidate named Cooper sold his stationery supply business and used the proceeds to pay the Yillahs to be included as a member of one of the three families for the bogus resettlement program. Two other candidates, Melvin and Tina, happened to be related to the wife of the vice head of state and they also had relatives from high places who accompanied them. At 11:15 a.m. when the ferry departed Freetown for Tagrin, at least my family was already thirty minutes ahead of them from Lungi en route to the Guinean border. It should take far less than four hours to reach the border from Lungi if the roads were paved, but they were not and the raining season also contributed to its worse conditions. In just an hour deep into our journey, we were still struggling to cover fifteen miles because road conditions posed hindrances that we had to deal with. At some parts of the road, our family rolled sleeves and took out shoes, descended the vehicle to push it through several hundreds of yards of muddy and rocky areas; in other cases we had to find rocks and sticks to fill in potholes and in other cases we had to use sticks and rocks to create quasi bridges aligned to the vehicle tires for grip, and with a good push as the driver accelerated, we went past one gallop after another, but I always stayed behind to dismantle the temporary fix so that other vehicles did not use the tracks and quick bridges that we constructed along the way. My wife noticed at one instance when I dismantled one quasi bridge after our vehicle crossed passed it, and she questioned why I should spend energy to do that when it should make it easy for other vehicles plying that road. For the candidates, there is no cause for alarm or anything to ignite their sense of urgency since their desire to snatch and convert refugees' program is paying off, and they are now about to reap the final benefit by going to the airport and waiting for me at the parking lot. Most of the passenger airliners that usually flew to and fro Sierra Leone had either ceased or reduced their respective routs and services because the country was at war.

The airport was mostly used by UN Peace Keepers and ECOMOG (Economic Community of West Africa Ceasefire Monitoring Group). On that particular Saturday, the departure time for the only passenger flight from Lungi International Airport to the United States via Europe was scheduled at 3:00 p.m. I estimated at least two hours between us: the candidates arrived at the airport parking lot to the time they should be expecting me to join them there. The vehicle that brought my family from Freetown to the motel in Lungi returned to Freetown morning with the ferry that anchored at Tagrin and must have ferried passed the other ferry that was bringing the candidates to Tagrin so it was not possible for that driver to have any contact with anyone of the candidates, and if by any chance he did, he can only name the motel where he took us, which should not be any cause for alarm.

At 12:30 p.m. the ferry from Freetown reached its destination at Tagrin and thirty minutes later they arrived at the parking lot at Lungi International Airport. There, they were joined by relatives and friends who accompanied them including the Yillah brothers. Together, while waiting, they shared final moments to remember. At 2:00 p.m. some of the relatives and friends along with Pa Yillah's brother decided to go into the airport to search for me. When they could not find me or any member of my family, they decided to make inquiries and every question they asked and whosoever they asked led them to more unanswered questions and as suspicion began to brew things became tense by the minutes. Now they found out that nothing on the flight manifest gave any indication about refugees travelling on resettlement program anywhere. Then the search for me and my family intensified. Minutes later, word reached the candidates at the parking lot that this whole venture might be a hoax and pandemonium broke up. Over fifty people organized themselves and spread out into small groups with the task to find me. In order that they are favored to get airport security help to find me, they decided to conceal the real issues involving the failed scheme to buy and use refugee resettlement program, so they misled airport security by saying that I was engaged in a human trafficking scheme involving vulnerable Liberian and Sierra Leonean children for sale in the United States. This alarmed airport security and before long ECOMOG and UN Peace Keeping personnel became concerned. Officers then delayed the flight for a couple of minutes as they search the plane and check travelers with the assistance of some of the persons who could physically identify me in person or any member of my family, just in case I was on board with a different name. The officers then called Mammy Yoko Hotel to inquire about me and they were told that I had not checked out yet, and in fact, I had extended my stay till Wednesday. The helicopter agency confirmed that I made a booking for that morning but rescheduled for Wednesday. These pieces of information were meant to lead them to think that my family was still in Freetown, but the blind man who happened to be farsighted wasn't buying that. He dispatched groups to check all the motels and the hotel around the airport to check for a family of seven (five children and their parents) and soon it was discovered and confirmed that my family did pass the night at one of the motels and were seen boarding a private transportation for upcountry. Then they contacted the few private transportation owners in the area and found the transportation company that I used, and it became clear to them now that I was on the way to Guinea.

It was around 3:00 p.m. when they began the chase after my family toward the Guinean border and though we were probably about an hour away from the border, we suddenly got into an unfortunate situation. The left back tire of our vehicle was punctured and the spare tire in the hood leaked air and was totally flat. The driver then suggested that he would have the vehicle parked in a nearby village with no less than ten huts occupied by few local farmers and then he would have to take off the tire and roll it over to a bigger town about one mile away where there is a gas station and a tire repair shop. I suggested that he should just drive the mile to the town, but his concern was for the rim and the inner tube, and I offered to buy a new rim, tire, and inner tube and to give him an extra tip. I had to get close to him and whispered the importance why we needed to reach our destination before 5:00 p.m. I told him that my wife's mother is dead in Guinea, and she has not yet been informed because her siblings wanted to keep it secret until she gets there. "Her mother is a Muslim, and she would be laid to rest by 6:00 p.m. today," I said. He turned around to look at my wife, and he shook his head in sorrow then he confined in me that he also had a similar situation when his dad passed the year before. He missed his dad's funeral and up till now he could not forgive himself. He finally drove the vehicle on flat tire to the big town, and we finally got the tire repaired even though I gave him the extra money for a new tire and rim and inner tube, which he pocketed but that was not my concern. He said that he would buy the new tire, rim, and inner tube on his way back at another town where they usually service their vehicle. We left the small town and after about a mile we were back on the main road and the fact that there were no new tracks meant that no vehicle had superseded us. But everything about me strongly felt that we were being chased, no doubt.

Chapter 69

We arrived at the Sierra Leone side of the border at 4:10 p.m. and it took so long for border officials to process us to the extent that I was beginning to think that they were delaying us to allow our pursuers to catch up with us. The distance between where border officials perform their duties and the Guinean side of the border is about two miles apart. Thanks to the lack of cell phones in this environments at the time and the faulty ground telephone and radiogram systems at the border, couple with inefficiency in the performances of border officers whose ultimate interest is geared toward tips from passengers order than performance ratings, none of them cared to pick up the piece of paper that lies in the telex machine sitting in one of the booths. It took about forty-five minutes to completely process us and that was because every one of them dragged their feet in fulfillment of the tipping policy: "Ou side den tie cow na dea e dea eat." After everyone was tipped, the process went on smoothly then we boarded the vehicle and drove two miles to the Guinean side. The chief security officer at the border already had information about my coming, so he welcomed my family and let us wait at his post while he processed our entry into the Republic of Guinea. While waiting, we were given food and drinks, and there was already a private Guinean Renault van waiting to take us in the capital Conakry where relatives of my wife were waiting to receive us. So we released the vehicle that brought us and bid the driver goodbye and at that point I had no more fear even if my pursuers catch up with me since my family was now on Guinean soil. Besides the support I had generated for my family in Guinea, the government is committed to our protection under the 1951 Convention and 1967 Protocol relating to the Status of Refugees once a valid and well-founded fear of persecution was established upon which asylum was granted once we arrived; therefore our pursuers must provide reasonable and legal basis through the Guinean legal systems to have me extradited to answer to a crime if indeed they can prove that I committed a crime in Sierra Leone territories. At around 5:00 p.m. when we arrived at the Guinean side of the border, another Mercedes Benz and a Land Rover loaded with my pursuers were indeed less than two hours away from the border. There were ten people in both vehicles: six in the Land Rover and four in the Mercedes Benz. Amongst them were the Yillah brothers, one uniformed military personnel from the Sierra Leone army whom they had convinced at the airport, the other military guy who once threatened me, and the rest was a combination of candidates and their relatives. Before leaving Lungi to pursue me, they sent a small group to Freetown to check the hotel there, my office, and other places to see if they can find me. One of the candidates who had a relative in the military informed that relative and convinced him to send a telex to the border authorities from the military barracks in Wilberforce, Freetown. The telex message which claimed that I was on the run after squandering $40,000 from Pa Yillah, arrived at the security post on the Sierra Leone side of the border five minutes before we arrived there, but no one checked the telex tray so the telex was not seen till the next morning. Meanwhile, the remnant of candidates and their sympathizers (relative and friends) left behind at the airport were forced to give authorities details of the allegations against me, and they built a case base on the already conflicting child trafficking fiasco, indicating that the five children in my family were vulnerable children that I took advantage of in order to trade them. This alerted and led ECOMOG officers to send radiogram to a contingent of their colleagues in various posts and also send telex to both the Sierra Leone and Guinean border authorities, which arrived there at 7:10 p.m. and 7:15 respectively. Both the first and second telexes sent to the Sierra Leone border authorities were not seen until on Sunday morning: one telex accusing me of money squandering and the others accusing me of child trafficking.

DYSFUNCTIONAL ONE

At 5:50 p.m. my family left the Guinean side of the border in a Renault van en route to Conakry to join my in-laws. We were barely thirty minutes on our way when our pursuers arrived at the Sierra Leonean side of the border. As they revealed the urgency of their mission to the authorities, they were given escort from the Sierra Leone security post to go after me quickly to the Guinean side of the border to alert the authorities and to continue the chase. The Guinean authorities, for their part, were told that I had stolen $75,000 from the blind man over a period of two weeks and was running away with a lot of cash on me. The blind man was there with some of the women candidates crying and gained a lot of sympathy, so after some plea from the head of security post from the Sierra Leone side, the Guinean border authorities reluctantly agreed to send their own security personnel after me to investigate the matter. We had gone passed Pamalap and mid-way toward Forecariah when a Guinean police vehicle on high speed with siren caught up with us and pulled us over. They took me out of the Renault van and place me in the police van and ordered the van to follow them back to the border. Before our arrival back to the border, the Guinean authorities received the telex that ECOMOG sent asking them to keep an eye for a Liberian refugee name John C. Davies, who is alleged to be in the process of trafficking five children. Before our arrival at the Guinean side of the border, there was already a confusion posed by the ECOMOG telex and the allegation as presented by the chief of border security from the Sierra Leonean side. As I was taken from the police vehicle and my family being led to a large parlor in the main border security post, the whole place was full with people, some of whom left their posts and other were curious people from nearby villages who came to see the man who suddenly became the talk of the border on both sides. It took a little while for investigators to talk to me or my wife. In that small window of time my wife, shocked, looked at me and whispered: "Why is all this happening?"

"You do not know anything, but I have received death threats for the entire family and all along I have been working on protecting us. So don't worry, we are safe, and you do not know anything." Moments thereafter, the Guinean and Sierra Leonean security confronted me with their compromising decision, first to jointly conduct a search of my family to see if there was any evidence of the kind of money my pursuers talked about and second if I have any evidence of birth certificates for the children in my family and third to have a secluded conversation with the children. I agreed to all of that, so they did a thorough search all of us, our travel bags, and every item in them and then I suggested they stripped search us which they did, and all that they found on my person and bag was Le.120,000 along with $300. Before they repacked our bags, I asked permission to open one of the folders in my travel bag and removed all of my children's original birth certificates including our original refugee registration documents including the United Nations High Commission for Refugee Travel Documents in which all of the children names and photos are tagged since 1990 when we entered Sierra Leone. I then provided six Liberian newspapers dated as far back from 1986 to 1990 all of which carried stories with photos of my entire family during celebrations of my Liberian National Chess Championships, which I won ten times in a row. Then I provided a small family photo album in support and at this point everyone was convinced that the children were my children and so by the time they talked to the children it did not take them long before they were overwhelmingly convinced. Then Pa Yillah when confronted to speak the truth finally confessed that this has nothing to do with child trafficking but for a resettlement program. Both border authorities investigating the allegations began expressing disappointment first with the telex message that the Guinean authorities received and the first claim about child trafficking which is now proven false, then about $75,000 claim that does not seem to add up. However, since it was getting late and the investigation had shifted to a third allegation about resettlement program the Guinean chief of security decided that our family be placed in a nearby motel with our travel bags and travel documents be held at their office and the investigation will continued and concluded the next day. The Guineans then rejected the Sierra Leonean security chief request to keep me over to their side of the border where all of my accusers would spend the night till morning. When the suggestion was made by the Sierra Leonean Chief of Security, for the first time my wife stood up and spoke using strong words in both English and French, and for a moment I could not believe she could sound so forceful, convincing, and strong. She cautioned the Guinean authorities about a statement that one of the men made threatening to use military force to suck their claim out of her husband. The man who made the statement was one of the two who threatened me in Freetown. The Guinean authorities asked the man if he made the statement, and he denied but admitted that he is a sergeant in the Sierra Leone army. Then he was asked how she knew he was in the military when he had on civilian clothing and he began murmuring and rumbling. He was then banned from the investigation and threatened disciplinary actions if he showed up there again the next day. At this the Guinean Chief of Security made a point clear to all of them: "The Republic of Guinea has granted this family asylum, and they are now under our protection. Under no circumstance would any member of their family would be turned over to anyone except if a probable cause is established in which case an extradition proceeding through our court system would be the only means by which he can be turned over to the appropriate authorities. Otherwise we do not have the authority to hand him over to anyone or to any country," he said. Then his deputy sealed the position expressed. "You guys made two seriously false accusations already that could cost this man his life at this critical times when there are all sort of havoc going on in your country and ours. In addition, the records here, including a recent newspaper from your country, show that this family was captive by one of the rebel groups for several days and one member from the family was killed coldblooded at Camp Waterloo when it was overran and taken over by RUF. How can we believe you guys that you are not after this man to kill his family, and we ended up answerable to our government for breaching the protection of a refugee that we are obligated to protect?" The Guinean Chief of Security pulled a drawer and took a bunch of keys, sprang up to his feet, and said to everyone "Bonne nuit, madam et monsieur, a demain." Leaving our bags, money, and travel documents in the custody of the Guinean border authorities, we were escorted by two officers to a nearby motel to spend the night and instructed to report to their office by ten o'clock the next morning.

Chapter 70

At ten o'clock on Sunday morning when we reported at the main office, we were taken to a courtyard at the back of the building. The Yillah team headed by the Sierra Leone Chief of Security at the border arrived at 9:00 a.m. At the motel where we spent the night, we managed to contact my wife's relatives overnight through one of the security guards and word passed around that we were being held on the Guinean side of the border. My wife's relatives then contacted higher government officials and word later reached the commandant of border operations who in turn talked with chief security officer at the border to urge the need for protection of my family. At the same time one of my in-laws made it on time with two of his gendarmerie friends to witness the investigation at the border. Also the nearby Paramount Chief of the town was alerted, and he also along with some of the elders in his district attended the hearing. At 10:15 in the morning, the investigation started and Pa Yillah took the stand. He was less than five minutes in his explanation when a Sierra Leone border officer came running in with papers in hand which he turned over to his boss who headed the Yillah team. Pa Yillah was momentarily interrupted as all attention focused on the officer who just came hurriedly in and for a moment I thought maybe it was a warrant for my arrest, but it was the two telexes that came in the day before which they missed. That led the investigators to reenter the premise that was settled. The investigators then asked Pa Yillah once more to clarify the telexes they received from ECOMOG and from the military barracks in Wilberforce in Freetown. He clarified that he did not understand how the reason for searching for Mr. Davies was misrepresented, but he learned last night that some of the people affected became frustrated and desperate to get help tracking Mr. Davies down so they said things like child trafficking, etc. After the clarification, he continued to make his case. He said he had been in the resettlement business for over thirty years before he became blinded, using his music band as a vehicle to resettling people in Europe and in America. He would slot them in as band members whenever his band is travelling abroad and then obtain visas for these people who would not return after the band traveled. So he became popular and people would entrust him with funds to assist them obtained visas to travel to various countries; therefore when he learned that Mr. Davies' organization, AccordOne, was resettling refugees, he contacted him and proposed to resettle some of his clients to which Mr. Davies agreed and received the sum of US $40,000, and yesterday was the day that dream was to be fulfilled to resettle a family of three totaling eighteen people. He concluded by saying: "However, Mr. Davies decided to double cross all of these people and betray the trust I placed in him and that is why we pursued him." He had difficulties explaining his case, stammering and rumbling through it which is mainly attributed to his consciousness that the deal is illegal. If it were an all Sierra Leonean investigation, he probably need not give many details in his explanation to put his point through to be favored. When he was done explaining, the investigation took a question and answer tone:

Q: Where did you obtain visas for all the people you have resettled using your musical band, and how many people approximately have you resettled?

A: I got visas from various European embassies and from United States embassy in Freetown, and I would say maybe I help about a thousand people resettled in these countries.

Q: To what country the current people were to be resettled by Mr. Davies as you alleged?

A: America

Q: What are their nationalities?

A: Sierra Leoneans (he said after a long pause and rambling).

Q: Under what status were these people allegedly to be resettled?

A: As Liberian refugees (again stammering through this answer after a long pause)

Q: You said you paid up to US $40,000 over a period of two months to Mr. Davies for resettling these people to the United States, how was these monies paid to him and where are the receipts? Did any of these people handed any money to him directly?

A: My brother would check the amount and put it in an envelope, and I would take it to Mr. Davies at his office. I did not ask for any receipt, and he did not issue any. And none of the people involved handed their money to him. They all paid through me, and I handed the envelopes containing the accumulated amounts totaling US $40,000 to Mr. Davies.

Q: At any of the times you handed him any money did you have witness or witnesses?

A: No. I trusted Mr. Davies and because he is the CEO of the organization so I had no doubt in dealing with him, and besides his organization processed all the people involved through medical, etc.

Q: Are there any of the people that were supposed to be resettled here at the moment?

A: O yes, about six of them here and the rest were left at Lungi International Airport yesterday.

At this point all six of his clients present were called, and they all stood up and came forward, and they were asked to state their names, which they did one after the other. They all gave their real names; I guess no one thought of the next question to follow. "What travel documents were you guys being used for the resettlement?" one of the investigators asked and unfortunately for three of the six who had their hand bags with them, pulled out their Liberian Lassaie passé and handed it over to the investigators who looked at the documents and asked the first one a question: "You just told us your name is Susan Thompson. How come you are carrying a travel document with the name Juan Nagbeh?" She buried her head and began to lick her lips and scratch head and other body parts. Pa Yillah sank in his seat, wiggled his eyes, and murmured something to himself. Inside the three travel documents are refugee registration cards dated as far back as October 1993 approximately two years before AccordOne was formed and before Pa Yillah admittedly contacted me to register his client for the Canadian Migration Application processing. So by the time questions as to when, how, and who issued them Liberian refugee ID was clarified, so many more individuals and institutions like the UNHCR and some Sierra Leone officials were implicated with aiding and abating crimes against refugees. One of the investigators asked Susan Thompson if she knew who the real Juan Nagbeh was and she paused, looked in the direction of Pa Yillah for help, and realizing that the blind man can't see her, slowly shook her head. Pa Yillah was then asked how these refugee IDs were issued to his clients and obtained by them. The blind man waggled his head and threw his eyes upward as though he was searching for something upward. Finally with his face twisted in anger, he asked the investigators how was he supposed to see and know the document they were talking about since he was blind and could not see. This ignited a mixture of uproar and laughter amongst all present as a deeply troubled and frustrated Pa Yillah struggled to keep investigators focus on what he referred to as the issue, the returning of the money he claimed I took from him for the deal. This aggravated investigators on both sides of the aisle and Pa Yillah was told in strong words that he was not going to dictate how the matter should be investigated. They as investigators were not going to shut their eyes to other aspect of a crime to look only at one aspect that favored an accomplice or mastermind of the overall crime. Pointing to the clients who produced their travel documents and refugee IDs, one investigator stressed that what had been established so far as of now before them for which serious actions can be taken are crimes against refugees and other criminal charges ranging from falsification of travel document to identity theft amongst others, which carried a good amount of jail time here in the Republic of Guinea if these transactions had taken place here. Then another investigator asked

Pa Yillah how the IDs were issued and obtained and he insisted that he cannot speak to that because he cannot see what document they were referring to and that the holders of these documents were adults and capable of speaking for themselves. Another uproar started again and everyone talking at the same time while others laughed, but I just kept quiet and played victim while waiting for my turn to prove that the only money that was received was from Pa Yillah's clients for processing of their Canadian Migration application and not from him directly. Argument between the Yallahs and their client ensued over the statement made by Pa Yillah. They felt that they should not be left alone to explain how they obtain the IDs when it was the Yillahs who actually processed the IDs for them in collaboration with the disappeared UNHCR program officer.

As they argued in English, the Guinean French interpreter, the two gendarmeries that accompanied my in-law who understood English started laughing uncontrollably so loud that the Guinean investigators and other Guineans present could not wait to hear what was being said and what the argument was about. Then one of the gendarmeries who accompanied my in-law, seeing that the interpreter could not control his laughter, took the floor to explain in French what the argument was about and almost instantly the over eighty Guinean people in the courtyard including the investigators were also laughing so loud that the whole place seem like a circus rehearsal. The Yillah clients felt betrayed and disappointed that Pa Yillah wanted them to explain how they obtained refugees' IDs when it was he who masterminded it all; it was he who brought a cameraman to take passport-size photos of them and baptized them with the names on the IDs. All they did was to appear and have their photos taken and to sign the ID forms that UNHCR staff processed to have the proper authority signature, sealed and laminated, and it was the Yillah brothers who handed them the finished IDs. So they expected him to be able to explain that to investigators instead of trying to escape liability and suggesting that he could not see to explain the documents.

By the time investigators were able to quiet down the place in order to proceed, two of the ladies had disappeared, leaving behind their travel documents and IDs. The two had taken excuse to use the restroom and never returned. It was reported later that the two were seen crossing the barrier dividing the two countries walking the two miles toward the Sierra Leonean side of the border. Since those two never returned, their IDs and travel documents were later turned over to the Sierra Leone Security Chief to do whatever that was necessary with it. Proceeding further after the short interval of arguments and laughter, the other four were asked as to how much money they paid Pa Yillah for the resettlement program and they reluctantly named amounts ranging from $7,500 to $10,000 per head to which Pa Yillah played tight lip when asked to confirm. Since he continued to dodge the questions, the rest of his clients present were asked if they ever handed money to me for their resettlement programs and they all responded no.

I was then asked to throw a light on the allegation concerning Pa Yillah's claim that he paid me $40,000 to help resettle eighteen of his clients. I categorically denied the allegation and asked the officers if I can have access to my travel bag. In a few moments my bag was handed over to me, and I took out an analysis pad together with AccordOne's duplicated receipt book. Then I asked permission from the investigators to ask the four clients present their refugee names, the names that they used when they came to my office for processing of their Canadian Migration Application processing, not their real names. When those were given to me along with the first absconded two, I flipped the receipt book pages and bent each duplicate receipt leaf issued them. The amount was Le.15,000 or US $25 on each of the receipt, and I explained the services that AccordOne offered. Now, I said if they can get receipt for this small payment why would there be no receipt issued for the bigger but critical amount that Pa Yillah is talking about? Pa Yillah was shaking his head and interrupted me couple of times demanding that I swear to it that he never paid me the amount to help him out with these people. I ignored him and continued with my defense. But when he kept interrupting me, I turned to his clients and asked when did they make the payment for resettlement to Pa Yillah? They said about two years ago. Then I asked Pa Yillah, how did he know two years ago that he was going to know me in June this year to help him with resettlement, about a year and half since he sold them a resettlement package, to justify his claim that I am a part of his scheme? The interpreter carefully interpreted my question and of course it resonated with all present, and Pa Yillah could not respond to my question. I said that aspect alone together with Pa Yillah's own record, which he explained here that he has been resettling people to many countries of the world over thirty years ago told the story. He saw my genuine Canadian Migration Application processing program as a stepping stone to cover for monies he had extracted from these people two years ago; monies he may have used on his big construction project and now he see me as a scapegoat for his agenda.

"This crime was committed over two years ago when I knew not these people, all of them including my accuser, and my accuser targeted me to use me in order to appease and delay the wrath of his victim, suddenly as you all can see, I am framed as a child trafficker, a dealer of refugee resettlement program, etc." I argued.

Then I asked: "Where is the evidence that Pa Yillah paid me $40,000 and for what purpose?" And I answered the question, "None, no evidence whatsoever." Before taking my seat, I asked this question while looking and turning around with my hands wide open: "Is there anyone in this courtyard who really believe that Pa Yillah was actually serious in chasing after me to catch me?" Everyone just looked at me with puzzle on their faces as the interpreter interprets my words and then I repeated the question again and turn around to view faces. Still no answer, then I said in soft words: "Pa Yillah actually wished that I was never caught, he wanted me and my family to have disappeared, gone so that he can simply placed the blame on me to appease his victims that I went away with their money, not $40,000 but the amount you see on that telex $100,000." As I was taking my seat, I could hear the Guinean crowd saying: "Oui, oui" and "C'vere."

The joint chiefs and all the officers left us in the courtyard and went into the main office to deliberate and in say ten minutes later they returned with their findings. The Guinean chief spoke and his interpreter interpreted after him in English word for word: "Mr. Davies and his family are going to Conakry, and we have their address there, and he would not be allowed to leave the country for a period of two weeks at which time Pa Yillah can proceed to institute charges against him if he so chooses in Sierra Leone. If the Sierra Leonean government needed Mr. Davies to stand trial they would request our government through the existing extradition treaty and if our legal system determine that he is liable for extradition, then he would be extradited. He has been granted asylum, and we are responsible to his protection at this time. We would keep his family travel documents for two weeks, and if there is no such request from the Sierra Leone government for his extradition, we would return his travel document to him, and he would be free to go wherever he wanted. The investigation is now suspended pending actions from your end, Pa Yillah."

There was a pause then the Guineans present embraced my family, the officers released our bags, and my in-laws took the bags in their vehicle. I overheard Pa Yillah saying that he thinks that I bribed the Guinean authorities but he was wrong, I did not. Pa Yillah was looking at justice through the eyes of the Sierra Leonean culture; this was justice. He got up with his team and he urged them to be patient. Once they arrive back in Freetown he would file a complaint and make sure that I am extradited to face justice. A bystander asked him how he intended to do that, and as he began to explain about his connections in Freetown and how different things would have been if I was caught on Sierra Leonean soil, the bystander clarified himself: "I mean, how are you going to have the government of Sierra Leone process a charge against him and institute an extradition proceedings against him when as of last night, fierce fighting in and around Freetown began and the whole city is in panic as we speak? Have you heard the news yet?" He asked. We were all stunned and clueless. Another bystander confirmed it by saying: "It is on the news early this morning that RUF has advanced and taken part of the city." We were all frozen as one officer turned on loud the radio in his car so we can all hear reports about the fighting, and it was reported that panic had gripped residence of Freetown the attempt by RUF to take over the capital city met fierce response from the military troops. As we all converged, shocked and confused about the news, Pa Yillah took a deep frustrating breath, placed his hands over his head, and in a callous-like manner uttered these words underneath his breath: "Well, I might as well seek asylum here in Guinea for now."

Chapter 71

Around 5:00 p.m. we arrived in Conakry and were placed in a one-bedroom apartment offered by my wife's cousins near Gbessia International Airport. Later that evening, few distant relatives that she never met before visited us, and it was ecstatic scenery as they all tried to connect the family tree from one generation to another and from one event to another. Some brought foodstuff and others brought assorted bathroom supplies which they offered us. For the rest of our two weeks stay, the hospitality we received from relatives and friends was cordial and encouraging even though most of these people were low income earners, some self-employed petty traders. But my wife's cousin, Papa Cakara, who assisted me while planning my family escape, was regarded as the backbone of the entire clan. He was a reputable mechanic who owned a successful auto repair garage located in the heart of Conakry, and he also imports scrap cars from Belgium, repairs them, and then puts them in the market for sale. His father held a high-ranking position in the government and was very instrumental in helping us with temporary asylum. It became an irony, however, that with all the hospitality and support accorded us and the strong ties my wife had in the Republic of Guinea, yet our oldest daughter, Elizabeth, who disappeared five years earlier at age six in 1990 during the heat of the Liberian war and was later declared dead in 1992, was still alive and living in the custody of her rescuers in Kankan, in the eastern province of Guinea while we were in the west, and we had no idea at the time.

By the time relatives and friends left the apartment late Sunday night we were exhausted and slept the night through. Early the next morning, my wife awoke me to discuss everything which she said looks like a dream to her and she wanted to know what went on in Sierra Leone and what is going on now and what our plans are. I talked about the threats that we faced in Freetown and my encounters with the Yillahs and how I skillfully defused some harm that might have happened. I said all along I did not want to have her involved with what I was planning so as not to give her cause to panic and increase anxiety and the pressure she was dealing with. She never allowed me to pause as I explained everything piece by piece and answered all of her questions and doubts one after another. By the time every aspects of the situation that she could think of was exhausted, she took a deep breath and reached for me, and we hugged each other so tightly like it was our first date.

Suddenly she slacked her grip of me and asked how we were going to leave on three hundred dollars. "Don't tell me that that is all we have left with five children to take care of and we certainly cannot depend on my relatives and friends here for long," she said. My wife has always been faithful to me, and I considered myself as blessed for having her. If anything, she is the one person that God place in my life to fill in the love and care that was so inconsiderably snatched away from me at age eight, something that has created a vacuum in my life that I needed. We have had some good times and indeed suffered together some serious hard times over the last five years and I knew what it would mean to her if I confirmed her fears that we only had three hundred dollars left, but for some stupid reasons I confirmed it and I said that "God will provide." The woman went from anger to being sad and in her frustration she asked: "When would God provide again for us when you gave away that entire provisions He provided our family? You became the Good Samaritan and took everyone else's problems as if you were entrusted with the welfare and security of all. Even those entrusted with peoples welfare saved enough for their own family. Now, after all these events, our hope for the United States just vanished and you blew up tens of thousands of dollars trying to please the world, and all we have left is three hundred dollars?"

She pulled away and walked into the sitting room and curled into a chair. Moments later I picked up one of the children's water flask that they used for drinking water while travelling and sat at the edge of the chair holding the flask and I asked her to unscrew the bottom and she asked furiously: "Why?"

"Unscrew it," I said. So she did and after unscrewing it she held the upper part in one hand and the bottom part in another and looked in them and there was nothing visible, then she asked: "Why am I doing this?"

"Get a knife and cut where you see the lining inside the bottom half," I said. Then she went into a cupboard and took a knife and carefully pierce open the plastic layer and find something rapped and lying flat on the surface of bottom layer; she ripped it off and opened it and found a thousand dollars. I stood by the room door and watched her face slowly transcend from twisted to clamor, and she asked if the other four flasks were like that. She found the answer in my eyes and rushed for all of them and after she did the second one I stopped her and said we do not need to expose everything as yet. Now she know we have five thousand dollars, but what she did not know yet is that we have another five thousand dollars in cash and another five thousand dollars in traveler's check carefully implanted into the children's hardback drawing books. She also had no idea that before we left Freetown I had taken her cousin's business address and mailed a package through DHL in his care addressed to me. In the package are two sets of children hardback drawing books along with some learning materials. Each of the drawing books contained six thousand dollars travel's checks. The delivery date of the package was scheduled for Tuesday, October 3, 1995; and before her cousin left, I had informed him that one of my staff would mail the children learning materials in care of him, and he assured me that immediately he received it he would bring it for the children. Another thing that she knew nothing about was that inside the metal handle of two of our travel bags contained two thousand five hundred dollars each, but all these would overwhelm her so I just kept quiet and watched her smiling at me as her excitement awoke all the children.

DYSFUNCTIONAL ONE

On the tenth day of October, the Guinean authorities released our travel documents and that same day our daughter Jacqueline turned five years old, so we rented a vehicle and we toured the city and dined in one of the most expensive restaurants downtown. The news about the war in Liberia and Sierra Leone continued to hunt us every day. People who knew that we were from both countries bring in bad news all the time and also the Guinean radio stations and television station spent most part of their respective broadcasts to talk and show images of the carnages, and we wish we could go someplace far away from the region. There were talks about cease-fire agreements to be signed between and amongst the warring fraction in both countries but trust has always been a big issue. Previous agreements had not been honored. Over the last five years, hundreds of thousands had been killed and millions more displaced as cease-fires and peace agreements were broken one after another. In implementing some of the peace accords the Guinean government in collaboration with ECOMOG had worked together in the region to ensure adherence and to improve access to humanitarian aids to support internally displaced Liberians and those fleeing the conflict in Sierra Leone. In the face of the current reported outbreak of fighting in and around the Sierra Leone capital, the Guineans are determined to make sure that their neighbors' wars do not spilt over into their country so they became tough on people fleeing and entering their country. In some Guinean towns along the borders with Liberia and Sierra Leone there had been incidents resulting in the death and injury of Guinean citizens that infuriated the Guinean people and the government, already under pressure had to do something to protect its border. Large groups of refugees from both countries were bypassing the various camps set up deep in the south and south east of Guinea and coming into the Conakry where there were no camps set up.

This influx of refugees in Conakry was in a sense adversely weighting on the country's economy as well as causing serious social and environmental problems. Arm robbery and other form of crime rates elevated drastically couple with foreign exploiters scrambled over the country's mineral deposits. Guinea had been going through its own share of political turmoil since the sudden death of its nationalist president, Ahmed Shekou Toure, on March 26, 1984. The Military Committee of National Recovery (CMRN), formed and headed by Lt. Col. Lansana Conte, took control of the government and began the process of dismantling the three decade structural institutions of the Toure's regime, which was branded as oppressive and authoritarian. The CMRN then abolished the country's constitution bringing about a Second Republic.

In the process, the one party political system was dissolved along with all of its massive wings built over three decades of the Toure's regime and all political prisoners released.

Growing up in the West African region as a little boy, it was easy to be brainwashed about African leadership; mostly stigmatized as dictatorship, authoritarianism, oppressive, totalitarianism, tyranny, and etc. But weighting with maturity the facts and circumstances surrounding these eras, it is fair to say that some of these descriptions do not hold true as some African leaders did or were forced to do exactly what was best for their countries given their respective circumstances. In the aftermath of slavery, colonialism, neocolonialism, and in the fight against extreme Western politicking, greed, and exploitations, Guinea, like many African countries, was forced into nationalist movements of some type and partnering with its neighbors in order to gain independence to free their respective countries from the threat of foreign exploitation and neocolonialism, which weren't pretty. The Guinea leadership strategy at the time included the preservation of the country's natural resources, which oftentimes were the target of interest to powerful extinctive forces. Then there were other serious foreign challenges in the midst of the Cold War period with Western powers bullying their way with African nations resulting to oppression, apathy systems, discrimination, economic and political picketing. All of these were different types of challenges in an era that demanded a different kind of leadership. One of the tools used by Western powers in the slavery era, colonialism, and neocolonialism eras has been the "divide and rule" strategy, which led to sectarianisms along a variety of fronts, which in turn laid the foundation for antinationalism, which over time culminated into greed, selfishness, tribalism, nepotism, and rampant corruption. By the time African countries achieved independence or their leadership prepped to assume governmental responsibilities from their so-called colonial masters, the byproducts that come with territory, the divide and rule policies, had already spread its roots deeply within the very fabric of so-called independence and all that Western powers will do when and where their interest is at stake is to pull strings from one or more of the various fronts to destabilize their subjects. These were some of the major challenges or aftermath of the challenges that still hunts some of the developing countries today.

Ironically, among the actions that the CMRN took to address and define the future of the country was the departure away from its nationalistic concept that the Toure regime represented and fought for. The CMRN encourages opened foreign investments, which opened the door to exploitation of the country's well-preserved mineral deposits in contrast to the sacrifices made over the decades and to the disadvantages of the masses. I would tend to think that when a country made such sacrifices, it would be for purposes of utilizing its resources to funding direct meaningful national development projects such as strategic human resource development growing from a free education system from elementary education to high school; making available educational loan at university level for its citizens without discrimination; providing subsidized health care system and a better social welfare system; implementing road projects and other infrastructural projects; promoting its economy in nationalistic ways by enacting legislatures and regulations to protect its business environment and to hold everyone else accountable for any breaches. In my opinion, opening the country's resources to unlimited foreign investment require very strict and strong protection and legal framework to guide and to control the playing field, and it also meant deploying of huge resources and formulating institutions to implement, enforce, and monitor regulations, etc. Liberia and Sierra Leone are statistical victims to these types of investments, allowing foreigners to explore their respective natural resources for pennies on the dollar for as long as possible while only a few citizen benefited from the nation's natural resources.

At the peak of the Liberian civil war in 1990, Guineans had passed a referendum for a new constitution and usher in the Third Republic with the establishment of a Supreme Court. Like old wine in a new bottle, the CMRN was dissolved and replaced by the Transitional Council for National Recovery (CTRN) composed of military officers and civilians with Lansana Conte still as president. The CTRN was mandated to manage a five-year transition to civilian rule, and by 1992, the door to multiparty system saw about forty political parties registering for the 1997 general elections. The parties needed to raise funds in preparation for their respective campaigning and war mongers from neighboring Liberia, Sierra Leone, and the Ivory Coast needed connections for their dirty deals and so Guinea became the central point of contact for some of the war mongers, flying in and out of the country to hold secret meetings or to trade blood diamonds with foreign investors, etc. These activities were troubling to some people and certainly within a short period of time I also became worried for all the signs that trouble was building up were visible. I was probably naïve, but I was not going to continue raising my traumatized family in Guinea after a few incidents inside the country and at its boarders leaving so many people dead, especially rebels posing as civilians. My family decided to fly to Dakar, Senegal, to live there. So on Saturday, October 14, 1995, we went to the nearby airport, bought air tickets, and flew to Dakar, Senegal.

Chapter 72

We arrived in the Republic of Senegal overnight. It was a spectacular view flying over the capital city, Dakar. There was sufficient evidence of electricity everywhere, lights stretching from the bank of the Atlantic Ocean to as far as one's eyes could see across buildings, skyscrapers, and landscapes. The children were ecstatic. They had never seen anything like that before. I guess they thought Freetown was the best place in the world compared to Waterloo Refugee Camp where we lived for about five years without any electricity. Freetown, the capital city of one of the richest countries in the world, yet the poorest, was a city in darkness for the most part of our five years stay. Electricity, the lack of which wrecked economies anywhere around the globe, was one of the many services that helpless citizens were forced to live without, imposed on them by a bunch of selfish, greedy, and ignoramus politicians and their foreign cronies, who in their lack of leadership and foresights sees themselves as the spotlights deserving adoration and worship from helpless citizens.

On the average, most areas in Freetown and other parts of the country received electricity supply few hours per week and lived without for the rest of the week. But for those who delighted in exploiting and sharing the country's wealth, they all have heavy duty generators at home and at their places of work, selfishly enjoyed their personal supply of electricity. At Dakar International Airport, we were all blown away by the beauty of the place, its neatness, and mainly everywhere were illuminated and airport workers and officers conducted themselves in orderly manner that amused me since I always seem to have an eye for seeing things in order and a brain for evaluating systems and the guts to fight against wrongs and injustices. As for the children, they would not believe that we were not already in the United States. It was like a fairy tale to them, and they fell in love with the place, and they insisted that they would like to settle down and live in Senegal forever. However, our fun fare at the airport shirked when airport authorities looked at our refugee travel documents and informed us that as a policy, we would not be allowed to leave the airport premise unless under UNHCR escort and if in seventy-two hours we are not received by the UNHCR we would be returned to where we came from. At first I could not understand it but I soon learned that there is no smooth place to live in the world without challenges and struggles of a particular type. I tried to convince them that even though we were travelling with UNHCR travel documents, we were capable of taking care of ourselves financially without being a burden on the government in any way whatsoever, but they are not buying it, and we were told that because of the children we would be allowed to take a suite at the airport hotel if we can afford it; otherwise we would be detained in their custody until UNHCR officers come and release us from their custody. The UNHCR offices were closed on weekends and Monday was a national holiday so we booked a suite at the hotel and from time to time a security would check on us. We were allowed to move around within the premise of the airport. The next morning we made friends with some of the airport workers including security personnel and later the seventy-two hours were extended to allow us time on Tuesday to contact the UNHCR office for them to pick us up. It wasn't until Wednesday of that week that the protection officer from UNHCR office came to the airport to have us released. When I spoke to him by phone the day before, he indicated that Senegal was not a zone of assistance for English-speaking Liberian and Sierra Leonean refugees. I urged him just to help release us since it was costing a fortune for my family to live in the hotel, and I also told him that we would try to live within their policy of non-assistance to English speaking refugees. So when he finally released us from the airport, he took us to the UNHCR office downtown and prepared an identity document for us which reads in English and French as follows: "This is to attest that the bearer of this instrument, whose photo appeared below, Mr. John C.

Davies, is to be considered a Liberian refugee in Dakar, Senegal. He is not eligible to any assistance outside of the assistance zones, Sierra Leone, Guinea, and Ivory Coast." The document had an expiration date and was renewable every six months. After it was issued to us, he escorted us from his office and at the entrance he bid us good luck as he returned to his office. We stood in front of the UNHCR building for about an hour just looking up and down the busy street hoping that we could see someone whom we can connect with to find a hotel or motel. One of the private securities at UNHCR office became concerned and was later helpful. He gave me a city map and provided me some tips on public transportation, restaurants, and cheap hotels. We found one hotel not too far away and after we checked in we decided to find some place to eat lunch. After lunch we chartered a taxi and toured the city to look around and to have a feel of things. That night, we weighted the risks and costs of traveling to another country in order to settle down and after looking at all options we decided by majority vote that we should settle in Senegal and beat the challenges before us, which included learning the local languages: Wolof and French. So we engaged a three-bedroom house in Dekele, Castor, bought new furniture and fixtures, furnished it, and then enrolled the children in a nearby private school named Groupe Scholiere Nolive at Liberty Six. Then we found and enrolled at a Catholic adult language learning program set up by CARITAS to assist English-speaking refugees learn the two main languages in order to integrate in the Senegalese society. So when the children are off to school my wife and I attended the two hours classes learning the two languages and late evenings after the family ate dinner we had a personal teacher name Cisse, hired to help us learn French and to help the children with their homework.

At the Catholic adult language learning program, we met with many Liberian and Sierra Leonean refugee parents and before long we became aware of the general English-speaking refugee community struggles and challenges in Senegal. The first problem was the wording of the attestation document that UNHCR gave all

English-speaking refugees such as the one they gave my family. Part of the wording of the document negates the very chatters and core of the UNHCR. Most places where the document is presented for any purposes the refugee would be told that they do not belong in Dakar and the countries listed on the document would be cited. In some instances, the document is interpreted as English-speaking West African refugees not welcome in the country where the UNHCR West African regional headquarter is located. Two of the countries listed on the document, Sierra Leone and Ivory Coast, were in a crisis where most civilians were fleeing for their lives. Refugee camps in the third country, Guinea, are overcrowded and obviously the country was not prepared to accommodate hundreds of thousands of refugees and more refugees kept fleeing the refugee camps set up in interior parts of the country to live in Conakry.

Apart from that, there have been incidents of shooting at the camps; in one such incident, about a hundred refugee women and children were caught in fierce fighting in one of the camps, and they were shot dead by Guinean troops who claimed that rebels were amongst the dead. In Senegal, however, there were other refugees from French-speaking countries that the Senegalese government and UNHCR recognized and accorded full support and services including a proper refugee IDs and also given travel documents. These are refugees who came from the Democratic Republic of Congo, Rwanda, Burundi in Central Africa and those from neighboring Mauritania and Guinea Bissau. These refugees are provided cash allowances, education, medication and housing while Liberian and Sierra Leonean refugees were abandoned by the UNHCR, on the basis of a bogus policy that practically refrained refugees from English-speaking West African countries from entitlement to any assistance in the West African Regional headquarter.

As a result, refugee children were left to languish without any education and many of them staved and homeless. These were the challenges on the ground that necessitated causes worth fighting for and I was not just going to sit back and watch other refugee parents struggle with their children while I play blind eye and deaf ears simply because I can afford to let my children attend private school and live well in a nice home while so many families are homeless and cannot afford to take care of their children. But I learned from experience that in order to fight causes like these, one must first identify and stipulate each one of the problems in clear terms, then to study their root causes how they come about. Then the next step was to research any laws, rules and policies, customs and traditions that barred or control every aspect of the causes, if available. These steps led me to finding solutions to real problems faced at Waterloo Refugee Camp even though the road toward these achievements could be bumpy and full of huddles but their resolution are feasible because the 1951 Convention & Rights of Refugees and the 1968 Protocol on the Status of Refugees laid out the foundation for benefits that these refugees are being denied. Also Article 26 of the Universal Declaration for Human Rights, and the Convention on the Rights of Children all to which Senegal is signatory, guaranteed free elementary education for all children as well as protection for children in other areas, so the task at that point was to see if there was any other rule that negates these provisions and to see if Senegal would back away from these commitments to which it is a signatory.

Chapter 73

Our first Christmas season in Dakar was a bittersweet experience. Although Senegal is predominantly Muslim populated, Christmas was observed as a national holiday and interestingly markets everywhere in the city were flooded with all types of children toys, Christmas artifacts, and a variety of decorating fixtures amongst others. The feelings of Christmas were unmistakably felt beyond our expectation, and my family did enjoy the holiday season but a lot of refugee families from the English community were in bad shape and needed helping hand especially those who were homeless. My family became easily empathic with their struggles. UNHCR Regional Office shared gifts among the French-speaking refugee communities and left out the English-speaking refugee community. The Catholic organization, CARITAS, later stepped in and provided food, toys, and clothing for all refugees without discrimination. On the last day at the Adult Language Learning Center at Route des Peres Maristes, I handed small transportation stipends to the entire English Speaking refugee families present to enable them pick up their gifts at the main Catholic office down town and I also extended invitation to a few of them especially those who were homeless to celebrate Christmas at my home. It was during that celebration that my family really became knowledgeable of the mal-treatments and segregation both UNHCR and the government agency responsible for refugees at the Department of Interior lashed out on English speaking refugees. Firsthand accounts of homeless refugee families spoke of how they were surviving in Dakar, the places where they spent day and night; some slept in a cemetery while other spent their nights in toilets in market places down town. Others were forced to send their children to join the local Talebay ritualistic tradition of solicitation on the streets of Dakar and from house to house collecting food remnants, leftovers from people that they do not know. My family was overwhelmed with sorrow and emotions by their stories.

A sister of one Liberian refugee woman recounted how they were both raped multiple times outdoors in front of the UNHCR-BOS Annex at Point E, Dakar, where they would sleep. Her pregnant sister was denied any medical assistance leading to her death in child delivery in front of the same annex. Her baby also passed after a few days. After the holidays in early January of 1996, my survival instincts kicked in and the question as to how English-speaking refugees would overcome their struggles and survive in Senegal became personal. At this time the Sierra Leone war had reached its epic and more Sierra Leoneans were fleeing the senseless carnages where hands and legs of citizens caught by the rebels were chopped off, from as young as one-day-old babies to as old as a hundred years old. Though the Senegalese authorities were tightening their borders to stop English speaking refugee from entering their country, yet through the cracks more Sierra Leoneans and Liberians seeking safe heavens traveled by road and by sea into Senegal and The Gambia to claim asylum. The challenges for me were of twofold: first, I needed to select among a few small business ventures I had researched to ensure sustenance of my family, and second, I had to formulate an approach to tackle the problem of education for English-speaking refugee children. Sometime in later part of November 1995, I had a meeting with the UNHCR Protection Officer, Mrs. Rogers. In that meeting I pointed out the challenges concerning education for the children and the fact that lack of education would come back to bite society if these children leaned toward bad influences. Although she claimed to appreciate my concern but she said I should not be worried about them when my own children were in private school. She assured me it was her organization's concern and that she was working in conjunction with the Ministry of Interior to address the problem. In early January, a group of Liberian and Sierra Leonean refugees met at my house to discuss the children education problem and to find solution. A committee was then formed headed by me to write a project document for education for English-speaking refugee children in Dakar. The project document was delayed because my family was in the process of moving from where we lived in Dekele, Castor to Grand Yoff. I had reached a decision to initiate home-movie business, a type of business that boomed in Liberia, in communities where cinema theaters are not located or where income groups cannot afford to meet theater costs. A study of the home-movie business showed there were none in existence in Dakar and since I had language barrier problems which held me back from working in my career environment, this was something that did not require fluency in speaking. I got an interpreter to interpret my business plan in French and then I used the document to contact the Commerce Department and obtained a license and an exemption to run that business as a fund raiser to help institute a suitable education program for English speaking refugees in Senegal. A temporary license was issued for a small fee, and it was renewable each year. It was agreed that since such a business was new to the department taxation would be determined and imposed based on reported annual revenue; therefore it was mandatory that accurate record of revenue be kept and submitted by-annually. It was also agreed that from time to time, inspectors would visit the business to evaluate it. I then leased a house with large parlor in Grand Yoff, a densely populated area where mostly low-income people resided, and then I had a carpenter built benches, billboards to placate postal of films and a podium where I placed my movie equipment comprises of a 76" flat TV, three VCRs, a medium size speakers, microphone and other apparatus including Canal+ Horizon transmission box.

Canal+ Horizon enriched the business by showing live events like European soccer matches, boxing, and etcetera. Then I bought a freezer to have my family sell cool aid, ice-cream, soft drinks and then I printed stacks of tickets and some flyers. Then I contacted the nearby video rental businesses to arrange film rental for my business. In the process, I got tips of the type of films the people like and a list of their best actors of which Jean Claude Van Dam topped the list. The weekend we started the business, I hired a cab and placed a local guy contracted in it with a loud speaker and stack of flyers to ride around this small town announcing and distributing the flyers spreading the good news. A new business was born. My plan was to show one movie in the afternoon and one at night but because of the mass turnout and demand on a regular basis we started showing two movies in the afternoon and two at night. Once a week on Sundays, we show two free movies in the afternoon only for the English-speaking refugee community.

By mid-February 1996, we had developed operational module to run the home-movie business and with the help of one local contracted, I find leverage to work on the education project for the Liberian and Sierra Leonean refugee children. The gathering of information for this project document was an easy task; almost every refugee knew something about why their children were not in school. The project called for the formation of a bilingual educational program to transition English-speaking refugee students from their current academic level into the French educational environment and to assist them continue with their respective English school curriculum until they are fit to transfer into the national French curriculum. When the project document was completed in early March 1996, it was distributed to various humanitarian organizations including UNHCR, churches and YMCA Dakar branch with a covered letter soliciting for their help to put resources together in order to provide durable solution to the problem. The YMCA branch in Dakar, located at Avenue Bourguiba X rue 12, Ben Tally, under the leadership of its Secretary General, Mr. Simon Lazarre Badiane, was the first to respond by calling for a conference on the issue and offering its compound to start the school.

But unfortunately many of the invitees discussed the project with UNHCR prior to the conference and withheld their respective participation on the basis that they have been contributing to assist the general refugee community through UNHCR and they would continue to do so and they are assured that UNHCR would address this problem. Other groups including staffs of Dakar Academy, a college preparatory, co-educational boarding and day school program primarily for third culture kids, offered to assist with training refugee teachers to meet the challenges for this project. At the conference, only a few Liberian and Sierra Leonean refugees who worked with me in writing the project document were present along with the YMCA represented by its secretary general. We however made some progress and the YMCA offered their open yard with benches and some desk to be used for classes. I provided the rest of the initial teaching and learning materials while many of the refugee teachers volunteered to work without pay to get the project off the ground. When the program started in May 1996, my five children were the first to attend the outdoor Bilingual Refugee School of Dakar. I had withdrawn them from the private school and enrolled them into the bilingual refugee program. The program had been politicized or rather caught in a web of UNHCR politicking and word had circulated that I had my children in private school while I try to manipulate the plight of poor refugee families who could not afford to put their own children in private schools. Meanwhile, both the Liberian and Sierra Leonean refugee communities had each formed their own association to fight for their rights and the UNHCR sees that as an opportunity to use them sabotage the refugee bilingual project at the YMCA. UNHCR officers had promised to support the two committees if they get their communities to boycott the bilingual refugee school project. But there is no doubt the fact that the project had place UNHCR on the spot and exposed them. A lot of the people and NGOs had no idea that some refugee children were not in any educational program under the UNHCR and now they are aware of the existence of the problem and it has gained momentum. Word went round to the refugee communities that my children had been withdrawn from the private school and now attending the new BRSD.

A Nigerian couple who had five children in their family also enrolled their children in the BRSD and as word went around some of the refugee families began enrolling their children. Despite the propaganda, within three weeks from the inception of the BRSD project, we had about a hundred and fifteen refugee children enrolled. But there were other major problems associated with refugee schooling that we did not take into account. Parents could not afford to transport their children on a daily basis to and fro the program and the next problem was hunger; no child would learn on empty stomach. While we were strategizing to resolve these two major problems to raise fund and to contract one of the local bus services to pick children from various points for school in the morning and to drop them home after school, to at least make snacks available in order to encourage the children to attend daily, UNHCR staff and their counterparts at the Interior Ministry were also strategizing to disrupt the program. They circulated a notice asking all English-speaking refugee parents to take their children to any Senegalese public school near where they lived to enroll them and bring evidence of their enrolment to the Ministry of Interior for verification as prerequisite to receiving educational allowance from UNHCR in the amount of twenty thousand CFA (an equivalent of $40) per head per term which means that a family would receive $80 as educational allowance for each child per school year. By this time everyone involved with the BRSD including all of the refugee parents were convinced that the project was best for refugee children. The public school system was not a solution for the children: (1) The children do not speak, read, or write French or Wolof, which are the official languages used in the Senegalese public school system. (2) The grade levels of the children are varied from kindergarten to twelve grade, and they all needed transition from the English school curriculum they were in before they fled from the war that made them refugees. (3) Besides language barrier there are verse cultural differences between the refugees and their Senegal host, and last but not the least, Senegalese public schools are free of any charges but overcrowded at least one hundred pupils in a classroom on the average and students are required to bring in their own learning materials. These traumatized refugee children could not learn anything from these environments other than being subjected to ridicules, bully and unnecessary punishment.

In fact there were accounts of refugee children being whipped in second grade at Ecole Machere in Grand Yoff because they could not cope with the compulsory Arabic lessons since they are from a Christian background. Therefore the UNHCR proposal did not make any sense to many why they would not recognize and appreciate the BRSD project and cooperate with it in fulfillment to the children's need as a durable solution. But who knows if the children's plight is not being used as a means to solicit funds or to misappropriate funds allocated? However, what was clear was that UNHCR staff felt exposed and threatened by the emergence of the BRSD project, and they can no longer conceal or suppress the problem because the line that closed that chapter of inactivity and neglect was drawn.

Chapter 74

In their quest to encourage the dissolution of the BRSD project, UNHCR staff and their Interior Ministry counterparts met jointly with officers of the Liberian and Sierra Leonean refugee committees, asking them to spread the news and encourage their members to take advantage of the education allowance they are offering. Using their divide and rule techniques, which they were good at, they increased the offer to thirty thousand CFA ($50) per term, which brought division amongst parents, some advocating against the offer while the majority insisting they would take the offer since they do not have any other means of income. A BRSD meeting was called immediately at the YMCA office attended by the English refugee community where parents expressed gratitude for BRSD project to providing education for their children but noted their vulnerabilities in caring for their families. They expressed their concerns about the problem they faced in transporting their children daily to and fro the project and to providing lunch for them, implying that their children would not learn on empty stomach. These concerns led us to formulate and agree on a strategy: Every parent would take their children and enroll them at public schools and become eligible for the UNHCR education allowance. After collection of the amount parents would simply return their children to attend the BRSD. Meanwhile, I volunteered to provide transportation and snack for lunch for the children and for teachers who are going to be attending. As usual, UNHCR staff knew how to keep an eye on refugee affairs through their divide-and-rule policies, so it did not take long before they learned about our strategy so they adjusted the eligibility process to counter our resolution, adding that after enrollment in public school, the refugee children must attend classes there for at least ten days without absence in order to be eligible for the allowance.

Someone from amongst us had leaked out our strategy but that was not new to me because of past experiences dealing with UNHCR. So my family started providing transportation and snacks for the few students and teachers in attendance while other avenues to improvise were being explored.

We then formed a board of directors and appointed some prominent individuals in the community who sympathized with our struggle. Three of the appointees were Americans, a Canadian, and two Liberians resident in Dakar and the YMCA Secretary General, Mr. Simon Badiane. The rest of the board members are a few refugees on the BRSD project committee. The Americans and Canadian on the board were expatriate educators who taught at Dakar Academy and the International School of Dakar where diplomats' children schooled. There was a lot of brainstorming behind the scene in order to keep the project alive while at the same time trying not to bring our new school board into conflict with UNHCR staffs and their counterparts in government.

Our new board chairman, Mr. Bentley, is the Canadian who happened to be a member of The Gideon, a religious group based in Canada. Through his connection, BRSD received donations in school supplies including Holy Bibles. Mr. Bentley and the Americans on the board came up with the idea to have the children pen pal with foreign students and they also had each student's profile documented, photograph taken and sent abroad in search for sponsors. These prospects encouraged parents to bring their children back to the BRSD project, hoping they would find sponsors to help support their children. Some of the first group of students whose profiles were sent abroad began to get favorable response and help. Other parents who never had their children registered with BRSD brought them and enrolled them with our project, and from henceforth a routine was established: first, parent would enroll their children with a public school and let them endure the pain and ridicule there for ten days or more and after the UNHCR agent visit the school to verify the children's attendance and declared them eligible for the allowance, the parent would collect the allowance and then bring their children back to BRSD. None of the children enjoyed their experience in the Senegalese public schools which had its own struggles: densely populated classrooms, poorly underpaid but exhausted teachers who apparently could not attend classes regularly

And on a personal note, Senegalese are hardly friendly with citizens of English-speaking African origin who does not speak any of the Senegalese local languages (French or Wolof). By mid-1997, many of our students gained sponsors and in the fall of that same year the pen pal project reach an interesting level where almost each BRSD student had at least a pen pal either in Canada or in the United States. Through Camp JAMANO, a summer camp located and operated in Senegal under a joint American-Senegalese initiative, a number of high school students from Oakcrest High School in Hamilton Township, New Jersey, led by then Vice Principal, Mrs. Lovie Lilly came in contact with BRSD students and faculties during the summer of 1998. As incentive to boost BRSD students' moral and confidence, sponsorship to enter Camp JAMONO was awarded to students with the highest academic standards in their respective classes and that is how the students who made it met with their United States counterparts. During a cultural exchange session, the history and challenges at BRSD were highlighted which the visitors considered an eye-opener. The plight of English-speaking refugee students then became the concern and interest of Mrs. Lilly and all of the Oakcrest High School students who then pledged to assist the BRSD students in any way they can and over the years they would make good that promise. Earlier that year, Professor Okrafor Williams of the Columbia University in New York visited his refugee family from Sierra Leone in Dakar and was impressed that his children were attending BRSD, so he visited the school to meet with its administrators and faculties to pledged his appreciation and full support and he also made good his promise. Nevertheless, the financial support we received could only cover about a quarter of the school's annual budget but the courage, dedication and determination of school officials and the teacher were unflinching as they work tirelessly without pay. Once in a while when we are short of anything, I would be obliged to make provision just to keep the project alive. In our quest to raise funds to sustain the project, our board chairman, Mr. Bentley wrote letters to a few selected millionaires in the United States that we thought would give us a lending hand but unfortunately none of them responded except for one, Mr. Ted Warner who responded at the time but declining our request. To make matters worse, some of the Senegalese locals in Grand Yoff had imitated the home-movie business and about ten others like mine had been established in the same locality. That competition sliced our business revenue by more than half and to make matters worse, by fall of 1998, the Department of Commerce ordered our business closed and our equipment seized for failure to pay assessed taxes. This posed some difficulties as subsidy to the school project and family expense ruined my financial position leaving me completely broke like a church rat once again leaving my family to endure hardship. With the home-movie business that subsidized the school project gone, and the burden of meeting school activity costs together with running a large family placed a toll on me, I was forced into executing plan B on my original list of prospective businesses.

Chapter 75

In the fall of 1995, I studied various types of small businesses to help sustain my family in Senegal. In that study, I highlighted a number of businesses that could be easier for a foreigner to operate. One of the businesses was popcorn making and vending, which was not popular in Senegal. Almost everywhere I visit in the capital city, popcorn was not seen anywhere, and most people I spoke to did not know what I was asking. There are different types of locally produced or imported corn kernels in the market but they do not pop no matter how one processed them. There was only one merchant I found in the heart of Dakar who imported on a quarterly basis about fifty cases of corn cannels at a time. His main customers were Americans and Europeans. When I spoke to him, he assured me that if demand for the product rises he can import hundreds of cases in relatively short period of time. Years before in Liberia, during the Tolbert era, I attended a trade fair in which a Nigerian national displayed incredible skills teaching how to build a manual popcorn making machine and his wife made some sugar-sweetened popcorn which I tasted, and it was good. But because electric popcorn making machines were everywhere in Liberia, the manual machine though admired, hardly attracted few people. Besides, sugar-sweetened popcorn was not something that was popular in Liberia. But seeing the way sugar is excessively consumed in Senegal struck me during my business research in the fall of 1995 and connected the idea of sugar sweeten-popcorn as a suitable business venture. This is a contrast in culture between Senegalese and Liberians. Like Sarah Palin would say: "The difference between a hockey mom and a pit bull is lipstick" so it is to say that the difference between Liberians and Senegalese is sugar. Senegalese are addicted to a special type of Chinese tea they named attire. The tea is so strong that it has to be brewed three times before its strength is wore out, and as a culture, those who are addicted to the tea says once one drank the first stages, the second and third brewed must be drank to complete a circle. The first brewed is considered strongest, the second stronger and the third strong. There must be at least one member in an average Senegalese family who knows how to brew this tea which is generally consumed twice a day in almost all households.

Senegalese takes a three hours break for lunch during a day, from 12 noon to 3:00 p.m. During these times majority of businesses such as shops, supermarkets, general markets, petty traders are temporarily closed, even public transportation are reduced until 3:00 p.m. when people get back to work. Rush hour is at 6:00 p.m. and most people scramble their way home to eat dinner with their families around 7:00 p.m. Families are so attached to each other that excuses for missing dinning are almost unacceptable and inexcusable. Every member in a family is expected to be home to eat dinner together from the same bowl placed on a special floor mat with everyone sitting on the floor. Twice in the day, during the three hours lunch time and after dinner at least one member of the family would brew the tea with incredible amount of sugar; for approximately every ninety-two fluid ounce of tea brewed a pound of sugar is used. One thing that came to my mind when I saw this much sugar being consume was the image of the sugar popcorn at the trade fair in Liberia long before the war. With the BRSD struggling and my family totally broke and struggling to survive and with the UNHCR politicking to take over the school project causing division between the teachers and administrator, I switched on to the popcorn project. Since I was penniless, I had to enroll all five of my children at the public school and chased the UNHCR office to get the education allowance for each child. After some heated argument and a strike demonstration the UNHCR finally paid the allowance and thereafter formulated a new policy to limit the number of children in one family that should be granted allowance. They then announced that educational allowances would only be given to maximum of three children in a family so any family with children more than three like mine would be given allowances for only three children. That did not surprise me since laws, rules, policies and procedures were made after my family almost everywhere we went. Part of the children allowance became seed money for the new popcorn project. I bought the materials, which included two giant pots, pipe, few sheets of metal layers and then I went over to a welder and produce him a sketch of the welding job I wanted done according to specifications to build two popcorn machines and sealing machine. The welders were curious as what they were building but I dare not tell them the truth because Senegalese people are very smart; they could throw me out of business before I even started if they knew what it was, so I told them I was constructing a soap making machine. The small movie hall was quickly dismantled and a small popcorn factory constructed. We made sure all doors are closed when we go into production. On the day we started all twelve bags of corn cannels we popped finished in approximately three hours. We were all stunned to see the number of people in the neighborhood who came asking for more. I had to go to the French merchant to pick up a case of the corn cannels and to convince him to import a hundred cases more as soon as possible. It turned out that at the peak of production, a hundred cases per week was insufficient to meet the market demand for "WOW!!! POPCORN FLAKES," which was the name of our product. The popcorn business grew like wildfire to a proportion where demand exceeded production on each given day. Our clientele grew from people in the neighborhood to shop vendors, street vendors, school cafeterias in and around the city of Dakar, ordering large quantities at wholesale prices and retailing to their customers. Before long we began experimenting flavoring the product and magically we created multiple flavors of popcorn: banana, pineapple, orange, mango, strawberry, coconut, barbecue, and etc. Then we created a template for label for each of the flavors with the brand name for the product, "WOW!!! POPCORN FLAKES." Below the red big bold brand name on the labels is description of the flavor and a list of components used to make the popcorn, but details of the components was not accurate for fear of losing monopoly to imitators. No one was allowed to enter our production room, and we were being careful not to even let anyone see what materials we were using, made sure that even our disposable garbage was never exposed. Many people attempted to imitate us by using the local corn cannels or applying the details of components but most of them ended up with either porridge or something else for popcorn. Others chose to interview my children but my wife and I had long prepared our children, and they fully understood the consequences of losing monopoly of our new venture. As the business grow at a very fast pace we realized that work requirement and work burden also grew, and we needed to employ people to assist us. We built more popcorn making machines and more sealing machines and hired two sealers and ten packagers. Then we bought a scraped Renault delivery van, repaired it and hired a driver whose job was strictly to do deliveries. This resolved the transportation problem we had and eliminated the delay in delivery that most of our customers were concern about. We no longer needed to contract people to carry large stock of popcorn on their heads or to wait for availability of public transportation to deliver orders.

As responsibilities increased, we needed to boost production to meet the insatiable demand, but though we could never meet the demand at any point in time, more importantly I decided to take the product to a new level by using it as a vehicle to distribute the thirty article of the Universal Declaration of Human Rights. I felt that that would help bring awareness through education, helping people understand these articles in a society where only a handful of educated people knew their own universal rights. At the time the only reward I thought it would garner was focused on school children, to help them understand what these rights mean to them and the society in which they lived. I was very conscious that ignorance of the rights was responsible, to some extent, for many issues within most African settings, but I did not fully understood the magnitude of this type of education on society and I underestimated its useful impacts. Armed with the English and French version of the Universal Declaration for Human Rights, we inscribed at random, one article of its thirty articles on the back of each of the labels so that when consumers are eating their popcorn, chances are that they could take some time to look at these articles to which their countries are signatories and compare the effect of these rights in their own lives. Although the preamble of the declaration promised teaching all nations and all peoples, schools etc, little has been done since 1948 to teach African people about these rights. In February of 1999, we started this circulation of the human rights articles on the back of each popcorn label and the demand level of the product elevated by 7 percent, an elevation which was mainly attributed to the orders we received for educational institutions such as West African Research Center, University of Dakar, Suffolk University of Dakar and some of the high schools around Dakar. But the mere circulation of the articles on the labels was not enough to catch the attention and concern of the majority of our consumer so we added a game with incentive to it. The game was for consumers to accumulate the labels from article 1 to 30 in order to earn twelve bags of the product. As winners began to turn in their thirty labels containing with each article and word goes around the demand continue to elevate as more people strived to collect all the articles. Some consumers even began trading labels amongst themselves, if they had labels in their collections of the same article, twice or more they would exchange them for ones they do not have so that they collect a set of the 30 articles. Although consumers were collecting the labels to turn them in only for the prize but they had to be encouraged to read the articles, so we added another challenge to it; we announced in May 1999, that anyone, especially school children who can recite all 30 articles word for word or read them their own terms without referral to the document would be awarded prizes from quartz watches, portable radios, tickets for three (Mum, Dad, and the student) to eat at one of the famous restaurants or to attend some live events etc. Although this does not move the penguin in terms of product demand, but it does challenges consumers to learn and to know their universal human rights.

In fact, I recalled the Director of the West African Research Center, Dr. Ndogo, commented once while I was having lunch with some folks at their cafeteria that "the popcorn message was quietly imparting knowledge and building up challenges for debate." Once every month from May 1999, at the YMCA compound we would host a price award forum for all those who believed they could recite the thirty articles of the Universal Declaration of Human Rights and it was impressively rewarding to watch young people reciting the articles, some in French and others in English. Those who fell short were encouraged to try again while those who passed the test collected their prizes. It was fun.

Chapter 76

As a direct result of the end of 1998/1999 school calendar year in June, production dramatically dropped by 40 percent but soon a strategy to chase students was implemented, which narrowed the 40 percent drop in production to 10 percent. It was summertime and the beaches were going to be flooded around Dakar, so we obtained vending permits and constructed small booths at various beaches and by retailing more of our products than wholesale we generate more revenue to cover school orders lost. At one of the beaches near Dakar International Airport, a hotel catering manager approached us, proposing that we sell our recipe for the various-flavored popcorn to the hotel management but when we could not do that he came back with his colleagues, a group of Lebanese businessmen offering a flowery partnership deal with more resources to promote WOW!!! POPCORN FLAKES on a larger scale to reach the over ten million population in various province in Senegal as well as exporting the products to other places and building factories in the not-too-distant future in other African countries. The flowery proposition was excellent, but we were apprehensive because of our knowledge and conviction of foreign exploitation in African, foreigners conniving with government officials and manipulating systems and in other instances influencing systems to enrich themselves at the expense of the poor and to the determent of communities. Since so many had been trying to get our recipe, and some actually trying to snatch away our command of the monopoly in the business, it might have been fair to say that we stereotyped and misjudged these businessmen, but there was another angle to this business which was very important to us: the distribution of the Universal Declaration of Human Rights which we believed was key to community development, and we do not believe that foreign businessmen who are good at exploiting

Africans would be in for educating them and opening their eyes, hence we declined.

In June 2000, the Senegalese Open National Chess Championships was announced and my love and passion for the game that has been my consolation ever since my youth became tested. I had to choose between chess and staying the course in the business at a critical time. My wife attempted several time to discourage me from taking part; she even reminded me of the ugly incident in the Sierra Leone National Open Chess Championships in which I was cheated in the finals in order to get me to concentrating on the business which needed my attention, yet I jumped her word and registered to take part in the tournament. Chess has always been my life; my whole life revolved around the game. But this made things difficult for me; doing chess and business at the same time. The tournament took off, and I went through all the other rounds until semifinals where I got whipped by Sir Winston Williams, a British national who instantly became my friend. Sir Winston Williams was then Regional Director for International Federation for World Peace & Unification (IFWPU) and his wife, Matta, whom till this day I considered my guardian angel, worked in the same organization. A year earlier their family, five children included, had made a strange sacrifice to transferred from Singapore to take up the challenges to unifying the world from that part of West Africa. The couple was drawn to the English speaking refugee segregation and maltreatment problems and before long their zeal and willingness to take up the issues head-on with UNHCR staffs and voicing out various concerns and proposing solutions became unflinching and noted by the refugee communities. Working with them under the umbrella of their organization made a big difference for me. I was taken to places and met people I would not have dream of.

One of their organization's challenges was to help change the Talibay children placed on the streets to collect ritual offerings for Marabous. Within the Talibay culture, people give food items, clothing or money as ritual sacrifices on their way to work or to wherever. In this tradition, the firstborn in the talibay family are assigned to each of these Marabous to collect sacrificial items from the general public in the streets or from one house to another and besides Arabic lessons, school is not an option. The children are so abused that their appearances, and awful odors tells the entire story one needs to know. Ironically, some of the very items they collect would end up in stores own by these marabous for sale. This somewhat recycling business puts marabous in advantageous position economically in the society. They intercede for their clients spiritually and predict their presence and future. The US Peace Corp had been trying to influence change to help these children get them off the streets and put in schools in the care of their parents but it is a deeply rooted tradition that powerful people in the government and in the private sector are involved with since most of them have their own marabous who predicts their lives by day; a culture that is almost unbreakable.

The Williams admired my popcorn project and the concept of human rights article circulations which they believed takes bravery and ingenuity. They were especially amazed by the momentum article 26 of the declaration had generated. The article addressed free education for all children at least at the elementary level and it is the responsibilities of countries that are signatories to the convention to ensure that these rights are protected and Senegal is a signatory. Parents from a cross section of the society were enlightened by the article and were discussing it and asking questions. Winston took a second job as English instructor at the Baobab Center where Americans and other foreign diplomas go to learn local and international languages.

Under the auspices of IFWPU I found myself in the company of diplomats and also attending diplomatic events. The first event I attended was the United States Independence Day celebrations on July 4, 2000. At the ceremonies attended by diplomats from other countries accredited to Senegal, I was introduced to staffs of the US embassy including Ambassador Thomas and her husband along with member of the other US missions. At that ceremony, we were able to get an appointment to meet Ambassador Thomas to discuss the Talibay children and the English-speaking West African refugee struggles. Two weeks later, the meeting took place in Ambassador Thomas's office at the US Embassy in Dakar. Those in attendance were Directors of USAID, US Peace Corp and other aids at the embassy. The other memorable event was the Indonesia Independence Day celebrations at the Indonesia Embassy in Dakar. This event, like the US Independent Day Celebration was attended by members of the diplomatic core in Senegal, government officials and interestingly staff of the UNHCR including the high commissioner. During the event, Winston, who had lived in Indonesia for many years, spoke one of the languages and was very much at ease with many of the Indonesian in attendance. During a cordial exchange with a group of Indonesians, Winston broke away, leaned over, and whispered in my ear not to turn around or look behind me. The point was that UNHCR staffs were not sure if I was the person they were seeing and they quietly argued amongst themselves. Finally one of their staff came close to check me out and she came so close that I did not notice until as she was leaving to go to the opposite side to tell of her findings. I slightly tilted my head, and I saw the perplexity in their faces, wondering why I was there or how come I was there. No refugee at my level was known then to be in frequent company of diplomats in Dakar. There is another place in Dakar own by a French millionaire who once sponsored the Senegalese National Chess Team to play in a chess tournament in Paris. This French national runs a chess open house every day of the week at his well-furnished mansion where people from all walks of life, mostly tourists from various countries, go to pass time with chess and do other businesses. I had no idea that such a place existed in Dakar until an invitation was extended by a some diplomats at the Indonesian Independence Day celebration.

Winston and I would spend most afternoons there. There was plenty of food, drinks, and desert, and we met good and wealthy people. When Winston took me there the first time and announced that I was the former ten-time Liberian chess champion, I felt flattered as eyebrows were raised and eyes were on me. Everyone wanted to play me, but the Frenchman himself overrode everyone and decided to play me first to see how Liberian chess looks like, and he was very impressed with the two games we played. Some people left their games to watch ours and when the Frenchman bowed in both games, not only that Winston's introduction of me was firm, but the games were a statement that I belong there, amongst the wealthy and the elite. The Frenchman extended open hands to me to come in anytime to entertain his guest. Thereafter, I visited frequently and met with some of Senegal's finest players as well as foreigners who took the game very seriously. We made a lot of friendship.

Chapter 77

Through its Regional Representative to West Africa, ASHOKA, an organization in the business of promoting social enterprises and entrepreneurship around the globe, nominated me as a social entrepreneur in October 2000 as a direct result of the impact of the popcorn project in communities in the capital city, Dakar. The project was widely noted for distributing and encouraging the learning of the Universal Declaration of Human Rights and using part of the proceeds generated to subsidize education for English speaking refugee children through the BRSD project that I initiated.

Indeed the impact of the popcorn project had been felt across wide sections of Senegalese communities in Dakar. Surprisingly, news of the projects had crossed the shores of Senegal across the Atlantic Ocean for consideration before the organizing committee responsible for selecting social entrepreneurs around the globe in response to the United Nations Millennium Summit, which took place in September 2000 at the United Nations House in New York. At that Summit, which happened to be the largest-ever gathering of world leaders, the United Nations Millennium Declaration was unanimously adopted: a statement of values, principles, and objectives for the international agenda for the twenty-first century. The document also set deadlines for many collective actions and in enhancing its values; civil societies around the globe are considered and committed as stipulated in its appendix as follows: "We stand on the threshold of a dramatic change in the way we perceive and practice global governance. Governance is not only for governments. The institutions of civil society which bridge the gap between individuals and states are needed, and are indispensable as partners, players and participators in the planning and implementing of policies aimed at creating a better world, a culture of peace."

DYSFUNCTIONAL ONE

Therefore "A Response from Civil Society Conference" was staged in New York on October 20–22, 2000, to engaged civil societies worldwide and to my astonishment the two projects I initiated in Dakar, Senegal, were recognized and I was invited to join the body of civil societies around the world to gather at the United Nations in New York for the conference.

The week of October 14, 2000, I had no idea I was nominated as a social entrepreneur and I also had no idea that I was selected to attend the upcoming conference in New York. I was busy going about my daily routing on Tuesday, October 16; in the afternoon I stopped at a cyber café to check my email account. To my surprise, one of the several emails I received came from a Civil Society Committee, congratulated me for a job well done and indicated that I am invited to attend the New York conference from October 20–22. My first instinct was to delete the mail after reading it because I thought it was one of the usual 419 schemes that were very frequent at the time. Even though I was connected to some members of the diplomatic core at the time but it did not cross my mine that I would be counted amongst global elites to have earned such accolades especially from my current status as a refugee. However, I replied the email and simply thanked the sender for their complement and expressed my appreciation for the invitation but indicated that I was a refugee without passport, visa, and money to purchase tickets less alone to cover travel expenses.

On Wednesday, October 17, I went down town to pick up labels from a printing press but there was a delay so I was asked to wait for about an hour before the labels would be ready. Across the printing press was a cyber café, so I went in to kill the time. To my surprise, a reply to the New York invitation email I responded to was sent almost immediately in the same hour I responded to it the day before but since I had no computers on my own, checking emails were done once every other day at a cyber café. The reply says that I am included in the Senegalese delegation to the conference in New York, headed by the Director of West African Research Center, Dr.

Ndogo, and that the invitation comes with a two-way Air France first class ticket with boarding expenses covered while in New York. I immediately printed the document and drove my delivery van to the West African Research Center to meet with Dr. Ndogo. When I arrived, I could tell that it was going to be difficult to see the director. His secretary claimed that I did not have any appointment to see him, so she did not think that I would see him, and she suggested an appointment for October 29, 2000 There were many VIPs and tourists with appointments waiting in the reception and at the launch to see him and there was an upcoming seminar that the director was preparing for that afternoon.

Knowing what I was there for was something time sensitive and would certainly not be necessary after the 22, and, also not sure as to whether the whole thing was a prank that would besmear me and ruin my relationship at the WARC so I convinced myself to wait around with hope that I might see the director any time he comes out, and I would just approach him at once and it won't take more than ten seconds of his time. Curious but determined to investigate the email, I instinctively walked through the corridor and tapped at the clerical door and when the senior clerk answered I opened the door and ducked my head in with a big smile on my face as I saluted him in Wolof. "Is Dr. Ndongo travelling to New York this weekend to attend a conference?" I asked. He nodded and asked me why I wanted to know. "I am a member to his delegation to the conference in New York but his secretary would not let me see him because I had no appointment and I need to see him urgently." He looked at me with a puzzled face expression, "You on the Senegalese delegation to the UN conference in New York?" he asked. I nodded and showed him a printed copy of the email messages. He picked up the telecom and dialed the director's number and spoke in Wolof, though my understanding of the language was not quite good, but I watched his countenance as the puzzle expression on his face faded and turned sweet as he spoke. Then he hung up, walked over to me, and extended his arm, congratulating me and asking me to wait at the reception for the director.

I barely took my seat at the reception when the director came hurriedly asking for me with joy and excitement and telling everyone in the room of my achievements from a refugee status. I was emotionally overwhelmed and fought hard to hold back tears but to no avail. My hands were over my mouth, and I still could not believe what I was experiencing; it was like a dream. He then took me into his office where a copy of the itinerary and my first class Air France ticket was handed over to me. He then disclosed to me how my inclusion came about. It was Williams who introduced my work to their organization's headquarters in New York and recommended me for the opportunity, but they had never said a word about it to me. I could not tell the director that I did not have a passport at the time since I was not sure how that would have played out. The conference starts on the 20; the itinerary shows that the delegation is scheduled to travel on the 18 at 9:00 p.m. just one day. I would have only today to obtain a passport because the next day, Thursday, is the only day in the week that the US embassy issued visitors' visas and if I do not get a visa then it would not make sense to come back after the conference date to request a visa. When I left the WARC, I sat in the delivery van for a while to get hold of myself because I was shaking, nervous, and emotionally overwhelmed and disoriented; it was all like a dream. I called a neighbor and ask them to let my son join me in town. Then I went to the Liberian Consular office to see if I can be issued a passport. The Consular told me their office ran out but one of his staff knew some people who sell them. My son joined me and we were accompanied by the consular staff in search for the people he knew that sells Liberian passports. Everyone he knew ran out too but one other person joined us to introduce someone else that the staff did not know.

The new fellow, Bobby, took us to his friend who had travel but left with his wife the only passport they had which they could not sell for a long time because it was a Liberian official passport, not the ordinary one. The woman's husband wanted $300 for that passport but Bobby, the middleman, added an extra $200 so I had to find $500. I advanced the $300 and Bobby held the passport and followed me to get the balance $200. We drove around town as I tried to raise the amount. It was late in the evening so I went over to the Baobab Center to meet Winston. He spoke with Bobby to turn over the passport to me and look up to him to make the payment the next day. Bobby needed a guarantee so Winston gave him his family camera, which cost over $500 and Bobby went away.

At 7:00 p.m. I had the passport on hand. The consular staff had informed me that they do not even have calligraphy service so it would be up to me to find someone with fine penmanship to write my personal information in the passport. My son and I drove to various places looking for someone who had done the job before or who can do it. We were referred to a Liberian at Warcam, who is said to specialize in this type of work. I was not satisfied with his performance when I gave him my information and provided a piece of paper the size of the passport and his performance was awful. It was about midnight; my thirteen-year-old son and I were hungry and exhausted so we decided to go home to eat and get some rest and to start our search again early the next day. I drove slowly in the quiet night as my mind and brain struggled for solutions to these suddenly queer challenges. I did not know how I would have slept that night; I am not the type who usually sleeps when challenged. We were about three hundred yards near our home when a thought struck me, and I abruptly stopped the vehicle and parked on the side of the road. Then I whispered something to myself and my curious son asked what was it that I said and what was going on. Then I spoke these words repeatedly louder: "I got it! I got it!"

"Got what?" my son asked.

"The right person whose penmanship fits the one we are looking for," I said.

"Who is he, daddy?" he asked.

"Monsieur Babacar Nydaie, your former public school director," I replied while watching his face for confirmation. But the boy is not used to seeing passports and probably don't fully understand what his dad was looking for. Indeed Director Babacar Nydaie was the man whose penmanship just clouded my vision. I remembered his writings on my children's school report cards and I was certain his writing would do for the job, but how can I get him to do the job was the big question. What approach to formulate to meet Monsieur Nydaie and to convince him to do this job was what I had to figure out overnight.

Chapter 78

Indeed, Director Babacar Nydaie was the right man for the job. Early on Thursday morning, I went with the passport and a pen I bought for the job to Ecole Marche de Grande Yoff and met with Director Nydaier. Director Nydaie, a five feet ten inches tall dark figure, spoke broken English and I spoke broken French. In the pass, we had challenged each other that whenever we met, I should practice my French-speaking skills when talking to him while he would practice his English-speaking skills, and we both had fun doing so each time we met; at times we would have fun correcting each other's mistakes. He admired the popcorn project, and he is sympathetic toward the struggles faced by the English speaking refugees in Dakar. Occasionally, he would support my children to become eligible for the UHNCR educational allowance by letting the UNHCR inspector know that the children are attending his school when they were actually attending the BRSD.

That morning when we met, I struggled with my broken French in explaining the scam I formulated overnight that I have recommended him to the Liberian Consular Office for a casual calligraphy contract to write in passports occasionally for a fee of $50 a passport. His eyes lightened when I said it, and he tapped me on the back for looking out for him. The director's salary was less than $200 a month and if he could get a second income he would certainly go for it as long as it was legal. I said that the consulate usually outsources these services to people with very good penmanship, and I thought he also could perform the services for a second income for $50 a passport because I always admired his writing which is by far better than some of the people now being used. In concluding I said that the consulate could not risk someone else's passport for a trial so the challenge is for him to do mine as a proof for the consulate to see his penmanship in order to outsource jobs to him. He then asked for the passport and I gave it to him with a couple of papers I had ready for testing. He closed his office door so as not to be interrupted. Then he took his time and made two test works as I keenly watched. I was impressed and wanted him to do the passport right away, but he wanted to do two more tests, so I waited and watched as the man perfected the job then he settled down on the passport itself and did a fine job.

I paid him the $50 and left. It was about 8:15 a.m. I drove to the Williams' resident to pick up Mata and to drop her off at the airport. She was travelling to South Korea where their family was planning to transfer for their next mission. At the airport, she offered a prayer for me to get the visa and charged her husband to do all he can to make sure the visa is issued. At about 9:45 a.m., Winston and I left the airport and drove to the Liberian Consulate's office where I had the Liberia official seal stamped and passport=size photos of my wife and I placed into the official passport making it ready to be presented to the US embassy. Winston and I went to the British High Commission's Office where he used a phone to call the Consular at the US embassy on my behalf. He was given a name and told to send me in, so I immediately drove there to meet the consulate staff I was sent to and he in turn sent me to the post office to pay for the visa and bring the receipt together with my passport back to him. When I returned with the visa payment receipt and submitted my passport, he gave me some forms to fill in, and my son Harry and I settled down in the waiting room where I filled in the forms and turned them over. The staff inspected the passport and was a bit skeptical, but I clarified his doubts and the fact that I further explained convincingly why, how, and where the passport was issued and complemented my explanation with references of meetings I attended at his embassy with Ambassador Thomas, the USAID, and Peace Corp directors he had no other alternative but approve the visa. Then I was now turned over to a female staff who was supposed to stamp the visa in my passport, but unfortunately she had some emergency for which the day care school that her daughter attended wanted her and technically it was over the visitor visa issuing time, put at 2:00 p.m. so she had closed her office and gone to the garage to pick up her car but fortunately for me she forgot her car keys in her office so she returned just in time when I was told to leave because she would not be coming back to work that afternoon because of her emergency. The staff who approved the visa was expressing his regret to me when suddenly she returned to pick up her keys. She then took a few moments to stamp my visa in the passport, and it was handed over to me. Suddenly, I felt as though a heavy weight was lifted off me and it baffled me to think that if I was told two days earlier on Tuesday, October 16, 2000, that I was going to be leaving Dakar on Thursday night for New York, I do not think I would have believed since I did not have it in mind let alone I had no passport, no visa, no ticket and not enough money and preparation.

Understanding my life, I can only classify this dramatic opportunity as God given. My son and I drove around as I settle a few things and made arrangements to assign responsibilities. Then we drove to the Baobab Center where I broke the good news to Winston and thank his family for their friendship and generosity. Then I bought a travel bag and two suits, a shoe, two shirts, and we arrived home a little after 7:00 p.m. As we broke the news to the rest of the family that I got the visa and would be leaving Dakar in about two hour's time, the house went ballistic with praises to our Heavenly Father. About an hour later my entire family was at the airport. Everything had happened so fast that none of us fully had time to consider how my separation from the family would impact each one of us. I learned later that after my departure that night everyone in my family in Dakar had sleepless night; they cried as though I was dead.

The French Boeing 747 arrived in France around 3:00 p.m. Airport workers including pilots were on strike so our delegation stayed in transit in France until late morning before connecting flights were made available. I left Dakar with a hundred and fifty dollars in my pocket and while in transit in France I bought phone cards and spoke with my family and paid for breakfast leaving me with seventy-five dollars, which was the amount in my pocket when I arrived at JFK International Airport in New York. For some unexplained reasons, the rest of the members of our delegation were put on another flight excluding me two hours earlier. I was placed on another flight, so when I arrived at JFK two hours later, the escort assigned to receive our delegation was no longer there, and no one with my name tag was there to receive me. The other members of the delegation could not account for me when they arrived earlier. This was my very first test in the United States with only $75 to my name with weather temperature below forty degrees, a condition that was not only strange, but I did not prepare for. Someone suggest that I bought phone card to call the number on my itinerary list. I did, but only got instructions to leave a message and someone would get back to me in twenty-four hours from Monday through Friday and this was Friday evening around 6:00 p.m. Next thing I knew as I held my travel bag roaming all over the place. I found myself among a band of hungry airport taxi drivers, some of whom talked me into their own ideas as to where they think delegates were lodged, and as a risk taker, I jumped into one of the cabs to the UN House. We arrived there and a security officer made a couple of radio calls before I was told to go to Hilton New York Hotel. When we arrived at the hotel, the cabdriver slammed me with a $325 bill and I thought it was $3.25 so I handed him a $5 note and told him to keep the change. "Is this some kind of a joke?" he yelled out.

"What do you mean?" I asked. He pointed at a meter and he yelled back at me: "Three hundred and twenty-five dollars, sir."

That almost ripped off my heart. I looked at the meter and whispered to myself, "Three hundred and twenty-five dollars?" I started perspiring and then I asked him to wait while I went into the hotel and asked the reception about the conference. I was directed to the hall where delegates were assembled having dinner. At the entrance was a long table with only my name tag on it. I told the ladies behind the table who I was and that I had transportation problem. They call someone from the logistic team and someone went out to the driver and settled with him. Then I had dinner and was escorted to Sheraton Hotel to share a suite for the night with a lawyer from the Bahamas also arrived late. The next day I was transfer to Hilton New York to share another suite with gentleman from the Liberian Justice Department who headed the Liberian delegation. My first night in New York was full of excitements. I had trouble in the shower and had to call the reception requesting them to help me with some hot water to shower. I was under the shower but the water started from cold to colder to coldest and I could not stand it. Someone had to come in to show me how the single faucet works to get hot water. I got laughed at when I later told my roommate who was not in at the time. After the shower. I put on my traditional Senegalese gown and decided to take a stroll and missed my way back. That night the weather was probably below twenty degrees, and it felt like I was placed in a freezer; it was something I never experienced before. I was shivering and my fingers ached so bad that I had to enter an electronics store to escape the cold, pretending I was looking for some kind of an electronic devise to buy. The merchant quickly noticed that I was new in town from my accent and the way I dressed. He and his friends struck a conversation with me then later they gave me direction to the hotel. That night, at the hotel, I stared through each of the windows in the suite and marveled at the beautiful views around me then I called my family to let them know where I was and what I have experienced so far. Then I watched TV till I fell asleep.

Chapter 79

Saturday morning came like a fairy tale revolution. The week's activities had been excitingly voluminous and challenging for me across two continents. I was so exhausted that it seems I was waking up from a coma. I could not believe where I was for a moment. Before I was fully awoken, it seemed I was still in Dakar. I went through my usual early morning rehearsal of things to do in my mind before I was fully awake. I went through things like, checking the popcorn order list, determining the volume of production for the day, making sure all equipment in the small factory are clean and all trash properly dispose of, etc. Faintly but gradually, sounds from the TV began to usher me into consciousness and suddenly it struck me that I was not in Grande Yoff, Dakar but in New York, the busiest city in the world. "Wow!" I whispered underneath my breath as I sprang from the bed and reached for copy of the conference agenda which read:

1. Opening Statements - Hilton New York, Oct. 20, 2000 10:00 a.m.   2. Reviewing the Millennium Declaration, UN House, Oct. 21, 2000, 9:00 a.m. - 5:00 p.m.   - NGOs as Partners in Debt Relief and Financing for Development   - NGOs as Partners in Values and Public Service   - NGOs as Partners in Strengthening the Family   3. Building Cultures of Peace and Leadership Oct 22, 2000 Hilton New York Hotel 10:00 a.m.   - Discussion Groups, 2:00 p.m.   - Closing Statements, 6:00 p.m.

The opening statements were delivered by selected NGO leaders and scholars who mainly examined and evaluated major points of the adopted Millennium Declaration. Ms. Deborah Moldow, co-chair of the Values Caucus, stressed how thinking about values and principles uplifts our consciousness, putting us in touch with our sense of purpose and that which is noblest in the human spirit. She expressed her belief that if all people share highest values and that a sense of shared values can be an important cross-cultural bridge to understanding and concerted action. In stressing her points, she cited the six values and principles in the Declaration: freedom, equality, solidarity, tolerance, respect for nature, and shared responsibility, which are reaffirmations of the principles of the U.N. Charter. Mr. Solo Dowuona-Hammond, president of the Olof Palme Peace Foundation spoke on the theme of development and poverty eradication, noted the lofty objectives in the Declaration, such as helving the world's extreme poverty by 2015. All of these goals hinge on the "recognition, promotion and protection of human rights and good governance."

Dr. Nicholas N. Kittrie, Chairman of the Eleanor Roosevelt Institute for Justice and Peace, addressed the theme of human rights, democracy, and good governance by first highlighting the chasm between the Declaration's espoused values and the reality.

Dr. Yvette Stevens, Office of the Special Coordinator for Africa and the Least Developed Countries, U. N. Department of Economic and Social Affairs, discussed meeting the special needs of Africa. She said that in the Millennium General Assembly there was general support for a comprehensive and integrated approach to be taken toward conflict prevention in Africa, including peace-building, poverty eradication, development, and democracy.

Dr. Allan Gerson, director of the War-to-Peace Transition Project at the New America Foundation, discussed strengthening the United Nations. He observed the post–Cold War period has been primarily characterized by civil wars and internal or intrastate wars. The other three major themes of the Declaration—peace and security, protecting our common environment, and protecting the vulnerable—were addressed by a reading of the relevant article of the Declaration itself.

This conference was an eye-opener for me as I struggled to fit in. The next day, delegates were taken to the United Nations House where item 2 on the agenda was covered. We ate lunch and dinner there between deliberations, had a tour of the building, and purchased souvenir items from the large collection of shops in the basement then we had a chance to meet with the UN Secretary General, Kofi Anna. During discussion groups at the Hilton New York Hotel the following day, one of female member of the Senegalese delegation in same group as me took offence of my narratives regarding the treatment of English-speaking refugees in West Africa as a direct result of UNHCR policies from the regional headquarters, Dakar. This culminated into some differences in opinion between us which were conveyed and settled down by the group. To my surprise, she extended our disagreement beyond the conference and allowed some of her Senegalese relatives who later visited her at the hotel that evening to confront me with threats. They charged me with being ungrateful toward their hospitality and with denigrating the good name and reputation of their country. This was not the case. I expressed the ill-treatment of English-speaking West African refugees not only in Senegal but in various West African countries and criticized the UNHCR mainly for their policies of segregation, corruption, mismanagement of resources, and sexual misconducts toward vulnerable refugee women. I also talked about selected cases of ill-treatments which occurred in Senegal for which many Senegalese people also disagreed with the UNHCR and condemned those occurrences. A comparison was even highlighted by another delegate from the Barbados who recounted that Kosovo refugees were provided the basic assistance from UNHCR: housing, food, and medical plus cash assistance of $800 a month per family compared to West African refugees who got $0.10 per day. However, the confrontation culminated into some bitter argument between us and eventually they described the popcorn project as a subversive activity in disguise, aiming at destabilizing the peace in their country so they declared their intentions to immediately work against it to shut it down. I never took their threats as serious so I did not say a word about this to my family when I spoke to them later that evening. That night, after the conference was officially over, most of the delegates packed up and left the hotel to spend time or visit with relatives or friends. My roommate also left to spend some time with his friend, leaving me to take his per diem, which was given the next morning. When I woke up the next morning, two envelopes containing $500 each addressed to my roommate and me with a "Thank you" message were slid under the door into the suite. I had used the change I had to buy souvenir items at the UN House and was wondering how I would move around or buy presents for each member of my family. My wife had emailed a long list of presents that every member of my family wanted me to present them upon my return, as if money grows on trees in the United States.

After I pocketed the thousand dollars with a great deal of relief, I decided it was time to follow-up on the honoring program that students of Oakcrest High School in New Jersey proposed for me upon hearing that I was in New York. On Monday morning, I created a kind of excitement when I called the vice principal of the school, Mrs. Lovie Lilly, to let her know I was attending a conference in New York. She had called the hotel and left me a message about the honoring programs that her students proposed and about some contributions they would like to make for the refugee school project in Dakar. Our last meeting was during the summer that very year when Mrs. Lilly and some of her students visited Dakar. So when I called her on Tuesday morning to say the conference was over and I would be leaving for Dakar that weekend, she decided to call me back during the day after all arrangements for the program was concluded. Later that afternoon, she called back to say they have decided to stage the honoring program on Thursday, October 25, at their school. Her husband who lectured at Columbia University in New York would pick me up from the hotel on Wednesday, and I would spend the night at her home; and on Thursday he would take me to the program, which would take place after school. The local press would be there to cover the event. Donations and pledges would be made for the BRSD. I made a request to my host to extend my stay at the hotel for one more night, and it was granted then I went out shopping for members of my family.

DYSFUNCTIONAL ONE

The next day, Mr. Lilly picked me up from the hotel at 4:30 p.m. and took me to their home in New Jersey where I spent the night. The next day he took me to the school where the honoring program was successfully held. The group of students that organized the program under supervision of one of their instructor, Mr. Joe Piecoski, and Mrs. Lilly shows how a few people can make such a big difference in changing the world. The students had divided themselves into groups and each group had been working harder to support the BRSD. The program started by each group leader taking the stand to explain what they had been doing since their returned from Dakar in support of our refugee school project; from fund raising to gathering donations in clothing, school materials and individual commitments. It was an extremely emotional program to see a bunch of teenagers caring so much and volunteering for underprivileged children across the Atlantic Ocean when those who the world entrusted with all the resources shows little or no interest at all. After I delivered my speech in which the plight of refugee children in West Africa was extensively highlighted, questions about the refugee school were posed to me by the audience and then I was decorated with Oakcrest High School badges and given the school's sweater, cap, t-shirts, and badges. The amount of $200 which the students had gathered from their lunch money was donated toward BRSD and entrusted to me. After the program, Mr. and Mrs. Lilly drove me to Philadelphia where I spent the night with Mrs. Gloria Tucker.

Gloria was a Sierra Leonean refugee in Dakar who was resettled a year earlier to join her husband and two children. She was once a member of our administrative team for BRSD. She was very close to my family in Dakar, and she also headed a little prayer group which met at my home every Friday. In our determination to overcome our collective struggles in exile, we were convinced that the answers rest with God and so we declared Fridays our holy day for prayer and fasting; therefore, we would meet at my home at 7:00 p.m. to break fast and Gloria would preside over the service. It was not a surprise therefore to find her preparing herself for pasturing a church in Philadelphia and also setting up missions in parts of Africa which has always been her dream. I had a good time that night with her family after Mr. and Mrs. Lilly dropped me off. The next day I set off for Maryland to attend an upcoming conference on the rights of refugees hosted by Layers Committee for Human Rights in Washington, DC. A delegate at the New York conference thought it expedient for me to attend that conference. The items I purchased for my family and the donations that I received from the Oakcrest students were all packed and stored in New York awaiting my return there.

In Maryland, I lodged with Ms. Charlene Davis, a member of the Oakcrest summer group to Senegal. She was excited about my coming to the United States and attending all these conferences and hoping that some kind of benefit would come from it to make a difference to the suffering refugee communities in Dakar where she had been and witnessed some of the heartbreaking situations there. At the Human Rights conference, I was stunned at the way and manner that the UNHCR representative side stepped some of the issues affecting refugees worldwide. At the end of that conference, I was extended another invitation to attend the Center for Economic and Social Justice conference on Capital Homestead at the University of the District of Columbia in Washington, DC. My new friend provided me with materials and references on the subject matter prior to that conference and he led me to the Martin Luther King Library in Washington DC where I visited for a number of days before the conference. On the morning before the conference, I called my family to inform them about my activities and to find out how they were doing, but sadly I received the news that opened another chapter of a new struggle. I was informed that our home was raided the day before by security officers who confiscated our factory equipment and ordered the closure of our popcorn venture. They had also threatened to incarcerate everyone in my family if they ever learned that the popcorn project was being operated with distribution of human rights materials.

It was heartbreaking for me to the point where I cancelled my attendance of the capital homesteading conference, but my new friend came searching for me when I did not show up at the point where he was to pick me from, and he convinced me to attend the conference anyhow. At the capital homestead conference, I had the opportunity to meet a handful of leaders, scholars, and civil rights activists. Because of my troubles, I daydreamed my way through the conference which was considerably informative and educative. I wanted to seek advice from Dr. Professor Norman Kutland and the Rev. Walter E. Fauntroy, a civil rights activist, then Pastor of the Bethel Baptist Church in Washington, DC, whom were introduced to me during dinner, but it felt like I was demeaning myself just after I was given a hailing introduction so I restrained from doing so and tried as much as possible to fit in. At the end of the conference, I accepted a nomination to become member of a new working committee formed to coordinate the conference resolutions. Later my new friend gave me a ride to Landover, Maryland, where I was lodged.

Chapter 80

That same night I called my wife, and we discussed the events that led to the threats, and she expressed her fears about what might happen to me upon my return. We both knew that I could be arrested, jailed, or harmed upon my return; but at the same time, it was a difficult but painful decision to stay away from my family. We looked at other possibilities to move to neighboring countries, but that option was somehow wearisome considering the troubles we had been through, escaping the Liberian war twice; rebuilding our lives in Sierra Leone; the ordeal of losing everything we had built in five years and being captives to RUF, one of the most ruthless rebel group in the world and our dramatic escape into Guinea; and finally our fulfillment to civil society in our effort to integrate in Senegal and the progress we have made in building our lives.

My wife reminded me about Dr. Ocrafor Williams whose children attended BRSD before his family was resettled in the United States. We found his Staten Island telephone number so I called him and explained my situation. He was excited that I was safe and still in the United States. Together we evaluated my prospect for seeking asylum in the United States, and he sort of estimated the timeline, which was actually depressing to me. He volunteered to file asylum application on my behalf and sent me a package containing the forms to fill out and to send back to him. In the package he enclosed a hundred dollar bill to help me out plus stamps to mail the package back to him after I had all the forms filled. At this point it became clear to me that I was in for a long haul. However, the forms were filed incomplete and weeks later when the Immigration Department returned the package to my Landover address in Maryland for me to complete and re-file, I was no longer at that address and I had no place to stay. I spent a few nights at a train terminal pretending to be waiting for a train to travel some place and during the day I go to MLK Library to do emails and read American history and newspapers.

My family had moved to another location for fear that something might happen to them considering the frequent harassment they were experiencing with people checking on them to see what they were doing and to find out when I was returning to join them. Earlier before I became homeless weeks before Christmas, my host had introduced me to Mr. Eugene Brown, Chairman of The Big Chair Chess Club on Sheriff Road, North East of Washington, DC. Chairman Brown, who also was little informed about Africa, doubted any quality chess-playing skills was even possible there let alone an African like me would match grandmaster level in the United States. When my host introduced me to him, he had promised to try me one day to see where I fit, but he had always put it off since he was also in the real estate business and was very busy. At the time, he was renovating their clubhouse on Sheriff Road. I called him one weekend and luckily he did not hesitate to pick me up from Union Station in Washington, DC. We ate lunch together at his house while he interviewed me about my chess life and my current living condition.

After lunch Chairman Brown cleared the dining table and set his giant chess set on to try me. My first instinct was to let him have things his way since he was contemplating on how to get me under a roof instead of me going back in the cold. My traveling bag was at an Amtrak station locker even though I was not traveling anywhere. But I remembered his zingers when I was first introduced to him as a grandmaster from Africa. He laughed out loud and asked what kind of chess was even played there, and I felt insulted so I was determined then that anytime he or anyone in the United States tried me, I was going to prove that that I am not a pushover for any one with this God-given gift of mine.

We played three games, all of which I won. The first game was a Danish Gambit; one of my favorite openings and once he took all three pawns offered, my attacking machinery became fiercely formidable and that game ended in a Novotny Interference (a move that caught two lines of defense leaving one open) in less than twenty moves. This was not to be for I could tell that the chairman was uncomfortable, and he gave me a scary look that was almost intimidating. But in chess, one does not win the first game against a new opponent and presume himself stronger than that opponent. Usually chess players like to take risks in a particular situation based on their knowledge of their opponents' strength, so it might well mean that he took those three pawns offered to see what I can do with Danish Gambit; he was disappointed. The second game was a Sicilian Defense and again the chairman honorably resigned within thirty moves. We took a short break after that game while he made telephone calls to some of his rich friends and members of their club. I could hear him pacing up and down on the floor above me and telling whosoever he was talking to that there is a fellow from Africa who has just kicked his ass convincingly, and he would like that person to make a few calls to get some people available who can beat me. We were in the middle of the third game when five men showed up. Four of them were in their fifties while the young man amongst them, named Tony, could be in his early thirties. They entered the house loud in their speaking and condemning their chairman for speaking so highly of me, an African. It did not take long thereafter when the chairman resigned in the third game and then the five men started arguing amongst themselves who should play me next. Their argument culminated into playing for money and soon Tony turned to me and asked if I dare play him for money. I had only my signature capital when I entered the United States, $75. I had sent much of the money I had to my family to help them move out from the place where I left them. Tony suggested $500 a game and I said we could start from $50. They all laughed out loud and he said $50 was waste of time. I said that I did not come with enough cash and that maybe we could do that some other day when I come prepared, so he finally agree and we settled down for the $50 a game. After the first game which I won, he argued with the others to play another one to complete a set. We increased the wager to $100. Tony lost the second game and one of the older guys took the seat and increased the wager to $200. By this time the men had split in opinion, two of them were now on my side betting against each other on the side. One of them who supported me said that he was going to give me an extra $50 for each game won. The amount of $200 for me was high stake, and I was careful not to lose any game nor draw any that day up to 4:30 a.m. when it all ended. The men drove away in their cars in the snow while the chairman allowed me to sleep in a couch in his basement. Around midday when I woke up Chairman Brown struck a deal with me to move into his club house that was under renovation and to help organize and implement their chess programs in return for living their for free. There was no heat in the clubhouse and some of the windows on the second floor where my room was weren't yet installed which made the temperature almost as cold as outdoor. It was not exactly where I needed to be but it was better than loitering all night long at train stations pretending I was waiting to travel and having to use public restrooms and eating all type of junk food. That afternoon, he drove me to the clubhouse on Sheriff Road, NE, and later I picked up my travel bag and settled down at the clubhouse. My earnings from the chess games netted $1,725.00 including my signature capital. In order to keep warm at night I had to bring the mattress downstairs and place it on the kitchen floor and then turned on the oven, periodically opening the oven door to let the heat under my blanket. During the day I would assist the carpenters and other contractors with their renovation work.

 The week before Christmas, Chairman Brown who was not only confident in my ability to play but respected my knowledge in other aspects of the game included me in the club's three member team to talk chess and its importance with school age children on DCTV. That evening I marveled at myself as I watched DCTV special thirty minutes presentation on chess, and it felt good that though I was cold and bundled up indoors lying on a mattress in a kitchen yet the viewers would be seeing what am seeing, men in suits looking elegant and dignifying, discussing what chess would mean to children to improve their learning skills, problem solving skills, critical thinking etcetera. That weekend, as though the finger print of God was crafting everything to do with my life, Mr. Greene, a member of the club who was also a school teacher announced he was leaving for Africa for a three-week vacation and wanted to get some tips and advices from me. As he broke the news to me and asking for my help, he sounded almost apologetic that he was not going to my country of origin, Liberia, but he was going to Senegal. "This is where my family currently leaves, Mr. Greene," I said, and his eyes widen. He agreed to take some of the things I had purchased and stored in New York, so I traveled to New York to pick up all the things that I and Mr. Greene was kind enough to take some of them for my family. My wife and children met him at the airport in Dakar and my son, Harry, was with him throughout his visit and made things easier for him.

Chapter 81

Renovation work at the clubhouse was completed in January 2001 and the rooms upstairs were converted into offices leaving me to find a place to live. I was still struggling with my first snow season and not quite adjusted as yet. To make matters worse, I was not getting paid for any work done and at the same time no one would play me in chess for money anymore because I was well known as being brutal in that little chess community. On the other hand, Chairman Brown would not encourage gambling in his newly renovated clubhouse where most of the chess programs were designed for the children in the vicinity, a policy that I fully supported. My visa expired on January 19, 2001, and I still had no idea that the INS had returned my incomplete application to my old Landover address which my host there returned back to the INS. All efforts to reach Professor Ocrafor Williams proved futile. The last time someone answered his phone, I was told he had gone on a mission out of the country, and they had no idea when he would be back. "It might take months," I was told. My reliance on the professor for my asylum processing and not knowing the status of the process at the time frustrated me. I was a little encouraged with his assurances that once the papers are filed with the INS, I should be fine living in the country for a year whether my visa has expired or not, and I would not be placed on removal proceedings, but I would not be allowed to work.

He also introduced the option of Temporary Protected Status (TPS) that undocumented Liberians in the country can take advantage of if they were here illegally. He had said that with TPS, I would be allowed to stay in the country for a year and be given work permit, but it is renewable every year if the president of the United States approved the status for the countries granted the privilege. If the president did not approve then all of those TPS holders are automatically considered illegal. The down side for me at the time was the fact that a TPS holder cannot leave the United States and return nor can they file any derivative proceedings on behalf of any of their family members to join them in the United States. This quick fix status was not something I would settle for so I chose to file for asylum, which when granted, would allow me to travel in and out of the country under parole and qualifies me as an asylee to file derivative proceedings to bring in my family. The narratives at the time suggested that I was in for a long shot but that was the new journey before me and I was determined to pursue this route. There were many people including my Landover host who tried to convince me to take the TPS offer, but this was something I could not accept under the circumstances. It sounded like breaking away from my family, betraying the trust and unbreakable bonds that we garnered over the years and neglecting my responsibilities as a father, husband and surrogate to many others who looked up to me and are inspired form the projects I initiated.

On the other hand, my living conditions in the United States was well below the extreme poverty line while my family's living conditions in Dakar had declined considerably forcing me toward accepting TPS so as to be eligible to work, to earn money in order to support my family. But many times I had to resist against it and believed that God would see me through the cause I thought was right for my family. Although I had many siblings and relatives in the United States, but our relationship had been dysfunctional for so long that I was used to living life outside of the terrain of siblings and relatives. Many of them have been influenced, brainwashed and hypnotized to think of me in contempt, others built evil perceptions of me or fed on the theory that I am the black sheep in the family, even though deep in their conscience none of them can really give a single account for anything wrong that I have done against them personally to warrant the volume of resentments and hatred they garnered for me or burdened themselves with. My mother who had been the architect of these complications was at this time living with one of my sisters in North Carolina having been affected and uprooted by the Sierra Leonean war. When I left the clubhouse in search for a place to stay, I was led to the Unification Church on Columbia Road in Washington DC through a casual friend from Rwanda named Lawrence, who himself was seeking asylum but was homeless. He had informed me of the possibility to be placed in a home by the church, but we would have to volunteer full-time services with different type of jobs. Through one of the pastors, we were placed in the care of two separate families for a short period of time. For his part, Lawrence traveled with the family that adopted him to live in another state, and I never got to see him again. After two weeks the Scheck family that hosted me had me transferred to one of the church's many homes occupied by people from diverse backgrounds on Upshur Street, off Sixteenth Street, North West in Washington, DC. It was a different kind of life for me. I was placed to share a small room in the basement with an Ivorian national named Jacob, who also was seeking asylum. The bunk bed in the room took two-third of the space. I slept on the bottom bed while Jacob slept on top. At 4:00 every morning, we were awoken to the call for devotion and tribute to "True Parents" the Late Rev. Sun Myung Moon and his wife. The couple's large photo was displayed on an altar in the worship room decorated with fresh fruits and worshipers comprising of people who are trapped, lost and unwilling to worship in that manner and those who are dedicated and willing would gather in the worship room barefooted in worship unto True Parents and to partake in the eating of the fruits. After that, Jacob and I would take a long walk to the church on Columbia Road to do all type of jobs like: sweeping, cleaning, arranging chairs for endless number of programs, running errands, offloading or loading stuffs in vehicles, compiling brochures for Sunday service programs, cleaning snow from part ways, etc. We are fed periodically from leftover food from various programs, or we buy food that is sold in the church or buy from elsewhere if we have our own money.

We did not get any stipends from the church despite the fact that all the pastors knew that we had our respective families in Africa, except if some Good Samaritan comes by and tipped us $10 or $20 once in a while. I was lucky once to get a $500 tip from a contractor who found out that I had a family to take care of and was sympathetic of my situation. The first morning that I was awoken for devotion, my perception was that it would be like the usual Christian devotion where the Holy Bible is read, songs of praises and prayers offered to The Almighty through Jesus Christ our Lord and Savior. So I was happy but my happiness was short-lived. I was taken by surprise and was terribly uncomfortable with the system of devotion totally new to me. I was introduced during the gathering as a new comer and the Japanese lady conducting the ritual looked me from head to toe, face twisted, and said my toes were stinky and that I needed to go clean my feet and put on a socks before entering the "holy" ground. I was embarrassed and felt all of the eyes in the room on me as I left to go back to the basement to wash my feet and to put on a pair of socks. When I returned into the worship room, I noticed that all of the Asian people and white people were barefooted while all the black people especially Africans had on socks. I thought for a moment that this could be strange—discrimination by feet?—and my thought was confirmed when a Ugandan lady later hinted that the Asian lady conducting the ritual called devotion was racist and did not like black people especially those who came from Africa.

Some religious books written for the Unification faith were read and at the end of the devotion everyone queued to take a piece of fruit from the alter. I was on the queue but did not take any of the fruits. The same Asian woman called me back and instructed me to take the fruit, and I said that I am not used to eating fruits or anything at that time of the morning. She insisted that it is imperative that I partake but I walked away, so she took offense and reported me to one of the pastors at the church, and I was chastised and given a warning. The next morning devotion all eyes were on me to see what I would do. I was prepared for it, so I brought home some fruits from the diner

I had in one Spanish restaurant the evening before. I switched the fruit I took with me into my paper plate and ate of it. Since that day I was always playing games either by skipping part of the devotion spending long time in the restroom or not showing up at all. Some mornings I would have Jacob say that I did not sleep in the room and he does not know where I was. And when I do showed up for the ritual I always made sure that I had my own fruits in my pocket ready to switch.

The Unification movement was very organized businesswise with tremendous amount of volunteer human resources at its disposal. The movement is good at utilizing certain of its members under the ternate of volunteering to raise funds through commercial activities like the buying and selling of flowers at strategic areas on streets. During Easter season in April, 2001, tons of flowers were ordered and hundreds of members allotted certain amount of the flowers and assigned at various places nationwide. Jacob and I joined many others under the supervision of Rev. Randall Francis to offload truckloads of flowers delivered at the compound at Upshur, for distribution to various volunteers of his district. Rev. Francis then assigned Jacob and me to two separate team to assist in selling some of the flowers but he made no provision to help us out with at least a little stipend. Jacob and I had work so hard for the church especially in preparation for Rev. Moon's "We Will Stand" fifty states tour. We walked long distances distributing invitations to other churches around Washington, DC and we clean up everywhere, floors, walls and ceilings, mowed lawns and trimmed trees and painted walls because of the anticipated visit of Rev. Moon. We were also recruited to serve the security personnel responsible for Rev. Moon's protection in Washington, DC and Delaware.

Just two days for the Washington DC chapter of the tour, we are being asked to sell flowers for the movement while our respective families languished in Africa. The theme of the tour we had worked so hard for was known as: "Rebuild the Family, Restore the Community, Renew the Nations and the World" so I asked the reverend what was in the flower sales for us to help us support our respective families that were in dying needs and he said point blank that all proceeds from the flower sales was to meet the church's administrative costs and not for benevolence. I then declined joining any team to sell flowers for the movement, and I persuaded the reverend to loan me about a thousand dollars' worth of flowers for my own venture. I was told to wait until after all the allotments to their members were made and if at the end of the day there were leftover flowers he might let me have them, but I would have to pay for it. That evening, he estimated the leftover flowers at $800.00 and gave me up to April 16, a day after Easter to pay for it before we go to the "We Will Stand" conference on that very day in Washington DC. I then got Louis Johnson, my best friend till this day, to borrow me the necessary equipment like buckets, cutters, tables and signboards and to transport me to and fro Route 50, Annapolis Road in Landover, where I started preparing bouquets of flowers from the eve of Easter. By noon on Easter day I completely sold all of the flowers for a total of $2,900. I repaid Reverend the $800 I owed and was left with $2,100. I immediately sent $1,500 to my wife, and we began a small import business with African craftwork and costumes. Two weeks later, I received the first consignment from Dakar addressed to the Unification Church. I started fund-raising in the name of the church and two-third of my customers was its members. The first consignment of goods were sold within a week, and I took things to another level by collecting information on what people would like and getting their orders, sizes for African clothing, handmade shoes, handbags. As I received orders, I passed them on to my wife using the church's telephone facilities and days later the second consignment twice the size of the first one came in and sales went faster than the previous one. In fact, a member from one of the church's departments ordered African drums and some other musical instruments and I supplied those along with costumes for their department. When that consignment arrived, I employed a part-time worker to help me sell the excess items at fleet market. By the time my fourth consignments arrived, some of the pastors in one of their committees held a meeting in which they discussed how flourishing I had been lately making money and employing a part-time work while using the church as a front without giving back. They have forgotten that I do all the jobs they wanted me to do without any pay at all. Therefore they concluded that when their procurement staff cleared the fourth consignment, they would like to take control of it by taking inventory of the items and I should declare my cost to them, and I would be working for them, reporting to them as head of the department I have created in their church. This was unacceptable to me, but I had no choice because the consignment is addressed in the name of their church and their procurement guy would clear it. They were going to discuss and determine what my remuneration would be following the sales of the consignment and then they would add more money to bring in more items in large scale to keep the business going. An insider from their committee hinted me not to accept the deal and suggested that if I wanted he would help me license a business, and I could operate in partnership with him. During that same period, Mata Williams emailed me to say she was contracted by a ballet group linked to Rev. Sun Myung Moon in South Korea to mobilize the diplomatic core in Washington DC for a theatrical play at the Kennedy Center in Washington DC. The email said she would arrive at Dulles Airport in Virginia so I met with her and for a week or two before the event I worked with her in rallying members of the diplomatic core; distributing tickets to the event amongst embassy staffs in Washington DC. She visited the church on Columbia Road and met with some of the pastors and staffs, many of whom she knew and worked with in the pass. When I disclosed the situation about my small venture she advised me not to accept their proposal, and she expressed distrust in dealing with the men involved.

  I respected her opinion because she knew them and worked with some of them in the pass. Mata knew that I could cook so she asked me to prepare a few African dishes for her at the hotel in Virginia where she lodged. She offered her visitors the food I cooked, and they all took interest in my cooking and one couple invited me to come over to their home to cook a few dishes for them. When I was done they paid me $500. Then Mata's younger brother, Ibrahim Daramy and his wife also called me in to do the same for them and they also paid me $500. So I created flyers for the cooking business, distributed them and began to get few contracts, though not much but it was prospective. After the Kennedy Center event Mata returned to South Korea and I took receipt of my consignment. The committee at the church banned me from marketing the products at the church and to their members so I started selling at fleet markets. This slowed down the pace in disposing consignments since I had no vehicle to move around from one place to another with large stock of goods and I also lacked the equipment to protect against rain and other weather conditions. Storage also became a problem as the committee banned me from all self-commercial activities.

Chapter 82

My relationship with the Unification movement and church was declining. Jacob and I had used the church's telephone to call our respective families in Ivory Coast and Dakar and that has increased the phone bills. The record showed that I out-used Jacob by three to one, and so I placed more charges on the bill than Jacob by far. I was with the notion that I cannot be used without pay so I took much of my pay on the calls I made which infuriated the church's administration. Jacob was the scary type, being over respectful to people who claimed to be godly but in a sense looked down on us and care less about our families more than they care about their own interests. I asked myself many a times why was I there, and I was also worried about my asylum application which I though Professor Ocrafor Williams was handling for me, but he had not responded to my calls for a long time, and we were now in July.

In another six months, come January 2002, my grace period would have expired and then I would join the batch of illegal immigrants or maybe forced to accepting the TPS. I approached members of the church committee one time for help with this, but one of their church's member who happened to be an immigration lawyer that they referred me to took some of my African handcrafts as fees for consultation alone and later charged me $5,000 to process my asylum.

On Friday, July 13, 2001, I received a call from Ibrahim Daramy for a cooking contract for the next day. He had promised to pick me up around 10:00 a.m. from Upshur. So on Saturday morning I prepared myself and waited for him. He promised to call me when he was near the house so that I can come out to join him in the car. He and his wife, Mary, strongly dislike the Unification church and its movement. They had always felt that it was a form of money-making entity and they disliked the fact that his sister, Mata, was a big supporter and follower and she is being used. I strongly agreed with them, but I cannot convince Mata about her faith, and I know within my heart that I was just there trying to find the water level. To me it was like I was just on the bumpy part of the road I find myself on but not really where I wanted to be but I was certain that there was something that God wanted me there for, and I still struggled to find it. But on this Saturday morning while waiting for Ibrahim, I came close to some of the answers. Knowing that Ibrahim would not enter any of Rev. Moon's facilities, I stepped out of the house at 9:30 a.m. and started strolling back and forth on Upshur near Sixteenth Street, then a grey vehicle came from Upshur Street slowly toward Sixteenth Street intersection. I was standing on the sidewalk. The vehicle came closed by slowed down and stopped just near where I stood and the driver winded down the passenger side window and tilted his head to talk with me. "Do you need a ride?" the driver asked. I lowered my head to see who he was and then I said, "No, thanks. I am waiting for someone". At this point the man behind the wheel and me recognized each other. He parked his vehicle and got out and with a big smile he called out my name and asked: "John, what are you doing here?" Without answering the question and overwhelmed with emotions I called out his name, "Mr. Best!!! Oh my god, am I dreaming?" I asked, and then we hugged each other. There was a lot to talk about between us.

The last time we saw each other physically was in 1989 after I defended the Liberian Open Chess Championship against a German national named Berndt. When I beat Berndt that find Saturday in Liberia, sport reporter for Mr. Best's newspaper, *The Daily Observer* took to me to their office for interview. The games took place at the YMCA on Broad Street in Monrovia; about fifty yards away from *The Daily Observer* office and Mr. Best congratulated me then. He had once hired me to teach his children chess in Liberia, and I used to go to his house in Paynesville, Monrovia, Liberia in the early eighties.

DYSFUNCTIONAL ONE

Mr. Best is a seasoned and respected journalist and was considered Liberia's best in the business. His newspaper, *The Daily Observer*, was the leading newspaper in Liberia. Besides, it was fair and nonpartisan but the Doe government burnt down its facilities shortly before the war and his family was forced into exile. It was a little over ten years since we met. The last I heard of him at the time was that he established *The Daily Observer* newspaper in the Gambia. For his part, he had mixed news about me; one of those was that I did not make it during the war and so he thought for a moment that he was looking at my ghost and not me physically. "What are you doing here?" he asked. "I live here," I said, pointing to the Unification house. His continence changed immediately, and I knew exactly what he was thinking. "I am not a part of this group," I said. I told him that I am just trapped because I did not get a place to stay but my main problem is my inability to know the status of the asylum application that Professor Williams filed for me, to know where I stood before expiration of the grace period. I explained how I have lost contact with the professor and don't know how to get about following up with the filing. Then Mr. Best disclose to me that that should not be a problem anymore. He pointed across the road to the Lutheran Church and said that he worked there. His office was just like thirty yards away from the Moony house. He said that our meeting was not a coincidence because he does not work on Saturdays and never once came by here on Saturdays. He forgot his reading glasses on Friday evening and has to do some private work at home so he decided to come get his glasses. He further said that when he drove into his office compound across the road he noticed I was standing out there, but he did not recognized me then. He sensed that I was either waiting for the bus so he decided he would offer a ride upon his return if I was going his direction. He then dropped the bombshell: "John, part of my job with the Lutheran administrative office involved immigration matters, and we do have an immigration lawyer handling immigration matters for people like you, so if you come on Monday we can try to find the status of the application that

Professor Williams filed on your behalf and if it happened that you need to file a new application we would be glad to handle it for you free of charge to the very end. It would not cost you a penny."

Anyone who ever carried a burden knows exactly how it felt the moment that burden is lifted off their shoulder especially if it is lifted at the moment they least expected. I cannot adequately express my emotions; it was as though one has just received a medical report saying that the cancer is no more in their system. I struggled to hold back tears as I thanked him and then it struck me suddenly as he drove away that the purpose I was in that Moony house, just 30 yards away from solving the one problem that has beset me was divine. For a long time since my surprise encounter with Mr. Best, I wondered how I would have met someone positioned exactly for what I most needed at no cost to me. What would have happened if I had taken off which was my first instinct when I was humiliated by the Japanese woman on my very first day at the Moony house devotion.

On Monday morning before the Lutheran Church opened its doors, I was there with a file full of papers to meet Mr. Best at the Jubilee Immigration Center. He was ecstatic when I produced several copies of his *Daily Observer* newspaper dated as far back as 1989 and 1990 that carried articles about my chess ventures and achievements in Liberia. He introduced me to the pastor of the church and then to David Rivera Esq., the immigration lawyer in charge of their immigration center set up to assist people like me. David scheduled me for an interview that week and a strategy was developed as to how we would proceed. First he would investigate the status of my original asylum application and the result from there would shape the next approach.

On July 19, 2001, he sent a form G-28, Notice of Appearance of Counsel announcing his representation of me to the INS attached to a letter enquiring about the status of my original asylum application. Days later the INS replied that the application which was originally filed on December 21, 2000, was return incomplete. So David decided to file a new asylum application and soon thereafter an INS interview date was set for October 2001. However, two weeks after I met Mr. Best, Ibrahim Daramy and his wife, Mary, adopted me to leave in their well-furnished basement down town Silver Spring in Maryland so I moved from the Moony house and washed my hands. Ibrahim then would send the amount of $400 every month to my family in Dakar and in return I took care of their catering needs. They were very busy, self-employed, and worked from home in their IT company called Edulearn INC. I was living with them when the notorious terrorists' attacks on the United States know as 9/11 took place. The attacks caused delays in refugee resettlement programs, and across countries where the programs were in progress, there were disappointments, anxieties, and frustrations amongst those refugees worldwide that were qualified, processed, or in transit as the United States tightened up its homeland security. I had my share of panic as internal security measure became tougher on undocumented immigrants and others but it was for a short period as David called to let me know that the INS has set an interview date for October that year at their Baltimore office in Maryland. On the day of the interview, the Jubilee Immigration Center provided my transportation to and fro and financed all other costs.

In early December 2001, David called to say that the INS has scheduled a date for the result of my asylum application shortly before Christmas. From the day, he told me to the day of the verdict I had my heart in my mouth. When the day came, David and I went together to join hundreds others in a big hall there to receive results of various applications. I am sure it was a day of emotion for all in that hall for many were called in and came back with tears running down their chins, "denied." David had another appointment so he left me there waiting for the result. At about 2:45 p.m. my name was called and immediately my feet weighted tons as my heart began pounding and blood running up my spine and my eyes began to dim. For many alien, the quest to live in the United States legally is pretty much the biggest burden for which when denied is like ripping their heart apart. The mere fact that I watched families after families coming from the offices with tears, some badly shaken, uncontrollably rocked me to the core; and when my name was called I seem like the next cow on the line for slaughter. I walked up to the uniformed officer, and I was directed to a window. The staff behind the window had a file with my name on it. I was already shaking when he called out my name to make sure it was me, and I responded by answering to my name. "Congratulations," he said, "you have been temporarily approved asylum in the United States pending FBI investigation on your background." I was not sure what I heard so I gasped "eh," and he repeated as he watched my nervousness transitioned into jubilation. I was given letters and references for the Social Security office and for assistance with various social networks and a date to obtain employment authorization ID. I left the building without taking the elevator. I took the stairs in three to four steps and almost fell. When I arrived on the sidewalk, I guess people on the sidewalk might have thought that I was another insane black man; I had my hands up in the air shouting praises unto God. I took the train from Roslyn Station and a man who sat near me became concern that I was shaking and murmuring to myself. He asked if something was wrong with me or if I needed help and told him what had happened to me. I had to tell someone to share the energy for I was overwhelmed emotionally. I forgot that I had a cell phone on me that Ibrahim bought for me so I asked to borrowed the man's cell phone to call the Jubilee Immigration Center, but he asked what was wrong with mine which I had strapped on my belt. I knew then that I had to calm down, but I just don't how. I called the center, but David was still out and I asked to speak to Mr. Best then I broke the news. I heard him telling the other staff in their office, and I could hear their jubilation in the background. I was the Jubilee Immigration Center's first success story, and we were all proud and excited that it has happened.

  On February 6, 2002, I received a letter from the newly formed Department of Homeland Security that the FBI completed their investigation of my background and my asylum status is cleared and is indefinite. Because refugee programs were suspended due to the 9/11 attacks, the operational strength and model for many of the nongovernmental organizations in the network dealing with refugee resettlements became adversely affected. Funding for the refugee resettlement program was cut, but many of these organization had resources that were not being utilized because refugees were not yet cleared to travel to the USA, so once I secured asylum approval, which is the criteria that is set for these organizations to release assistance to refugees and asylees within the borders of the United States, I found myself in the middle of so many organizations extending generosity toward me. I had to pick and choose what services I needed and from whom for there was multitude of benefits but just a handful of beneficiaries. I had to choose which one of them I liked and I ended up with the International Rescue Committee (IRC). Two of my IRC counselors: Caroline and Buryke, were volunteers. Caroline and her husband are retired US diplomats and Buryke and her husband are from the Netherland on mission in the United States. Her husband was Director of World Water Projects at the World Bank in Washington, DC. The two women were said to be bored home so they volunteered their time helping out with counseling services for these non-governmental organizations and I was blessed and privileged to have fall in the hands of these wonderful ladies whose care and friendships helped heal some of the wounds. They went beyond the call of duty to extend extra humanitarian considerations to my family and also to the BRSD. Burkye and her husband took me to the World Bank one day to take receipt of learning materials and computers from the book store project there. And during Mothers' Day in May 2002, they loaned me $1,000 to purchase flowers for fund-raising. They also helped out with transportation and all of them with their children who were on vacation from Europe along with my good friend Louis Johnson helped on that day to sell all the flowers. The fundraising generated net profit of $2,020 after all expenses plus the loan amount was settled and the net profit donated to my family. I was already working as an associate for ROSS Dress for Less at the Conventional Plaza in Rockville, Maryland. According to the terms of the IRC contract, I was bound to take any job that the social worker found for me so he placed me with ROSS where my job was to offload truckloads of incoming goods. It was not the kind of job that I preferred, but as always, I looked for a divine reason why I was placed there. It wasn't long before I figured out why. The 40 percent discount on all personal purchases that the company offered its employees was just enough reasons why I was placed there. Much of the money donated to my family was used to buy clothing for me and my family members. I was on the job for less than a month when I acquired a better job with the help of Caroline and Barkye as a program assistant with the Immigration & Refugee Services of America (IRSA) now named U.S. Committee for Refugee & Immigrants in Washington DC. The wardrobe I acquired from my first job was just appropriate for my new job. Day by day, I swanked.

Chapter 83

In early May 2002, David and I started the process for derivative petitions for my family to join me in the United States from Dakar. In December 1996, a little over a year of my family arrival in Senegal, my wife delivered our seventh child, a son I named after me. This made six children in our custody living with us until my travel to the United States in October of 2000. On the last Sunday in May, just a day preceding the scheduled filing date for the derivative petitions, I experienced a miracle that would live with me for the rest of my life. S. B. Daramy, the elder brother of Ibrahim Daramy, invited me to fellowship at the Temple of Praise International Church in Beltsville, Maryland. His wife, Nike Daramy, was the senior pastor of the church at the time while he was head of the deacons. The senior pastor stepped to the podium after praise and worship songs to delivering her sermon. She led the church in prayers in preparation for her sermon, and right after the prayers, she paused for about a minute while the anxious congregation waited patiently to hear her sermon. "I have my prepared sermon before me but for some reason the Holy Spirit is leading me to deviate from it and inspiring me to speak about divine hope," she said. Continuing, she said, "I don't know who this is for, but I believe the message of divine hope, not just hope. Divine hope is an extraordinary message for someone in the congregation today," she concluded. She said it was strange that she has never felt that way before to deviate from her prepared sermon to speak about something that she did not prepare for then she urged all to receive the blessings of divine hope. So she put aside her prepared sermon and started preaching using the theme divine hope. At that very moment, my cell phone rang, and I felt embarrassed for the distraction. I thought it was on vibes but it wasn't. As I scrambled to find it in my coat pocket the pastor paused again waiting for the distraction to end, and some people in the congregation following the sound of the phone looked in my direction, which made me feel nervous and embarrassed. I stood up and ran out of the hall and on the way the phone which was still out of my reach stopped ringing after the seventh rings it was program for was exhausted. So I stood outdoors and looked at the caller ID and saw that the number was foreign. It was a call from the Republic of Guinea. "But who could be calling me from the Republic of Guinea when I have not given my number to anyone there?" I thought.

As I was thinking and trying to make sense of it, the phone rang again and this time it was my wife calling from Dakar, Senegal. I took the call and right on the spot noticed the emotions in her voice, but there was noise in the background so I had trouble hearing clearly as usual. My heart began pounding as my psychic tells me something abnormal had happened. I spoke with her early that morning and everything seems normal. Besides, I always called to save my family the cost involved in initiating calls. "What happened?" I yelled out. "Elizabeth is found!" she yelled back in an almost broken voice as though she had been crying. I paused and still could not figure out what she meant or how to make sense of it. Confused, I momentarily almost convince myself that this must be a crossed-line or the caller might be talking to the wrong person. Then she asked: "Are you there?"

"Yes, I am here," I said. "What do you mean by Elizabeth is found?" I asked.

"Our six-year-old daughter Elizabeth who disappeared in the Liberian war in 1990, has been found. She was not dead as we concluded," she uttered. As her hoisted voice pierced through my eardrum and her words began to resonate, I screamed and my body shook uncontrollably. I felt like a chilly touch at the back of my neck, and it was as though I was passing out. Then I sat on the door step to the church entrance. I could faintly hear my wife still on the phone asking if I was there, but my mind in a snapshot was wandering through the six months of search for my daughter in 1992 and the memorial service we already had as a closure in June 1992. A couple

DYSFUNCTIONAL ONE

entering the church notice I was sitting in their way on the steps which was unusual, so they stopped to ask if I was alright and I nodded. Then I responded to my wife who kept asking if I was still on. "Is she there with you?" I asked.

"No, she is currently in Guinea. The Red Cross contacted us, and we spoke for about an hour. I interviewed her, and I am convinced she is our daughter," she said. She went on to explain many personal things in our family that only Elizabeth would have known: all the nicknames I forged and labeled on everyone in the family; the names and other details of the then housemaid and nanny, the school she was attending and names of her teachers from kindergarten to second grade together with names of her best friends and school events, etc. Then she disclosed that she had given her my cell phone and that she may be calling me soon. As she was explaining I imagined what Elizabeth looked like and all type of images of her comes to me and fear grabbed me and my body began to tremble. Instinctively, I ran into the church uncontrolled and shouting praise to God Almighty and for a moment the preaching stopped as the congregation focused on me. Some members of the church later said that they thought I had gone out of my mind while other thought I must have seen the Holy Spirit. However, the deacons surrounded me and took me into another room where they found out the reason for my ballistic emotions. But that was not the end of my miracle that fateful day, there was one more mind-boggling event of the day to come.

After the service, the senior deacon and another member of the church took me home and spent some time with me there. IB and Mary joined us at the dining room discussing this wondrous event when suddenly the house phone rang and IB pick it up and said it was the immigration lawyer, David Rivera, on the line, wanting to talk to me. David had never called me on weekends let alone on a Sunday afternoon, but this day he had called me to inform me that he was filing the derivative application with the INS for my family first thing the next morning, and he wanted to clear with me if I had anything to add or subtract before he proceeded. I became speechless and lost in wonder so I told the deacon to speak to David about Elizabeth. David had earlier learned a lot about me and my journey when he was preparing me for my asylum interview. We agreed to postpone the filing while we go back to work to get Elizabeth included in the application. Meanwhile, the resurrection of Elizabeth changed my life affected my efficiency at work as I daydreamed events after events. I could hardly stop thinking about her, what she looked like, and soon anxiety began building up. I was already suffering from anxiety and depression over missing my family for the two years we had separated, and then Elizabeth's situation drove me deeply into these conditions. I barely slept at night as I would call either Guinea or Senegal to talk, mostly just to hear her voice and recalled her telling me stories after stories that she remembered and also how she ended up in Guinea. My coworkers and employer had no knowledge what state of mind I was in especially when my performance was being criticized, but I was a sleepless man at night when lines are accessible and clear and the international phone rates and minutes are maximized to talk to Africa. During the day I could feel that I was no longer that energetic person I used to be. So I decided to take a ten-day leave during Christmas to travel to Africa to spend time with my family in the Gambia. At the same time I used the opportunity to take the learning materials I had accumulated for BRSD.

On September 11, 2002, the United States Department of Justice issued me a Refugee Travel Document, and on December 29, 2002, I obtained a visa to visit the Gambia where members of my family assembled for our well-deserved emotional reunion that helped to heal the wounds and scars that our long separation had inflicted on all of us. Everyone arrived in the Gambia long before my arrival on December 30, 2002. I would have loved to spend Christmas with them, but my vacation leave matured few days after, and I had only ten days to return back to work from December 29. It was good to see everyone in the family in one place once again, and it was very special to have Elizabeth as our very worthy Christmas gift; a gift that filled us all with unending jubilations and praises to the Most High.

Chapter 84

My family's appetite to spend more time together was short-lived as ten days quickly passed by leaving me with no choice but to return to work in the United States. There were plenty of tears at the airport on the day of my departure. We all wanted to spend little more time with each other, but we realized that I had to return to deployment in the United States like a soldier in the military. I had to continue watering the seeds that I sowed to resettle my family in the United States. Shortly after I returned on January 12, 2003, I obtained my driving license and purchased my first vehicle, a Mitsubishi Gallant. Later that same month, Mr. Raleigh Seekie, a former Assistant Minister of Finance in Liberia in the Doe regime, who later became one of the leaders of ULIMO (one of the warring fraction), was in search of a job in Washington DC. He applied for a teller position at the nearby Bank of America branch at DuPont Circle. One of the bank staff and me casually spend part of our lunch time playing chess at the circle. This staff, having met Mr. Seekie after his application was denied, suggested that a Liberian (me) could be of help to him with his job search. So Mr. Seekie came to my office and scheduled an appointment through the receptionist to see me. Before our meeting, he had no idea I was the person he came to see. I visualized his image when I saw his name on the visitor's slip that reached my desk but I refused to convince myself that it was the same man I knew in Africa; the flamboyant assistant finance minister turned rebel leader now interested in teller position with a bank and now seeking a clerical position.

This must be someone else with the same name, I thought. When he walked into my office, little did he know that it was me, the one that he harassed and terrorized in Kono District, Sierra Leone for a hundred dollars he loaned my friend, Fred De Shield, and me to repair an old Ford vehicle we had bought on credit to make a living for our respective families in 1990. The meeting was a surprise for both of us. During his early days affiliating with ULIMO in Sierra Leone, the rebel group that terrorized, killed, and displaced so many people in Liberia and in villages and small towns in Sierra Leone, Raleigh Seekie was elegantly dressed, carried a commanding stature, and was greatly feared. But all that had gone when he entered my office; I saw and smell a differently shabbily dressed figure almost fit the profile of a severely stressful character and he looked terrified. We greeted each other and in that moment the air in the room was a mixture of surprise, embarrassment, and disgust. He chose then to play a boldface forgetful card trying to say that though he recognized my face but he could not remember where he knew me from. The man was assistant minister of finance while I was also assigned to the Office of the Controller at the same ministry, responsible for the government cash flow statements and reporting to the minister of finance. I had taken over the job from an expatriate named S. Ramachandra, contracted by the Liberian government. Mr. Seekie and I attended the usual Monday morning meetings at the finance minister's office at the time. This was how we knew each other and that was the reason why he loaned us a hundred dollars when we approached him in exile in Sierra Leone where we needed help at the time. He could hardly look me in the eye after I reminded him where we last met, at Kono District in Sierra Leone in 1991. The incidents were not discussed; just the place and year when he bullied us was named. I then invited him to lunch with me so we drove in my new Mitsubishi to Philips Restaurant at the Waterfront where we ate lunch. I was able to lure him out of his uncomfortable conscience to bring him to the place where he at one point lifted his shirt to show me marks from beating he took from then President Charles Taylor whom he claimed falsely accused him and others of planning a coup d'état. He portrays himself as a victim and expected sympathy from me and I hypocritically played along. He admitted that life was rough for him in the United States and that he was staying with a brother in Virginia who wanted him to find any job to help with the bills. It was hard to believe that a man of such high stature in Africa who pursued me in Sierra Leone and had me detained for a couple of days for owing him $100 would now be asking me to help him with transportation money and to help him find a job. While we were eating, I asked him if he really forgot where we last met and he blinked his eyes multiple times and finally bowed his head as I reminded him about the incident at Kono District. Since then our eyes never met without him bowing his head or scratching some part of his body. I helped him out with a $20 bill and he thanked me and never again showed up to see me. Somehow, I predicted that he would not come back to see me and he never again visited me or followed up his job search with me. When I told my wife about the incident, she was amazed and annoyed at me for showing this man any kindness. She recounted the suffering he caused our family during the Kono District incident and thought that he did not deserve any kindness from me but we both agreed that somehow he needed the way I treated him not only to fulfill the anecdote that "no condition is permanent" but also to help him man up to understand the next anecdote and the law of retributive justice that "whatsoever a man sows so shall he reap" either in this life or wherever.

In the fall of 2003 I lost the IRSA job due to oversight to confirm flight schedule information to one of our agencies on behalf of a refugee minor who ended up stranded at JFK Airport. The fourteen-year-old kid arrived from a foreign country and our airport coordinator at JFK missed putting him on a connecting flight to his destination in Bowling Green, Kentucky, because I failed to send the advice on time. I don't know how that happened but things became tough once more after I lost the job. It became difficult to take care of my large family and at the same time meet my personal bills on time: my monthly rent and car note at $1,250 and $600 respectively plus other living expenses. To meet these expenses without a gap, I immediately became a car salesman, first at Tischer Acura in Laurel, Maryland, and later at Darkars, 355 Toyota in Rockville, Maryland.

Since this was a commission-based job and the car sales business is somewhat seasonal, things began declining for me and for my family. At Tischer Acura, I became salesman of the month in the first month I worked there, but the salesmen I met there teamed up against me and my production dropped badly in the following two months and I was fired. I learned the hard way that in the car sales business, one can be fired if they do not meet their quota of sales.

At 355 Toyota, the same thing happened to me. My first three months were good as I was able to sell over the quota for these months. But on the fourth month when I could not meet the quota I was fired. In fact, Darcars was different from the other dealerships I explored. Darkars feeds on the plight of job seekers as a special niche to boost its income. It was a cleverly set up scheme to generate income from all potential applicants before they are contracted. The dealership constantly puts out ads through various medias seeking salesmen with fine print incentives but applicants were charged a certain fee for being trained by the dealership to sell their cars. The charges were never mentioned in any of the fine print ads. In my case, when my job application was being processed I was sent over to the Darcars' training department on Cherry Hill Road in Silver Spring, Maryland, for training and upon my arrival there the amount of $175 was demanded as training fees before I was allowed to attend the class. The company knew that a certain percentage of their sales teams in all of its branches are bound to fall short in selling vehicles to meet their assigned monthly quotas at each of its branches. In addition, the company also understood that by keeping surplus salesmen at each branch would help prevent most of them from reaching the goal of selling vehicles to meet the quota. So an unending pool of candidates to fill in these positions for a fee was ongoing, boosting the company's income at the expense of job seekers. I asked the man in charge of training why I should pay the company a fee for training to sell their vehicles but his explanation was that they were imparting a skill that potential salesmen could use elsewhere. But he refused to answer questions why that was not being disclosed in their ads, and he cannot confirm any case where an applicant only came there to attain their certification only to seek car salesmanship elsewhere without working for them. As to whether Darcars salesmanship certification is recognized as an accredited licensed institution, he ignored the questions and referred me to talk with the management of the dealership if I care to know all that. However, my experience in the car dealership educated me about inequality in the car sales business. It is fair to say that there is no guarantee that the same price is paid for the same type of vehicle anywhere. The final price of a vehicle is based on individual negotiations despite the Maroni price tag and finance interest rates differs from one financier to another predicated upon many factors relating to individual buyer. Once I got into the car sales business, I realized that just as there are companies targeting newcomers to exploit them as I learnt from my job with the Immigration & Refugee Services of America, so was the same with dealerships and financiers targeting and teaming up to exploit first-time buyers especially those without credit history or with bad credit history. It did not take long for me in the car salesmanship business to figure out that my own vehicle which I have been cherishing was a rip off, which made things more painful for me. The Maroni price tag at the time of my purchasing the vehicle was $16,500 but after they were done loaded me up with all of the extras, some of which they claimed were compulsory, (which I now found out were not true) together with the maximum finance rates since I had no credit history, I was locked in a $32,000 car loan contract, and, set up to paying a monthly car note at $598. Excited at the time to see myself in a brown new car with less than five miles on its odometer; the fresh smell and sweet talks of the first major credit transaction to building credits to enable me buy homes and owning whatever, I fell for it. But all the flowery talks and the excitements it brought me then at the time of transaction went away when I became an insider and seeing the same vehicle sole for $14,500 and some buyers with bad credit paying as low as $175 monthly for their car note for the same vehicle, I felt violated and cheated and a sense of burden instantly took its toll.

The situation became compounded when my fellow salesmen learned about the situation and began to mock me implying that I was stupid to have accepted such a deal. Some of them were driving Mercedes Benz, Lexus, and other luxury cars and none of them were paying car notes over $500.00 a month. As the unending mockery turned into irritation, I went back to the dealership where I purchased the vehicle to renegotiate the payment terms but that made a more laughable stock than I thought. Consequently, I choose what I thought was an easy way out by stopping to make the payment and the vehicle was subsequently repossessed. Two days after the repossession, I sold a Toyota Tundra to a man who came into the dealership wanting to trade-in his deceased father's 1995 Nissan truck. He refused the dealership offer to credit him $50 for it on the basis that his deceased father, who was a retired United States naval officer would have rather donate the vehicle to a humanitarian organization instead of trading it for even a thousand dollars. So he then decided to purchase the Tundra without the trade-in. But when he turn to me and ask me if I knew any nearby humanitarian organization he could donate the vehicle to, I knew then and there that his deceased father and my deceased father, who also was a retired naval officer, must have been watching over their sons I said to him that I knew a humanitarian organization name John Davies standing right before him now that can use the vehicle. He laughed and thought I was joking, but when I told him I was a refugee without a vehicle and would gladly use the mini truck if he donated it to me; he immediately said that was something that would have please his late father. So he donated the Nissan mini truck to me and I issued him a receipt and transferred the title and obtained a new tag from Motor Vehicle Administration (MVA) the next day.

So when Darcars fired me about a month later for not meeting their sales quota, I had the pickup truck that propelled me to my new venture. I signed a new contract with *The Gazette* to distribute their newspaper on Wednesdays in some areas in Silver Spring for a $300 fee biweekly. Since that amount was not enough to pay my rent as well as taking care of my family I ended up putting all my belongings in a storage facility and became homeless, living in my truck. My new monthly income was being equally split between me and my family in Dakar. A few months passed by then I signed up with a currier company in Washington DC, to deliver mails and packages between offices during the other days of the week besides Wednesdays. It was low commission paid contract that depended on a number of delivery to beef up the income per day, but since I was new to the business, dispatchers would assigned the hefty pick-ups and deliveries to special contractors and the little less trips assigned to new comers. So it was not profitable for me at the time as much as just to be added to my Jack-of-all-trade repertoire and the many places and routes I had come to know in the metropolitan area: Washington DC, Maryland, and Virginia. Soon the wear and tear on the mini truck began to take its toll so I could not continue with the currier business that does not cover repair cost.

Chapter 85

On June 28, 2004, after two years of the filing for my family's reunification, the INS finally approved the petitions. This was great news to my family, and we were all very happy, but we soon realized that the months ahead would be tougher as the good news opened up new challenges to test our faith, our resolve, and our guts. The consular office at the U.S. embassy in Dakar confirmed receipt of INS approval and communication for processing of my family and their visa interview was scheduled for December 1, 2004. In 2002, when David filed the derivative reunification petitions with the INS, I consulted with the UNHCR for assistance to have travel documents issued to each member of my family but their protocols and red tapes was making things difficult and it became clear that we were on our own in this family reunion project. So I started processing Liberian Laisse-Passer for my family use as travel document from the Liberian embassy in Washington DC and also obtained attestation that the institutions responsible for the provision of certificates of births along with certificate of marriage were destroyed during the Liberian civil unrest but the embassy attested our nationality as Liberians and also attested that my wife and I were a married couple and the children are our blood children. I had these documents ready for my family and sent them by DHL to my wife in Dakar.

On the very day in June 2004, when my family's I-730s were approved by the INS for our reunion, I went to a subway at the Layhill Shopping Center at the intercession of Layhill Road and Bel Pre Road. I ordered a turkey sandwich and sat at the last table facing the entrance. There were not many people and most of the seats were empty. While I was eating, a man came straight passing by the other empty tables and asked if he could share my table. I nodded and he took that seat opposite me and almost immediately he struck a conversation with me. He started by talking about his preferences in Subway sandwiches and I thought that was weird because preferences don't matter to me at that point in my life. He finally got me to say something and then we started talking. Soon he noticed my accent and became curious about my origin. "There are lots of Africans in my congregation," he said.

"You are a pastor?" I asked.

"Yes, my church is around the corner, the Free Methodist Church. What church do you attend?" he asked. I told him that I was a member of Oak Chapel United Methodist Church just a few yards away from the Subway on Layhill Road. He talked a little about his diversified congregation, some youth programs that they blended with after-school programs, the program he crafted to help trouble kids in the vicinity, how helpful that has been, etc. I commended him for that and expressed the need for such programs especially in refugee camps in Africa where there were so many parentless and misguided children. Then I mentioned a chess program I once designed and implemented at Waterloo Refugee Camp that helped a couple of traumatized children, many of whom had no parents and expressed regret that once I became employed the program ceased to carry on because I had to travel long distances to work and by the time I returned the whole camp would be in darkness because of lack of electricity. When I mentioned chess, he became excited and wanted to know more about my chess credentials; the only accomplishment that no man on earth dare demine and the only accomplishment I felt comfortable talking about even if you don't ask me. It turned out that chess is one of the games used in mentoring in his church's youth programs, and they really never had any one like me to help with that component of their programs. He then wrote his mentoring program schedule at the back of his complementary card and ask that I stop by whenever I am chance to evaluate their chess tutorial program. But when he asked for my address, I had to tell him the truth that I was homeless and that struck him hard.

"You are joking, John," he said, looking straight into my eyes.

"No, I am not," I said with a smile. I told him that I spend most nights in my mini-truck at the back of the Subway in the shopping center. "I used to sneak in sleep in the Oak Chapel UMC basement, but apparently that irritated the junior pastor so I had to change course stay in my truck until I can find a job and prepare to bring my family from Africa to join me," I said. Then he asked me personal questions about how I became homeless and about my family and whether I thought it would be easy to bring all of them into the country, on and on. When we were done talking he extended an invitation to fellowship with his congregation the following Sunday and then he went over to the man behind the counter and prepaid for seven sandwiches for me with instructions to have each released to me one per day over the next seven days. As he was leaving, he asked that I greet both Pastor Boye and his assistant Pastor Schnider of Oak Chapel UMC on his behalf.

Early on Sunday morning the caretaker of Oak Chapel UMC allowed me to shower at his quarter and then I drove over to Acorn Storage at the corner of Aspen Hill Road and Connecticut Avenue in Silver Spring where I stored my stuff, to dress up for fellowship with the Free Methodist Church congregation. After the service, Pastor Dick introduced me to some of the people involved with his youth programs including some of the youths and everyone was excited that I was there. Apparently he had told them about me. One of the youth programs was scheduled for 6:00 p.m. that Sunday and they all wanted me to come and observe, so I came back to the church annex where the youth sessions took place that evening. It was nice spending an evening with a bunch of curious youths who wanted to verify what they had been told about my chess skills. I was forced to play two simultaneous blindfold games with the kids who thereafter took interest in me. Pastor Dick was glad to see me around that evening. We discussed his big ideas to expand the youth programs to embrace trouble youths all over Silver Spring and just before we dispersed, he took my cell phone number and promised to call me sometime during the week.

DYSFUNCTIONAL ONE

On Wednesday, July 21, 2004, I stopped by his office at noon when I was distributing *The Gazette* in the neighborhood and he told me to come see him the next morning. When I met him on Thursday morning he took me into his office and disclosed to me that since we met he had not been comfortable with the idea that I live in my truck. He feared that I could be attacked overnight in the truck so he had arranged for me to temporarily lodge in one of the church's youth camp houses at Peach Orchard Retreat Center on Peach Orchard Road in Silver Spring. He called the church's secretary, Lean, who took me there and set me up. It was a one-room camp house about 15' × 15'. In the room was a bed, one table and two chairs and a small cupboard. Lean brought me new bedspreads, two pillows, towels, some toiletries, and some fruits. The large general bathrooms, restrooms, and kitchen are about twenty yards away from the small camp house. There is a large tabernacle on the left from my assigned camp house about twenty-five yards away. This large piece of land on which the camp is located had a number of similar camp houses to house over a hundred people but I was alone there at the time. There were thick bushes and large trees and large playground in the center. After Lean showed me around and turned over the key, I drove to the storage to get some of my stuff: cloth, computer and printer, and a portable television. I set everything up and took a shower and then spent my first night on a bed with enough legroom different from the sleeping in the truck where I had to curl my lets all of the time. I watched TV that night and slept well. It was only when I was planning my day on Friday morning that I realized that the Thursday was my birthday. I was so stressed out living life for my family that I had forgotten my own birthday. It turned out that the camp house was my birthday present.

Chapter 86

On Wednesday August 18, 2004, I picked up the allotted bales of *The Gazette* newspaper and brought it to the camp for packaging. Before I started living in the camp, I had problem finding a suitable place to package the newspaper before distribution. I sometimes do the packaging at the Oak Chapel UMC compound, but I don't think the then junior pastor liked that either. It was a great relief that I now had a large place where I can take my time do packaging without having to look over my shoulder. On this day, the printing press added accessories to be inserted in the newspaper before distribution. Among the accessories is a booklet containing names and addresses of religious groups in Montgomery County, Maryland. After I was done packaging and distributing, I had a few leftovers and as usual I would retain a copy for reading at my leisure. So I settled down in my camp home late that evening and started reading the newspaper with each of its inserts, then suddenly, like a voice whispering in my head, it occurred to me that the religious booklet would be the starting point to seek the appropriate resources to help my family reunification project. After thinking it over I was convince this was it, the sign of good things to come, so I sprang into action and went to work; grab some plain sheet of papers and a pen and started working on a plan. On the top of the first paper, I listed my objective with step by step goals to achieve the overall objective, which is "to reunite Davies family in the United States." After I was done listing goal after goal, I realized that the cost involved would be astronomical beyond my financial capabilities. I had distributed my resume and had two interviews already, but my current income was not enough to take care of my family and my needs. The first goal was to reach a selected religious group for assistance in a convincing way so that it does not look like a scam or a fluke.

DYSFUNCTIONAL ONE

To achieve this, I prepared a standard letter of request narrating my family's struggles and the type of help my family needed from them. Attached to the letter of request would be each family member's INS approval record along with their particulars, photographs and contact address all of which I thought would be convincing. I then selected four hundred churches in Montgomery County for the experiment. I recalled the volunteer job that Jacob and I did at the Unification Church in 2001, distributing invitations to various churches in Washington, DC to facilitate Rev. Sun Mung Moon's 50 States "We Will Stand" tour as a preparation for my own need at this time, and I was confident this would be the way to resolve my family situation. The cost of this very first goal was estimated at $1,000, to purchase at least a few rims of plain paper and photo papers, inks for the printer to make four hundred colored copies of photographs multiply by eight, photo copies of INS documentations, four hundred large envelops and stamps at $1.30 per each plus transportation cost. To be inserted in the package was a list of all the requirements with estimated cost per each: visa interview fees, medical fees and visa fees for all eight members of my family, air tickets, airport charges, etc. My next goal was to follow up with the groups that I mailed the packages to and to follow up with responses as well. I had an Excel spread sheet set up for the processes. When I was done with all these planning I realized that there is one goal that had not planned for: where was I going to get all the materials, administrative support, etc., that I needed to reach these four hundred churches? By the time I reached this brick wall it was bed time so I say my prayer and went to sleep, but as usual in my sub-consciousness, the quest for resolution lingered.

When I woke up on Thursday morning, I had thought of what to do with my plan so I went to Pastor Dick to seek counsel. He took a good look at the plan and decided that we should pray together which we did. After the prayers, he called Lean into his office and submitted my plan to her and instructed her to work with me and use all available resources to get these packages out as soon as possible. The next few days I worked with Lean to have the packages completed and sent out to all four hundred churches. The last fifty packages were mailed out on Wednesday, September 8, 2004. On that fateful day I distributed *The Gazette* newspaper and returned to the camp around 5:00 p.m. I was physically exhausted as was always the case on Wednesdays when I am done distributing the newspaper so I rested for about an hour and then I decided to shower before it get dark since I was already scare living in the place like I was living in the wild with no human movements or sound around. Shortly after 7:00 p.m. I was eating diner when I turned on the TV. Almost instantly, the local channel that the TV was tuned to was giving snapshots of the news to come within the hour. I became completely startled, helpless, and dumbfounded at one of the news headlines which ran like this: "A man is out there with a perfect plan scamming churches in Montgomery County, details at 8:00 p.m.!" The food in my mouth turned sore, my appetite died as my stomach somersaulted. "Am I dreaming?" I asked myself so many questions. "Is this news about me? What if details of the news released at 8:00 p.m. referenced my plan directly? What does it matter if it is me or not, the damage was already done, whatsoever the story would be or whosoever it may refer to, a cloud of skepticism is now hanging over every request put forward to churches especially by strangers like me," I concluded thoughtfully. Discouraged and disoriented, I left the food and pace inside the small room, my mind wondering as the clock slowly but painfully tick toward 8:00 p.m. Finally my worst fear ended at 8:00 p.m. when footage of the news came on as I watched with special interest. It was a man who claimed his sister was suffering from cancer on top of her head. He was quoted as saying that her insurance coverage does not cover certain treatment needed for her survival and that doctors have given her ultimatum that would be fatal if she did not raise the fund to pay for that particular treatment. A pitiful photo of the woman undergoing surgery was displayed, showing most part of her head cleaned up and little hair sporadically left on other parts of her head. Another photo of the same woman was shown when she was normal before she became ill. It was all a scam that many churches fell for, donating funds. In an interview with reporters, one pastor, whose church became victim of similar scam, recalled many other scams churches are experiencing every day and warned against well-organized scams going on across the country. When it was all done I was left with mixed feelings as to the status of my request with the churches concerned in light of the current story.

Now, why would God allow me to go through all these only to see this kind of story that is obviously toxic to my request? I thought. *Does it mean that God did not approve my plan? Why this story right now, just today when the last fifty packages of the total of four hundred are mailed out?* Like we were two in the room, I asked why and demanded an answer. To the other person I said: "This is not about a man who scammed churches using a fake sister cancer story, the timing here shows that this is about me, my family reunification plan. Was it not you who showed me what to do? Did not I prayed about this plan, and did not Pastor Dick and Lean also prayed for the success of this plan? You must tell me tonight why this now." I opened the door and walked across the slightly dark bushes toward the tabernacle like a madman I shouted the name of God and demanded that He appear to tell me the meaning of my sufferings. "The worst punishment for any man is to be separated from his loved ones," I shouted loud inside the slightly dark tentacle, crying as tears purring my chin. I called Him out to talk to me but I was the only one there.

Suddenly, I imagined hearing something. I was not sure what it was and fear gripped me and I ran off toward the camp house and quickly entered locking the door behind me. That night I experienced a terrible nightmare. When I came out of the nightmare I realized that the room was very cold. Cold air from outside was coming into the room because a piece of board that I attached to cover a hold in the window had fallen off leaving that part of the window opened. I was so frightened that I curled under the blanket trembling as I watched the window. Something happened that night that I just can't explain.

I was always afraid of crawling reptiles and would do everything possible to avoid being outside at night. How I got the bravery to leave the camp house to go to the tabernacle in the dark, I had no idea till this day. I did not recognize the answer I was desperate for since I was preoccupied and overwhelmed with grieve over what I thought might ruin the work already put in place, to hinder the objective of reunification of my family, which means my whole world at that point in my life. Putting things in biblical perspective, it appeared as though the heart of churches would be hardened to provide the assistance I am asking to have my family reunite. Only 1 percent of the four hundred churches contacted responded to my request. However, I followed up with all of them calling by phone to enquire if they did received my package which all of them acknowledged but the majority declined to even talk about it.

One church official even said over the phone that: "We are not here for this. We have our own problems," she said and hangs up on me. For the most part I could sense resentment directed at me from the other end of the line but I persisted to call one after the other and updated my Excel sheet to guide me. One harsh response after another deterred the next call, but I kept my eyes on the ball and continued, hoping to break through. By midday on September 22, 2004, I completed my review and follow-up exercises with all four hundred churches and updated my spread sheet. I could not find a single prospect to follow up on and it all seems a dead-end. In my frustration that afternoon, I went back to the tabernacle to talk to God. For some reason I thought in my mind that I was in the wilderness and that the tabernacle was my Mount Sinai, where He and I talked to one another. I was not crying this time, but I challenged Him to appear and tell me how happy He was that I am being tortured and traumatized. "Where are you in all this?" I yelled out laughing but serious. "Four hundred churches, all in vain? What happened to the 'Ask and ye shall receive...and the knock and the door would be opened' thing? Why are all four hundred doors closed on a genuine cause but opened to non-genuine causes? I will stay here until you answer these questions. Aren't you the Most High of whom it is said according to Ephesians 3:20 that is able to do exceeding abundantly above all that we ask or think, according to the power that work in us? Okay, it is now my fault, there is not much power working in me, is that it? Talk to me, tell me something." I went on and on with my crazy talk with God in the tabernacle until about an hour later my phone rang. A woman identified herself as Prophetess Sarah of Glory Temple Congregation called me by my name and asked if it was good time to talk. She said that she was going to call me late last night after she had time to read my request and felt the pain of separation my family is going through but she figured it was late hour to call me. She spent part of the night praying for my family, and she wanted me to know that the Lord has already appointed a man who will shoulder my pain like it was his. I thanked her for her prayers and ask for the man's name and contact information. Then she sighed and there was a brief pause. "Are you there?" I asked maybe twice or thrice and she said: "Do not worry. He will contact you," and she said she had to go. We said good-bye and then hung up. "Prophetess Sarah," I whispered her name to myself, and I reach for her caller ID, but it was "unknown" that registered for her caller ID. I returned to the camp house to check my spreadsheet and there was no such name as Prophetess Sarah nor was there any church named Glory Temple Congregation. I looked at the source of my spreadsheet; the booklet containing the addresses, and there were no such names either. Then, lying across the bed and contemplating on the call and everything else, I fell asleep that afternoon for a couple of hours and when I woke up about three hours later, everything that happen that day and the day before all seemed like a dream.

Chapter 87

The next day following my crazy talk with the Almighty, I went over to the Burtonsville Public Library to check my email and found an email from a Pastor Richard Hogue of Liberty Grove UMC. The email reads:

<u>Response from Liberty Grove United Methodist Church</u>
FROM: Richard Hogue
TO: John C. Davies
Thursday, September 23, 2004 11:31 AM

Dear John,

    I have received your letter and would like to meet with you to talk about it. I can meet with you next Monday or Tuesday. Could you please call me at 301-421-9166 or respond to this message by email? Thank you.

Rev. Richard Hogue

At 1:21 p.m. that day, I responded to the email and later called the Reverend who happened to be the senior pastor of the church. In my mind I kept questioning if he was the one that Prophetess Sarah was referring to. Clearly this pastor could not have seen my letter, it may have fallen in the wrong hand because spreadsheet tells me that someone at the church said this was something that they could not subscribe to and I was referred to the Catholic Charities for help. However, the big question kept popping up: is he the appointed one or do I have to look for another? So far he seems so. My meeting with the pastor on Monday, September 27, 2004, was fantastic. He disclosed that he was happy to have received my letter because they have had a surplus in their annual budget as a result of unused refugee fund which was being carried over each year since September 11, 2001, when the resettlement of refugees were put on hold as a result of the terrorists attacks. He was going to have the committee responsible for that fund ready for our next meeting and when that is done he would contact me. This first meeting was for him to get all the facts about my situation for better presentation to the committee. I left the meeting very happy, praising God for reopening one door out of the four hundred closed doors. I thought that after all, desperate crazy talking could be the best way of communicating with God; setting Him down in an empty chair, a method which Client Eastwood may have later copied from me and applied at the 2012 Republican Convention in Denver. On September 28, 2004, I went to check my email at the Library and found another email dated September 27, from Richard Eckert, a deacon at First Alliance Church on New Hampshire Avenue in Silver Spring. That email reads:

Your Request For Help
FROM: Richard Eckert
TO: John C. Davies
Monday, September 27, 2004 5:24 PM

Greetings,

My name is Richard Eckert. I represent the Deacons of First Alliance Church in Silver Spring. Our pastor received your letter and passed it along to me for response. I was wondering if you'd be able to meet with me this week at our church to discuss and pray further on your request? It is located on New Hampshire Ave, just south of Bonifant Road.

Would Wednesday evening (9/29) at about 6pm work for you? I have prayed for you and hope to see you soon.

Many blessings!

In Christ
Rich

I replied the email and agreed to meet Richard at First Alliance Church on the next day, September 29, at 6:00 p.m. But there was another email that really touched me emotionally as I read it. I felt the writer really related to my pain as I read it. Every word struck me so that I could feel the compassion that the writer felt. It was an email that came from a Pastor Steven Pettit of Derwood Bible Church and it reads:

Ref: <u>my response</u>
FROM: Steve Pettit
TO: John C. Davies
Tuesday, September 28, 2004 4:01 PM

Dear John,

    I can't begin to tell you how deeply I feel for you and your family. I read your letter sent to me this past week. I wish that we could help you but we can't. We are presently helping a man in your same situation from the Congo. It is costing us a fortune to help him and this in addition to 18 different ministries we have around the poorest places of the world. My daughter just got back from Liberia and we know of your suffering. I am praying that someone else will step forward from the hand of God on your behalf.

                                             I wish I could do more,
                                             Pastor Steven Pettit

I replied to his email on September 29, thanking him for his sincere response and prayers. On that same day I met with Richard Eckert at First Alliance Church. A team assigned by the church's deacon headed by Richard met with me and examined my story along with all of the documents enclosed in my request. They concluded that they would assist my family with airport charges if all goes well and my family is making the trip. The conclusion did not seat well with me since airport charges was the last item on my request which comes and became possible only if the preliminary expenses are met.

But I thank them for the offer, and they prayed for me and we bid each other good-bye and then I started walking my way out of the church when another man, struggling on his knees came after me at the entrance. "Are you not John Davies?" he asked. I turned around and looked at him, hesitated and said yes.

"I know you from somewhere" he said while handing me a sealed white envelope with my name written on it. I took it from him while searching in my head where I may have known him but nothing clicked in my memory of him anywhere. I would have remembered a man who walked crookedly because of his bad knees, but I just can't remember him. "Thank you" I said as I took the envelope from him. Then I asked if he can remind me of our meeting anywhere, but he took cannot remember only that he thinks that he knew me from somewhere. He stretched his hand and introduced himself as Donald Allen, one of the deacons of the church, but he was in the church's vestry with the choir while the other deacons met with me. He said he read my request, and he had been restless ever since. On the left top of the envelope was his name, address, and telephone number. He would like me to attend their church on Sunday, and in the main time if I needed anything, I should not hesitate to contact him. We bid each other well and I left. In my truck, I paused to open the envelope to see what was inside. It was a hundred dollars. I drove down the road to the nearest store to buy some groceries and phone cards to talk to my family and then returned to the camp house. The weather was bad later that night. It was raining heavily and the winds caused havocs. Shortly before midnight, my phone rang and it was Donald Allen expressing his concerned over my safety and wanted to know if I was fine. He then offered to let me sleep over at his house for the night, but it was difficult for me to make such a decision for someone I just got to know the same night. I told him I was considering his offer and would surely call him back if I think I can't make it. He even offered to drive where I was to pick me up if my truck couldn't make it through the weather. I was skeptical and indecisive. Here was a man who claimed to know me but could not remember where, and I can't remember either and he personally offered me a hundred dollars and now offering me to spend the night at his house the same night. I have hardly met anyone that kind for a long time. Most people would take some time studying me or getting use to me and over time they would extend that kind of kindness. I was actually threatened by the weather but since I could not just make the decision, I told him that I was safe. However, the next day he called again to check on me and I began to sense that he was actually a caring and compassionate person, but I never thought of him as fit the prophesy and prayer of Prophetess Sarah and Pastor Steven Pettit as the "someone who will step forward from the hand of God on my behalf."

The weather was bad that weekend and Donald Allen kept calling me to find out how I was doing. At one point he said that he could not sleep well because he was thinking about me throughout the night and the more I postpone coming to his house the more he is becoming worried about me. Then I visited the First Alliance Church on Sunday. I watched Donald singing in the choir and after the service he walked over to me another envelope, in it was a new key wrapped in a small paper US flag with his home address on it and a hundred dollar bill. On the next day, he call me while at work and said I can go to his house anytime and described the guest room where he wanted me to occupy as long as I would like to until my situation improved. So I went to his house at East Light Drive in Silver Spring, inspected the room and moved in before he arrived home from work. That evening I found out that he and I were not alone in his house. He had assisted another man named Michael Isaacson who still lived in his basement free of charge. Donald who was sixty, at the time, was an employee of NASA. His wife had worked as a secretary at a US Naval Base before she passed ten years earlier. When I learned that Donald himself was also a retired naval officer, it was evident that some spiritual naval connection that cannot be explained in a natural sense or understood in an educated way was taking place again. Later that evening, Mike who worked with Marriott Hotel returned home and Donald introduced me as a member of the family. Then he took us to dine at one of the restaurants in the neighborhood where we also got to know each other a little. Donald found out that night that I was up till 4:00 a.m. struggling to get clear line to talk to my family about our reunification plans and about other issues of interest to our family. I did not notice when Donald and Mike left that morning for work. But Donald came back home at lunch time and we ate lunch together. Over lunch, he showed empathy for the pain in separation that we both suffered; for him, his deceased wife and for me my family across the Atlantic Ocean. On the dining table, we both shed tears when he shared stories of late wife and I took the initiative to pray for us. There was a long silence then strangely Donald broke it by asking if I could sing. It was the first time in my life that someone ever asked me about singing. It was funny to me so I started laughing and then he gave his reason for asking me. He wanted me to join their church choir and invited me to their rehearsal that evening. I had no idea why the choir team including their director approved my voice after a couple of rehearsals with the anthems for the upcoming Sunday service. I was accepted into their choir and assigned a robe. I don't know how Don, as he was affectionately called, felt about my prayers for his late wife and his loneliness during lunch that day, but he seem to telephone everyone he knew in church and told them about the prayer and the peace of mind he felt. He even told of his feelings of the presence of the Holy Spirit during the prayer. I was flabbergasted that someone would paint me as a saint. At the end of the choir practice the director asked that I offer the closing prayer. My feet almost crumbled underneath me. I was not expecting that and everyone in the room noticed that I was bashful, but they all urged me saying they have heard of the prayer I offer that afternoon for Don, and they also wanted to receive the same blessing. I, however, overcame bashfulness and offered the closing prayer.

In that prayer, I selected a line from one of the songs that we had just rehearsed, which asked "God to send down the rain" and then I asked God to turn a blind eye and deft ear to all our early bickering of the rain that was sent to us that day, which many in the room earlier condemned, calling it nasty weather that is responsible for slippery roads and slow traffic that ruin their errant during the day. And I challenged them to put themselves in the places of those experiencing draughts and just imagine how they would feel if they were to received the blessings of rain. This little prayer made a great impact. When I was done, hands were placed over mouths in amazement, and Don could not have been prouder of me as everyone realized the hypocrisy or ignorance in their reactions to the weather as they expressed their disgust prior to the rehearsal but selected a song that asked the Lord to send down the rain. As we dispersed, everyone appreciated me with hugs and welcomed me on board as a member of the choir.

Chapter 88

In mid-October, Pastor Richard Hogue called to inform me that their refugee committee would like to meet with me. I had not informed Don or anyone about my dealings with the Liberty Groove UMC. I believed then that since they ran a budget for refugees that was in the surplus, my family had a better chance to be assisted for our reunification. I attended the meeting and the pastor formerly introduced me to the members which included a few Africans, amongst them a Liberian woman whose brother was once my client prior to the war in Liberia. Another member of their committee was an immigration lawyer who already checked the authenticity of the INS approval documents. The pastor presented my case in his opening remark and the committee members asked a few questions and then I explained the status of the process, what was needed then, and what would be needed in the near future before and after the visas are issued. A secretary took notes. The meeting came to an end and the next step forward was said to be determined in another meeting that they would schedule and let me know. I went away enthused and happy that things were progressing.

Behind me the Liberian woman told the group that she had doubt that I am a Liberian. She told stories of people from other African countries that are not at war buying Liberian papers and imposing as Liberian refugees to get benefits. Therefore she was sent to the Liberian embassy to check on me. She went to the embassy the next day and received overwhelming and convincing confirmation that I was a Liberian but that was not enough. The next huddle of doubt created was that I could just as well be scamming by using people who may have paid me money to bring them to the US and claiming that they are my family. As fate would have it, the day after she visited the Liberian embassy to enquire of me, I was driving from

Washington DC and while going passed the embassy on Sixteenth Street, NW, I decided to stop by to talk with a friend I had not seen for a long time. It was then I was told that this Liberian lady from the church came in to inquire about me. During our next meeting at the church, the Liberian lady did not attend and so do many of the members of the committee, and I was treated with cold shoulder by the few members present. I sensed that something was not right, but I had no choice. From that juncture, they turned me around and things ended up taking me in circles with no substance moving forward. Sometimes I would be told that they had no quorum to meet to decide issues and I had to just keep waiting interminably. Other time, the immigration lawyer in the group was working out some verification process for them with consular staff of the US embassy, and they would get back to me when she completed. Things were not as I thought they were and my risen hopes and convictions crumbled. The group I was banking on had let me down, and I had given up hope in my dealings with them. The evening that I last contacted them I returned home totally disappointed and depressed. Don noticed that I was not happy so he thought he could guess what the matter was. He thought maybe I was missing my family and not being there with them was taking a toll on me, and I just conceded. Don had earlier defended me at the First Alliance Church and I had no idea then. The pastor of the church had also commented that my plight was a scam and that he did not believe I had a family of my own. That night Don heard me crying on the phone late in the night while talking to my family, and he was overwhelmed with compassion for my plight. The next morning he left for work as usual at 6:00 while I was asleep. Around 9:00 a.m. he returned to the house. This was unusual for he had never come back that early. I was still asleep when I heard sound of the front door being unlocked. Then I realized it was Don when he called me out by the name he usually called me:

"Hey, fellow, you still sleeping?" he shouted from the sitting room. "Get up, I have something important to tell you that is why

I came back from work this early," he said. When I heard him say that, my gut sunk down my stomach and my head spun. The first thought that cross my mind aligned with the feelings of rejections, disappointments, and betrayal I had been experiencing lately. These, coupled with pain of missing my family and my inability to protect them had impacted my energy and I was depressed. *Is Don going to kick me out?* I asked myself. *Have I done anything wrong, or has he been persuaded to kick me out?* I thought. He patiently waited for me while I took care of myself and few minutes later I was seating face-to-face with him at the dining table. He brought some tacos for breakfast and handed me one of the bags. He had also brewed some coffee ready. I was still on the edge and eagerly wanted to hear what he was about to tell me, so I could not eat even though he beckoned to me to start eating.

He started by saying: "Fellow, I realized that if I continue to listen to what people are saying, I will never do what God wants me to do. Ever since I read your letter of request, I prayed over it, and even before meeting you, I have been restless in my spirit and burdened by your family circumstances. Then when I met you, it was as though I knew you already and I have never had a full night rest since then without being burdened by your family situation. I want you to know that I can no longer delay what God wants me to do even though it might be questioned by man. From today, you are my brother and your family is mine too. We are both in the project of reunifying your family together from now onward," he said with a smile and then he paused. By this time I was becoming relieved that he was not going to kick me out after all. Then he released the bombshell. "Now I am going back to work, but I would like you to go in my room and use my computer to search for airline tickets for all eight members of your family and for your newly born granddaughter too. When I return from work, I will make the payment online for all the tickets. In the meantime, you can send them this." He placed an envelope on the table containing a thousand dollars. "To take care of other urgent needs in the process there in Dakar."

At that very moment, I don't know if I believed my hearing or if I was dreaming or hallucinating. I have always kept a watchful eye so as not to miss out when an opportunity arose, but this moment beat my discernment. I did not think of Don as the one prophesized to "step forward from the hand of God" to fulfill the dream. My mood transformed from instant panic, anxiety to amazement and I became dumbfounded at how God works behind the scenes out of pure love for us. I laid my head on the table and Don noticed I was sobbing uncontrollably so he came over and massaged my shoulders. "Fellow," he said, "it is not me but the Lord who made everything worked for the good for all that place their trust in Him." I thanked Don then he urged me to send the money by Western Union right away, so he drove me to the shopping center on his way back to work. Even the Western Union worker noticed something sweet about me that day. He had watched me purchased phone cards almost every day and now he noticed something different about me which he never knew about me. Surely, a great burden had been lifted off my shoulders and some positive energy seems to be flowing. I went back to the house and researched three airlines and air tickets. When Don returned from work he looked at all three options and selected the most expensive among them: Air France. We were told that the duration of the ticket is for six months so Don went to work to pay for all nine tickets for a total of 12,350.20. That night I called my family and told them about Don and what he has done and they were all amazed and greatly relieved. I never got any call back from Liberty Groove UMC anymore as was promised, and I never bordered to ask them for anything. I would visit the church once in a while because in my first meeting with the pastor, the question of my faith, denomination, and place of worshiped came up and I revealed that I was a member of Oak Chapel UMC, so a transfer was arranged between the two churches, and I was transferred from Oak Chapel to Liberty Groove. On days when I attended services there, I usually came across some of the members of the refugee committee, but not one of them ever raised the issue about my family reunification, and I also would not ask. In fact, the Liberian lady on the refugee committee usually greeted me with a big smile and hugs and I also reciprocated. Somewhere inside her head she believed and enjoyed some gains for suppressing the progress of a brother but on the other side I had something out of her reach that she cannot control, let alone suppress. So we both smile and hug on the surface but in the inside I knew it was different.

With a sound piece of mind comes an intensive job search to develop a solid income base to take care of my family when they do join me. But Don had business ideas. He wanted to sponsor me to take AICPA exams to be certified as a CPA in the United States or to study the insurance business in order to establish an agency to serve insurance companies in the country. I selected the latter since the timeframe was shorter, so he enrolled me with AD Bankers to take insurance classes, and after I passed the board exams and was certificated as insurance producer in the State of Maryland in January 2005, he decided to blend that with the American Cash Flow Corporation certification and soon I was also certificated as a cash flow consultant. With the two certification on hand, Don hired a corporate lawyer and registered Davies Capital Funding, LLC, in which he gave me 75 percent shares while he took 25 percent. His intention was to position me so that when my family arrives, we would have some income strings to fall back on. His major interest was to go to Guatemala to build a motel for hosting missionaries and to build a school for underprivileged children there. He had traveled there on missions many times before and had developed a way to serve there after his retirement in four years. Because he knew that I am a chess freak, he bought Chess Master 8000 program and installed it on his computer and offered to surprise me if I could beat it in championship mode. When that eventually happened and the program generated a certificate saying I beat it in championship mode, Don upgraded my membership with the United States Chess Federation and offered to sponsor me to take part in the U. S. Open Chess Championship in Phoenix, Arizona after the arrival of my family.

Don would call my family in Dakar every weekend, and twice a month he would send them money. He knew everyone in the family by name, and he also knew their date of birth and sends them birthday presents as well as calling to sing birthday songs over the phone. He took me to MVA when my vehicle tag expired and paid up all my delinquencies, removed red flags, and helped me obtain a new tag. I was heading for my first insurance contract with American Income Life Insurance Company one day when my truck broke down on Interstate 495. When Don learned that I was stranded there, he took excuse from work and came with a tow truck and towed my truck to a garage where he paid for repairs and had all four tires replaced with new ones. By now, we were both permanent on the First Alliance Church choir, and we attended rehearsals three times a week. There were few people at the church who felt that Don was being used and that I actually had no family but was using that as a way to scam him. A cousin of his deceased wife who is member of the congregation felt that way and therefore she and other closed members were treating me with contempt, but Don asked that I ignore all of them and look up not even to him but to the "man above." The senior pastor of the church felt the same way and tried to convince Don, but he later realized his mistake and apologized. Don made a reference to it several times, and he would say that if he listens to what people are saying, he would not be able to do what God put on his heart to do and usually he would tap my shoulder, laughed out loud, and reaffirm his first words to me on the day we first met: "We have met somewhere before and I think I know you," he would say. Like many other events in my life that I cannot explain or make educated sense of, this was one of them. All that I can say is that Donald Allen was the appointed and anointed one that the anonymous caller at the tabernacle that goes by the name Prophetess Sarah and the email from Pastor Steven Pettit prophesized about. This man stood up above four hundred churches and makes the greatest impact in the life of an extremely distressed family.

Chapter 89

My family had their first interview on December 1, 2004. On that same day, I received an email about the status of the interview from the Immigrant Visa Unit Chief, Mr. Ousmane Cisse at the US Embassy in Dakar. The email reads:

> Dear Mr. Davies,
>
> Your family came in this morning with the packet III with some civil documents issued by the Liberian Embassy in Washington and the UNHCR. We instructed them that in order for us to accept the packet III and proceed with their cases, they need to obtain the proper Liberian civil documents from the competent authorities in Liberia and these documents: original birth certificates for all of them, marriage certificate for the mother and the Senegalese birth certificate for the child who was born in Senegal. As soon as these documents are available, we will accept the packet III and proceed with these cases.
>
> Sincerely,
> Ousmane Cisse
> Immigrant Visa Unit Chief

When I received this email, I realized there would be a delay with the estimated travel schedule we predicted, which we thought would have been around December 10, 2004, since we believed the visas would have been issued during the interview date on December 1, 2004. There have been and would be many refugees worldwide travelling either through resettlement programs or reunion with families, relatives, or friends without birth certificates or marriage certificates obtained from the proper civil and competent authorities from their respective countries. It is a common pattern that most people who abruptly fled a crisis mostly fled for their lives without a single ID card let alone with birth certificates and marriage certificates. Even the proper authorities who issued those documents are themselves on the run without any single ID to identify themselves.

Normally, UNHCR would play the role of providing certifications for refugee families to facilitate their travel, but UNHCR Dakar had blatantly neglected to provide the needed certifications to facilitate my family travel. In 1997, for education purposes, UNHCR had provided all refugee children with birth certificates to facilitate their enrollment in public schools. Our family had copies of these birth certificates along with the ones issued by the Liberian embassy in Washington DC, all of which the Consulate rejected and claiming that they should be issued by the proper authorities in Liberia.

So many questions came to my mind: Why are others in our exact situation provided traveling documents by UNHCR but my family denied? What was the content of the Liberty Groove UMC enquiry about my family to the consulate office at the U.S. Embassy in Dakar? Does not the consulate email inferred that my family's nationality is being questioned? Why would they not respect the birth certificates issued by UNHCR years ago? The answers to these questions only led to nowhere. What led somewhere was to go after the required document to prove everything that the Consular challenged, which would take a lot of time. When Don saw the email, he was equally as disappointed as I was. But we both knew that there were enemies spiritually in high places also at work, so we prayed over it and discussed a strategy to move forward. First, we had to cancel the tickets that he purchased and obtain refund before those tickets expired. To obtain a refund meant that some percentage of each ticket cost would be relinquished as cancelation charges, but on the other hand, leaving it as it is and not knowing exactly when the certified documents from proper authorities in Liberia would be obtained might result into the expiration of the tickets, hence, the loss of all its value. Since South African Airline was also flying to and fro between Dakar and the United States and their tickets are durable for a year as oppose to Air France's six months, we decided to switch over to South African Airline and because their ticket was cheaper compensated for the cancellation charges incurred from Air France.

It was a difficult process for me to see the refund being done because Don was under tremendous pressure from so many people who were not in support of my cause, and I was afraid he might change his mind. There were some white people at First Alliance Church who never even would respond to me when I greeted them. Don's late wife cousin had spread her fears that the way she sees things, Don might even will his property to me and that she believed that Don's kindness toward me was not ordinary, implying that I must have been doing some form of voodoo to weaken his heart.

But Don was steadfast and resolute in his decision. Then we set off to find trustworthy people in Liberia to mediate and expedite the processing of passports to help process their birth certificates along with the marriage certificate for my wife and I. Since our son, John, was born in Senegal and my family was still there, it made it easier to obtain his birth certificate but for Jacqueline who was born in Freetown, it was a challenge as well as the others that were born in Liberia. In processing these documents, other documents were required to empower those who mediate for us. These involved power of attorneys, recent photographs, notarizations, etc. I spent sleepless nights working through mediators through different types of bureaucracies, red tapes, and personal interests, tips, bribery, and the phone companies also benefitted. After two agonizing months with a lot of money spent, at least $600 per each traveling document, $700 for marriage certificates, and $325 per each birth certificate plus over $2,000 used to expedite the processes, the documents were completed. Don and I put resources together since I was gainfully employed with American Income Life Insurance Company to meet the cost of these documents. Mr. Kenneth Y. Best had traveled to Liberia for a few weeks to arrange for reestablish of his newspaper. I contacted him, and he collected all of the documents and delivered to me in the United States upon his return.

JOHN DAVIES

By early February 2005, we had obtained all of the certifications for presentation to the consular office for the visa interview. Elizabeth's birth certificate was the last to obtain because they had to undo her death record and nullified it before the processing of her birth certificate began. With all of the certificates mailed to my wife, I then replied Mr. Cisse's email of December 1, 2004. My email reads:

Appointment and visa processing
FROM: John Davies
TO: US embassy dakar
Monday, February 7, 2005 6:15 PM

Dear Mr. Cisse,

Thank you once again for attending to my family for the second time. They have obtained the Police Clearance documents you lately requested from them two weeks ago. Furthermore, the "proper Liberian civil documents from the competent authorities in Liberia" you earlier requested: Birth Certificates and Marriage certificates are now handy for your records. Also Birth Certificates for our daughter, Jacqueline, who was born in Sierra Leone in 1990 and our son, John, who was born in Senegal in 1996, are also now available for your records.

Accordingly they would be coming on Wednesday, February 9, 2005, to submit all or the documents required of them to have their cases processed in order to obtain the visa to facilitate their travel over the weekend.

Let me add that we have only ten days remaining for the forfeiture of their travel tickets as we have twice canceled and rescheduled their travel with the airline due to the delay in receiving the documentations you requested. Thank God Almighty that everything you wanted is now handy.

I look forward to your kind assistance to this matter.

Sincerely
John C. Davies, II

DYSFUNCTIONAL ONE

The last paragraph of my email was meant to humanize the situation to urge Mr. Ciese to expedite my family cases but that did not go well. My wife dropped off the original documents to the consular office at the U.S. embassy in Dakar, and she was told that she would be contacted within ten business days. But two and a half weeks passed by and there was no contact. So I sent another email which reads:

Fwd: Appointment and visa processing 1
FROM: John Davies
TO: US Embassy
Thursday, February 24, 2005 10:59 AM
----- Forwarded Message -----

Dear Mr. Cisse,

I understand you were on vacation. I hope you had a good one. The reason I am sending this message is that my family is in suspense concerning the processing of their visa III cases. While you were away they got the police clearance you lately requested and fortunately all of the other original documents from the proper authorities in Liberia, Sierra Leone and Senegal respectively you initially requested of them: birth and marriage certificates were all finally obtained and submitted to your office.

My wife was told that she would be called upon. She has waited 2 weeks and some days now and there has been no call yet. I have advised her to go back to the Embassy to see you because we do have a time sensitive arrangement for their tickets which has already expired and I have managed to pull off a grace period on them which when expired will leave us loosing the total value of all 9 air tickets. Please let me hear from you concerning this issue as soon as possible.

Thank you very much for your kind consideration to this matter.

Sincerely
John C. Davies, II

This email did not seat well also. It was as if the evil forces were determined to do everything to strengthen the weakest link in their camp. My wife did not get any call from the consular office, and I never got a reply until on March 18, 2005, after I made several telephone calls to their staff. Their reply reads:

RE: Appointment and visa processing 1
FROM: US Consular, Dakar
TO: John Davies
Message starred
Friday, March 18, 2005 8:36 AM

Dear Sir,

Please be informed that the interview date for the Davies family will be on May 11, 2005 at 7:30 a.m. Please bring your original civil documents with you:

- birth certificates or affidavit of birth,
- Police certificates for applicant over 16 years old,
- 8 front photoes and 2 profile,
- medical report (please see attached info)

Please bring with you copies for all of the above mentioned documents as well.

Best Regards
Consular Office

On May 11, 2005, when my family appeared for the interview and to receive their visa, the consular staff came up with another huddle. This time they want DNA for all members of the family to prove that the children in our family are my wife and I natural-born children. It was for the same purpose that they had requested birth certificates and marriage certificates from "the proper Liberian authorities" before they would conduct the interview and process the cases and issue the visas. It was as though someone in the consular office was disappointed that we were truly Liberians contrary to their mental state of mind or hoping that we would never have been able to obtain the civil document that were requested. They now scheduled DNA sample collection for my family to take place on June 2, 2005, at 4:00 p.m. to be executed by the embassy contracted medical officer, Dr. Djoneidi at his Clinic on Rue AX-1 Point E in Dakar. The fee for collection of the DNA per person was 10,000 FCFA equivalents to $50 per person. The total cost of the DNA test itself which was to be conducted in the United State along with the sample collection and transportation of the DNA samples from member of my family from Dakar was put at $5,000. Don drove me to the laboratory in Baltimore where he made down payment and my DNA sample was collected by the laboratory. Then he made the payment to cover collection of the DNA from all nine people involved to the US embassy in Dakar. On June 2, 2005, my family went to the US contracted doctor's clinic where Dr. Djoneidi collected their DNA and turned them over to be transported to the laboratory in Baltimore, Maryland, by the embassy in Dakar as required.

Like the UNHCR refusal to issue travel documents for my family, so also was the Internal Affairs Ministry (IAM) refusal to issuing clearance for my family to leave the country. It felt like we were in a hostage situation. A family friend named Josh Moore became concerned and decided to intervene. Josh, an American journalist assigned with Africa Consultants International, based in Dakar, Senegal, took the initiative to accompany my family to the IAM once again. Frustrated, he later involved his personal attorney, Mark Milland, to represent my family at the IAM before its commissioner. In the mist of the stressful crossroads that burdened me emotionally, mentally and physically, Josh sent me an email that helps to absorb some of my pain and mystery; adding a little life back into me as I read with tears running down cheeks. The email reads:

JOHN DAVIES

To John Davies
From Josh Moore
May 11, 2005

Hi John,

    I know this will be hard for you but I also know that you are a very strong spirited person who can overcome any obstacles. I went with your family this morning to sign for their clearance from the Internal Affairs Ministry but they would not issue it. This time they want you and your wife's DNA along with the children, especially that of Elizabeth who was not registered as your daughter with UNHCR Dakar when you registered your family here in October 1995. We got all the DNA forms from them and I need you to send me a fax number where I can send it for you to do yours and have the Laboratory sent directly to the address indicated on it. Your wife and the children would have theirs done here at the General Hospital. If we can have this done as soon as possible the clearance will be issued. The officers at the IAM says there are no further time frame, it all depends on when they received the DNA results then they will immediately issue their clearance. I tried my best but it seem to me that someone may be trying to frustrate your family for your activities here in the pass which, may be considered subversive in the eyes of a fraction of the authorities while others applauded. There seem to be a mixed feelings about your Human Right initiatives. I did not want to discuss this on the phone this morning with you as you know how unreliable the line system is here. Anyway, rest assured that when the DNA process is completed they would have no other huddle to bring because I have also involved my Attorney, Mark Milland. He has announced your representation and also obtained the IAM position from the Commissioner. Let us continue to pray that your family remain save for your reunion. I am awaiting a fax number to send you the forms. Be of courage John and all will be history soon.

Yours,

Josh

Chapter 90

Up till this point, I had lived my life for the family I loved unconditionally; a family that I can lay down my life for any day, but, how far would I go or how much would the pain be if a child in this family turned out to be someone else from the DNA result, was something beyond my imagination. This was a challenge that increased my anxiety level and drove me into frequent hallucinations, leaving me wrestling with a number of what-if scenarios over and over again. At times the world around me is shut down leaving me isolated. I told myself that it would be better to have a leg amputated without anesthetic or to have an eye plugged out than to be put in that position. How could I undo my love and affection for a child that I have considered mine for many years? Or how would that child undo their love and affection for me, if they found out that I am not their dad? Why the consular staffs did come up with this after all they had asked for and the time wasted? Do they just enjoy the torturing that DNA tests has been causing families after families or is it the devastations that it caused especially African families that amuse them? If DNA test, which is not popular in African culture, is conducted for families across the board, the results could turn the entire continent upside down. The stakes were too high; negative results from the DNA would also affect Don considerably. How would he face the people of the church who doubted my story and never wanted him to support my cause in the first place? He would have been betrayed and maybe forced to withdraw from the cause, leaving me to live my life with the irreparable pain that could lead me to my early grave. I remembered the few cases I had witnessed in Dakar during the late 1990s.

In some of the cases, families were torn apart, and in one such case, a fourteen-year-old kid may have committed suicide a few days after he learned the shocking news from DNA that the man he had known, loved, and called his father was after all not his father and the brother and sister whom he had known, loved, and called his brother and sister was only a half-brother and half-sister. Worst of all, he was going to be left behind while his mother and other siblings traveled to the United States to join the man he knew as his father who filed the petition for them for which they traveled from Freetown to Dakar. The consular office dropped him off the list, and he was terribly shocked, leading to his death. The father himself was said to be devastated to the point where he also divorced his wife and dropped her off the list. Because of unrest in some West African countries at the time, Senegal was the point of visa processing, and I have witnessed many of these type cases like replica of the Maury Show in an African setting. It was painful because many of these people were already victims of war now becoming victims of DNA. I have always thought then that one day if I have the resources, this would be one area I would involve myself to provide counseling and therapy for these type of victims. So for the Consular office to demand DNA after all my family went through just left me tortured for months to come, and my performance at work was badly affected causing me to withdraw from the work. My family reunification became my full-time work.

During the Sunday, May 15, 2005, service, the DNA situation was announced following an update of my situation, which was a frequent thing that Don usually responded to asking for prayers on my behalf. This caused widespread concerns, mixed feelings, and misconceptions. At this time the junior pastor of the church had left to take up a new mission in another state and the senior pastor also left to take up a new mission outside of the country. The church's board was interviewing candidates to fill the two positions. Since we were expecting my family in May, Don had negotiated to have the junior pastor's house in Burtonsville, Maryland, rented out to me for my family to live in. I had just acquired my first insurance contract with American Income Life Insurance Company and at the same time plans were underway for the establishment of our newly register corporation: Davies Capital Funding LLC. There were so many good things going on at the same time when suddenly the DNA imposition changed everything. Some of the preparations for my family coming resulted into waste since the DNA across country lines would take a couple of months. We were now obligated to pay rental for an unoccupied house while in the process of several arrangements for office to house our business, the purchase of furniture, fixtures, equipment, and supplies for our new cooperation, which was already registered in Maryland.

On the week that the consular imposed DNA testing on my family, a three-day men's retreat of First Alliance Church was to take place in Gettysburg, Pennsylvania, and Don insisted he was not leaving me behind to lament about our disappointment, so I joined the men's retreat team and that made a lot of difference. It was a good thing that I attended the retreat, which greatly benefited me and prepared me for the tough days ahead. Some of the men at the retreat showed their solidarity with me and embraced me as their brother, and I was truly touched.

Mr. Richard Price, a member of our choir, wrote a check for $500 to Don as his contribution toward the cost of the DNA test. Later at church that Sunday, another member of the choir, Ms. Marsha, also wrote a $2,000 check to Don as contribution toward the DNA test. Despite the bickering and mongering and gossiping by others, there were few others that have come to put faith in Don's initiatives. To see him standing steadfastly with me from September 2004 up to that time, sharing his experience in interacting with members of my family and how they called him from Dakar during his sixty-first birthday in February to sing and wish him well on the phone was moving. Minds had been changed because of this one man.

After the retreat, Don started preparing for his knee surgery in Texas. He said that one of the best experts in that type of surgery was in Texas, but he wanted to go there because he had a half-sister called Linder who lived there. Many times he had asked for prayers for Linder to be relieved from drugs and other type of unpleasant activities. He wanted to spend some time with her during his recovery after he is discharged from the hospital. On June 2, 2005, Brian, the church secretary and I escorted him to Ronald Reagan National Airport in Virginia to make the trip to Texas for his knee surgery. At the airport parking, we prayed for healing and for his safe return. He wrote his half-sister's name and contact information on a piece of paper, and he handed over to me just in case I could not reach him at his cell phone. He said his cell phone would be open for communication but after his operation on both knees he would be lodging with her for a while before returning to back to Maryland where he had lived for about forty years. We talked about some of the things we needed me to do while he was away, our new business and about his car and a few housekeeping items. His flight was announced and he left.

When he arrived in Texas, Linder was there to accompany him straight to the hospital. The next morning he called to update me and to share the biblical verse for the day as usual. On June 4, the surgery was done on one knee, and he called to explained how painless it was, frequently referring to the doctors as the best in the country. The next day, surgery was done on the other knee, and he called again to express amazement how easy and painless it was. We praised the Lord, and I updated him about preparations for our new business and the lease we were supposed to sign to house the business. He had told Linder all about me and my family during this period, and on two occasions he wrote three checks totaling $12,000 and asked her to put it in the mail addressed to me while he was still at the hospital recovering.

On Tuesday, June 7, he called to say he had signaled that his car in Maryland was being used. It was Michael who used his car and the alarm system notified Don at the hospital in Texas. Michael said he was only washing the car, and Don and I joked about it because we both knew he was using the car without his permission. On Wednesday, June 8, he was discharged and before he left the hospital he called twice. First, it was early in morning when he shared

DYSFUNCTIONAL ONE

the verse of the day and to ask me to tune my TV to a certain channel to watch Dr. Charles Stanley, one of our favorite preachers.

The second call was when he was about to leave the hospital to spend some time at Linder's home. Hours later, I called her home number to speak to him and he said he was doing fine. He said he would be traveling back on Tuesday or Wednesday the following week, but he would let Brain and I know as soon as his flight details were confirmed so we can pick him up at the airport.

On Thursday, the ninth, he did not call and I was concerned, so I called his cell phone as well as Linder's home phone several times and no one picked up. I left messages and no one responded.

Friday, the tenth, I called and no one answered. My wife and I spoke on the evening, and she disclosed to me about a terrible dream she had the night before so she stopped all the children not to leave the house that day. Some of the children wanted to go to the beach to swim, but she warned them to stay home because the dream was not ordinary according to her. In her dream, she saw a white man being stabbed multiple times and was brought to her front door to die. The dream scared me because I had not spoken to Don for two days and that too was unusual.

On Saturday, the eleventh, First Alliance Church had yard sales so I went there in the morning to buy a few items. The items I bought were a few paintings and artwork for my family house. So when I left the church, I drove to my family house in Burtonsville to drop off the items. I was there fixing the paintings on the wall when my cell phone rang and the caller showed it was Don. I rushed to answer the call, but it was Linder asking my whereabouts in Maryland so I asked why and she said that she was in Maryland at Don's house and would like to see me immediately. I asked for Don and she said: "Just come as quickly as possible. I am waiting."

I jumped in my truck and drove to Don's house where I met her. She opened the door for me and the whole living room was clouded with cigarette smoke. I entered and greeted her but disturbed by the smoke. After our greetings, she waved me to a chair, but I was still standing when she said: "I am sorry, but your friend passed in the early morning hours yesterday." Those words hit me like a truckload of bricks. My vision became dark and my feet weaker and crumbled from underneath me, and I fell on the ground and for a moment I passed. When my vision became clear, and I looked up over me still lying on the ground, Linder's eyes and mine met, and I saw something in her eyes that told me more truth than any word that came from her mouth. It was the kind of cold but unmistakably unemotional eyes of a cold-blooded murderer. There was no doubt in my mind that Don was murdered probably because of my family.

Chapter 91

I was lying on the floor, pounding my fist against the ground and crying out loud: "Why you let this happened Lord, why?" Linder was still looking down at me with those scornfully cold but emotionless eyes, cigarette between her fingers with smoke pouring from her nostrils. After a couple of minutes I asked her how it happened. She rambled and stammered her way through it all as she avoided any eye contact with me. She said after Don was discharged from the hospital, she took him home, and he was doing fine but late that night he had a heart attack, and he was rushed back to the hospital where he was resuscitated and later discharged on Thursday afternoon. Then Don decided to shop for her daughter (his niece) on their way home from the hospital and she (Linder) tried to stop him but he insisted so they made a stop at a computer store where Don bought his niece a laptop. When they arrived home Don told her that if anything happened to him, he would like his body cremated.

In the early hours on Friday, he had a second heart attack and never recovered from it. He was taken back to the hospital where all efforts to have him resuscitated did not work out, and he was pronounced dead in the early hours on Friday. As she finished telling her story she then looked into my eyes to ask if I had his will. She also wanted to know if he had a safety deposit box anywhere that I know of. I asked why she was asking me those questions when according to her Don had the time to take her daughter shopping and also told her if anything happened to him he wanted to be cremated. "Why did he not tell you where his will was and where he had a safety deposit box if he told you what he wanted done to his body after his death?" I asked.

In answering, she rambled again and said that Don told her that I knew everything about him and that I was his closest confidant.

She had already ransacked his room searching for his will, his house mortgage documents, his vehicle title, and for any other document that she considered important. Then I asked where his body was and she told me that it was already cremated that morning while she was on her way to Maryland. I asked if she had called to informed anyone at First Alliance Church where Don have been member for decades, serving as deacon and member in several committees? She answered no. I asked if she called and inform his work place and she said that she planned on doing so on Monday. I asked if she already informed Don's sister-in-law who attended the same church and it was at that point that she asked me back for her telephone number. The church directory was always on a shelf in the dining room, so I pointed there and she reached for it.

Then as she was searching for Don's sister-in-law's phone number she came back to ask if I was sure that I did not have even a copy of his will because Don told her that nothing of his were hidden from me, and she was surprised that I said that I had no idea. I then referred her to the church. "I don't know what to say to you at this very moment, but as a matter of fact, there is a yard sales going on at the church right now and most of its members and leaders are there. I suggest that you go there to meet with some of the church's leaders and tell them all these things that happened and ask them for the information you are asking me for," I said in a rather sarcastic tone. She declined either because she did not have the guts to do it, or she was running out of time with her insidious plans that brought her to Maryland. So after a while, I decided to go to the church to break the news of Don's death, and everyone present there was saddened upon hearing the news. When I returned to Don's house, I met a U-Haul truck being loaded with his household possessions: TV set, computer, office, and household furniture and many other item were being loaded into the truck to be take to Texas. She had his clothing in trash bags outside of the house and told me to take those. I remembered Don was planning a trip to Guatemala in the fall of that year, and he had bought bails of used clothing so I took the

DYSFUNCTIONAL ONE

trash bags full of his clothing and later gave them to the Guatemala missionaries he was to make the trip with.

I couldn't take any more of Linder's meanness and boldness so I walked away that Saturday afternoon and drove to my family home in Burtonsville, leaving Michael and Richard Eckert who had just moved into Don's guest room shortly before his trip for the surgery in Texas. At my family home I found one of mail that Don had sent me during the week, and it contained a $6,000 check that I was to add my own contribution of $4,000 to make the initial lease payment for the premise in Green Belt, Maryland, where our company's office was to be housed. I decided immediately to deposit that check in our company's bank account because I knew exactly what Linder was going to be doing in Maryland on Monday morning. She was going to alert Don's bankers that he was dead and give them instruction not to honor any checks payable to me or to our company from his personal account. But if I can move quickly and deposit the check and on Monday morning withdrew all of the amount since the company's bankers would let me spend the money on the face value of the deposit then there is no way that Don's bank would not honor another bank's transactions when the funds are available in Don's account and the check I deposited was a genuine check that he issued before he passed. So I rushed to our company's banker, Sun Trust Bank, and they were already closed but still doing business with customers that were inside. I called one of their staff who I was friendly with, and he opened up for me to enter and I was able to make the deposit. I was now left with only one check that Don had written to me in the amount of $2,000. His bankers can only cash up to $2,000 a day for a noncustomer, so I had to wait on Monday morning. With any luck I would cashed it before Linder makes her move Monday.

Later that evening, I was grieving Don's death when a phone call came in from South African Airline to inquire about a call they had received from a man posing as Don requesting them to cancel the tickets that were purchased for my family and to refund the payment. The caller had no knowledge of the ticket references, and the debit or credit card that they quoted from which the original payment was made was also wrong. Don's correct address was also wrong and moreover the call came from Texas and not from Maryland where the transactions originated. The airline suspected something was not right so they had called Don's home phone number on file earlier that morning before Linder arrived in Maryland. This alerted me that Linder may not be working alone in the murder of Don. There must be an accomplice, probably one of her ghetto buddies, and they seem to be doing everything they can in order to maximize benefits from his estate. What they do not know at the time was that Don had changed all of his credit and debit cards after the purchase of the tickets. He and Michael went bowling one weekend long after those tickets were purchased and Don's wallet went missing from the locker room at the bowling place. So he reported the loss to the credit card companies and to his banker and new cards were issued that the airline would not recognize as the card used to purchase the tickets. Furthermore, the airline had no idea that Don was dead. Linder had been using his bank card and credit cards after his death to shop. She used it to buy her air ticket to come to Maryland, and she also used it to pay the funeral home in Texas to have his body cremated and to hire U-Haul to transport his properties from Maryland to Texas and of course to feed her drugging and drinking appetite. The gentleman on the line from the airline said that they suspected the caller was imposing as Don because he could not provide accurate information that the purchaser would have known, but he was calling to alert me since my name is on file with them as the initiator of the transaction and my family was the passengers on file. I thanked him and informed him that Don may have passed away in Texas on June 10 under mysterious circumstances and the person requesting the refund was an impostor who apparently had ulterior motives. I stressed the point that the tickets which have already been issued should not be refunded under no circumstances.

"The tickets are property of the Davies family for which the airline can be held liable in Dakar if the Davies are denied there use when the time comes in a month or two. Any refund must be legitimized by a court order from Don's estate, not just anyone, relative, or family member," I emphasized. The man agreed with me, and I could hear him typing something on the record. At this juncture, I began to examine the theory that Don could have been killed because of my family. That same evening Michael called to ask me to pick up some items of mine from Don's house because he and Richard had been asked by Linder to vacate Don's house as soon as possible as the house would be put on sale as early as Monday. At church the next day, many questioned the abnormal circumstances surrounded Don's death, but no one cared to go the extra mile to find out the truth. I was told that according to the system in America, Linder was the next of kin to his property where there is no will but that was not my contention. Even if there was a will, my contention was that the circumstances surrounding his death were pointing to foul play. Everyone agreed that Don had never indicated that he wanted to be cremated upon his death let alone to be cremated within twenty-four hours of his death without any announcements at the place where he had lived for over forty years.

On Monday morning, I went to the bank to cash the last $2,000 checks that Don had issued me before his death. Linder was already at the bank to alert its management of his death, and she had with her a death certificate. She was very prepared, and she was moving quickly with her plans which made me think that she must have planned earlier enough and she succeeded in luring Don to confine in her, having him fell straight into her smear. When I presented the check, the teller referred me to see the manager. The manager then claimed that I would have to hold on to the check because the issuer's account is temporarily closed. I asked him if the bank has a court order to close the account until administrators to his estate were appointed or whether the mere receipt of a customer's death certificate by the bank means that all genuine transactions the customer entered and checks that they wrote to pay their bills prior to their decease would be unilaterally put on hold by the bank?

"Of course if there was any fraud reported then there would be an issue, but anybody can die any time, and your bank would deprive the living for a genuine cause without a court order?" I asked. After a couple of exchanges and subsequent phone calls that he made to clarify the bank's position, the manager signed off on cashing the check and the teller brought the money in an envelope to me in his office.

Linder was still waiting even though she was done talking to the management. She watched the manager escort me to the door, and I walked past by her without a word being said. When I left the bank, I went straight to our company's bankers and withdrew all the money we had left including the amount for the $6,000 check deposited on Saturday afternoon. I knew the bank would be processing that check through Don's bankers that afternoon, and I knew that there were enough funds in Don's personal account to honor and clear all checks he wrote for various purposes. The risk was to hold on to the check until Linder succeeded in legalizing her hereditary powers and began to reverse and dishonor every transaction in progress prior to Don's death. By midweek, she had cleaned up Don's house and had a second U-Haul truck on the way to Texas.

Then she contested the $6,000 check with Don's bankers and our company's bank got involved and called me up, but I advised that they would have to deal with it as every position I took was legitimate. The checks were issued by Don to take care of a legitimate business, and Linder was the one who mailed them to me, and I have all rights to cash checks legitimately made payable to me, and I am not obligated to tell anyone why the check were written to me except when legally required to do so. Linder flew to Texas that weekend and called me from there with threats that he would have my head spin if I have any more issues to do with any of Don's bank accounts so I threatened her that Don's original will and testament would soon be released to the FBI to investigate his death. She never called me again, but I planned to go to Texas to investigate his death, especially so after I obtained a copy of his death certificate and called the hospital where his knee operation was conducted and introduced myself as Don's business partner and got their version of the story, and I also called the funeral home where his body was cremated and got their side of the story. Then I called the FBI hotline and spoke with someone who listened to my story and sense there may be foul play, but it might be hard to prove since the body was already cremated. They however transferred me to their Texas branch and details of the information I provided were taken down, but I was told pretty much the same line that was given me.

    One of our choir members advised me to drop my plan of going to Texas and to leave everything with God as nothing that I would do on my own will bring Don back, but the Lord would take care of the situation. He said Don would have wanted me to fight to bring my family, and he would have been happy so I should concentrate on that. I told my family about Don's death, and it was as though he died there in Africa before them. It was very hard to console all of us over his death.

Chapter 92

On July 9, 2005, I received a package containing my family DNA results from State Department. The rhythm of my heartbeat changed gear the very moment I opened the package and read the cover letter telling me that each of the seven sealed envelopes contained the DNA results of each child in my family and that the same had been forwarded to the US Embassy in Dakar. I had earlier promised myself that the best place to unveil the result would be at the tabernacle located at the Free Methodist Church Retreat Camp where I used to live on Peach Orchard Road. So I placed the package inside a Holy Bible that Don had earlier presented me as a gift and placed the Bible under my pillow. Despite my restlessness that night and sporadic temptation to open the envelopes I stuck with my earlier commitment to open them only at the tabernacle. Now that the one that was chosen from the hand of God has left the battle with me though I was confident that he was still in it with me spiritually, the best place to unveil the result would be at the holy place where I received the first prophesy.

I was also fearful of the pain it might cause me if the results turned out negative for the most part. Tension was building up in the air momentarily as the time for unveiling the results drew near. The pressure on me was like being summoned on the Maury Show seven times the same day. Since Don's death I had not been able to rehearse or sing in the choir without crying in the middle of a hymn or when one of his favorite songs came up. All my life I had never sung in choir until Don initiated me. He said then that he believed in me and indeed he was my inspiration. We were singing alto together and always seating side by side on the same bench during rehearsal and during Sunday services. I was beginning to feel chill once I sat on the choir bench. It feels as though he was present near me, and I would imagine him being there, which often times saddened me to the point where I would start sobbing.

On Sunday, July 10, I took with me the DNA package to church and after the service I drove to the tabernacle and laid the package on the altar. There were campers around but no one was near the tabernacle. Then I offered thanks to God for having Don in my life and for his soul to rest in peace. Then I prayed for all those who had been disappointed and devastated with DNA results, and I prayed for my family and for all the content in the package to turn out 100 percent positive. In my prayer, I asked for God to grant me peace even in event that any of the results turned out negative. At that point it was like making a covenant with God with the determination and courage that whatever the results, all of the children would remain as is, children of the Davies family, without any discrimination. After all, they have all suffered too much to be abandoned and isolated or disowned at this stage of our struggle. When I was done praying, I spent some quiet time just sitting there and watching the birds singing, enjoying the wind, and watching few children in the playground recreating while waiting for the time to strike 2:00 p.m. before I started opening the envelopes one after the other starting from the youngest child, John, my namesake, who was born in Senegal. His DNA matched both parents' by 99.99 percent, so he was cleared, and that was a good start.

Then it was Jacqueline's turn, and she also matched her parents by 99.99 percentages so she was cleared. Then it was the second twin, Shirley and Gracious, and they too matched both parents' DNA by 99.99 percentages. Then it was the first twin, Harry and Harriette, and they too matched both parents' DNA by 99.99 percentages.

By this time it was six cleared out of seven. Then it was Elizabeth's turn, but her DNA only matched her mother 99.99 percentages and 0.00 percentages with me. I stood there shaking and trying to come to grips with reality and looking back twenty-two years what might have happened. My wife had been faithful, loving, caring, and honorable all these years; and she had never cheat on me.

I told myself maybe she was seeing someone else during her school days when we just met then in 1983. I wondered how poor Elizabeth would take this news. She is still my girl, my oldest daughter, and if I had the power, she was not going to see this DNA result for the rest of her life. But I suspected that the embassy would be disclosing the information and probably denying her the visa on the basis that the principal applicant is not her father.

So after everything, I drove home and called my wife and broke the news to her. She was devastated and for the first time she disclose to me her inner secret about herself twenty-two years ago when we just met. She broke down over the phone and confessed that she was raped. She would have told me about the incident, but she was afraid that I would have turned away from her because women who are raped in our culture are considered and treated like outcasts; they are ridiculed in most cases so they hardly came forward to say what has happened to them. I told her that I am at peace with the result and that I was not perfect too. "I probably had a child somewhere that I don't know about before we met because I did some stupid things too when I was young," I said, but we both were afraid that the result would devastate Elizabeth, especially if they deny her the visa, and she finds out that I am not her real dad. So I decided I would figure out something before the visa interview date.

So I contacted David, our immigration lawyer, and acquainted him with the situation and he decided that we could make a special appeal for Elizabeth with the INS and also for Harriette's baby, Christina, who was not included in the original I-730 application. Things later worked out for Elizabeth. After the consulate disqualified her and denied here visa, David and I were busy working with the INS for reconsideration under the circumstances and a few weeks later the consideration was granted, and she was finally approved. During the period, I had to call her and speak with her from my heart about everything, and she showed tremendous maturity and understanding, through it all; although of course, there was some pain, but knowing that I was committed to be what I have always been, a loving and caring dad, she was assured and we all were able to find the part toward healing our wounds.

During the last week in August 2005, the consular office finally issued visa to all members of my family except for Elizabeth whose approval came late. On September 7, 2005, they travel on board South African Airline from Dakar International Airport to JFK International Airport in New York. Before their travel, and knowing that Elizabeth was to follow soon, we brought my wife's mother to Senegal to take care of my granddaughter, Harriette's daughter, Christina, who was also denied. There was a lot of support from First Alliance Church and its members, especially members of the choir. The church had been blessed with a new pastoral staff headed by Pastor Mike Mercurio, who allowed the use of the church's van to go to JFK International Airport to pick up my family.

The church secretary, Brian, and Frank, the youth pastor, accompanied me to New York on the eve of my family arrival and we slept in New York. I spoke to my family at the airport in Dakar and instructed them to alert me when they were about boarding the airplane just so I can believe that they really departed Dakar because it was just unbelievable that they were finally cleared and the long awaited reunification clouded with unpredictable challenges was just a matter of hours away. It was still unbelievable when the flight arrived and all the passengers were processed and attended to by airport authorities but my family was out of site. We called on an immigration officer to inquire if there was a refugee family by name of Davies on board the South African flight. He replied that if they were then they would be the last to process because they would have to be photographed, fingerprinted, and work permit will be issued them along with the document they would use to obtain their social security numbers etcetera. *What a blessing,* I thought.

When I arrived in the country, it took me up to sixteen months to obtain a work permit and Social Security number, but for them, each one including John who was just eight years old was issued a work permit upon arrival. We waited behind a barrier that created a fence from where newly arrived passengers comes through when they exited the area where airport authorities cleared them. People who waited for their love ones waited at the entrance of the barrier to hug, kiss, and so forth. At various points over head the barrier, a sign in big bold letters reads: NO ENTRY or VISITORS NOT ALLOWED TO CROSS THIS AREA. All the while we were there waiting I watched many who had come to receive someone waiting behind the barrier until their love one reaches the entrance to the fence.

After two hours of waiting (which seemed one of the longest two hours), I saw my sons Harry and John, behind them were two of my daughters, Shirley and Gracious. At that point, the signs and the barrier disappeared, and I instinctively and uncontrollably found myself over the fence as I leaped over it like an athlete leaping over huddles, my food hit the top part and I tumbled, landing violently on the ground. Simultaneously the children were running toward me and I landed with my back in the prohibited area they came falling on me and I find myself hugging and kissing while lying on my back. Two officers who saw what happened came to see if I was hurt. "Sir, are you all right?" they asked, but the smile on my face said it all. "Yes, I am fine forever," I said. As I was sitting up, one of them came very close and said, "Are you sure?" I looked up and in a flash I thought that he looked just like Don. I remembered what Don has always said that when my family arrived they would ride the coolest limousines from New York to Maryland. He pulled me up by the hand and as I was standing he asked again: "Are you all right? Are you sure you are all right? Do you need help, sir?" "Yes, sir," I said with a smile. "Call one of the coolest limousines in New York to ride my family to Maryland for our big reunification ceremony." The officers chuckled and helped me get on my feet as the crowd watched with puzzle looks on their faces. I kissed my beautiful wife in the frenzy of things, and we all walked toward the end of the fence where Brian and Frank waited with their cameras. They had planned to capture our family's first reactions, but my tumbling over the fence caught them by surprise. They had not turned on their cameras. I guess they thought it was the normal-type protocols where we all waited at the entrance and everything else is staged. No this was a desperado type of reunion, crazy style.

We then drove in the church's van from the airport and seven hours later we arrived in Maryland. On the way to Maryland we made several stops to eat and to use the restroom. I watched my two sons ate up a bucket of Kentucky chicken as they slept through part of the trip. The first place we went was at the church for prayers before Brian drove us to the house in Burtonsville.

Chapter 93

Don was the motivating force behind the First Alliance Church family. He was one of a kind, always willing to lend a helping hand to someone in need in obedience to the almighty. In my case, as the one chosen from the hand of God, he wrestled against all odds in support of the cause to help my family resettle in the United States. His resolve and steadfastness later encouraged others during the struggle. On the first church service my family attended, the skeptics and the unbelieving Thomas came to grip with reality. It was an emotional moment for my family during the first Sunday service when we were placed on stage to be recognized and welcomed by the congregation, and we had to speak before the congregation.

For me, this emotional moment resurrected Don, the man who made it all happen against all odds. It felt as though he was there seating in his favorite seat watching and feeling very proud and hoping this event sent a positive message to those who always think and stay inside their own box. How proud he would have been seeing his critics and the unbelieving Thomas in the congregation hugging and kissing my children, some offering to take them shopping or to show them around, etc. I was pretty certain that there were many others, probably in all four hundred churches I had contacted for help, who would now be willing and happy to go the extra mile in showing affection and kindness. After the services, on the church parking lot, many brought stuffs that were in their cars that they donated to us.

Over the next two weeks the church assigned Brian to drive my family around in the church's van to help transport us to take care of some of the most urgent integration processes like: obtaining Social Security cards, various inoculations, and medical examinations necessary as prerequisite for the children's schooling. Then the children were enrolled in various educational institutions: Harriette passed the ITT Tech aptitude test administered at their Virginia Campus, and she was enrolled there in a four years bachelor of science degree program to study business administration. Shirley, Gracious, and Jacqueline enrolled with Spring Brook High School in Silver Spring and John enrolled at Burtonsville Elementary School. Harry later enrolled with TESST College to study information technology. On the last Sunday in September 2005, we visited the Free United Methodist Church on Bonifant Road and Pastor Dick joyfully introduced my family to his congregation. His secretary, Lean, was very excited that things worked out from the work we did together.

One Sunday in October, we visited Oak Chapel United Methodist Church. Pastor Boye, who was the senior pastor there, had retired. I once had him talked to my wife in Dakar, and he was also helpful a couple of times when I needed some food money when I was homeless. Pastor Schneider was now in charge. I was given a chance to introduce members of my family to his congregation, and I thanked them for their prayers. One thing that saddened Don was the fact that out of four hundred churches I contacted requesting assistance, only 1 percent responded. He would gasp and shook his head in disappointment most times when we talked about it and he would say: "Truly, many are called but only few are chosen, feller." It was troubling to him that they could have replied just to say at least that they do not have the resources to assist, but they are praying and they should actually pray to show empathy for a family. I once wished I had the resources and the time to visit all four hundred churches with my family when they arrived just to document reactions from all four hundred churches.

On the last Sunday before Thanksgiving Day 2005, I took my family to Liberty Grove United Methodist Church where I was already a registered member. The church would hold three services on Sundays because of its large congregation, and it has a tradition to hear from those in attendance who may have something to share;

a prayer request or praises for any kind of experience etcetera at the end of each service. Usually the last service on Sunday is the most attended and that was the session that my family attended. Toward the end of the service, the Pastor Richard Hogue as usual, moved amongst the congregation with wireless mike in hand that he would give to anyone who had their hand up as having something of praise or a prayer request to share. I had my hand up and so did others who had prayer request or something to share. The pastor walked down the aisle and then noticed it was me. His countenance changed, and he later admitted that he thought I was there again to ask for prayers for my family still stranded in Dakar. I stood up, took the mic from him, and then I thanked all of those who had remembered my cause in their prayers and then I said that prayers have been answered: "My family finally arrived in the country in September, and I just wanted to thank God mostly for his unconditional love and care." Then I started introducing members of my family, from my wife to all six children present. I said my oldest daughter Elizabeth has also been approved by the INS, and she would be joining the family in December. As each member of my family stood up one after the other when I called their names, the pastor stood fixed with a perplexed countenance and at that moment only God knew what was going through his head; although he later confessed that it was a moment of truth in the life of his ministry as a pastor when he came to grip with himself to ask where things might have gone wrong. He said it was beyond his expectation.

The immigration lawyer lady on their Refugee Committee who had contacted the US consular office in Dakar to verify my story, an action that was unnecessary, was sitting on the bench adjacent to mine. She had her hand over her mouth and behold one of my children was sitting next to her since the ushers could not seat all of us on one bench. When I noticed her, I was reminded of the inquiry they made at the Liberian embassy in Washington DC, and I have always believed that their inquiry at the embassy in Dakar may have sparked the DNA test that was proposed by the consular. So I expressed gratitude to God almighty that through all of my troubles the DNA test that the US embassy unnecessarily requested turned out to prove that all of the children in my family belonged to the family and that also had given me a peace of mind. The Liberian lady too who had negatively instigated and influenced members of the Refugee Committee was sitting upfront with her head turned to the wall avoiding looking my way.

The church applauded when I was done and after the pastor finished with the convocation, a crowd that would have otherwise walked past me by surrounded my family to express how glad they were that we made it. On the way out, the pastor asked if we had time to lunch with him and few elders of the church. We had lunch with them at one of the nearby restaurants where he expressed regrets over the way I was treated without trying to cast blame on anyone. Then he extended my family an invitation to eat dinner with his family on Thanksgiving Day. Pastor Hogue was an easygoing man whom I believed had good intentions but for bad influences that led him to do otherwise in my case. They were not forced to assist me, but they should not have raised my hopes by saying they would and then pushed me around for a while and started verifying my story to all the wrong places and finally branded me as a scammer without any proof and I ended up being ignored.

We had dinner with his family on Thanksgiving Day and witnessed the pastor himself in cooking gears in the kitchen. We had a good time with his family and in the difficult months ahead he rendered us some assistance.

Elizabeth's approval for travel did not go well as expected. The consular office at the US embassy in Dakar delayed her processing for almost a year. My wife became pregnant shortly upon arrival in the United States on September 7, 2005; and on June 10, 2006, when we were about to commemorate the one-year anniversary of Don's death when she gave bath to a bouncing baby boy in the same hour that Don passed a year earlier. The doctor had projected her delivery date for June 12, but on the eighth, she was experiencing labor and was then admitted at the Laurel Regional Hospital in Laurel, Maryland. I left the hospital on the night of the ninth and in the early hours of the tenth I received a call from the hospital that she gave birth to a boy. I rushed to the hospital to see her and the baby. We hugged and kissed then she whispered in my ear: "Remember the dream I told you about a year ago about the white man that was stabbed to death and laid before our door?" she asked. I nodded, and she went on: "Well, I had a rejoinder to that dream last night. This time the white man that was stabbed slowly awoken, stood at the doorstep, and all the stabbed marks were no longer there. He knocked at the door and when I opened it, he just smiled at me and handed me a marble with the initial DAD on it. I held the marble and looked at it for a while, but as I lift up my head to ask him the meaning of it, he just was not there anymore. Moments later I was awoken by the pain and then gave birth to the child," she explained. Later she took a piece of paper under her pillow on which she wrote in bold letters: DAD. "Does this mean that we should name the baby after your dad?" I asked. She flipped the paper over and the name: DONALD ALLEN DAVIES (DAD). We looked at each other and smiled, followed by a long period of silence, and we both realized what we always knew that some things are not meant for us to understand. But we do understood that we do not have to commemorate June 10 as the death anniversary of Don any more than we should be celebrating his birth onto our family. The man that was prophesized to be the hand of God has been manifested into my bloodline.

Davies Children in Maryland 2008

First Christmas in the US 2005

First Sunday in the US 2

First Sunday in the US

First Thanksgiving with Pastor Hudges and family 1

Donald Meade Allen 2004

John Chea Davies
United Nations House
New York October 2000

About the Author

John Davies was born in a little town call Kissy Mess-Mess in Freetown, Sierra Leone in 1954 and was forced into becoming a street-boy at age eight. He attended elementary school there but dropped out from grade seven when life got messier, following a long absentee record.

John later went to Liberia in 1971 to continue schooling and attended Lincoln Secretariat Institute where he took interest in book keeping & accounting. He dropped out sooner this time when things became messy and went back to Freetown.

In 1975, after failed attempts to become a permanent seafarer, John returned to Liberia with a commitment to finish schooling. He learned a great deal and had taken an interest in chess during his first failed seafaring attempts, which became a solace for his disappointment and mediocre living. The bargain he made at Lincoln to clean the school as payment for his attendance luckily worked out. John was able to graduate with an A in 1977, which propelled him to a senior book-keeper position with the world's largest rubber plantation.

With resources at his disposal, John then enrolled with the Metropolitan College and the London Educational Association to further improve his education. Here he took up other related corresponding courses. John won the first Liberian National Chess Championship in 1980 and defended the title ten years in a row. He also became president of the Monrovia Chess Club in 1981. He worked as contractual counterpart at the Ministry of Finance and later merited the status of a public accountant and established Davies & Associates, Certified Public Accountants.

Recently John graduated with an MBA from Colorado Technical University and just started working on his Ph.D. John founded

Global Alliance Solution, LLC, a consultancy firm providing strategic management services in dynamic environments for companies seeking competitive edge in global markets. The company is located on Capitol Hill in Washington DC, 20 F Street 7th Floor. Website is www.globalalliancesolution.org

CPSIA information can be obtained at www.ICGtesting.com
Printed in the USA
BVOW08s1437260515

401593BV00001B/1/P